PHILOSOPHICAL DILEMMAS:
A Pro and Con Introduction to the Questions
THIRD EDITION

Phil Washburn

Source material from:
Washburn, *Philosophical Dilemmas: A Pro and Con Introduction to the Questions, 3rd edition*
978-0-19-531464-9

Oxford   New York
OXFORD UNIVERSITY PRESS

OXFORD
UNIVERSITY PRESS

Oxford University Press is a department of the University of Oxford. It furthers the University's
objective of excellence in research, scholarship, and education by publishing worldwide.

Oxford   New York
Auckland   Cape Town   Dar es Salaam   Hong Kong   Karachi
Kuala Lumpur   Madrid   Melbourne   Mexico City   Nairobi
New Delhi   Shanghai   Taipei   Toronto

With offices in
Argentina   Austria   Brazil   Chile   Czech Republic   France   Greece
Guatemala   Hungary   Italy   Japan Poland   Portugal   Singapore
South Korea   Switzerland   Thailand   Turkey   Ukraine   Vietnam

ISBN 978-0-19-045462-3

Methods and Techniques: Facts and Concepts   *58*

Understanding the Dilemma   *60*

1.5 IS FAITH AN ANSWER?   62

Yes: Believer. "Accepting Limits"   *63*
  Critical Questions   *67*

No: Questioner. "Faith and Its Consequences"   *67*
  Critical Questions   *70*

Methods and Techniques: Consequences   *71*

Understanding the Dilemma   *73*

1.6 IS BELIEVING IN GOD NECESSARY FOR A MEANINGFUL LIFE?   75

Yes: Meaning Theist. "The Meaning of Life Is the Submission to God"   *76*
  Critical Questions   *80*

No: Existentialist. "The Myth of Ultimate Meaning"   *81*
  Critical Questions   *85*

Methods and Techniques: Objectivity   *85*

Understanding the Dilemma   *88*

CURRENT CONTROVERSY

1.7 IS BUDDHISM PHILOSOPHY?   92

Yes: Buddhist. "The Philosophy of Buddhism"   *93*
  Critical Questions   *97*

No: Specialist. "The Difference Between Religion and Philosophy"   *97*
  Critical Questions   *101*

Methods and Techniques: Definitions   *101*

Understanding the Dilemma   *103*

Connections: *Transcendentalist or Naturalist?*   *107*

CONTENTS

Preface to the Third Edition   xvi

Preface   xvii

Historical Parallels   xx

Introduction   1

Chapter 1. God, Immortality, and Faith   15

1.1 DOES GOD EXIST?   16

Yes: Causal Theist. "In the Beginning"   16
  Critical Questions   18

Yes: Design Theist. "Design or Chance?"   19
  Critical Questions   22

No: Atheist. "The Retreat of the Gods"   22
  Critical Questions   25

Methods and Techniques: Arguments   25

Understanding the Dilemma   26

1.2 IS GOD LIKE HUMAN BEINGS?   29

No: Abstractionist. "God Is Love"   30
  Critical Questions   34

Yes: Personalist. "The Projection Theory"   34
  Critical Questions   37

Methods and Techniques: Meanings of Words   38

Understanding the Dilemma   39

1.3 CAN GOD ALLOW INNOCENT SUFFERING?   41

No: Contradictor. "There Is No God"   42
  Critical Questions   45

Yes: Reconciler. "Character and Contentment"   45
  Critical Questions   48

Methods and Techniques: Consistent Beliefs   48

Understanding the Dilemma   49

1.4 IS THE SOUL IMMORTAL?   52

No: Mortalist. "Immortality"   53
  Critical Questions   55

Yes: Survivor. "For and Against an Afterlife"   55
  Critical Questions   58

Chapter 3. Happiness, Obligations, and Values   205

3.1 IS PLEASURE THE ONLY VALUE?   206
Yes: Hedonist. "Hedonism"   207
  Critical Questions   209

No: Pluralist. "A World of Values"   210
  Critical Questions   215

Methods and Techniques: Facts and Values   215

Understanding the Dilemma   217

3.2 CAN WE UNDERSTAND HAPPINESS?   221
Yes: Definer. "Happiness"   222
  Critical Questions   224

No: Skeptic. "The Elusive Dream"   225
  Critical Questions   227

Methods and Techniques: Essential Properties   227

Understanding the Dilemma   229

3.3 IS MORALITY RELATIVE?   231
Yes: Relativist. "Moral Relativism"   232
  Critical Questions   236

No: Absolutist. "Right for You, Wrong for Me?"   236
  Critical Questions   240

Methods and Techniques: Ad Hominem   240

Understanding the Dilemma   242

3.4 IS HAPPINESS THE STANDARD OF MORALITY?   244
Yes: Utilitarian. "Utilitarianism"   245
  Critical Questions   250

No: Formalist. "The Principle of Morality"   251
  Critical Questions   255

Methods and Techniques: Moral Theories   256

Understanding the Dilemma   257

3.5 IS SOCIETY THE SOURCE OF VALUES?   260
Yes: Functionalist. "An Objective Basis for Morality"   261
  Critical Questions   263

No: Moral Theist. "The Current Crisis and Its Solution"   263
  Critical Questions   266

Methods and Techniques: Necessary Conditions   266

Understanding the Dilemma   267

CURRENT CONTROVERSY

3.6 SHOULD DOCTORS EVER END PEOPLE'S LIVES?   270
    No: Protector. "Having Reasons for Moral Decisions"   *271*
        Critical Questions   276

    Yes: Euthanizer. "The Complex Issue of Euthanasia"   *276*
        Critical Questions   280

    Methods and Techniques: Justification   281

    Understanding the Dilemma   283

    Connections: *Humanist or Objectivist?   287*

Chapter 4. Free Will, Mind, and Human Nature   293

4.1 ARE WE FREE?   294
    No: Hard Determinist. "One World, Not Two"   *294*
        Critical Questions   297

    Yes: Metaphysical Libertarian. "Free Will and
    Common Sense"   297
        Critical Questions   299

    Yes: Soft Determinist. "Verbal Disputes, Facts, and Free Will"   *300*
        Critical Questions   303

    Methods and Techniques: Introspection   303

    Understanding the Dilemma   305

4.2 ARE WE RESPONSIBLE FOR OUR ACTIONS?   308
    No: Excuser. "Rejecting Responsibility"   *309*
        Critical Questions   311

    Yes: Judge. "No Excuse"   312
        Critical Questions   315

    Methods and Techniques: Infinite Regress   315

    Understanding the Dilemma   317

4.3 IS THE MIND NOTHING BUT THE BRAIN?   320
    Yes: Materialist. "Body and Soul"   321
        Critical Questions   323

    No: Dualist. "The Inner Life"   324
        Critical Questions   326

    Methods and Techniques: Possible and Impossible   327

    Understanding the Dilemma   328

4.4 CAN COMPUTERS THINK?   331
Yes: Mechanist. "Can Computers Think?"   332
  Critical Questions   335

No: Mentalist. "People vs. Machines"   336
  Critical Questions   339

Methods and Techniques: Analogies   339

Understanding the Dilemma   340

4.5 ARE WE ALWAYS SELFISH?   343
Yes: Psychological Egoist. "No Free Lunch"   344
  Critical Questions   346

No: Psychological Altruist. "Is Love Selfish?"   347
  Critical Questions   349

Methods and Techniques: Generalizations   349

Understanding the Dilemma   351

4.6 DOES PERSONAL IDENTITY DEPEND ON MEMORY?   354
Yes: Lockean. "The Binding Thread of Memory"   355
  Critical Questions   359

No: Sartrean. "The Essential Self"   359
  Critical Questions   364

Methods and Techniques: False Dilemma   365

Understanding the Dilemma   368

CURRENT CONTROVERSY

4.7 ARE THE DIFFERENCES BETWEEN MEN AND WOMEN
PHILOSOPHICALLY SIGNIFICANT?   372
No: Unifier. "Men, Women, and People"   373
  Critical Questions   377

Yes: Complementer. "Who's Afraid of Difference?"   377
  Critical Questions   382

Methods and Techniques: Classification   383

Understanding the Dilemma   385

Connections: *Reductionist or Spiritualist?*   389

INTRODUCTION

What is philosophy? This book is intended to help you understand philosophy and to develop your own philosophy. Where should you begin? Perhaps the best way to start is with the word "philosophy." What comes to mind when you hear that word? What do you think philosophy is? To some people, "being philosophical" means being very steady and self-controlled in the face of disappointments. It means accepting loss or pain without becoming emotional about it. "They didn't hire him, but he was philosophical about it," someone might say.

At other times people use the word differently. They say, "His philosophy is 'Eat, drink, and be merry.'" Or "Do unto others before they do unto you. That's my philosophy." In these cases the word "philosophy" means a slogan or maxim that people hold, which sums up their beliefs about the world or their values. Other examples of such principles are "Live and let live," "Che sera, sera" ("What will be, will be"), or "The world is a crazy place."

Sometimes people involved in a discussion will say, "That's a philosophical question," where they mean that the question is about semantics, fine shades of meaning, or splitting hairs. For example, scientists disagree over whether animals can learn a language, and some say it depends on what we mean by the word "language." Often the reply is, "Well now the question is merely philosophical," or "You are making a philosophical distinction."

Finally, you may have heard someone say, "Oh, he is something of a philosopher," where the speaker meant he is a crackpot or a crank. If a person is a vegetarian, or has a scheme to eliminate all government, or tries to communicate with aliens from outer space, others might say, "Don't pay any attention to him, he's just a philosopher."

These examples show that the word "philosophy" has various connotations and images associated with it. Thinking about these uses of the word "philosophy" is valuable because it makes us aware of what many people already believe about philosophy. It reveals *common assumptions* and things people take for granted about philosophy. You should be aware of your own preconceptions as you try to acquire a more complete understanding of philosophy.

Which of the meanings is correct? Is any of these the true meaning of the word? Probably not. Philosophy is too large and complex to be summed up in one or two phrases or uses like these. And while common expressions reveal people's assumptions, they are not the best way to understand what philosophy is. (The word "astronomy" might call up certain images or beliefs in people, but those widespread beliefs would not give us a good understanding of what astronomy is.)

On the other hand, these usages may contain a grain of truth. For example, most philosophers would probably agree that philosophy is a search for general principles that explain the world and guide our lives (like "Eat, drink, and be merry"), although it is more than that. So the second common meaning of the word has some truth in it. Philosophy also requires very careful analysis of key ideas and general concepts (like the concept of language), and therefore the third sense is partially correct. Moreover, if you study philosophy and take it seriously, you will probably find yourself set apart from others, who may regard you as a little strange. And finally, if you study philosophy, you will probably gain some tranquillity and peace of mind. But each of these four ideas is too sketchy and superficial to convey a reliable picture of philosophy.

Let's try a different approach. Instead of surveying ordinary expressions and assumptions, let's look at the *origin* of the word "philosophy." The word comes from two Greek words, *philo* and *sophia*. *Philo* means love, and *sophia* means wisdom, so originally "philosophy" meant the love of wisdom. A philosopher is one who loves wisdom or wants to be wise. But what is wisdom? Well, wisdom is a kind of knowledge, or understanding. So philosophy is the pursuit of wisdom, a kind of knowledge. In this way it is similar to other subjects taught in colleges and universities. Those subjects are also pursuits of different kinds of knowledge. So if we compare philosophy with other subjects that are more clearly defined, we may reach a better understanding of what philosophy is.

PHILOSOPHY AND OTHER SUBJECTS

Biology is the pursuit of knowledge about living things. It is knowledge of life, or living organisms. (This word also comes from the Greek, *bios*, which means life, and *logos*, which means word or speech.) Geology is the study of the earth, and it sums up all the knowledge we have of the earth. Sociology is the study of society; psychology is the study of the "psyche," or mind. All these subjects pursue knowledge about different aspects of the world.

But while a philosopher seeks knowledge (i.e., wisdom), it is a different kind of knowledge. For one thing, philosophy is the study of *all* of life as we live it and all of human experience. It is not limited to living things, or the earth, or society. Philosophy wants to understand the *whole* of life, not one aspect of it. A philosopher might ask, for example, how our knowledge of living things is *related* to our knowledge of the mind, and how they are both related to society— in fact, how everything we see and do is interconnected.

Another difference between philosophy and these other subjects is that these subjects pursue factual knowledge, whereas philosophy pursues something different. A biologist wants to learn and discover facts about plants and animals. If you read a book about biology you will learn a lot of interesting facts about what cells are made of, how organisms grow, how they get food, and so on. But philosophy does not consist of facts like these. Instead, philosophy tries to make sense of the facts, especially the basic facts about our lives. It tries to understand what the facts mean and how they fit together; it does not try to discover new facts.

For example, it is a well-known fact that we all die. What does that mean for us? Is it very important, or not so important? How is that fact related to other parts of our lives? Does death mean that everything I do is ultimately meaningless? Biology will tell us about the physical and chemical changes that occur when a person dies, but those facts won't answer the philosophical questions. The basic facts of human experience are already known. Philosophy tries to put the facts together in a way that makes sense.

It is also a fact that some people are deliberately cruel. They intentionally cause an innocent person to suffer or to be unhappy. That is a fact, but what does it mean? How is it related to other parts of our lives? Moreover, when we read about cases of cruelty in the newspaper, such as abandoned children or beaten wives, we feel a strong revulsion and maybe anger. That is a fact, but what does that fact mean? How should we understand the cruelty, and our reactions to it? Should we say cruelty is morally wrong, and we know it is wrong because we feel so strongly about it? Maybe, or maybe not. Should we say the cruel person should be made to suffer in the same way he or she makes others suffer? Maybe, or maybe not. But the facts from sociology and psychology are not going to tell us what is morally right or wrong, or what we should do about it.

Philosophy is a search for knowledge, but the knowledge it seeks is different from other kinds of knowledge. Philosophical knowledge, or wisdom, is more inclusive than the knowledge of biology, sociology, or other subjects. It is about life as a whole. Moreover, the example about cruelty and morality shows that philosophers try to find knowledge about values as well. Philosophers want to understand how we should live. The basic facts about life are known, but the best way to live is not so clear. And in asking how we should live, philosophy is not asking for more facts. It is asking how we should respond to the facts.

The knowledge that philosophy seeks is wisdom, and wisdom is different from other kinds of knowledge. Furthermore, the *search* is different from the other subjects like biology or sociology. These subjects are sciences, and what makes a subject a science is the *method* it uses. Biologists try to learn about organisms by following the scientific method. That means, first, that they carefully observe something, such as a seed that grows into a plant. Second, their observations lead to questions in their minds, and they think of possible answers, which they state as hypotheses. Third, they perform an experiment to test the answer, to see if it is correct. Wherever possible biologists try to measure what they observe. Geology, chemistry, sociology, psychology, and all the sciences follow the same basic steps of the scientific method.

Philosophy does not follow the scientific method, because that method would not lead to the kind of knowledge philosophers want. What method does philosophy use? It isn't easy to say. Philosophers use many different methods. They try to understand human experience in many different ways. Different philosophers have said that a person can gain wisdom in different ways, and they disagree among themselves about the best way.

So far we have considered only the sciences. But we can get a better focus on the methods of philosophy if we compare it with other subjects that are not sciences.

PHILOSOPHY AND THE HUMANITIES

Philosophy is not like the sciences: it does not seek facts and it does not follow the scientific method. But is it like the *humanities*? The humanities include art, literature, and history. Those subjects try to understand human experience as a whole, as philosophy does. Educators sometimes say that the humanities try to understand what it means to be human. In other words, they seek to understand human experience in general. But their methods are different from those of the sciences. Artists and writers do not conduct experiments or try to quantify things. So in both these ways (i.e., in studying the whole of human experience, and in using nonscientific methods) philosophy is closer to the humanities than to the sciences. But the methods of philosophy are different from the methods of other subjects in the humanities.

For example, philosophy is different from art. Artists try to express or explain aspects of human experience through sights and sounds. Painters use colors and shapes, composers use sounds and rhythms, choreographers and dancers use movements, and other artists use other media. Artists respond to the whole range of life as we live it and try to make sense of it. If you know how to "read" their works, you can learn a lot about human experience. But philosophers try to put their ideas into *words*, not images. They try to explain human experience by describing what we can see or what we do, rather than painting it. And they try to put their results into general concepts and principles, rather than images or musical themes.

Literature is another subject in the humanities, and writers do put their ideas into words. They tell stories about all kinds of people and places, such as the story of the wandering hero Odysseus. Or, in dramas and films, they write dialogues that actors speak on a stage. But while philosophy uses language, it is different from literature because philosophers do not tell stories. They do not describe characters like Odysseus or what happens to them. Instead, they try to understand what experiences mean in general terms. They might use certain incidents and individuals as examples, but the examples are only means to understanding a general truth about life. For example, Odysseus' wife, Penelope, remains faithful to her husband for twenty years while he is away. Homer tells the story beautifully. But the philosopher is more interested in the significance of the event. Is Penelope admirable for being so loyal, or is that degree of loyalty unreasonable? Is love that strong? Can it last for twenty years with no contact between the lovers?

In other words, a writer like Homer wants to understand one example of love in detail, but philosophers want to understand love in general, based on many different examples. That is, they want to understand the concept of love. They want to find the truth about love, which they can state in general principles, like "Love is the strongest motive humans know," or something like that.

Another difference between literature and philosophy is that writers tell stories that are not strictly true. A writer invents characters and events, because writers want to entertain readers as well as enlighten them. Philosophers, however, seek only the truth. They are not interested in "a good story" for its own sake. But that brings us to another part of the humanities, namely history. History is also truth, not fiction. It must be based on known facts. A historian may try to organize his or her information in the form of a story, maybe even with a main character, but the story must be completely true, down to the last detail. And many historians do not tell stories at all, but describe a period of time, or one aspect of a past society. Not only do historians seek the truth, as philosophy does, but they also try to understand all of human experience. While historians have usually concentrated on political events, some also investigate the history of religion, the history of science and knowledge, past societies' moral beliefs and practices, social classes, agriculture, and other parts of life. How is philosophy different from history?

One obvious difference is that historians study the past, while philosophers are interested in all of human experience—past, present, and future. And philosophers do not try to determine the facts about some period or event, like the American Revolution, or even why it happened. They are less interested in the facts than in the judgment of the facts, or what the facts mean. For example, a historian might ask how Thomas Jefferson's contemporaries responded to the Declaration of Independence when they first heard it. On the other hand, philosophers might ask if the ideas expressed in the Declaration of Independence (equality, liberty, self-determination, the pursuit of happiness) are really the best guidelines for society. Or they might ask what historians mean when they say that the American Revolution was *caused* by the desire for self-government. Can historians really find causes in the past? How can the historian know that something was a cause of the Revolution? Is there a universal law that says that when a desire for self-government exists, then a revolution will occur? If not, then how can the historian know that the desire caused the Revolution?

These philosophical questions are at a higher level of generality than the historical questions about specific facts and causes. That is the difference between philosophy and history. Philosophers think about the broadest, most inclusive aspects of human experience, and about how the different aspects are related. A philosopher wonders about the nature of knowledge in general, and asks how a historian can know about the past. Or she wonders about the idea of cause and effect, and asks how some events in history can cause other events.

BUILDING A WORLDVIEW

Philosophy is like other subjects because philosophy seeks knowledge. But it is different from other subjects in the kind of knowledge it seeks and in the way it seeks knowledge. Philosophy is the love of wisdom. Another way to put this is to say that the goal of philosophy is to build a coherent, adequate worldview. A worldview is a set of answers to questions about the most general features of the world and our experience of it. In trying to build a worldview, philosophy attempts to answer the following questions:

1.   What kind of being am I? What does it mean to be human?
2.   What is the best way of life? What goals should I have?
3.   How am I related to people around me? How should society be organized?
4.   How can I find answers to these questions? What can I know with assurance?
5.   Does religion provide the answers? Does God exist?

These questions indicate the most basic, fundamental aspects of human experience: (1) human nature, or self and identity; (2) moral values and action; (3) society and one's place in it; (4) knowledge and understanding; and (5) transcendence. Philosophers try to answer each of these basic questions, and put the answers together into a unified outlook, or point of view, that makes all of experience understandable. The goal of philosophy is wisdom, and wisdom means knowledge of the basic features of the world and your place in it. It means knowledge of who you are, how you should live, how society works, and how you can find out these things.

There are many possible answers to these questions, and thus many possible worldviews. The answers that you accept make up *your* worldview. They make up the beliefs and values that define you as a person.

The concept of a worldview raises many interesting questions itself, and throughout this book you will be thinking about various aspects of worldviews. For example, how do you acquire a worldview? Do you simply adopt the worldview of your parents, or your teachers, or your friends? Do you take one part from one source and other parts from other sources? Does everybody have one? How do you judge a worldview? What makes a good worldview or a bad worldview? Does it matter what my worldview is, or what my girlfriend's or boyfriend's worldview is? Can I change my worldview? You will think of additional questions as you work through the book.

One thing to notice about worldviews is that they are not simple. Each of the basic questions above can be broken down into more specific questions. For example, to answer the first question (what kind of being am I?), you need to answer some other questions included in it: am I free, or are all my actions caused by something outside of me? Will I survive the death of my body, or am I a physical machine which breaks down at death? Can I know myself better than others, or do other people see my real traits better than I do? Am I basically self-centered, or basically giving and self-sacrificing? Each of the other questions also includes more specific questions.

As you read about different answers to these questions, you will often have difficulty deciding what answer is best. For example, one difficult question is "Does God exist or doesn't he?" Some people struggle for years with this question. Was the world created for a purpose, or did it just appear, accidentally? How can you decide? Shouldn't you decide what God is like, or what kind of God we are talking about, before you decide whether or not he exists? These are not easy questions to answer, and it will get more complicated when you read different, conflicting answers, each of which may seem plausible.

Shaping and refining your own worldview is not something you can do in an hour. It takes some effort. At least it does if you want a satisfactory, mature worldview. In building a worldview you can live with, there are some commonsense guidelines you should follow. The guidelines are based on the nature of philosophy itself. They will help you gain an understanding of who you are, how you should live, how society works, what is real and what isn't, and how you can find answers. One guideline is that your worldview should be based on *human experience* in the widest sense. Your beliefs and values should make sense of your experience and the world as you encounter it. It would be very frustrating (and irrational) to hold beliefs and values that are in conflict with your ordinary life and the things you see around you.

Nevertheless, many people do hold beliefs that are out of date, or expected of them, or flattering to their ego, but are not based on their real day-to-day lives or experiences. Voltaire portrays a perfect example of such an irrational worldview in his great classic, *Candide*. Candide's friend Pangloss, the philosopher, maintains that our world is "the best of all possible worlds." Meanwhile, Candide is shipwrecked, betrayed, tortured, and almost killed in an earthquake. It is very difficult for him to accept the idea that the world cannot be improved. So your experience is your starting point and your standard for building your worldview.

But of course you cannot ignore other people and their experiences either. Obviously you can learn and benefit from other people's experiences, since they can do things and go places you cannot. They may have thought about things more thoroughly and more deeply than you have. So you should step back and look at your own experiences, and listen to others, when you try to answer these philosophical questions. The whole point of philosophy is to find answers that make sense of life and human experience.

Another guideline you should follow is to think about how the parts of your worldview fit together. Your answers are *interconnected*. For example, how does your answer to the question "What kind of being am I?" relate to your answer to the question "How should I live my life?" Think about this example for a moment. One traditional answer to the first question is that you are a combination of two things, a soul and a body. Bodies live about seventy years on average, but souls live forever. And this traditional answer also says that the quality of your soul's eternal life depends on the way you live now, while you are still inhabiting this body. If that is true, then of course you should live your life the right way now, since this life is relatively short compared with your soul's life after it leaves your body. The point to see in this example is that the different parts of your worldview are interconnected. The answer to the question "What kind of being am I?" influences the answer to the question "How should I live my life?" and vice versa. In fact, all the questions are interconnected. Your answer to one will have an impact on your answers to the others.

That is why you should think about how the parts of your worldview fit together. They depend on each other. If you accept an answer to one question, and another answer to another question, but the answers are *incompatible*, then your worldview will be unstable and very difficult to hold. For example, a person might answer the question "What can I know with assurance?" by saying that we know what we can see. The test of knowledge is to see something with one's eyes. If you can see it, then you know it, and if you can't see it, then you can't be sure about it, according to this theory. But the same person might answer the question "What kind of being am I?" with the traditional answer mentioned above (i.e., I am a combination of body and soul). This person would have a problem, because no one can see a soul. We can see a body, but we cannot see a soul. But if I can know only what I can see, then I cannot know that I have a soul. This person would have no good reason to believe his answer about being a combination of body and soul. In other words, two parts of his worldview are in conflict. His worldview does not make sense of things, but only adds one more layer of confusion to his beliefs. He should give up one of these answers and replace it with another that fits in with his other answers.

A third guideline you should follow is to accept answers that are clear and *understandable*. After all, the purpose of developing a worldview is to understand the basic features of human experience. You should try to state your answers in words that you and others can understand. A vague feeling, a gesture, a grunt, or a simple slogan is not an answer.

Finding clear, explainable answers can be difficult. For example, you could say that the foundation of society is each individual's unalterable human rights. Human rights should be the guiding principle of all government. That is your answer to the question of how society should be organized. Now this sounds very noble. But do you really understand this part of your worldview? Can you explain what rights are? What is a human right anyway? Can you explain what rights people have? Does everyone have a right to a job? To the best medical care? To make remarks that may offend someone? Can you explain why people have rights? What is it about me that gives me certain rights? Is it my intelligence, my moral sense, my ability to make choices, or something else? If I do not know the answers to these questions, then I do not know what you mean when you say people have human rights.

There is no doubt that *some* people can answer these questions clearly. They can explain their views. But if I cannot explain *my* answer—if I just say I know people have rights and that's the end of it—then I do not really have an answer. A mere slogan, like "Each individual has human rights," is not an answer, because I do not understand what it means. Unfortunately, many people who write about philosophy use words and phrases that they cannot explain. They might talk about "seven levels of consciousness," or "cosmic harmony with the World Spirit," or "being open to the aura of the other." I have no idea what any of these phrases mean, and the writers who use them do not explain what they mean. They are not related to any experience of mine, nor do they help me understand any experience I have had. The main purpose of phrases and sentences like these is to make the reader feel better, not to help him or her understand anything. These words have an emotional effect. They inspire feelings of awe and mystery, of tremendous importance, and perhaps of secret, privileged knowledge. But they are not answers. They are not part of a worldview, because they do not help anyone understand anything.

WHY BUILD A WORLDVIEW?

Constructing your own worldview is a long, challenging process. First you must discover what you believe about these important matters now. Maybe you never asked yourself seriously, "What can I know with assurance?" or "What kind of being am I?" Or if you asked yourself, you may not have worked out a complete answer. As you begin to think explicitly about your beliefs, you must try to formulate them clearly, so they are more than just vague phrases, like "human dignity," or "for the people," or "hard facts." Then you must test your answers against your experience. Do you have good reasons to accept your answers, reasons based on what you have seen, or done, or learned from others? Or are you accepting some answers just because they sound impressive, or your friends accept them? Next you must compare the answers to different questions, to see if all the answers fit together. Your basic beliefs about human nature might be in conflict with your beliefs about society, or knowledge, or something else. If that happened, you would have a kind of philosophical "split personality." You might be a kind of Dr. Jekyll on questions of transcendence, and a Mr. Hyde on questions of knowledge. But don't worry. It's very common, and it can be cured. The cure does require some effort, however.

Why should you take the time and make the effort to build a coherent worldview? There are many reasons. One is that the process is a lot of fun. People are curious. We all want to know more about the world and ourselves. And we want to know not only the facts but how the facts fit together. We are curious about the big picture. One of the most satisfying things you can do is understand something, especially if you have been puzzled by it for a long time.

Another reason to build a worldview is that people have a strong desire to define themselves and to know themselves. Everyone needs a sense of identity. People want to know who they are, and how they are like and unlike other people. The most important element of the sense of identity is one's beliefs and values. I may have light or dark hair, I may be tall or short, but those things are not what makes me who I really am. I may own a sports car or a pickup truck, I may wear designer jeans or cotton work clothes, but those things do not define me either. What makes me the person I am is what I *think*. Do I believe in God or not? Do I think people are basically trustworthy or not? Do I want to own fine things or do I want to improve the world? Do I get angry at rich people spoiled by wealth, or at poor people living off others' labor? Some people answer these questions one way and others answer them another way. The answers make you the person you are. These basic beliefs and values, and the actions based on them, are the core of one's identity. In a real sense, building your worldview is building yourself.

You can see how important beliefs and values are if you simply imagine the following case. Suppose you want to get to know a person, such as a new coworker or a new neighbor. What do you need to know before you can say you really know that person? Her taste in clothes? That might be a small clue, but it certainly isn't enough. The car she drives? Another clue perhaps, but it could be completely misleading. What you really need to find out is what she thinks. How does she answer these basic questions? What are her fundamental beliefs and values, about people, goals in life, right and wrong, God, society, and herself? If you can find out what she believes about those things, then you will really know her.

Some people say that philosophy is not practical. Nothing could be further from the truth. Philosophy is an attempt to find credible answers to the basic questions about life, and the answers a person accepts will have a tremendous impact on his or her life. Think for a moment about the different parts of a worldview. What kind of being am I? Your answer to this question will influence your self-image, and your feelings about yourself. What goals should I have? Obviously your answer to this question will virtually determine the direction of your life. How should I relate to others, or society? Your answer here will influence the kind of citizen you will be, your participation in political affairs, or lack of it, and the kind of changes you will work for. What can I know with assurance? Can I be sure about what I believe, or are most beliefs just shots in the dark? The way you answer this question will influence your confidence or doubts about your beliefs and worldview. What kind of world do I live in? Is it hospitable or hostile, predictable or chaotic? Your answer will certainly affect your outlook and feelings about your surroundings, and might even influence your choice of a career (if you are impressed enough to become a scientist and study the natural world). Does God exist? If you say yes to this question, your fundamental attitudes toward everything—yourself, other people, the natural world, death, morality, belief, everything—will be different from the attitudes you will have if you say no. If "practical" means it helps you to succeed in life, then philosophy is the most practical subject there is.

Philosophy helps you achieve success in your life as a whole, not necessarily in your pursuit of money. It is a very rewarding activity, and it may give you peace of mind, or inner strength, or confidence. Or it may not affect your feelings at all. The purpose of philosophy is not to make anyone feel better. The goal of philosophy is wisdom. It is motivated by curiosity and the desire to understand, not the desire to be happy. Sometimes knowledge is actually painful, but philosophers want to know the truth anyway.

Philosophy is not the same as "self-help." Everyone has seen or heard about self-help books. They are very popular. They have titles like *The Power of Positive Thinking*, *How to Overcome Stress*, *Slay Your Own Dragons*, and *The Cinderella Complex*. These books all have the same basic pattern. First they describe one or more personal problems that people have, such as loneliness, procrastination, too much stress and anxiety, low self-esteem, obesity, feelings of powerlessness, and so on. They recount specific case histories of people with these problems. Next they offer advice on how to solve the problem, often in the form of several steps you can take. For example, one book on feelings of powerlessness says that to overcome these feelings you should practice being honest and open, practice taking control, practice being your own person, and practice changing your habits.

Some people turn to philosophy because they expect philosophy to solve their problems for them. Studying philosophy is very rewarding, in a special sort of way, and it may change a person. But philosophy is different from self-help in two fundamental ways. First, self-help books are aimed at people with emotional and behavioral problems, problems that interfere with their normal lives or that make them unhappy. In other words, the problems self-help books discuss are problems in a person's feelings or behavior. The solution lies in changing the behavior, or perhaps in changing some beliefs that lead to bad feelings. Thus, in self-help books the answers are valuable only if they help a person stop procrastinating or stop feeling lonely or whatever. The answers are valuable for their effects on behavior or emotions.

The priorities of philosophy are different from self-help. In philosophy, convincing answers are valuable for their own sake, whether or not they change a person's behavior or feelings. Whereas self-help books place the emphasis on bad feelings, and look for answers to change those feelings, philosophy places the emphasis on answers themselves, regardless of people's emotional reactions to the answers. The only "feeling" philosophy tries to satisfy is curiosity. The test of an answer in self-help books is "Does it make me feel better?" The test of an answer in philosophy is "Does it explain human experience, is it consistent with other things we know, and is it clear and understandable?"

There is a second fundamental difference. Self-help books are about problems that only some people have. Most people are not so anxious or lonely that they seek help. But philosophy is about questions that apply to everyone. Philosophical problems are universal. They are not limited to one group or another group. The questions about the existence of God, human nature, the organization of society, and so on, are questions about human experience in general, not your experience or my experience or one group's experience. Moreover, the solutions in self-help and philosophy are different as well. A self-help book offers solutions that apply only to the individuals with the emotional problem. Usually the solution is to change one's feelings or one's behavior. But philosophy looks for solutions that are acceptable to everyone. It seeks answers that are convincing to any reasonable person.

This contrast between philosophy and self-help books is a little abstract, and mainly negative. It says philosophy is not self-help. In fact, much of this introduction has been negative in the same way. I have talked about how philosophy cannot be summed up in common catchphrases, how it is different from science, literature, and history, and how it is not the same as self-help. I have only indicated in very broad outlines what philosophy is all about. It is about constructing an adequate worldview, and finding answers that make sense of our lives and that fit together. But you cannot understand philosophy by reading a description of it, like the description in this introduction. You must get involved in philosophy to understand what it is. You can read a definition of philosophy, but that will not give you much of an understanding of what philosophy is all about. You can even read about great philosophers and what they have said, but that is not enough either. It is better than reading a definition, but it does not give you a real grasp of the subject matter or the methods of philosophy. Understanding philosophy is like understanding tennis, cooking, mountain climbing, or anything else: you have to try it yourself before you can understand it. To understand philosophy you must get involved with philosophical problems, you must weigh different solutions or theories, and decide which are convincing. You must *do* the same things that philosophers do. Reading about it isn't enough. The only way to understand philosophy is to practice it.

This book is designed to help you practice philosophy, that is, think about philosophical problems, try to understand the questions, examine the alternative answers, consider the pros and cons, and decide which answer is best.

CHAPTER ONE

GOD, IMMORTALITY, AND FAITH

1.1 DOES GOD EXIST?

Theist or Atheist?

All the questions that philosophers ask are important, but of all their questions, this one is probably the most important. Think of the consequences. If there *is* a God in the traditional sense, then He created you, He is watching you, He knows all your thoughts and feelings, He expects a great deal from you, and He will judge you at the end of your life. He will give you tremendous rewards or punish you severely (according to Western religions). He is also able to help you now in many ways, since He is able to do anything. Every human being was created by God, and therefore everyone deserves an absolute respect. It also means He created the world. The world is not an accident, but was planned. The world as a whole and everything in it has a design and exists for a purpose. We can understand that purpose by understanding God's plan. The world in a real sense is our home, built for us by a loving parent.

On the other hand, if there is *no* God, then we are alone in the universe. We cannot look to any transcendent source for help. Our destiny is entirely in our own hands. If we want moral standards, we will have to make them ourselves. If we choose to disobey them, nothing guarantees that we will regret it. Wicked people prosper and good people suffer; the world is not just. There is nothing divine or special about human beings; we are merely highly evolved animals. We have very strong, competitive instincts. The world around us is often hostile and dangerous. There is no reason behind things, nothing has any purpose. We cannot understand the meaning of nature because it has no meaning; it just is. So our whole outlook on life, and the way we live it, depends on how we answer the question "Does God exist?"

This section includes three essays. The first tries to prove that God exists based on the causal connections among events. What caused the things we see around us, and what caused those causes, and what came even before that? Mustn't there be a beginning? If you think this essay is convincing, then you are a causal theist. The second essay argues that the world is wonderfully ordered, like a complex machine, and therefore must have been designed by an intelligent creator. If you think the second essay is persuasive, then you are a design theist. Finally, the last essay tries to show that there are no reasons to believe in God. If you do not believe in God, then you are an atheist.

YES: CAUSAL THEIST

"In the Beginning"

Most people who believe in God believe on the basis of faith, or on the basis of a personal experience of Him. But aside from faith or experience, it is perfectly reasonable to believe in God on the basis of what we all see around us. In fact, rational considerations show that God must exist.

Two simple facts, taken together, show that God exists. First, it is a fact that everything in the world has a cause. Nothing just happens for no reason whatever. We see causes and effects all around us. For example, the rain causes the plants to grow, accumulation of moisture in the air causes the rain, the heat of the sun causes the evaporation and accumulation of moisture in the air, and so on. If you catch a cold, it was caused by germs in your body. The germs grow rapidly because you are tired from lack of sleep. They entered your body because they were floating in the air and you breathed them in. They were in the air because someone sneezed.

So whenever we think of anything in the world, we can always ask, "What caused it?" And when we find the cause of something, we can then ask what caused the cause, and what came even before that. In other words, we can trace the causal chain further and further back in time.

But this leads to the second important fact. We cannot imagine the causal chain going back forever. Our minds stumble when we try. We cannot grasp it. Try to imagine a chain that extends infinitely, without end. You cannot. Of course, you can think of it going very, very far, but when you think of the chain, you think of a definite object, with limits. You cannot think of an unlimited chain.

The same applies to the "chain" of causes going back in time. You can think of your parents, who caused you, and their parents, who caused them, and so on. But the line had to begin somewhere. You cannot imagine the list of your ancestors going back infinitely, without end. There had to be a beginning.

Some people maintain that we *can* imagine an infinite chain of physical causes. We simply say it is a chain "without end." But what kind of chain is that? "Without end" is a purely negative characterization, and negative characterizations only tell us what something is *not*; they do not tell us what something *is*. Therefore they do not help us understand anything. Suppose I say that I can imagine a new color. What sort of color? Well, it's not green, not yellow, not red, not blue, etc. Now do you know the new color I am thinking of? With that description, you have no idea what I am imagining. That kind of negative characterization does not give you a concept of a new color. Neither does "without end" give you a concept of an infinite chain.

It is true that mathematicians work with "infinity." But all they are doing is laying down some rules for manipulating abstract symbols (numerals), and then seeing what one can and cannot do within the boundaries of those rules. For example, an infinite series defined by one operation is said to "converge" toward its "sum," while an infinite series defined by a different operation is said to be "divergent." But these terms do not describe real series. They are artificial constructs. Mathematicians do not claim to be talking about the material world when they apply their rules.

The fact is that the series of causes we see around us must have a beginning. We cannot imagine it going on forever. And there is another reason to believe in a beginning. The great Catholic philosopher of the thirteenth century, Saint Thomas Aquinas, explained it this way:

> Now the series of finite causes cannot go on to infinity because in every series of causes the first cause is the cause of the intermediate cause, and the intermediate causes cause the last cause, whether the intermediate causes are many or one.

In other words, if *A* causes *B*, and *B* causes *C*, then *A* is the first cause, *B* is the intermediate cause, and *C* is the last cause (or last event). For example, (*A*) a salesperson presses a button beside the front door, (*B*) the button sends a current to the doorbell, and (*C*) the doorbell rings. Aquinas continues:

> However, if you take away the cause you also take away its effect. If there is no first cause among the efficient causes, there will be no last or intermediate cause.

He is saying that if (*A*) does not occur (e.g., no one presses the button), then neither (*B*) nor (*C*) will occur. The electric current will not flow, and the bell will not ring. He concludes:

> But if we proceed to infinity in the series of causes there will be no first cause, and therefore no final or intermediate effects would exist—which is obviously not true.

If the causal chain extended infinitely, there would be no first cause. But if there were no first cause, the later effects would not occur (just as the doorbell would not ring without a cause). But obviously we see effects happening all around us. So the causal chain cannot extend backward infinitely. There must be a beginning.

Now we are ready to put our two facts together. The first fact is that everything in the world is caused by something. The second fact is that the series of causes cannot extend back in time infinitely. Therefore, there must be a First Cause. And that is God. God is the source and origin of the world. He created the world, and therefore He created you and me. All rational people must accept the existence of this First Cause. They may not call the Creator "God," at first. But if they meditate on the true meaning of this conclusion, they will begin to acquire a more religious attitude.

Key Concepts

universal causation	causal chain	infinite series
imagine	negative characterization	First Cause

Critical Questions

1. What two facts, when combined, prove that God exists, according to the essay?

2. What is a negative characterization? Can you give an example of a negative characterization of something?
3. Do you think we can imagine an infinite chain of causes? Can we think of things that we cannot picture in our imaginations?
4. If we cannot think of something (maybe because it is self-contradictory, e.g., a square circle), does that mean the thing cannot exist? Could square circles exist?
5. The essay says we cannot imagine the causal chain going back without end. Why does Aquinas believe the chain cannot go back infinitely?
6. Does a causal theist believe God is caused or not? Does he or she believe God is infinitely wise, infinitely powerful, or infinitely good?
7. Has the essay proven that God exists, in your opinion?

YES: DESIGN THEIST

"Design or Chance?"

Like many people, I have often felt the overwhelming majesty of the world. Looking at the stars at night and thinking about the vast numbers and spaces, hearing a newborn's cry and thinking about her miraculous arrival, sitting by a lake and seeing the incredible harmony of multitudinous animals, plants, and environment are all enjoyable experiences. But the powerful feelings I had were more than merely emotions. They were an intuition of something more pro-found. I gradually realized that what affected me so deeply was the *order* of the world. It is magnificently ordered, like an incredibly vast machine. I think the strong feelings were a perception of an important truth. It is important because it convinces me that the world was created by a wonderfully wise and power-ful Designer.

Some people do not see or feel the order of nature. To them, the world is more like a junkpile than a fine Swiss watch. They see nature as a heap of un-related objects, jumbled together helter-skelter rather than a carefully con-structed machine, with parts that mesh and support each other.

The different perceptions are very important, and not just a matter of aes-thetics. If the world is like a heap, then it could have appeared by chance. It doesn't present any special problem in understanding why it works the way it does. It doesn't have any particular order, so there is nothing to be explained. It just happens to work that way. (There is still the problem of why there is any kind of world at all, why there is something rather than nothing. But that is a different question. The question here is "Why does the world exhibit *order*?")

On the other hand, if the world is like a *machine*, then it is impossible to believe that it appeared by chance. Swiss watches do not spring up out of the ground, or appear randomly like seashells on a beach. Every machine, without exception, is made by an intelligent *designer*. The parts of a machine must be deliberately assembled in a particular way, not thrown together haphazardly.

In other words, if the world is more like a machine than a junkpile, then we must suppose that some Designer put it together. I believe that the world is wonderfully ordered, regular, and harmonious, and that the order is evidence that it was created by an intelligent Designer.

Nature is like a machine in many ways. For one thing, all the manifold diversity we see is made up of only ninety-two basic parts—the ninety-two natural elements (hydrogen, helium, etc.). Every substance, whether natural or manufactured, every mineral, plant, and animal, is composed of these few "nuts and bolts." The only differences are due to the proportions. Machines, too, can be disassembled into their component parts, which are usually some type of metal, plastic, or rubber.

Another machinelike feature of the world is the interdependence of the parts. In an organism, for example, every part depends on every other part. If the heart or nerves malfunction, every other part will soon malfunction, too. In an ecosystem, like a forest, or a bay, all the plants and animals interact and depend on each other. If humans interfere and feed the deer in the winter, for example, or catch all the lobsters, then the balance is upset and severe problems appear. The parts of machines are interdependent in exactly the same way.

The interactions in nature are incredibly complex and precise. Your brain continuously monitors your body. It maintains a constant temperature of 98.6 degrees Fahrenheit. It keeps you balanced so you don't fall. It uses the liver, the kidneys, and the lungs to regulate the precise levels of sugar, water, and oxygen in your blood. It keeps you alert during the day and puts you to sleep when you need rest. All of these processes depend on extremely minute chemical changes, either in the blood or in the nerves. The precision is like the hundreds of electrical pathways and switches on a tiny computer chip, but much more exact.

When we think of machines, like watches, cars, or typewriters, probably the first thing we think of is repetition. Machines operate in a repetitive, regular way. The wheels go round and round in the same pattern over and over, the spark plugs fire one after the other, the typewriter carriage slides across and returns. And we see exactly the same regularity in nature. The lawfulness of the world is perhaps its most remarkable feature. Night follows day, season follows season, children follow parents. In our own bodies, the heart contracts and pumps blood into the arteries, it flows through the parts, and eventually returns to the heart to start all over again. The more we learn about the world, the more lawful, orderly, and regular it appears. It looks more and more like a vast, complicated machine.

Nature is like a machine in being orderly, exact, and made of interdependent, interchangeable parts. Since every machine is created by an intelligent designer, I conclude that the natural world was created by an intelligent Designer as well. The world is inconceivably more complex, precise, and grand than any machine. But that shows how much more powerful and intelligent than us the Designer of the world must be.

The heart of the argument is the resemblance between the world and a machine. But someone could challenge the other part of the argument, which is the connection between machines and intelligent designers. Today many people say that nature is lawful and made of interdependent parts, like a machine, but it *could* have grown up naturally. It could have evolved. They say that the regularity, the precision, and the interdependence do not require a Designer to be explained, but are the result of chance. Random combinations of elements, plus natural selection, can produce the admittedly astonishing precision and harmony that is so evident in the world.

But this seems illogical. It is surely obvious that no machines can occur by chance, not even the simplest ones. Can openers do not grow on trees. So how could the marvelously complex natural world, so much like a machine, spring up by chance? People say "evolution." But if that were enough, we should see machines grow up through evolution.

It isn't sensible to think that random combinations of atoms could produce the human body and mind. Do people *understand* or merely believe it because the present authorities say it is true? I for one do not understand it, although I have studied the theories. And I dare say that those who profess to believe it do not really understand it either, because it is too far-fetched. It is like believing that if the waves pound the beach long enough, they will eventually recombine the elements to produce a fine watch. A person might *believe* in miracles like this, but he or she would not *understand* how it happened.

We can add the idea that some combinations are more adaptive than others. But that isn't enough. The theory of evolution still holds that the end result—humankind—is the product of pure chance, one accidental change after another. Some changes work better than others. But that doesn't explain how the process of random combinations would produce such a complex being as a person. No one believes machines could be produced this way. But people are much more intricate than machines. Therefore, no one should believe people could be produced this way. The growth of the world might have taken millions of years, but it must have been guided by intelligent choice.

If the world is like a machine, and all machines require designers, then the world requires a Designer. Now, if the two premises are true, as I have tried to show they are, and if the inference is correct, then perhaps our attitude toward the natural world should change. We should show a little more respect for God's handiwork. Many people today see plants and mountains and birds as accidents, mere matter, or monstrous agglomerations, without plan or reason. Instead, perhaps we should try to appreciate the ingenuity of their design. If we look at nature in the right way, we might get a glimpse of infinite wisdom.

Key Concepts

machine	interdependence	evolution
lawfulness	designer	random combinations

Critical Questions

1. The essay says that if the world is like a machine, then God must exist. Why? How can one go from the first statement to the second statement? What is the intermediate step (or steps)?
2. In what ways is the world like a machine, according to the essay?
3. A design theist admits that the world is incomparably more complex and precise than any machine. Doesn't that prove that the world could not have been designed?
4. Can you think of any other similarities between the world and machines? Can you think of any differences between the world and machines?
5. Why does a design theist think the theory of evolution cannot explain the order in the world? What is wrong with the theory?
6. Does a design theist assume that humanity is the goal, or purpose, of biological change? If one rejects that idea, and believes that humanity is not the goal, but is only an accident, only the most complex species to appear so far, could one then accept evolution as an adequate explanation?

NO: ATHEIST

"The Retreat of the Gods"

People fear what they do not understand. Religious belief is a response to such ignorance and fear. It is an attempt to cope with a capricious, unpredictable, and potentially hostile environment. It teaches people to bow down, submit, beg for forgiveness, give gifts, and make sacrifices to try to appease the inscrutable gods. But fear is a self-defeating response. It encourages resignation and fatalism. Who could stand up to the gods themselves? Better to submit. But such passive attitudes perpetuate ignorance, and therefore fear, and therefore religious belief, in a futile cycle.

Since religion feeds on ignorance, religious belief has declined steadily over the centuries as knowledge has increased. Today the grounds for religious belief have disappeared completely. In our day there is no reason for anyone to believe in God. We can trace the decline of religion through six stages. In each successive stage the gods retreat farther and farther from ordinary life, they diminish in number, and they lose their recognizable, human characteristics.

1. Before the dawn of history, our primitive ancestors believed in countless "spirits" all around them. Primitive peoples today, who are at the same

stage of development as those prehistoric ancestors, believe that trees, animals, the sky, springs, magic herbs, weapons, and other objects possess spirits of their own. Everywhere they turn, they see or hear a spirit. And they try to influence the spirits by offering gifts or promising service of some kind. Such an attitude is an understandable response to ignorance. If a fruit tree bears abundant fruit one season but little fruit the next season for no apparent reason, the primitive farmer might decide that the tree has a will of its own. It seems as unpredictable as people are. Since he couldn't influence the tree through natural methods, he might be able to influence it by flattery, gifts, or promises.

2. As civilization advanced, people learned more about the natural world and the causes of things. By the time of the ancient Greeks (500 B.C.E.), the spirits, or gods, had retreated to one place—Mt. Olympus—and they had diminished in number. There were only a dozen or so major Greek gods, plus various nymphs, naiads, sprites, and so on. The Greeks still regarded the gods as humanlike beings, and the gods controlled the important natural processes, like the seasons and the movement of the sun across the sky. But not every object or place was inhabited by a spirit, according to Greek religion. They understood how bees fertilized flowers, for example, so they did not need to believe in a "spirit of the flowers."

3. A further advance took place with the appearance of monotheistic, Western religions. The idea of one God probably originated with the ancient Hebrews before 1300 B.C.E., and evolved over the centuries in Judaism, Christianity, and Islam. The one God differs from polytheistic gods in several ways. He is not to be found anywhere on earth, but resides in a distant, transcendent heaven. He guides history in a general way, but rarely intervenes directly. We can see the contrast in Homer's *Iliad*, representing Greek religion, and the Jewish Scriptures (or Christian Old Testament), representing monotheism. In Homer's *Iliad*, the Greek gods frequently appear and talk to the heroes, they hide their favorites in a cloud, or turn aside a threatening spear. In early books of the Scriptures, the one God is similar to the Greek gods, in that he walks on the earth, appears directly to people in a bush or a whirlwind, and performs miracles. But as the monotheistic tradition evolved, God appeared less and less in human form. People realized that there were better explanations of why a spear failed to hit its mark. They did not need to evoke God to explain every little event.

4. Around 1600 the Scientific Revolution began, and within two hundred years the human race discovered more about the natural world than it had in the previous two thousand years, or two hundred thousand. Sir Isaac Newton, building on the mechanics of Galileo, systematized a set of precise laws that explained virtually all motion, from the distant planets to a flying cannonball to a clock's pendulum. Consequently religious attitudes changed. Educated people of this period adopted a form of religion known as "deism." They removed God even further from human affairs. God was now conceived to be a rational Being who designed the great world-machine and set it in motion, but who then retired and let it run by itself. People explained events by reference to prior causes, not by imagining that a supernatural God continually watched and interfered. There was no need for such a belief. Furthermore, since the Divine Being was less involved with human events, he might be less human himself. Deists still believed that God was rational (a sort of super-Newton), but he did not exhibit all the changing emotions of the Judeo-Christian-Muslim God, such as jealousy, anger, pity, and so forth. There was no reason to believe in such characteristics.

5. Newton's triumph was in physics. The next development was in biology. In 1859 Darwin published his *Origin of Species*, wherein he explained how the human species had evolved from simpler types of animals. We now understand why we have the human shape and human capacities that we have. They are adaptations to the environment, slowly built up over the eons by the blind process of natural selection. This new understanding has undermined religious belief even further. Deists had believed that a God was required to design the human body and human mind. Since they conceived of God as a kind of Divine Intelligence, they still believed that the human intellect was "in God's image." But now we know that the human mind and body grew up naturally, accidentally, through random mutations and natural selection, like other species. No one drew an original blueprint for humanity. There is no reason to believe that our human intelligence is a copy of God's nature. There is no reason to believe that God is intelligent or has a mind. Thus as we learn more, the need for God becomes smaller and smaller.

6. The last chapter in this story occurred in the twentieth century. As humanity has progressed throughout history, the idea of God has shrunk and receded. Educated people no longer believe that God is present, guiding physical objects like automobiles. They no longer believe God has emotions as we do. In fact, Darwin's discoveries removed the need for any human qualities of God at all. But if God was not human, religious people asked, then what was he (or it)? Maybe God is a "force" or "energy" that flows through all things, or maybe it is Being itself. Physicists believe in forces and energy, but what made the God-force different, in the minds of religious people, was that God was *good*. Whatever God was, it worked for the best, they insisted. But the horrors of the twentieth century have undermined that last characteristic. The pain and suffering of the wars, famines, and tortures, culminating in the Holocaust, have made it impossible to believe in a good God. A good God could not permit such things. But if we take away that last characteristic, what is left? Nothing. The idea of God has finally disappeared.

It has disappeared along with our ignorance and has been replaced by knowledge. The knowledge of physics, biology, and history may be difficult to accept, but it has the virtue of being based on reality rather than imagination and fear. Moreover, it leads to further progress rather than fatalism and stagnation.

The long retreat of the gods is one aspect of humanity's maturation. The story of spirits replaced by gods replaced by a distant God and so on is really the story of the childhood and adolescence of the human race. It shows our growing acceptance and mastery of the real world. With the final disappearance of God, we have reached adulthood. We no longer need fabulous stories to comfort us. We can face the world in a more mature way.

Key Concepts

spirits	monotheism	intelligence
polytheism	Deism	the Holocaust

Critical Questions

1. How was the evolution from primitive tribes to the ancient Greeks a decline in religious belief, according to the essay? How was the evolution from the Greeks to monotheistic religions a decline?
2. Do you agree that these changes were *declines*?
3. In what two ways did the idea of God change after the Scientific Revolution (i.e., in stage 4)?
4. What impact did Darwin's theory of evolution have on our image of ourselves, and on people's conception of God?
5. Do you think it is possible to believe in God but believe he or it is nothing at all like humans? Could we call a galaxy, or heat, God?
6. Do you think it is possible to believe in God but believe he or it is evil, or neutral, i.e., not good?

Methods and Techniques
ARGUMENTS

These essays are all philosophical because of the question they address. But they are also philosophical for another reason. They are intended to persuade you, the reader, to accept a certain conclusion. They are not telling a story, or describing anything, or trying to entertain you. Instead, each essay presents an argument. In philosophy, the word "argument" has a special meaning, different from the ordinary meaning. Ordinarily, an argument is a dispute or disagreement or fight. But in philosophy an argument is a set of reasons to believe something. "In the Beginning" and "Design or Chance?" both present reasons to believe that God exists, while "The Retreat of the Gods" tries to persuade people that God does not exist. Other philosophers propose reasons to believe that the highest goal in life is pleasure, or that we can never be certain of anything, and so on. They give reasons to accept their conclusions, and you must decide how strong the reasons are. Philosophers want to know what they should believe about these general topics, so they study reasons for holding one belief or another. Therefore, to a large degree philosophy is about arguments.

Writers could try to get you to accept their conclusions in a variety of ways. They could threaten you. They might say that if you do not agree with them they will come to your house and shoot your dog. Or they could plead and beg you to accept their conclusion. They might say that otherwise they will lose their jobs. Or they could try to bribe you. They could say that people who agree with them are more popular and have 23 percent fewer cavities. But of course these writers don't stoop so low. Like all philosophers they base their conclusion on well-known facts that anyone can observe. The first essay emphasizes the fact that events have causes. The second describes a number of established facts about the physical world. The third describes historical changes. In other words, they try to come up with objective evidence to support their conclusion. They think that the evidence should convince anyone that they are right.

These writers' appeals to facts illustrate an important point about arguments. All arguments have two parts, called "premises" and "conclusions." The facts are the premises. They are the reasons that the writer uses to try to make you believe something. The belief that the writer wants you to accept is the conclusion. For example, in the first argument, the premises are that everything has a cause, and that the chain of causes cannot go back in time forever. The conclusion is that God exists. The premises of the second argument are that the world is like a machine, and all machines are created by intelligent designers. The conclusion is that the world was created by an intelligent designer, i.e., God. You should enjoy isolating and stating the premises and conclusions in the other essays in this book. If you analyze a person's point of view very carefully in this way, you will be surprised at how sloppy some people are. Their writing may sound very eloquent and persuasive, but if you actually state the premises and conclusion, you often find a big gap: the premises don't support the conclusion at all. You may find gaps even in these essays.

With practice you will get better at picking out premises and conclusions, and seeing flaws in people's arguments. Of course the point of doing this is not to criticize people. The point is to make sure your *own* beliefs are based on good, solid reasons.

Understanding the Dilemma
THEIST OR ATHEIST?

Does God exist? If you answer yes, then you are a *theist*. If you answer no, then you are an *atheist*. "Theist" is a general word for a person who believes in some kind of divinity. A monotheist is a type of theist who believes in one god (monotheism), while a polytheist believes in many gods (polytheism). There are other variations, but for now you should concentrate on the basic division between theism and atheism. Is there a God or isn't there? Are you a theist or an atheist?

The essays in this section should help you decide. The first two support theism, and the third supports atheism. Which point of view is more similar to your own? You do not have to agree with everything a writer says. The essays simply present contrasting ideas to help you think about your own beliefs. If you found yourself nodding in agreement as you read "In the Beginning," then you are a theist. The second essay also supports theism. If you answered the study questions about "Design or Chance?" and, after reflecting on the various things in it, you decided that the observations and the conclusion were likely to be correct, then you are a theist.

On the other hand, if "The Retreat of the Gods" seemed accurate to you, then you are an atheist. If you agree that all the reasons for believing in God or the gods have disappeared and have been replaced by scientific explanations, then you are an atheist. The essay doesn't prove that there is no God. It only shows that the reasonable conclusion is that God does not exist.

There are different types of atheists and theists. In this section you have read about two types of theists, *causal theists* and *design theists*. Anyone who accepts the first essay and believes that facts about causes and the causal chain prove that God exists is a causal theist. People who accept the second essay are design theists because they look at the order and design in the world, and those facts convince them that God exists. A causal theist and a design theist agree with each other that God exists, but they have different reasons for believing in God. Both, however, disagree with the atheist. The main choice you face in this section is between theism and atheism.

Throughout this book you will be presented with choices between two alternatives, like theism and atheism. The decisions you make will determine your worldview. They will form a kind of network of your basic beliefs and values. It is difficult to make these choices. It is difficult to decide what you think. So most people try to avoid making a choice. They put aside the whole subject and ignore it. Or they try to find a middle ground, so they do not have to choose one side or another. In some cases a middle way may be possible. In other cases it isn't.

Is there a middle way between theism and atheism? The answer depends on what we mean by the word "God." In other words, the atheist says there is no being who created the world, who knows everything, can do anything, and watches us. A theist says there is a God, but some theists might define "God" differently from the atheist. One theist might say he or she believes in God the Creator but does not believe God knows everything, or can do anything whatsoever, or watches us. Is this a middle way? Could an atheist and a theist agree that such a being exists? To answer these questions you should read Section 1.2, "Is God Like Human Beings?"

Many people say they have found another middle way between theism and atheism. They say they are "agnostics." An *agnostic* is a person who believes that no one can *know* whether or not God exists. If you ask them "Does God exist," their answer is "I don't know." But an agnostic is *not* a person who cannot decide, and it is not a person who hasn't studied the issue or thought carefully about it. Real agnostics understand all the evidence and reasons theists and atheists give, but they have another theory about knowledge. They have studied the different ways of knowing (science, direct experience, logic, art, intuition, etc.), and have concluded that none of them gives good enough reasons to believe or not to believe in God. (You will read about knowledge in Chapter 5.) Is this a middle way between theism and atheism? Not really. It is more like giving up on finding any answer, rather than finding an answer that lies between the two sides.

So the issue for now is theism vs. atheism. Does God exist or doesn't he? Is the first essay right, or the second, or the third? If you are unsure about your answer, then you should make a tentative decision for now. Later, of course, you can change your mind. Making a decision will help you understand what it really means to hold a particular belief, because you will be personally involved. It will force you to think hard about the ideas because they will be your ideas.

The following statements may help you make up your mind. The first set consists of statements that a theist might make. They are beliefs that many theists hold. The second group includes statements that atheists might make. Of course not every theist believes every statement listed here under "theist," and the same is true for atheists and the other list. But these beliefs are generally characteristic of the two positions. Which statements do you agree with? Which sound true to you? Are you a theist or an atheist?

THEIST

1. Everything must have started somewhere, or must have come from something, and that beginning source of everything is a Supreme Being.
2. Everything that happens is observed and guided by a mind or power beyond the natural world.
3. The world was created for a purpose and is fulfilling that purpose.
4. I am not just an animal; instead, I am related to a higher being outside the material world.

ATHEIST

5. The world may not have a starting point, and if it does, that point is not God.
6. What we can see, touch, and investigate scientifically is all there is; belief in God is just prescientific superstition.
7. The world is completely comprehensible; everything that happens can be explained by circumstances and prior causes.
8. Human abilities are more developed than animals' abilities, but are not different in kind.

FOR FURTHER STUDY

Historical Examples

THEIST: Thomas Aquinas. *Selected Philosophical Writings*, edited by Timothy McDermott. Oxford University Press, 1993. Thirteenth century. Aquinas offers five famous proofs for the existence of God.

ATHEIST: David Hume. *Dialogues concerning Natural Religion*. Many editions. Originally published posthumously in 1779. In part 5 Hume presents several arguments against the design theist's position.

OTHER SOURCES

John Hick. *The Philosophy of Religion*. 4th Edition. Prentice-Hall, 1990. An excellent, even-handed discussion of all the issues. Chap. 3 is an examination of arguments against God, based on sociology, Freud, and modern science.

Sam Harris. *The End of Faith: Religion, Terror, and the Future of Reason*. W.W. Norton, 2004. A passionate attack on what Harris sees as the irrationality of religion and its consequences in behavior.

Brian Davies. *Introduction to the Philosophy of Religion*. 3rd Edition. Oxford University Press, 2004. Chaps. 5 and 6 present the pros and cons of the causal argument and the design argument, and Davies concludes that both arguments are persuasive.

Bertrand Russell. *Why I Am Not a Christian, and Other Essays*. Allen and Unwin, 1957. A witty, lucid demolition of the causal and design arguments, a skeptical appraisal of Christ's teachings, and a rejection of the moral value of religion.

George H. Smith. *Atheism: The Case against God*. Prometheus, 1979. Clear discussions of faith, arguments for God, and the consequences of atheism.

Frederick C. Copleston. *Aquinas*. Penguin, 1955. Readable, sympathetic exposition of Aquinas' philosophy, including his arguments for the existence of God.

Richard Swinburne. *Is There a God?* Oxford University Press, 1996. Argues that the existence of God is a simpler explanation of the world than the existence of material objects by themselves.

J.J.C. Smart, J.J. Haldane. *Atheism and Theism*. Blackwell, 1996. Smart criticizes the standard arguments, while Haldane defends religious belief.

1.2   IS GOD LIKE HUMAN BEINGS?

Abstractionist or Personalist?

A large majority of people in the United States say they believe in God, but I would guess that many of these people have never examined their concept of God very carefully. How should we describe God? What do we know about God? Did he walk in the Garden of Eden with Adam and Eve? Did he allow Moses to see his back? These descriptions from the Bible make God sound almost human, even to the extent of having a humanlike body. But most religious people would probably deny that God has a body. If he has no body, does he have a personality? Is he an introvert or an extrovert? Is he primarily a thinker, a feeler, or a doer? This doesn't sound right either. It is very difficult to say *what* God is like. Often the most that religious people can say is what God is *not*: he is not physical, not male or female, not limited by personality traits, not conscious in the way we are, etc.

But if a person cannot say what God is like, then it may be impossible for that person to believe that God exists. If a person knows very little about the nature of God, then there is very little for the person to believe. Consider an analogy. Suppose you visit a friend at her house, and she tells you that behind one door, which is always locked, is a wonderful gliptor. You have no idea what a gliptor is, and your friend cannot answer any questions about it. Is it alive, is it large or small, what is it made of, what does it do? Your friend cannot say. All you know is the name. Can you believe the gliptor exists? There is no question that your friend uses the word and says she believes in the gliptor. But can you believe the gliptor is behind the door?

The following essays are about the ways people think of God. The first takes the idea that *God is love* and tries to develop and defend it. It defends an abstract concept of God. The second examines the idea of God as a *father-figure*, and asks if it is reasonable to think of God that way. Is it reasonable to believe that God has personal, humanlike qualities?

NO: ABSTRACTIONIST

"God Is Love"

Karen McAlister, age 14, was angry. I had just begun teaching my regular Sunday School class for young teens when Karen raised her hand. "You keep saying God is wonderful, and we ought to thank Him for everything. But He doesn't sound so wonderful to me," she said. The other kids fidgeted and looked embarrassed. Karen went on. "We started this year with Genesis and God's creation of the world and Adam and Eve and everything. That's all fine. But later when God keeps sending plagues to the Egyptians and wants total obedience from the Hebrews, He just looks like a big baby who has to have his way."

Karen was clearly upset, and a few of the other kids began to agree with her. We spent the rest of the class period talking about the way that ideas of God change and evolve in the Bible. Karen's feelings are not unusual. Many thoughtful young people outgrow the simple, mythological picture of God, but cannot find a more mature, adult conception to take its place. Karen was in this transitional phase. She wanted to believe in God, but she could not accept the stories about a bearded grandfather-God that she had been told all through her childhood. And she was put off by the stern, violent God of the Old Testament. Now, at 14, she was searching for a more spiritual way of thinking about God.

Many people—not just children—have literal, cartoonlike images of God as an old man sitting on a throne, dressed in a white robe. When they think of God they think of Michelangelo's wise father-figure on the ceiling of the Sistine Chapel reaching over to give life to Adam. But that picture is much too limited. Other people cannot believe such a being exists. But since they cannot conceive of God in any other way, they stop believing in God altogether. And that's even worse. They need a deeper, more challenging, "mind-stretching" concept of God.

As we grow older, and live through more complex experiences, we can grasp deeper, more subtle ideas of God. When young children hear words like "wise" and "powerful," they understand them in terms of their own experiences. Their father is "wise" because he knows the entire multiplication table, or he knows the four food groups, or the answers to other questions. He is "powerful" because he can carry them in his arms, or open windows that are stuck. Wisdom means factual knowledge they can understand, and power means physical strength they can see. But when these children grow up, they go through a number of transforming experiences. They make friends, lose friends, fall in love, get rejected, get married, have children, and sometimes get divorced. They struggle with a career, succeed, fail, bend their principles, grieve over deaths, and watch their children grow. During this process, words like "wise," "powerful," "beautiful," and "love" take on whole new levels of meaning they didn't have before. Now, as adults, they are able to understand powerful emotions of ecstasy or anguish, and subtle shades of feeling. They understand the complexities of relationships, the wonder of free choice, the solemnity of commitment, the burden of responsibility, and a range of other ideas that children cannot grasp. They understand those parts of life that are profoundly moving, vitally important, and above the intellect. They become aware of the inner, non-physical, *vital* part of life. It is not automatic or guaranteed, but if they work at it, their spiritual lives become much richer. They become capable of experiencing multitudinous aspects of life that are far beyond the physical concepts and feelings of children.

If they work at it, they can develop a more spiritual way of thinking about God. I believe that all the things we tell children about God are basically true, but we must know how to understand those truths. God is not a grandfather in the sky. Instead, God is love. The true essence of God is love—pure, absolute, unconditional love. We say that God is love often enough, but we don't take it seriously. If we take the time to think about the characteristics we usually attribute to God, we will find that they all add up to love. Let's consider them one by one.

1. "God is the creator." Some people think of God as a kind of magician who can make objects appear suddenly out of thin air. But that is literal, childlike thinking. The real creative force in the world is love. Love inspires a man and a woman to create life. There is nothing more miraculous and wonderful than that creation, an act of love. Love of others brings people together to cooperate and create new ideas, new ways of living, new discoveries. Human creativity of all kinds derives from love, whether it is love of another person, or of a group.

We can even think of love as a metaphysical principle, if we stretch our minds a little. Love is a kind of attraction. And in a way, attraction is the most fundamental force in the universe. It explains all the galaxies, planets, continents, plants, and animals that make up the world. All that order and structure is the result of the attraction of some elements for others. Over the eons, matter and energy became more organized, more complex, more structured, through the combinations of more and more structures. Everything that exists is a group of atoms bonded together by mutual attraction. Materialists see only the atoms and decide that the world is a lifeless mass. But if we step up to a more spiritual level of thinking, we can see the *process* at work with the material, and the *pattern* in the matter, which is just as real as the matter. We can see the force of attraction that weaves through all things, creating order out of chaos and life out of lifeless particles. At a higher level we can recognize that it is the same mysterious force that draws us to other people, and generates all that we create.

2. "God is eternal." Some people think of God as an old man, because He lives for such a long time, namely, forever. So He is incredibly old. But it makes more sense to think of God as love. Love is eternal. We can know this in two ways. First, the force of love is not limited to you or me or any couple or any group of people. Even if love in one person ceases to exist, it continues in other people and other places, and even in the natural world. It is the source of all the structure in the world, so it will continue forever. We can know this in a second way through our own experience. When we are in love, we are drawn beyond our selfish, individual concerns toward something more important. We sacrifice our personal desires for the sake of the beloved. We transcend ourselves. In that experience we get a glimpse of eternity. We move closer to something—pure love—that is so much greater and stronger than any single person and his or her momentary desire. We begin to understand how love is not limited to any single person's feelings, but is infinite and eternal.

3. "God is all-powerful." In Exodus God is able to part the Red Sea, turn the Nile to blood, and perform other miracles. He is represented again as a kind of magician. But if we are looking for a more spiritual power, we can find it in love. "Love conquers all," people say. A man who is in love will climb mountains, cross deserts, and face all kinds of terrors in order to be reunited with his lover. And love gives him the strength to do it. When Gandhi wanted to liberate India from British rule, he could have tried to organize an armed rebellion, but he believed nonviolent resistance would be more powerful. He counted on people's decency and love of their fellow man, and he was right. Love proved more powerful than empire, greed, and fear.

4. "God provides guidance." Some people believe God gives them signs, like a book falling open to a certain place, or missing a train, or some other striking event. Or they think God talks to them. Most people, however, do not hear God's voice, and they regard the "signs" as coincidences. But we can find guidance in love. If we are confused and don't know what to do, we can stop and reflect on love. For example, a man quarrels with his wife and then notices how sympathetic his young, attractive coworker is. Should he

sleep with her? Or a woman feels bad for the homeless in her town, but she wants to work extra hours to get a promotion at her job. Should she devote some time to volunteer work? Love shows the way. If the man really loves his wife, he will recognize a brief, sexual infatuation for what it is, and remain faithful to her. If the woman really loves her neighbor, she will make some sacrifices to help him. People have always said God is the source of morality, and they were right. God is love, and love is the highest and truest morality.

5. "We are made in God's image." In other words, we are similar to God. Some people think this means God has two arms and two legs, or at least a face. But others cannot believe that God has a body or a face. On the other hand, if God is love, then we could be made in the image of God. Love is what makes us fully human. Animals mate and raise offspring, but they do not consciously, willfully feel love. The real center of our human nature is our ability to love. And the more we are filled with love, the more like God we are. When we give love to people, we are expressing the divine, God-like part of our nature.

6. "God is within you." God is not waiting for us in some distant heaven. He is not removed from the world, "above" us, or watching us, like Orwell's Big Brother. God is part of each of us, residing within our own hearts. God is as close to us as our own thoughts and feelings. He is the love that we feel inside ourselves. If you wish to know God, look within your own heart. Look at the unselfish, beautiful love that you find there, and you will begin to understand. Look at the pure devotion you see in a new mother, or in the cheerful social worker at the soup kitchen, or the nurse in the cancer ward. God is all around us, as well as in our own heart. We only need to know how to look.

People say all these things as they grow up, but too often they continue to think like children. The ideas are all true, but we must try to understand them in an adult way. We must give them a spiritual meaning. If we do, then we will have a more mature concept of God.

It took a long time for Karen, the teenager, to get over her anger. She felt that her religion was trying to spoon-feed her fairy tales. She even decided that if God is a vengeful, violent magician in the sky, then He does not exist. We have talked many times about the nature of God, and I've tried to explain that God is love. God, or love, is not simple or easy to understand, and Karen is still learning and growing. But there is one thing she understands completely: there is no doubt whatever that love exists.

Key Concepts

God	love	spiritual
identical	human nature	moral guidance

Critical Questions

1. When you think of God, do you think of a powerful, wise old man? How would you describe God?
2. Do you think children are incapable of understanding many things that adults understand, like love, commitment, responsibility, or betrayal? Can 16-year-olds understand all these things?
3. Abstractionists claim that their concept of God is more spiritual than most people's concept. What do they mean by "spiritual"?
4. Does love really provide answers to moral questions? For example, in the cases the abstractionist mentions, suppose the man says he loves his young coworker, or the woman says she loves her work. Then what guidance does love provide?
5. In general, how does someone prove that one thing, X, is identical with another thing, Y? For example, how does a scientist prove that lightning is identical with electricity? How could Lois Lane prove that Superman is really Clark Kent?
6. The abstractionist claims that all the beliefs people have about God are also applicable to love. Can you think of any beliefs people have about God but do not have about love? For example, do people believe God hears their prayers?

YES: PERSONALIST

"The Projection Theory"

One of the oldest and most common critiques of religious belief in God is the assertion that the concept of God is a projection of idealized human qualities onto nature. God, it is claimed, is imagined to be all that frail, frightened humans would like to be themselves—infinitely powerful, aware of the future, morally confident and irreproachable, and above all, immortal. There is no such being, the critique claims, just as there is no Santa Claus who will bring children whatever they ask for. Both characters are products of wish-fulfillment. That is, in both cases people want something to exist so strongly that gradually they decide that it really does exist.

As old and familiar as this critique is, the majority of people still believe in God. Are all these believers stubbornly irrational? Or is the critique flawed or inconclusive in some way? Does the theory undermine belief in the traditional God? This theory, which can be called the projection theory, needs to be evaluated. Is it true, and if it is true, what does it prove?

The projection theory has taken different forms over the centuries. As long ago as 520 B.C.E., the Greek philosopher Xenophanes said:

> If oxen and horses had hands and could draw and make works of art
> as humans do, then horses would draw their gods to look like horses
> and oxen like oxen.

But the projection theory was elaborated in more detail in the mid-nineteenth century by the German philosopher Ludwig Feuerbach. He based it on the psychological assumption that human beings strive to reach self-consciousness, but that they can do so only by seeing themselves reflected in their environment, in their art, their manufactured goods, their tools, and especially in other people's reactions to them. In a sense, they project themselves onto their environment, and then read the results to gain self-knowledge.

But a high level of development is required before a culture realizes that parts of the environment reflect our own selves. And it is very difficult to know which parts of the environment are reflections of ourselves, and which parts are independent of our effects. For example, primitives believe that a tree or river has thoughts and intentions of its own. They mistakenly project their own intentions and feelings onto inanimate objects without realizing that they do so.

According to Feuerbach, the modern concept of a single deity is another form of the primitives' projection. The believer's own thoughts and feelings are not projected onto particular trees or the wind, but are focused on a single Being who is not localized in a particular place. However, the monotheistic God has entirely human characteristics and emotions. Therefore, Feuerbach inferred, it was not God who created humans, but on the contrary, humans who created God. Humans created God in our own idealized image, as omnipotent, omniscient, and immortal, without realizing what we were doing. After the image was formed, it seemed—like Pygmalion's statue—to take on an independent life, issuing commands and making promises.

Feuerbach also concluded that religion prevented humans from fulfilling our potential. We worship the power and creativity of God, when we should realize that we possess all the magnificent qualities ourselves. Not as individuals, but as the species, humankind. The species is potentially omnipotent, omniscient, and even immortal. Humans should worship ourselves.

The most famous form of the projection theory is due to Sigmund Freud. While Feuerbach proposed some psychological assumptions as the basis of his critique, Freud developed a comprehensive, complex theory of the mind as the basis of his view of religion. First, he established that a large part of the mind is unconscious, but still effective. People have unconscious memories and desires that nevertheless affect their behavior. He further explained that the desires or memories are unconscious because the individual cannot bear to admit them consciously; they are too painful or embarrassing. A neurosis results when the individual attempts, indirectly or symbolically, to act on the desire or memory. An example might be obsessive hand washing, which could be an indirect expression of an unconscious desire to atone for sins. In addition, Freud discovered that a man's or woman's childhood experiences often exert a strong influence over their later lives, even though the adults do not remember the earlier events.

These aspects of mental functioning explain humankind's belief in God. As a young child, each person feels completely secure, protected, and provided for by a supremely capable father. But as people grow older they recognize that their fathers are not perfect, or infallible, or immortal. They face the terrifying prospect of being alone, of dealing with the hostile and threatening world by themselves. For most people, this possibility is too frightening. Most people unconsciously decide to remain children, if not physically, then psychologically. They are determined to hold onto the feeling of security and being cared for, even if they have to invent a surrogate father. As Freud says:

> The psychoanalysis of individual human beings teaches us with quite special insistence that the god of each of them is found in the likeness of his father, that his personal relation to God depends on his relation to his father in the flesh and oscillates with that relation, and at bottom God is nothing other than an exalted father. (*Totem and Taboo*)

People imagine an ideal father who is in complete control, who knows all, and whose favor can be won by obedience and devotion. Their real fathers appeared to have these qualities when the children were very young. As adults, their powerful, unconscious desire to be watched over by such a father leads them to believe, consciously, that such a supernatural Father actually exists.

How persuasive is the projection theory? Does it prove that religious belief is irrational, or even that God does not exist? How should the theory be evaluated? First notice that, even if the claims are true, and a theist's concept of God is nothing more than an enlarged concept of his father, the theory does not prove that there is no God. The theory (if true) describes only the way some people think about God. It says nothing about whether or not some sort of God—like a father or not—really exists. It is possible that God really *is* like a perfect father. The fact that people want very badly for such a father to exist does not rule out His existence. It is also possible (even if the projection theory is true) that God exists, but that He/She/It is not like a perfect father.

Notice in the second place that the theory does not apply to people who conceive of God in some way other than as a perfect father. It is true that Western religions (Judaism, Christianity, and Islam) describe God in anthropomorphic terms. But if other religions conceive of God as nonhuman, and not possessing fatherly wisdom, compassion, and strength, then the theory does not apply to them.

In the third place, the projection theory does not apply to people who have objective evidence that God exists. The thrust of the critique is that belief in God is irrational. Freud assumed that religious believers have no other reason to believe in God besides their childish desire for a perfect father. Their real reason for believing in God is merely their wish that He exist. They may talk about theology, miracles, philosophical proofs, or evidence from history, but these are all embroidery, according to Freud. These ideas do not move people. The real basis of their belief is not evidence or facts or any conscious knowledge at all. The real basis is their unconscious desire to remain in a state of childish dependency.

This is the crux of the issue. Is Freud's assumption correct? Do people who believe in God have any objective reason to do so? Is their belief based on any real evidence? Or is it only wishful thinking? The strength of the projection theory as a critique depends on the answers to these questions. If believers have some independent evidence that God exists—such as a direct encounter, or a philosophical argument—and base their belief on that, then the projection theory is not a serious criticism and proves very little. If they can point to sound reasons for believing in God, then their belief is not irrational.

However, if they do not have any evidence, independent of their personal desire to believe in God, then it would seem that the projection theory applies to their particular case. And then their belief in God *is* irrational. Believing something solely because one wants it to be true is the epitome of irrationality. It is a flight into a dream world and a failure to accept reality. It is confusing one's own subjective feelings with the objective world, like a person who believes he is Napoleon because he wants to be powerful and respected. Believers certainly may want God to exist. There is nothing irrational about that. But they must have some reason, beyond their desire, to believe that He exists.

Therefore the projection theory proves nothing by itself, *even if it is true*. It does not prove that there is no God. It does not apply to those believers who conceive of God as nonhuman. And it does not necessarily prove that the belief in God is irrational. If the believer has good reasons to believe in God, in addition to a strong desire, then the belief may be perfectly rational.

Key Concepts

projection theory	anthropomorphic	infantile
critique	unconscious	irrational

Critical Questions

1. On what psychological assumption is Feuerbach's projection theory based?
2. Why is belief in God harmful, according to Feuerbach?
3. In Freud's view, why do people believe in God?
4. Freud probably developed his theory with monotheism in mind. Does it also apply to polytheism, in your opinion?
5. The essay states that, even if the projection theory is true, it is still possible that God exists. How? If God is a projection of our minds, doesn't that mean he is imaginary?
6. Do you know of any religion in which God does *not* resemble humans, and does not have human qualities?
7. How does the essay define irrationality? Does a personalist think that believing in God is irrational?

Methods and Techniques
MEANINGS OF WORDS

Philosophers want answers to important questions, such as "Does God exist?" They realize that an essential part of discovering good answers to these questions is understanding the terms or concepts in the question. They realize that before they can know whether or not God exists, they must know something about what God is like, or what it is that does or does not exist. In fact, it may not be going too far to say that philosophers are just as interested in figuring out what the questions and answers mean as they are in knowing which answers are correct.

Many of the questions philosophers ask are explicitly questions about the meanings of terms or concepts. What is happiness? What is a person? What is justice? Just as many people say they believe in God, so many people say their goal in life is happiness. But they cannot say what happiness is. The same is true of justice. Everyone says it is a good thing, but no one knows exactly what it is. Furthermore, two people can argue for hours about the justice or injustice of a policy if neither person has a clear definition of justice. Often what people call "philosophical" arguments are arguments over the meanings of abstract words. But while some think these arguments are a waste of time, in reality they are extremely important. People cannot have any solid beliefs about God, social justice, happiness, or other important issues, without having clear definitions of the key terms. Getting clear on what the words mean is a necessary precondition for finding any answers.

Both these essays try to explain what people mean by the word "God." The abstractionist's approach is to say that one thing—God—is really identical with another thing—love. In other words, two things that everyone thought were separate and distinct are actually the same. This one thing was merely looked at from two different points of view, so to speak. This is progress, because it reduces the number of problems we face. It simplifies our outlook. We no longer have to understand (1) God, which is very vague and confusing, *and* (2) love, which is clearer and easier to understand. If God *is* love, then we only have to understand love, which is already clearer than the traditional concept of God.

Other philosophers may use the same procedure. For example, one could survey many examples of happiness and propose that they all amount to pleasure. Happiness is really just pleasure. The idea of happiness is vague and hard to pin down, but the idea of pleasure is more specific and easier to understand. The experience of pleasure is simple and familiar to everyone. Now this is a controversial theory. Is it really true that every case of happiness is really a case of feeling pleasure, and nothing else? (You will read about this issue in Section 3.2, "Can We Understand Happiness?") The point of this example is not to define happiness. The point to see is that philosophers often try to explain a puzzling idea by showing how it is really the same as a simpler idea.

The second essay also tries to explain how people think about God, but it uses a different method of clarifying the idea. It emphasizes the *origin* of people's idea of God. And it points out that people may not realize what the origin is, because the origin is unconscious. The essay says people may imagine a powerful, protective Being, who is a substitute for their fathers. It not only asks *how* people think of God, but also *why* they think that way. Why do we define the concept the way we do?

One can ask the same question about other concepts, such as the concept of justice. A person might propose that our concept of justice begins in early childhood when we play games with other children. Maybe the first thing that very young children learn when they play with others is "be fair." If I may do something, then others may do it as well, and if I do not want others to do something, then I should not do it either. Philosophers might try to explain why we learn this rule. Here philosophers are trying to explain our concept of justice by uncovering its origin. That is one way to understand important concepts.

Understanding the Dilemma
ABSTRACTIONIST OR PERSONALIST?

Theists are different from atheists insofar as theists believe in God. But there are different kinds of theists. I have already mentioned monotheists and polytheists, causal theists and design theists. Besides the questions of one or many, and cause or design as evidence, part of believing in God is deciding what God or the gods are like. If you are a theist, what kind of God do you believe in? If you are an atheist, what kind of God do you deny exists?

The essays in this section present opposing views. An abstractionist believes God is an abstract, universal power, the power of love. Love is real, of course, and an abstractionist claims that love has most of the properties theists usually associate with God. But love is not a person. It is not conscious, it does not have thoughts or feelings, it does not listen to us. When speaking of love, we say "it" rather than "He."

The personalist describes a more traditional concept of God. According to this "personal" view, God does have human qualities. He makes plans and then carries them out, he feels approval and disapproval, he communicates with people, talking and listening, he knows about the world (in fact, he knows everything), and so on. Abstract powers or processes have none of these characteristics. Theologians may argue over which human traits God has. (For example, is God male, female, or neither? Does God feel anger, jealousy, regret, and other negative emotions? If God thinks, does that mean he can change his mind? But if he is omniscient and perfect, why would he ever change his mind?) Although they may argue among themselves, these theists are convinced that God is like people in some ways.

How can you choose between abstractionism and personalism? One thing to consider is why you believe in God. The kind of God you believe in is related to your reason for believing in God. For example, if you believe in God because you see evidence of divine power all around you, in the creation of the world, in the infinite power that creation required, in the direction of history, and elsewhere, then you may be an abstractionist. You may think of God as the power that created and organizes all of existence.

On the other hand, you may believe in God for different reasons. You may have had a personal encounter with God. Some people say they have heard God's voice, or felt his presence, and they are certain that it wasn't just their imaginations. If you have had such a life-shaking experience, then you probably believe in a personal God.

Both the essays contrast mature ways of thinking and immature ways. For an abstractionist, the very idea of a personal God is immature. An abstractionist says that theists need a more spiritual concept of God. A personalist says that the idea of a personal God is not itself immature, but some people's *belief* in a personal God is immature, because it is only a wishful projection of a father figure. No one wants to be immature, but the two essays have slightly different views of what is immature.

Which of the following sets of statements are you inclined to accept? Which describe the kind of God you believe in? Of course if you are an atheist, none of these statements seems true to you.

ABSTRACTIONIST

1. God cannot be visualized.
2. God is more like a force, a spiritual magnetism, or energy, or a pattern, than a person.
3. There are good people, and there is the quality of goodness itself, and God is more like goodness itself than like a particular good person.
4. We should try to enlarge and stretch our idea of God, and go beyond the concrete images we had as children.

PERSONALIST

5. God knows about me and cares what happens to me.
6. God is like a father-figure, but much greater.
7. Some things make God happy and other things make him sad.
8. Without emotions and thoughts and plans, God would not be comforting, would not give hope, would not be a being you could talk to.

FOR FURTHER STUDY

Historical Examples

PERSONALIST: Martin Buber. *I and Thou.* Macmillan, 1978. Originally published in 1923. Buber argues that a relation with a "thou" is fundamentally different from a relation with an "it," and that relations with finite, limited "thous" make us want a relation with an eternal, infinite "Thou."

ABSTRACTIONIST: Paul Tillich. *The Courage to Be*. Yale University Press, 1952. In the last two sections of the book, "Theism transcended," and "The God above God," Tillich tries to explain his more abstract conception of God.

OTHER SOURCES

Don Cupitt. *After God: The Future of Religion*. Basic Books, 1997. Argues for a "poetical theology" in which God is not an objective being, but a symbol of universal love.

Sigmund Freud. *The Future of an Illusion*. Norton, 1989. Originally published in 1927. A brief, clear analysis of religion as a form of self-delusion and dependence on an all-powerful father-figure.

John F. Haught. *What Is God? How to Think about the Divine*. Paulist Press, 1986. An attempt to explain some difficult, abstract ideas in comprehensible terms.

C.S. Lewis. *Beyond Personality: The Christian Idea of God*. Macmillan, 1945. Fireside chats in plain language about the Trinity and other Christian ideas about God.

Sallie McFague. *Models of God: Theology for an Ecological, Nuclear Age*. Fortress Press, 1987. Discussion of various metaphorical ways of thinking about God, from a feminist perspective.

J.B. Phillips. *Your God Is Too Small*. Macmillan, 1953. Easy-to-read critique of immature concepts of God, and defense of the Christian, personal conception of God.

James D. Collins. *God in Modern Philosophy*. H. Regnery, 1959. Broad-ranging history of philosophical thinking about God from the Renaissance to the present.

1.3   CAN GOD ALLOW INNOCENT SUFFERING?

Contradictor or Reconciler?

The problem of evil is a standard, traditional problem in philosophy. But for many people it isn't an academic, theoretical problem at all. It is an urgent, emotional cataclysm in their lives. When something terrible happens, people naturally ask why. We try to understand why a loved one died, or why a natural disaster devastated a whole community. To understand means to put the tragedy into some larger context. We try to see how it fits in with our other beliefs and values regarding the goals we should have, human nature, society, or God. This question probably brings more people to philosophy than any other question.

The issue is usually called the problem of evil. But what most philosophers mean by "evil" is innocent suffering. When a child contracts a lingering, fatal disease, that is evil because the innocent child suffers. When one man kills another for his money, that is evil because the victim and his friends and relatives suffer.

Anyone can ask why these things happen. Is there any reason for them? Do they serve any purpose? What do they tell us about the kind of world we live in, or the nature of human beings? But the question is particularly pressing for people who believe in God. If God knows about the suffering, and if he can do whatever he wants, then why does he stand by and let it happen?

In the first essay below, the author claims that there is no answer. The only explanation of evil is that God does not exist. In other words, the existence of evil "contradicts" the existence of God, so to speak. Since we see evil all around us, and it is incompatible with God, we must conclude that God does not exist. The second essay says that evil is compatible with the existence of God. Evil can exist and God can exist, too, because God has a reason to allow evil to occur. God and evil can be reconciled.

NO: CONTRADICTOR

"There Is No God"

I am continually amazed by religious people. They remind me of contortionists who bend their bodies into weird, unnatural shapes. Religious people go to great lengths to bend and twist the facts to try to support their beliefs. But facts are stubborn. They won't go away. Eventually we have to learn to live with them, whether we want to or not.

To a normal person (not a mental contortionist) a few facts demonstrate that religion is misguided. Think for a moment about the world that standard religions say God created. It is obvious that the world is not a perfect place. In fact, it's pretty lousy. Suffering, pain, and tragedy fill every newspaper. War, famine, disease, and crime are so common that we hardly notice them; we take them for granted. I could go on and on, but it's too depressing. Some of this evil and suffering is caused by people. One man murders another, a woman abandons her family, we hate and torment each other. Other suffering is caused by the natural world. Disease strikes a young child, floods and fires destroy families and whole regions. Natural disasters cause just as much pain and sorrow as human faults.

How can all this evil occur, if there is a God? No one denies that people suffer, but *why* do they suffer, if there is a God? God is supposed to be all-powerful. He can do whatever he wants. And he is said to be benevolent. He loves his creation. If he is all-powerful, then he *can* eliminate suffering. And if he loves us, then he *wants to* eliminate suffering. But suffering occurs. How is that possible? If God wants to eliminate it, and he can eliminate it, then why does it still happen?

Look at it this way. Imagine a person who is walking along the street and decides he wants to buy a newspaper. And imagine that he is able to buy a paper. He has fifty cents in his hand and he is standing beside a busy newsstand. He really does want the paper, and he really can buy it. If these conditions exist, then what are the chances that he will buy a paper? It's a sure thing. There is nothing to prevent him, so long as he really wants to, and he has the means. Why wouldn't he go ahead and buy it, if he does want to and he is able to? The same question applies to God. How is it possible that he does not eliminate suffering?

It is possible only if (1) God does not *want* to eliminate it, or (2) he is not *able* to eliminate it. If he wanted to, and he were able to, then suffering would not occur. But it does occur. So either (1) or (2) must be true. (In other words, either there is no being who wants to eliminate suffering, or there is no being who can eliminate it.)

But if either (1) or (2) is true, then there is no God. A being who does not want to eliminate suffering is not loving and merciful, not God. Likewise, a being who is not able to eliminate suffering is not all-powerful, not God. Since suffering occurs, there cannot be a being who is both benevolent and all-powerful. We must give up belief in one of those traits, and that means we must give up belief in God.

Someone might continue to believe in a supernatural being who is able to make a better world, but who doesn't care about us, or who even takes delight in our anguish. Such a person would be like the character in Shakespeare's *King Lear* who says, "We are to the gods as flies to young boys: they kill us for their sport." But a being who is able to kill people for sport, or who even watches impassively and coldly as people suffer, is not God. That is more like a monster.

Or someone might believe in a supernatural being who cries out at the pain in the world, but who is just as powerless to prevent it as we are. That isn't God either. God is supposed to be the creator of everything. Surely if there were a being who created the world from nothing, then he could modify a few of the parts. So if the Deity is not able to eliminate suffering, that being is not God.

Of course apologists for religion have tried to squirm out of this bind in various ways. The standard maneuver is to claim that God is certainly able to eliminate suffering, and wants to, but he wants other things even more, and those other things require suffering. For example, they say God wanted human beings to be free, so we could freely choose to worship him. But if we are really free, then we have the capacity to do evil as well as good. Regretably we misused our freedom; we have chosen to kill and torment each other. And that is why evil occurs. It isn't God's fault; it's ours. This is "the free will theory" of evil.

But it is a very poor theory. There is other evil besides human evil. Who is responsible for earthquakes? Earthquakes (not to mention dozens of other natural calamities) cause tremendous suffering of innocent people, and earthquakes have nothing to do with free will. The free will theory fails for another reason. God must have *known* that people would misuse their free will when he made us. He is supposed to be all-knowing. He must have foreseen the hatred, violence, deception, and cruelty that people would spread around the world if he gave us free rein. If he knew it would happen, and he created us with free will anyway, then he bears responsibility for the consequences.

Others offer a different theory. They say that suffering tests us and teaches us to be humble. Like Job in the Bible, our faith is being tested, and the purpose is to teach us how insignificant we are and how great God is. But this is absurd. Imagine a baby who is born with a horrible disease and who dies in convulsions after six weeks of pain. Suppose the parents and relatives do learn to be humble. Does that lesson justify the child's suffering? Is the parents' humility that important? Can a loving God use children like laboratory demonstrations to teach his lessons? This theory makes no more sense than the free will theory.

To be perfectly fair to believers, let's consider an additional point. They say that innocent people who suffer will be rewarded by God with unimaginable blessings in heaven. And that makes up for the suffering. Does it? Suppose the child who dies in agony is later rewarded in paradise. Does that really give God the right to torment the child in the first place? Does it prove that God is a loving father? If the answer isn't perfectly clear to you, then apply the same standards to a human parent. Here is a (human) father who beats and abuses his child. But he says he has a good reason. He wants to teach his other children to be humble and submit to him. And besides, after beating the child senseless, he rewards her with toys and chocolate and a vacation. Is the beating justified? No one with a sense of justice can say it is. If this kind of behavior by a human parent is brutal and vicious, then the same kind of behavior by God would be brutal and vicious.

Religionists are grasping at straws. There is no way to hold on to the idea of an all-powerful, benevolent God in the face of the suffering we see around us. The reasonable conclusion is not that there is a powerful but indifferent being out there, and not that there is a compassionate but weak being mourning with us. The reasonable conclusion is that there is no God at all. Some events are simply tragic. No one is pulling the strings, no one planned it all, no one is trying to teach us anything. There is no God.

Key Concepts

evil	dilemma	free will
suffering	omnipotent	humility
benevolent		

Critical Questions

1. What are the two main types of evil that the essay describes?
2. What are the two most important characteristics of God?
3. The essay describes a dilemma facing theists (people who believe in God) that is created by the existence of evil. What are the two sides of the dilemma?
4. A contradictor says that if we accept either side of the dilemma, then we must give up our belief in God. Why? Do you agree?
5. Why doesn't our free will explain evil, according to the essay?
6. If God wanted to teach us not to value this life and the things of this world, but to live for the next life, how could he do it? Wouldn't he have to make us suffer?

YES: RECONCILER

"Character and Contentment"

In every society and every age, some people believe in God and some do not. The proportions change, with first one side in the majority and then the other side. But the division is always with us. Though I cannot prove it, I feel sure that when cave men huddled around their campfires at night, some professed their faith in a Divine Creator, and others scoffed at their primitive superstitions.

Not only is the debate part of the human condition, but the sources of the disagreement are perennial and universal as well. Part of the human race is convinced of God's existence by the majesty of the world around them, and by the insistent voice within the inner chambers of their hearts. The other part denies that God exists because they say the world is horribly flawed. They see the catastrophes that take uncounted lives every year: the disasters of flood, fire, famine, pestilence, and quaking earth. No God worthy of the name would create such a botched, toilsome world, they believe. These disasters have always seemed, to part of the human race, incompatible with belief in a wise Creator. Thus the debate continues.

I will not end the debate with these few remarks. But I would earnestly appeal to you, the reader, to think carefully about your allegiance to one side or the other. In particular, I urge you to weigh on a just scale the alleged evidence against God. The nonbelievers are making a serious error. They rail against the pain and suffering of the world as if they would remove it altogether. They say that if they could make the world over again, they would eliminate all the hardships that we endure in this world. But they are shortsighted and see only the surfaces of things. Pain is a necessary part of life. It is part of what makes us human.

Is this mere fatalism, the exhausted resignation of the battered and defeated? No. My thesis is life-affirming, a plea for human dignity. I say pain and struggle and even loss are necessary for men and women to realize their true humanity. The greatest good that an individual can create is *character*. Strength of will, unflinching acceptance of the truth, determination to go on, to prevail, rising above the petty and the trivial, above all, disdaining self-pity: these virtues have been recognized in all ages as the components of character. They are the bones and sinews of a mature personality. They are not all of a person, but they are the sturdy framework, without which nothing else can hold up or last.

Everyone has character to some degree, but not everyone possesses it in the same degree. Some individuals are more reliable, more steadfast, more responsible, than others. Some people are the kind of people you would want to have with you in a crisis, such as being lost in a forest, or stranded in a lifeboat. And you undoubtedly know others whom you would *not* want with you at difficult times. But character isn't only valuable in emergencies. We all enjoy and admire integrated, stable people at other times as well. We trust them. We look up to them. We try to emulate them. In fact, they embody the ideal of human nature: the fully developed, self-possessed, strong personality. How do these integrated personalities acquire character? How would you try to instill character in your growing child? There is only one way. An individual must face challenges and overcome them. He must go through difficult tests, in which he draws upon all his personal resources, and discovers abilities of which he was not aware. He must sometimes fail, and learn from the failure, so he will not fail the next time. He must acquire a wide variety of experiences, so he can face a new situation with the confidence that he has worked through something like it before. He must learn about frustration, about pain, about the dejection following long, persistent efforts that come to nothing, so these feelings will not overwhelm him in the future. Therefore, suffering is necessary to form character.

Those embittered people who complain about the tragedies of life, and say that God should have eliminated them, do not realize what they are asking. Try to imagine a world in which there is no suffering at all. No one is ever hungry, no one ever falls and gets hurt, no one cuts a finger or breaks a bone, no one gets a headache or the flu or indeed any kind of illness. It never rains too much or floods crops, there is no drought, there are no quarrels, no anger, no jealousy, no crime, and finally, no death. Would this be an ideal world? I do not think so. The nonbelievers seem to think it would, but they are making a mistake about values. They are assuming that contentment or continuous pleasure is the highest value in life. But they are wrong. This pleasure-world would leave out the most important thing. The highest value is character, and in this world no one would have a chance to develop character. The necessary challenges are missing. No one would learn to extend himself, to strive, to be resourceful, or to be patient. Since all desires would be satisfied, no one would be forced to meditate on human limitations or on what is most important above all in life. No one would be wise.

A moment's reflection will bring to mind many examples to illustrate these general ideas. Abraham Lincoln is, of course, one of the most loved and admired figures in American history. Why? Because of his gentle, unbreakable soul. His beautiful Second Inaugural Address is perhaps the best expression of character in the English language. But the words and the personality behind them can be understood only in historical context. Lincoln had lived through the Civil War. He had seen the hospitals in Washington, he had made frightfully difficult decisions, he had searched almost desperately for a competent Union commander. And besides these matters, during the same years he had lost his young son to illness, and his wife was increasingly unstable. The photographs of the man from the 1850s to 1865 tell his story more eloquently than words. In spite of the tragedies, he maintained his perspective and his determination to bring good out of evil. In 1865 he was able to write:

> With malice toward none; with charity for all; with firmness in the right, as God gives us to see the right, let us strive on to finish the work we are in; to bind up the nation's wounds; to care for him who shall have borne the battle, and for his widow, and his orphan—to do all which may achieve and cherish a just and lasting peace among ourselves, and with all nations.

Lincoln shows us, by example, the very best that humanity can be. Few reach his stature, but all can aspire to the standard he set. It is not his intelligence, or even his compassion, that shines so brightly down through the years. It is his character. And his character would not exist without the soul-wrenching challenges that he met and mastered.

In the sharpest possible contrast to Lincoln, some people lead pampered, protected lives. They or their parents are well-off, they live in nice homes, drive expensive automobiles, buy gadgets and trinkets on a whim, order others about, and generally get what they want. In my experience, people from such backgrounds are spoiled. Beneath the surface, they are arrogant, insensitive, and utterly bored. They have never learned what is really important in life. Sometimes they not only lack character, but they even lack all moral sense whatever. The young man who strangled his girlfriend in Central Park in New York City a few years ago went to private schools and enjoyed a privileged life, but he never learned what is important in life.

Please understand me. I am not trying to persuade you that all suffering is good. It isn't. Nor am I advocating the popular idea that pain is a "test," and that when bad things happen God is trying to see if our character will hold and if we will remain faithful to Him. The "test" idea assumes that God is a suspicious, cruel being, and it assumes that we already have the quality of character *before* we are tested. I believe both assumptions are obviously false. Pain is not a test but an *opportunity*. Tragedy makes it possible for an individual to grow and learn and be stronger. In struggling to carry on, to rebuild, or to find purpose, an individual can discover within himself a clear vision, a center of gravity, and a focus that he has never known before, and that adds up to character.

Pain, then, is a complex and subtle gift. It is not good in itself, but it makes a genuinely human life possible. Moreover, it is only an opportunity, not a guarantee. The decision is up to us to take advantage of the opportunity. We must choose to face the challenges, to wrestle with them, to make our mightiest efforts, before we can grow and reach a higher level. It is a gift, but it is one we must have courage to use. Character is not a trait like eye color or dyed hair. It is not inborn and it is not easy to get. A person can only acquire real character through long, difficult experience. It is the result of experience and could not exist without experience. Thus a world that had no pain or suffering in it would also have no strong, complex men or women in it. I believe a world where character is possible is infinitely more valuable than a world of mere contentment.

Key Concepts

character	nonbeliever	contented life
suffering	value	opportunity

Critical Questions

1. What is nonbelievers' evidence against God?
2. How does one acquire character, according to the essay? If God is omnipotent, why couldn't he simply create people who are born with character?
3. A reconciler says nonbelievers are making a mistake about values. What is their mistake?
4. Do you agree with the essay that a world without pain is *not* an attractive world? Would you prefer to live in a painless world, or in our world?
5. What is the "test theory" of evil? Is there any difference between the reconciler's theory of God's plan regarding suffering and the test theory? If so, what is it?
6. Do you think God was being kind and generous when he created cancer and earthquakes? Is tremendous suffering compatible with belief in a loving, all-powerful God?

Methods and Techniques
CONSISTENT BELIEFS

Everyone has seen a movie or TV program about a trial. At some point in the program a lawyer will cross-examine a witness, looking for *inconsistencies* in his story. For example, Smith, the witness, might say that he met Brown on Thursday. "But wait a minute," the lawyer replies. "Brown was in New York on Thursday, but last week you said you stayed in Miami until Friday. You could not have met Brown on Thursday." In other words, the witness has made two inconsistent statements. He stated that he met Brown on Thursday (in New

York), and that he stayed in Miami until Friday. He must be lying about Brown or about Miami.

Lawyers look for inconsistencies in a person's story because they are strong evidence that the person is not telling the truth. Two statements are inconsistent if they cannot both be true at the same time. For example, (*a*) "I was in Miami all day Thursday," and (*b*) "I was in New York all day Thursday" are inconsistent. If one is true, the other must be false. The following pairs of statements are also inconsistent [i.e., (*a*) is inconsistent with (*b*)]:

a. Brown is over six feet tall.
b. Brown is under six feet tall.

a. Green is single.
b. Green lives with his wife.

a. Black is an ardent tennis player.
b. Black never enjoys playing tennis.

a. White is a sincere democrat.
b. White opposes equality of political rights.

In each case, if (*a*) is true, then (*b*) must be false, or if (*b*) is true, then (*a*) must be false. In everyday language, we can say that (*a*) and (*b*) are *contradictory*, and that a person who stated both had contradicted himself. (In logic, the word "contradiction" has a more narrow meaning. Two sentences are contradictory if they cannot both be true, and cannot both be false. But we need not worry about that here.)

Consistency and inconsistency are very important in philosophy for the same reason that they are important in a courtroom. If two of your beliefs about God or human nature or society are inconsistent, then one of them must be false. So philosophers try very hard to eliminate any inconsistencies or contradictions among their answers to important questions. The most common criticism of philosophical theories is to show that in some way they involve a contradiction.

That is just what the contradictor tries to do in "There Is No God." He claims that statement (*a*), "God exists," is inconsistent with statement (*b*), "evil occurs." If one is true, the other must be false. And it is obvious that (*b*) is true. So (*a*) must be false. In contrast, the reconciler tries to show that the two beliefs, "God exists," and "evil occurs," are consistent, not inconsistent. They are consistent because a loving, all-powerful God could *want* evil to occur. It is an opportunity for us to build character, the most valuable thing we can have.

Understanding the Dilemma
CONTRADICTOR OR RECONCILER?

A reconciler believes that evil can be reconciled with the existence of God, and a contradictor believes it cannot. In other words, a reconciler says we can believe in God and recognize evil in the world at the same time, while a contradictor says that God and evil cannot exist at the same time. One "contradicts" the other. Furthermore, since evil obviously exists, the contradictor says, God must not exist.

So the question in this section is the following: "Are God and evil reconcilable?" Is it possible to believe in both at the same time? Could anything explain how God could create evil? The reconciler represented here argues that God could allow evil because evil enables humans to achieve their greatest good, the creation of character. We can admit that evil occurs, but also believe that God loves us, because the evil is a sort of blessing in disguise; it makes growth and maturity possible. Suffering is a sort of necessary evil. A world without evil, the reconciler claims, would actually not be as good for us as our present world, so the present world is an act of love by God.

A contradictor claims that making innocent people suffer cannot be an act of love. A greater good might require inconvenience, perhaps, or a little pain, but the kind of grotesque, monstrous evil we see in the world could not be justified by anything. The beliefs in God and in evil contradict each other.

The contradictor says the issue is like the paradoxical question some people ask: "What happens when an irresistible force meets an immovable object?" The only thing that can happen is that one has to give way. Either the force is not really irresistible, or the object is not really immovable. They cannot both exist in the same universe. If the force really is irresistible, then the object cannot be immovable, and vice versa. To say that something is irresistible is just to say that there are no immovable objects. Therefore you cannot believe in both at the same time.

The reconciler, however, says the issue is more psychological. Could God love us, but at the same time make us suffer? What purpose could God have in allowing evil to occur? What could his motivation be? What is he trying to accomplish by making us suffer? There are several possible answers. The reconciler says God's purpose is to give us a chance to build character. Does this make sense psychologically and morally? Reconcilers believe it does.

The key issue is consistency. Do your beliefs fit together intelligently? Or do you say one thing at one time, and something else, in conflict with the first statement, at another time? Both theists and atheists might have inconsistent beliefs. A contradictor claims that the theist's belief in God and evil are incompatible. But a theist might say that the atheist's belief in scientific laws and harmony in the world is incompatible with her belief that there is no God to create the order.

Similar conflicts exist in people's personalities and behaviors. Some men behave like dependent children when they are with their parents; like experienced, confident playboys when they are with their girlfriends; and like disciplined machines when they are at work. Which is the real person? Most people strive to integrate and unify their personalities, and decide which basic attitudes make up "the real me." Philosophers try to do the same thing with their beliefs, which are an important part of one's personality.

CONTRADICTOR

1. Nothing could justify the creation of a world in which innocent people suffer the way they do.
2. Even if suffering built character (which is doubtful), the character is not worth the cost in pain and anguish.
3. The universe does not exist for our sakes; it is beneficial in some ways and harmful in others, but the universe doesn't care at all.
4. Reconcilers are emotionally dependent on the idea of God, and they will believe and say illogical things to keep that idea.

RECONCILER

5. Suffering is a terrible thing, but in the long run it makes us better human beings.
6. God expects a lot from us; we should not think that he treats us like fragile children.
7. A life of challenges and accomplishments is better than an easy life of pleasure.
8. God is not a complete mystery; we can understand why he allows people to suffer.

FOR FURTHER STUDY

Historical Examples

CONTRADICTOR: David Hume. *Dialogues concerning Natural Religion.* Many editions. Originally published posthumously in 1779. Part 11 contains Hume's classic formulation of the problem of evil.

RECONCILER: John Hick. *Philosophy of Religion.* 4th Edition. Prentice-Hall, 1990. In chap. 4 Hick presents a version of reconciliation based on the views of Irenaeus, a Christian theologian of the second century.

OTHER SOURCES

Nelson Pike, ed. *God and Evil.* Prentice-Hall, 1964. A collection of classic and contemporary pieces on both sides of the issue.

C.S. Lewis. *The Problem of Pain.* Macmillan, 1962. Argues that pain is God's way of getting our attention and making us aware of our dependence on him.

Fyodor Dostoyevsky. *The Brothers Karamazov*. Many editions. Originally published in 1880. Book 5, chap. 4 is a vivid, fictional statement of the problem of evil, together with two contrasting responses to it.

Carl Jung. "Answer to Job." In Joseph Campbell, ed. *The Portable Jung*. Penguin,
1971. Jung proposes that Job's God is so vast, powerful, and unreflective
that he encompasses both good and evil.

Brian Davies. *Introduction to the Philosophy of Religion*. 3rd Edition. Oxford University Press, 2004. Chap. 3 is a defense of reconciliation on the grounds
that God is neither moral nor immoral.

Harold Kushner, *When Bad Things Happen to Good People*. Schocken Books, 2001.
Argues that God regrets innocent suffering as much as people do, but cannot prevent it because he is not omnipotent.

1.4   IS THE SOUL IMMORTAL?

Mortalist or Survivor?

If you want to know what the weather is like in Australia, you can go there
and find out. After a week or two, you can return and tell your friends about
it. But suppose you want to know what death is like. Death is not like Australia
(although some disappointed tourists might disagree). You cannot visit the land
of the dead for two weeks, and then return to the land of the living and tell
them about it.

Many people want to know what happens after they die. But we cannot
apply the standard procedures to find out. We cannot make observations, conduct experiments, or take measurements. "Dead men tell no tales," as the saying goes.

Is there any other way to find answers about death, short of experiencing
it oneself? Great writers have *imagined* what death is like. Homer describes
Odysseus' visit to the "gibbering shades" of the underworld, and Dante
paints a fascinating picture of both heaven and hell (and purgatory, too). But
these are merely interesting stories. Philosophers want answers that they can
believe.

The first essay in this section claims that by analyzing certain key ideas we
can know what happens after we die. Or, more precisely, we can at least know
what could not possibly happen. It argues that we could not possibly survive
the death of our bodies. Death terminates our lives. We are mortal. In the

second essay, the writer looks for indirect, circumstantial evidence, and tries to decide what the uncertain hints and clues add up to. The evidence is not conclusive, but it offers some support for survival, according to the second essay. If you agree with this position, you are a survivor.

NO: MORTALIST

"Immortality"

Many people say they believe in "life after death." But how can there be *life* after *death*? Death means the end of life. Maybe what they mean to say is that no one ever dies; life continues forever. But how could anyone believe that? We see people die every day. Everyone knows that there are only two certainties: death and taxes. Actually these people do not believe in life after death, because the very idea of immortality is inconceivable. People may hope that they will never die, but they cannot believe that they will live after they die. It doesn't make sense.

The best way to begin untangling the confusion is to ask how the idea came about in the first place. It is easy to understand how people arrived at this confused notion of "life after death." You can imagine what the world will be like after you have died. You can imagine your grieving family, the people attending your funeral, the changing seasons, the daily routines that continue. Picturing the events in one's mind is very similar to imagining that one is *watching* these things. Of course imagining something is not the same as watching it, but they feel similar. But part of the situation is that one's body has been buried. So if one is watching events, then one must be invisible or insubstantial in some sense. In other words, it is easy to imagine how life goes on after one dies. Since that is a little like watching life go on, it *seems* easy to imagine also that one goes on oneself, but without a body.

But that is strictly impossible. If a person has no body, then he or she has no eyes either. But a person with no eyes cannot watch other people. With what would one watch them? Moreover, a person with no body would have no senses at all, no hearing, no sense of touch or taste or smell. How could there be any contact with the physical world if there was no way of getting information about it? There could be no interaction of any kind between the person and the world. A person without a body could not talk or affect the world in any way. He or she would be completely cut off.

From what angle would things appear to a person without a body? If there is no body, then the person is not located in space. Would one watch another person from above, or below, right or left side? The question cannot be answered, since the watcher has no body and no position relative to what he or she is watching. But if one watches or sees something, it must be from some specific point of view, from some angle. There can be no seeing except from some point of view.

Everyone agrees that our *bodies* will die and disintegrate. But some people insist that another part of themselves will continue to live, but without a body. But this makes no sense. It is impossible to think of a *person* without a body. The concept of "person," or "human being," includes certain essential characteristics that depend on having a body. For example, "person" is defined in part as a being with senses that provide the individual with information about the environment. People (by definition) learn about their surroundings and react to them. They have minds (by definition) and their minds are filled with sights, sounds, smells, and so forth. A being with no senses whatever, no influences from the environment, would not be a person, as we understand the term.

Another essential property of persons is that they have personalities. Each one is unique. And that uniqueness depends in part on the sort of body each person has. The personality of someone who is tall, athletic, and thin will be different from that of someone who is short, awkward, and plump. It is impossible to separate the personality from the kind of body one has.

A third essential property of persons is being located in space. There may be some things that are not located in space, like the number seven or Beethoven's Fifth Symphony. But you cannot conceive of a person, who exists, but doesn't exist anywhere in particular. It is like trying to think of a table, but a table that is neither square nor round nor rectangular nor any other shape. It's impossible; it makes no sense.

Here is another essential property. If you continued to exist without a body, would you be male or female? Without a body you would be neither. But can you really conceive of yourself as neither male nor female? No, you cannot.

The problem I am describing is not that we lack imagination. Artists and writers have taken the most amazing flights of imagination in dreaming of a world of heaven and hell. Hieronymus Bosch painted fantastic creatures and scenes of the afterlife that stretch anyone's imagination. But however bizarre the inhabitants of the afterlife, they have some sort of bodies. The problem is a matter of concepts, not imagination. The concept of a person includes having a body. You cannot separate the two, just as you cannot separate the concept of a triangle and having three sides, or the concept of a bachelor and being unmarried. We know that there cannot be any bachelors who are married. There is no point in trying very hard to imagine a married bachelor. The phrase "married bachelor" doesn't make sense.

The phrase "disembodied person" is similar. You cannot conceive of yourself or any person existing without a body. It is like trying to think of a triangle with four sides. People only think that they can, because they can imagine the world continuing after they have died. But imagining the world continuing is not the same as imagining oneself without a body. They are not really imagining themselves *in* that world. They are only imagining the world by itself. What is the difference between that world *with* you in it—but with no body—and that world *without* you in it at all? There is no difference. If you have no mouth or voice or hands you cannot affect people or the world in any way. Without any sense organs, you could not be affected by the world in any way. With no interaction whatever, you are not really in the world. So people are not really imagining themselves continuing to exist without a body. They are only imagining the world after they have died.

We can imagine the world continuing after our death. But it is a mistake to think that we can imagine being in that world, but with no body. The very idea of immortality makes no sense at all.

Key Concepts

imagination	essential property	position in space
inconceivable	senses	personality

Critical Questions

1. What makes people think that they could survive their own death? What mistake are they making?
2. Why couldn't a person be aware of the world after the death of his or her body?
3. Do you agree with the first essay that one's personality depends in part on one's body type? Is being male, or female, an inseparable part of one's self?
4. How does the mortalist show that people are only imagining the world after they have died, and not imagining themselves *in* that world?
5. If you cannot imagine something (e.g., being in two places at once, being your own grandfather or grandmother), does that prove that it is impossible? Can you believe that something is possible when you cannot imagine what it is?
6. Do you think the mortalist has shown that immortality is *impossible*?

YES: SURVIVOR

"For and Against an Afterlife"

There are three words that are very difficult to say. I'm not thinking of "I love you," although those require courage and humility. Even more difficult are "It's my fault." Hardly anyone has the strength to say those, and mean them.

I'm thinking of the difficult words "I don't know." Especially nowadays, with our information-based economy and university degrees, those words are difficult because having answers confers status. In addition, the progress of science makes us think we can know everything.

The words are most difficult to say when it comes to the most important questions, like "Does God exist?," "What is right and wrong?," and "What happens when I die?" With regard to the last question, the fact is that no one knows what happens after death. No one has experienced that state and returned to the world to tell about it. Therefore, it is *possible* that human beings survive the death of their bodies and continue to live in a different form. And it is possible that we do not. We simply don't know. Anyone who claims otherwise lacks the strength to say those three words.

Even though we can't be sure of what happens after death, we can look for evidence for and against an afterlife. And the evidence gives us a small degree of hope.

Evidence for an Afterlife

Several kinds of evidence make it probable that we will survive the death of our bodies. First, throughout history people have reported seeing apparitions of recently deceased individuals. Often groups of people have seen such beings, and even animals have reacted to them. C.J. Ducasse describes some cases in his book *A Critical Examination of Belief in a Life After Death*. The important thing is not to savor the strangeness of such cases, but to ask if they really happened, and if there is a natural explanation of them. The fact that several people have reported seeing the same apparition, and that animals—who do not lie—have reacted to them, suggests that they are real.

Second, some people report speaking with men or women who have died. Occasionally, the voice, or spirit, will inform someone of something he could not possibly have known if he had not had contact with the deceased. For example, the spirit may tell someone of the location of something that only the deceased knew.

In other cases, the spirit, who speaks through a living medium, or channel, will elaborate a profound, complex philosophical system, unlike any current philosophies or religions. The medium is often an average person, usually with a modest (perhaps high school) education. It is highly unlikely that the medium could develop such a set of beliefs and advice by himself or herself.

One of the most famous mediums was Madame Blavatsky, who founded the Theosophical Society in 1875. She said she was in spiritual contact with two long-dead Tibetan monks, who guided her writing of *The Secret Doctrine*. The book demonstrated a thorough familiarity with esoteric Tibetan religious doctrines and practices, which Blavatsky could not have known. How did she write such a book? The simplest explanation is that the deceased monks helped her.

It is true that the majority, in fact almost all, of such cases are fraudulent. The apparition was a hoax, or the person acquired the knowledge in some other way. But a few cases have been thoroughly investigated by people who know all the tricks. They defy explanation, except that some people survive the death of their bodies, and contact those they left behind.

The third kind of evidence is near-death experiences, or NDEs. Many people who have almost died (e.g., by drowning or in surgery) report remarkably similar sights and feelings. After they have recovered, many say they felt a deep calm and sense of release. They say they left their bodies and watched the doctors trying to revive them. They were moving through a dark tunnel toward a brilliant light. They met and talked with deceased friends and relatives. Many dying, unconscious patients in hospitals have later accurately described the machines and techniques the doctors used to resuscitate them. Some even described what was happening in other rooms in the hospital.

The best known study of NDEs is *Life After Life*, by Raymond A. Moody, Jr. Moody describes numerous examples. The similarity among very different people's experiences is quite remarkable, and suggests that they are not simply hallucinating or fantasizing. After all, if twenty witnesses of an event all agree on the details, then it is probable that the event really occurred, and the witnesses are telling the truth.

Moody thinks that another fact, besides the unanimity, is even more persuasive. He asks

> How is it that the patients can give such elaborate and detailed accounts of resuscitations, explaining in their entirety what the doctors were doing to bring them back to life? How can so many people explain what was going on in other rooms of a hospital while their bodies were in the operating room being resuscitated? To me, these are the most difficult points for the NDE researchers to answer.

Skeptics can question all this evidence. Undoubtedly some patients are simply imagining things. Some writers have proposed that chemical changes in the brain, such as lack of oxygen, can explain NDEs. But while that could explain the agreement, since everyone's brain would react in a similar way, it could not explain the knowledge of other rooms that patients have.

Evidence Against an Afterlife

The evidence against an afterlife is that a person's mind or consciousness is completely dependent on his or her body. Anesthetics and other drugs affect consciousness, a blow to the head can temporarily remove consciousness, light and sound impacting on the eyes and ears cause a person to have certain sensations, and so on. All this implies that if the body is destroyed, then so is the mind. Some skeptics go so far as to say that we can't imagine a mind existing without a body.

But this evidence is not persuasive. Centuries ago people probably couldn't imagine plastic surgery, or being hypnotized, or hearing a symphony thousands of miles away, or other things we take for granted. As for the body influencing the mind, there is just as much evidence that the mind influences the body. I decide to stand, and my body moves. A decision—a mental event—influences my body. If I am frightened, then my hair stands up and my heart races. Anxiety can interfere with digestion and cause ulcers. All these are cases of the mind acting on the body.

Suppose some fourth graders like to play with computers during recess instead of going outside. And suppose those computer fans get better grades and are generally better students than the kids who play outside. Should we say that playing with computers leads to being a good student, or that being a good student leads to an interest in computers? As far as we can tell, the influence goes in both directions. It's impossible to say that one is dependent on the other. And the same is true for mind and body. The influence goes in both directions.

Conclusion

It appears, then, that all the evidence that the body influences the mind is balanced by just as much evidence that the mind influences the body. Therefore, the evidence against an afterlife is neutralized. It is canceled out. As far as the evidence is concerned, it is just as reasonable to believe that there is, or that there is not, an afterlife.

But we still have the evidence *for* an afterlife. It is far from conclusive. The bottom line is that we do not know what happens when we die. But on the whole, this evidence makes it probable that we do survive the deaths of our bodies.

Key Concepts

apparition	fraudulent	evidence
medium	near-death experience	neutralized

Critical Questions

1. The survivor seems to believe in ghosts. On what grounds? Would you say this belief is rational?
2. If someone like Madame Blavatsky claimed to communicate with the dead (e.g., Tibetan monks), how would you test her claim? How would you decide whether she really could communicate with the dead?
3. Suppose someone said people near death all have similar experiences because their brains and bodies undergo similar traumas. Why wouldn't that undermine the evidence, in the survivor's view?
4. In your opinion, which of the three kinds of evidence of life after death is most plausible?
5. How is the evidence against an afterlife "neutralized," according to the second essay?
6. Does the "neutralization" test apply to the evidence *for* an afterlife?

Methods and Techniques
FACTS AND CONCEPTS

These two essays provide several contrasts. They are very different, not only in their conclusions, but also in their methods. The first essay uses a *conceptual* argument. It bases the argument entirely on the *meanings* of the crucial concepts—person, see or aware, and body. It claims that the very idea of being aware of one's surroundings is tightly connected with the idea of having a body. They are so tightly connected that they cannot be separated. That is, we cannot imagine a person who is conscious and aware, but who has no body.

The mortalist would say the situation is comparable to Paul Bunyan's cook, who, the legend says, could make pancakes so thin that they had only one side. This is a cute story, but we know that one-sided pancakes are impossible. Not just extremely difficult to make, or rare, but absolutely impossible. We cannot imagine such a thing. If someone says that he seems to remember eating a one-sided pancake, or that he once had a fleeting glimpse of a one-sided pancake, we do not investigate further. We do not search for other witnesses, or conduct laboratory tests to find out more about these remarkable pancakes. We know that the person is mistaken, however sincere and honest he may be. We know he is mistaken because the concepts "pancake" and "one-sided" cannot be put together. The same is true for "conscious" and "bodyless."

The method in the second essay is completely different. The survivor admits that we cannot have any verifiable, certain knowledge of the afterlife, but thinks that various reports provide some evidence of an afterlife. The question is "How reliable are these reports?" Can we believe what people say about their experiences?

Credibility is a problem not only for philosophers, but also for journalists, scientists, and ordinary citizens during an election. Whom can you believe? Often people give conflicting reports about some event, or a person's story may be inconsistent, or the person may have some ulterior motive for telling the story. (For example, if a person says that he encountered aliens from outer space, he may become a celebrity and appear on TV. But that prospect—not respect for the truth—may be his motive for saying he encountered aliens.)

The second essay considers a variety of reports and tries to apply standards of reliability to them. One important standard is agreement. Are there several witnesses, and do the witnesses agree among themselves? Another standard is bias. Do the witnesses have any reason to lie, or would they profit from lying? Another test it applies is alternative explanations. Is there another explanation for the experience besides the one the witnesses give, and which explanation is the simplest?

The second essay also compares conflicting evidence, i.e., evidence for an afterlife and evidence against an afterlife. And it tries to weigh the two sides to decide which is more persuasive. The evidence against is the mind's dependence on the body. But the body is also dependent on the mind. The survivor argues that the evidence against is "neutralized," and so the evidence *for* an afterlife is stronger.

Philosophers search for believable answers to the most important and difficult questions we ask ourselves. They must consider many different experiences, reports, facts, and theories, all of which are in conflict. Philosophers must continually try to decide which reports are believable and what evidence is strongest. The second essay is an example of that process.

Understanding the Dilemma
MORTALIST OR SURVIVOR?

What happens when you die? A survivor believes that you will continue to exist in some way. You will probably be conscious of your surroundings and other people, and you may interact with physical things. You will survive the death of your body. A mortalist disagrees. He or she believes that dying is like going to sleep and never waking up again. You completely cease to exist. Death will terminate your existence.

Survivors believe we are immortal, because they believe a human being is a duality. They believe a human being is made up of two distinct parts. One part is the body, and the other part is the soul, or mind. The body dies, but the soul continues to live. That is possible because these two parts are completely different. The body is a physical object, with mass, shape, color, solidity, and all the characteristics of other objects. It is subject to the same physical laws as other objects. It is restrained by gravity, it can be frozen, burned, divided into smaller parts, and eventually it disintegrates, like other physical objects. But the other part of a person, the soul, is not physical and not subject to physical laws. The soul is the part that thinks, remembers, feels emotions, and enlivens the body. It is the active part of us. It is the part that is happy or sad, shy or bold, intelligent, creative, lazy, or arrogant. It has no weight, shape, or location in space. Since these two parts are so different, survivors can be called *dualists*. They believe that at death the two parts are separated. The body dies, but the soul continues to exist, separate from the body.

Mortalists, on the other hand, believe a human being is just one thing, a physical body. In contrast with survivors, they are *monists*. The word "monist" comes from the Greek root *monos*, which means single, sole, or alone. We have already encountered the same root in the word "monotheism." Mortalists think a human being is one complex entity, not two entities tied together. We are physical objects, but we are extremely complicated physical beings, with brains, nervous systems, sense organs, hormones, and muscles. Unlike simple tables and chairs, we are physical objects who are capable of thinking, feeling, and acting. Mortalists do not deny that people think and feel. They simply say we do not need to believe in a separate, nonphysical soul to do these things. The body does them. In fact, they believe we cannot imagine a thinking, feeling person without a body. The idea of a nonphysical soul, separate from the body, does not make sense, they say. So they believe we are one thing, a complex human body. And since everyone agrees that the body dies and disintegrates, they are mortalists. They believe we are mortal.

The two essays in this section are very different. They approach the issue of life after death in different ways. The second considers different kinds of evidence, or observations, that may support belief in an afterlife. But the first considers the very *idea* of an afterlife, and analyzes what the idea means. Another difference is in their assumptions about human nature. The survivor in the second essay is a dualist, while the mortalist is a monist. But the main difference is in their conclusion, and that is the main decision you should make. Are you a mortalist or a survivor? When you die, will you continue to exist in another form, or will death be the final end of your existence?

MORTALIST

1. I am so intertwined with my body, and my very idea of myself is so dependent on my consciousness of my body, that I could not possibly exist without my body.
2. It is impossible to imagine (clearly, in detail) existing and interacting with the world without a body.
3. All the images and ideas of heaven or an afterlife are simply images of earthly life with the defects removed; no one has described any so-called disembodied existence.
4. All the alleged evidence of "life beyond the grave" can be explained by purely natural means (such as optical illusions, unconscious memories, etc.).

SURVIVOR

5. I use my body just as I use my car, but I am not the same thing as my body.
6. Spirits of the dead sometimes speak to people, send us messages, or move objects, start fires, break glasses, and so on.
7. Belief in life after death is not just wishful thinking, but is a rational conclusion based on a sober assessment of objective, factual evidence.
8. Life after death will be unlike anything we can possibly imagine.

FOR FURTHER STUDY

Historical Examples

MORTALISTS: Lucretius. *On the Nature of the Universe*. Penguin, 1951. First century B.C.E. In Book 3 Lucretius presents about a dozen arguments designed to show that the soul ceases to exist when the body is destroyed. Most, but not all, are based on his atomism.

SURVIVOR: Plato. *Phaedo*. Many editions. Fourth century B.C.E. Plato claims that we have a kind of knowledge that is eternal and unchanging, and that we could acquire such knowledge only if our souls existed independently of our bodies.

OTHER SOURCES

William Dudley, ed. *Death and Dying: Opposing Viewpoints*. Greenhaven Press, 1992. Chap. 5 presents short excerpts, pro and con, from books and articles on survival, near-death experiences, and the relevance of survival to the meaning of life. Easy to read.

Terence Penelhum. *Survival and Disembodied Existence*. Routledge & Kegan Paul, 1970. Penelhum argues that the existence of one's soul without a body is impossible.

Hywel D. Lewis. *The Self and Immortality*. Macmillan, 1973. Chap. 8 is an attempt to explain how one could exist without a body.

Howard P. Kainz. *The Philosophy of Man*. University Press of America, 1989. Chap. 11 discusses paranormal phenomena, and chap. 12 defends the possibility of survival, based on some careful analyses of key terms like "soul" and "existence."

Peter Carruthers. *Introducing Persons*. Croom Helm, Ltd., 1986. Chap. 7 is an imaginative (but skeptical) consideration of resurrection, reincarnation, and problems of personal identity, using science fiction thought experiments as well as other arguments.

John Hick. *The Philosophy of Religion*. 4th Edition. Prentice-Hall, 1990. Chap. 11 is an examination of the Hindu doctrine of reincarnation.

Raymond Moody. *Life After Life*. Mockingbird, 1975. People's stories of neardeath experiences, told by a survivor.

Paul Edwards, ed. *Immortality*. Prometheus, 1997. Edwards explains the positions and issues in a long introduction, and includes thirty-four selections from Plato to Parfit.

Alan F. Segal. *Life After Death: A History of the Afterlife in Western Religion*. Doubleday, 2004. Large historical survey of many societies' beliefs, and a plea for an open mind.

1.5   IS FAITH AN ANSWER?

Believer or Questioner?

It is not easy to say what religion is, or what makes a person a religious person. Is believing in God enough? There are many ways to think about God, and some beliefs might not be enough. For example, suppose a person believes that God or the gods exist but is terribly afraid of them. Or suppose the person doesn't like God, or even hates him. Is that person religious? He believes in God, but it sounds odd to say he is a religious person.

Or imagine another example. Suppose a philosopher studies the concepts of cause and effect and time, and after careful reasoning decides that something caused the universe to exist. The nature of the world requires a Creator, or God. This philosopher also believes in God, but again, he does not seem to be a religious person.

If believing in God is not enough, then what else is necessary to be a religious person? One answer is faith. That is, a religious person is a person who has faith in God, and believes in God on the basis of faith. That is why neither of the two people in the examples above is religious. Neither has faith.

But it looks as if we have answered our question with another question. The original question was "What makes someone a religious person," and our answer was faith. But what is faith? Is faith in God like faith in your family doctor, i.e., trust that he will do the right thing? Or is it like faith in electricity, i.e., belief that it exists even though you cannot see it or understand it? Or is it something else? There is no simple answer.

The following essays explore different aspects of faith. In the first, the writer tries to explain why he has faith in God. He says it is OK to believe in God even though he has no evidence at all for his belief. We can call anyone with this position a "believer." The second essay says the believer's attitude has terrible consequences. It argues that a person should have some good reasons to back up anything he or she believes. A person who agrees with the second essay is a questioner.

YES: BELIEVER

"Accepting Limits"

I have reached the point in my life where I am beginning to feel the need to sum up what I have learned. I want to start tying up loose ends. I've had a long, full life, and now I want to take stock. What was it all about? What was it for? What has life made of me?

I could talk about my accomplishments in my work. And, to be honest, I would have to talk about some failures, too. I could spend hours thinking about the happy times with my wonderful wife, Jean, and our daughter, Chris. But should I include my first wife? Of course. That big mistake was part of my life as well.

However, I can't talk about everything at once. For the present, I want to describe one particular way that I have grown over the years. I want to explain why I believe in God. I didn't always believe. It is a part of me that has gradually changed. I am not going to discuss religion. Religion is not the same thing as belief. Actually I do worship with my congregation regularly, I work with the people there to help the less fortunate, and I try to live by our religion's principles. Religion has become more important to me in the past few years. But I want to go back to the foundations, which is belief in God. I practice religion because I believe in God, not the other way around. The belief is primary.

I will begin with an observation. It is a fact (I think) that more elderly people believe in God than young people. If you took a poll of one hundred college students and one hundred retired people, asking each group "Do you believe in God," I think that a higher percentage of retired people would answer yes than college students. Why is that? Why do more people tend to believe in God as they get older?

The most common answer is that older people are more afraid of death. They feel death approaching, it is frightening, and they believe in God because the belief is a comfort to them. It is a way of denying death. But that is not why I believe in God. To me, death is a puzzle rather than a terror. I have lived my life. I am ready for it to end. In fact, I'm a little curious about dying.

I have come to believe in God by a different route. What my life has taught me is that we human beings are not all-powerful and all-knowing. We are limited. There are some things we simply cannot understand. With all our science and technology and learning, the world is still, ultimately, a mysterious place. Elderly people have seen enough failed experiments and heard enough shallow, empty explanations that they know about limits. They have lost the blind optimism of youth.

Accepting limits is the first step toward belief in God, and it is a difficult step to take. As a young man, I denied it. I worked hard in school, and I was fascinated by the incredible wealth of knowledge and information accumulated in universities. After college, I went on to study medicine, confident that science could defeat the age-old enemies of mankind—famine, disease, war, and even death itself. For a number of years I practiced medicine, relieving pain, helping some, extending lives, and, through my research, adding a little to our medical knowledge.

But as the years passed, my doubts began to grow. I began to wonder how much of the world and man I really understood. How much did anyone really understand? The science of medicine has grown tremendously in my lifetime. But it seems that for every breakthrough we also confront new problems. Take one example. In the sixties, some brilliant surgeons developed the heart transplant technique. In those days the possibilities seemed endless. If we could transplant hearts, then perhaps we could transplant other organs. And as the transplants wore out, we could replace them with new organs from accident victims. Theoretically a person could live forever. One little problem was that the bodies of the patients kept rejecting the new hearts. They treated the new heart like a foreign invader rather than a life-saving improvement. We assumed that a few minor adjustments could solve the problem, but the adjustments didn't work. We could suppress the rejection for some time, but blocking the rejection led to other problems. We learned from our "advance" that the immune system was much more complex and subtle than we realized, and that heart transplants were not the great triumph we thought they were.

And now of course there is AIDS, an incurable, fatal disease of the immune system. Hundreds of thousands of people worldwide have already died, and many more have the infection. Why? Where did it come from, and what can stop it? We don't know. It seems almost as if nature is cruelly taunting us for challenging her. The more we learn, the more we realize we don't know.

I practiced medicine for over forty years, and I'm glad I had the opportunity to serve my community. I helped a lot of people heal themselves and get back on their feet. But there were tragic cases. Some were beyond hope, some I might have treated differently if I had a second chance, some were just baffling. During the first decade or so the deaths were very difficult to take, but I was able to snap back. I was confident that science could fight death. But a physician is in a paradoxical position. For a doctor, the greatest enemy is death. Injury and disease are challenges, but death is the ultimate defeat. And yet, every patient will eventually die. We can avoid it for some time, but death is inevitable.

As the years passed, and I witnessed more and more deaths, I began to think about death in a different way. From asking "Why did this patient die," I began asking "Why does death happen at all?" Why does everyone die? I read a good deal of the scientific literature, and I discovered that, beneath the jargon and the studies of cells and organs, the fact is that no one knows why death occurs. We can describe the process. But we don't understand why the body deteriorates to the point of collapse. It is just one of the limits we must face.

Death is a limit in two different ways. Obviously death limits each person's allotted time on earth. That was disturbing and painful to me, but I could continue living as I had with that limit. However, death is also a limit in another way. It makes no sense. We can't understand why it happens. It is a limit on our proud intellects. Even if we learn more about cell processes, we cannot answer the larger why. Why do we have such a strong will to live if we are all doomed to die in the end? Why does the world work this way? I realized I couldn't answer these questions, and that realization gradually changed my whole outlook on life. I was no longer the confident, optimistic young man I had been. I finally had to admit that we do not have answers, that there are no rational reasons for everything, and that the world is really beyond our comprehension. That was a completely new way of thinking. It made me a much more humble person.

Once I admitted some limits on our understanding, I discovered others. As a young man, I had assumed that the astronomers would eventually explain the origins of the universe. But all they talk about is the "Big Bang." They have nothing to say about what came *before* this Big Bang, or why it occurred. Here is another example. When I began my career, I thought I was in control of my life. I thought I surely understood myself and what I wanted. But somehow I found myself married to a woman I didn't love, behaving in ways I didn't want to behave. I was an overconfident, ambitious fool. Moreover, I didn't understand others any better than I understood myself. I thought expanded education and government aid would inevitably lead to a better society. But in spite of vast government programs and billions of dollars, we still have rampant crime, homelessness, broken families, and crippling debt. We seem to be in decline.

One of my greatest pleasures now is music. The rhythms, harmonies, and tone colors are always delightful, and sometimes the sheer beauty is almost overwhelming. Can anyone explain that beauty? Why do I feel that way? And how did Mozart create such wonderful, inspiring sounds? No one knows. All we can do is bow our heads in the face of such mysteries.

We are like children around a campfire in the forest at night. Within the little circle of light everything is cozy and comfortable, but we are surrounded by a huge, black darkness filled with strange shapes and unidentifiable, frightening noises.

What I have learned in my threescore and ten is that the world is greater than we can know. We have a little knowledge, but we are severely limited in what we can understand. Why am I here? Why do I die? Why does the world work the way it does? Why do I do what I do? We cannot find answers to these questions through science or reason. Therefore, I have *chosen* an answer. I choose to believe in God, an all-powerful, all-knowing, all-loving Creator. He created me to worship Him. That belief provides answers to all the other questions. It tells me why I am here, why I die, why I do what I do, and why the world is the way it is.

I cannot find answers to these questions in science or philosophy, so I have *faith* that God exists. I have never been impressed by miracles (though they may occur). I have never heard a Voice of God commanding me to believe. In fact, I do not have any evidence that God exists. What I have learned is that some questions can't be decided by evidence or facts or reasons, because reality is just too complex and obscure for us to understand. For answers to these questions I rely on a different part of human nature and a different method. I have faith. I choose to believe the answer that seems best to me.

This is a two-step process. First we must admit that we cannot understand everything. Then, after recognizing our weakness and impotence, we can take the second step of freely choosing to believe in God. Where science and intellect cannot provide answers, faith and commitment can. Faith is not proof. It is not even rational. Indeed, where we have proofs and reasons, faith is out of place. But in so many areas, I have learned, we have no proofs or evidence or reasons. When we realize those limitations, faith is the next step. It is beyond proof and argument.

I am aware of my critics. Some people will say I am wrong and should not have faith. But if scientists cannot explain death or the universe or beauty, then how can they say that my answer is wrong? If they knew why we die, or how the universe began, then I would listen to them, and I would believe their answers. But they don't have the answers; they don't know what is true or what is false. They cannot prove that there is or that there isn't a God. So how can they say my belief in God is wrong?

Many people agree with me that scientists and philosophers do not have all the answers. But many refuse to take the next step and believe in God because of their pride and misplaced confidence. I am not so confident. Since we cannot find answers based on evidence and reasons, I have accepted an answer on different grounds. I believe in God on the basis of faith.

Key Concepts

limits	death	faith
understand	mystery	God

Critical Questions

1. What lesson should we learn from the heart transplant technique, according to the believer?
2. How did the believer's reflections on death lead to a basic change in his outlook on life?
3. What are some examples of things we cannot understand, according to this essay? Do you agree that no one understands these things?
4. If you agree with the essay that we do not understand these mysteries, do you also believe we will *never* understand them?
5. How does the believer reply to his critics, i.e., those who say he should not have faith? Is he right?
6. Does the believer think that he understands God? If not, but he has beliefs about God, then why couldn't he have beliefs about death, or other things he does not understand?
7. Consider an analogy. It is very difficult to know what works in education. No one knows for sure why some children succeed and some fail. Should teachers, therefore, have faith that success depends on genetics? Or diet? Or parents' income, or something else? No one knows for sure what cures cancer (if anything). Should a patient with cancer have faith in one type of cure, e.g., injections of extracts from calves' brains?

NO: QUESTIONER

"Faith and Its Consequences"

In many religions faith is held up as an important virtue. In his letter to the Corinthians, for example, St. Paul specifically lists "faith, hope, and charity" as Christian virtues. Faith may be even more central to Islam. The very word "Islam" is derived from an Arabic word that means submission, and the first of the Five Pillars of Islam is to acknowledge that there is only one God. Other religions place more or less emphasis on faith as well.

But is faith a virtue? Is someone who believes something on the basis of faith acting in a praiseworthy manner? A consideration of the *consequences* of faith shows that it is actually *not* a virtue. People should not believe things on faith. In fact, faith can be very dangerous.

To say that you believe something on the basis of faith is to say that although you do not have good *evidence*, you believe anyway. For example, many people decide to believe that an omnipotent, loving God created the universe. They have no evidence for the belief. They admit that all the "proofs" and disputes through the ages are inconclusive. The few facts we do understand can be explained by scientists using natural laws. So there is no evidence that God exists. But they decide to believe in God on the basis of faith, not on the basis of evidence.

What is evidence? To say that there is *evidence* for some belief is to say that some established facts make the belief *more probable*. For example, a prosecutor in a trial presents evidence that the defendant is guilty. The evidence might be bloodstains at the scene of the crime, which are the same blood-type as the defendant's. The two facts—blood stains and matching blood-type—make it more probable that the defendant is guilty. They aren't proof, but they are evidence of guilt. If nine out of ten patients who take a drug are cured, and all the patients who did not take the drug remain ill, those facts make it probable that similar patients who take the drug in the future will be cured. This is evidence, not faith.

Another example of faith is belief in immortality. There is no good evidence that people continue to exist after they die. The alleged "voices from beyond the grave" and other ghost stories all turn out to be hoaxes perpetrated by swindlers on desperate widows and grieving relatives. At least the cheated widows are looking for evidence, however bogus it is. But some people say they believe they will go to heaven after they die, even though there is no evidence that heaven exists. They say they do not need evidence. They simply have faith that they will never really die.

The desperate widow believes that her dead husband still exists somewhere. Why does she believe it? She has faith, people say. But that just means she decides to believe, even though she has no real evidence. *Why* does she have faith? Why do people have faith that God exists? It is a personal decision, people say. But why do they make that personal decision? The facts and objective evidence do not persuade them to believe. If they did, it would not be faith but a rational inference about probability. So why do people have faith?

There are two possible answers. One is that some *authority* tells them to have faith. For example, parents tell their children (directly or indirectly) that they should believe in God. They cannot point to convincing evidence that God exists, but they still say he does, and they expect their children to believe, too. After the children grow up, they never question what they have been told. Priests and rabbis are also looked up to as authorities. They tell people to have faith, and since people trust them, they do what the religious authorities say.

Besides authority, the other reason people have faith is comfort. The belief makes them feel better. This is obviously why the desperate widow believes her dead husband still exists. Believing that he is out there somewhere, listening or watching, makes her loss easier to bear. The same motive explains why many people believe that *they* will be immortal. The prospect of their own death is so terrifying and painful that they can't face it. So they decide to believe that they will never die. They have faith.

Both these ways of thinking lead to terrible consequences. The first way is to decide to believe something (to have faith) because an authority says it is true, even though there is no evidence to support the belief. But if people follow authorities, they will never learn to think for themselves. It is very easy to believe something because an authority says we should. We just submit, sheeplike, and avoid all responsibility. In contrast, it is very difficult to search out all the facts on some question, weigh the evidence for and against, and then make a reasonable decision. And yet the difficult path is better than the easy one. In the long run, people will be happier if they think for themselves, and society as a whole will be better if it is made up of reasonable, inquiring citizens rather than obedient sheep.

Furthermore, if people submit to authorities in matters of religion, they will soon submit in matters of politics, social policy, education, personal relationships, and other areas of life. People who habitually accept their priest's word in matters of religion will probably accept their Congressman's word in matters of foreign policy, or government expenditures. Such slavish obedience is degrading. And such tremendous power over people on the part of authorities is very dangerous, because power corrupts. In addition, if people follow authorities in matters of belief, then they will soon follow them in matters of action as well. Beliefs are the basis of action. If you decide to believe in God because your minister says you should, then what will you do when your minister says you should donate more money to the church, or convert your neighbor to the true religion, or report on any irregularities you see among your neighbors? (Literally thousands of followers of Sun Myung Moon, who lives near New York, have allowed him to choose their own spouses for them, usually complete strangers. He also decides when they should consummate the marriage.) Submitting to authorities is a bad way of thinking. Many of the horrors of history began with that seemingly innocent decision.

The consequences of this kind of faith are clear. The consequences of the other kind of faith are perhaps more difficult to see, but for that very reason they are more dangerous. The other kind of faith was when people decide to believe something because the belief makes them feel better. If people believe in God on the basis of faith, then they will believe other things on the basis of faith. It is only natural. If the method of thinking works in one area, people will use the same method in other areas, particularly when the method is comforting.

But consider the consequences. I would feel better if it were a fact that men are intellectually and emotionally superior to women. The *evidence* on the issue of men's and women's abilities is confusing. Some studies seem to support one conclusion; other studies seem to support the opposite conclusion. So there is no hard evidence one way or the other. Therefore, I will simply *choose* to believe that men are superior. Why? Because it is a very comforting belief. It makes me feel better about myself. This is the way of thinking of people who believe in God on the basis of faith. That idea makes them feel better, so they decide it must be true. But the consequences of this way of thinking are terrible. It leads to sexism. Believing that men are better than women just because it makes me feel better is blatant sexism. Of course it could just as easily lead to racism, superpatriotism, and other forms of chauvinism.

Other consequences of this kind of faith are just as bad. It is very difficult for people to accept responsibility for their actions, especially when they fail or make a mistake or do something wrong. Guilt, shame, and embarrassment are painful feelings, and everyone wants to avoid them. How easy it is to simply deny the charges. "I didn't want to do it. The system made me do it!" "I was out of my mind. I didn't know what I was doing." "The pressure from work was so intense that I had no choice but to lie." "Hey, she had it coming to her anyway." How easy it is to believe in one's own innocence, when the belief is so comforting and soothing to the conscience. The evidence may be inconclusive. It is very difficult to know why someone did something, even oneself. It is often difficult to know for sure what was right and what was wrong.

But the belief in one's innocence is sometimes a sham and a lie. Having faith because it makes one feel better is a bad way of thinking. Denying responsibility is not only false in many cases, but it also creates bad feelings among others, it sets a bad example, and it makes it easier to do even worse things in the future. If more and more people think this way, then in the long run, it will undermine society.

It comes from the practice of believing something because the belief makes one feel better. Beliefs should be based on evidence, not comfort. Our beliefs are supposed to be about the world as it really is. That is what beliefs are. Therefore, we must make every effort to find out exactly what the world is like. We do that by observing, analyzing, experimenting, and collecting information, not by obeying authorities, massaging our own egos, or letting our fantasies run wild. The consequences of basing any beliefs on faith would be disastrous.

Key Concepts

faith	authority	consequences
evidence	comfort	chauvinism

Critical Questions

1. How does the essay define "faith"? How does it define "evidence"? Can you make up an example of each?
2. Why do people have faith, in the questioner's opinion?
3. What are the consequences of trusting authorities, according to the essay?
4. Do you think accepting the authority of one's religion really would lead to the results described? Don't we all accept and believe scientific authorities?
5. How would faith lead to sexism and racism, according to the questioner?
6. Where exactly do the questioner and the believer disagree? Does a questioner think we can understand the things a believer says we cannot understand?

Methods and Techniques
CONSEQUENCES

Let's focus on the second essay for the moment. It tries to persuade you to accept a certain point of view, a thesis. The thesis is that people should not have faith in God or anything else. How does it try to get you to agree? Well, since it is a philosophical essay it tries to offer good reasons to support the thesis. Remember that if you offer reasons to believe something or do something then you are making an *argument*, in the philosophers' sense of "argument."

The essay uses a type of argument that is very common. It says you ought not to have faith, and the reason is that having faith leads to slavish obedience to authorities and stereotypical thinking. In other words, having faith leads to bad consequences. You have seen the same type of argument many times before. Some people say we ought not to show violent programs on TV. The reason is that violence on TV leads to real fighting and shooting among people who watch the violent programs. Or people say we ought not to smoke, because smoking leads to lung cancer. Your mother told you that you shouldn't leave the milk on the table all night because it will spoil. All these arguments have the same form. They try to persuade you not to do something. And their reason is that doing it leads to bad consequences. The *form* of the argument is the same in each case, even though the *content* is different.

Here is another example. A controversial topic today is euthanasia, or "mercy killing." Some people say that doctors should not help patients with terminal illnesses die, because that would lead to terrible consequences. Once we take that first step, they say, then doctors or hospitals might want to put to death old people who are still healthy, or retarded people, or handicapped people. And that result would be horrible for society. This argument has the same form as the others. It tries to persuade you not to do something (i.e., encourage euthanasia). The reason is that doing it leads to bad consequences.

I said earlier that a big part of philosophy is the study of arguments. As you read the essays in this book you will begin to recognize the writers' arguments—their conclusions and the reasons they give to support them. And you will also begin to see *types* of arguments, that is, arguments with the same form. In other words, one philosopher might be writing about God, and another might be writing about the best society. Their conclusions and reasons will be different, since the subjects are different. But they might still use the same type of argument. The two arguments might have the same form, just as the arguments about violence, lung cancer, spoiled milk, and euthanasia all have the same form. Learning to recognize the form of an argument will help you analyze and evaluate a writer's position.

The argument in the second essay is the same type as the other examples. We can call it the "negative consequences" argument. Now the interesting question about an argument is "Is it convincing?" Should I accept the conclusion? Are the reasons strong enough to support the conclusion? Philosophers consider several factors in deciding whether or not to accept an argument, but the most important is the *truth* of the reasons. Before an argument can be convincing, the premises must be true. (Remember that reasons are also called "premises.") So, should you smoke? It depends on whether or not smoking really does lead to lung cancer. If smoking *does* have fatal consequences, then you shouldn't smoke. Should TV show violent programs? It depends on whether or not violent programs really do lead to violent behavior by those who watch.

Thus when you see a negative consequences argument, you should ask, "Does the action really lead to bad consequences?" (You probably think this way already, but it helps to be more self-conscious and methodical in your thinking.) How do you know whether smoking leads to lung cancer? How does anyone know? The best way is to find examples. If there are many examples where a person smoked, and the smoking caused the person to get lung cancer, then you can say that smoking leads to lung cancer. If there are many examples where watching violent programs on TV caused a person to commit acts of violence himself, then you can say violence on TV leads to violence in reality. (Of course, it is difficult to prove that watching TV *caused* the violent behavior.)

Finding examples is easy in some cases. Leaving milk on the table overnight really does lead to spoiled milk. I have done it myself. In other cases it is more difficult. Can we find examples of euthanasia leading to the killing of handicapped people? I don't know. You would have to do some research on medical practices around the world and throughout history. The practice of euthanasia is rare, so it is difficult to know whether the premise is true. If the premise is *not* true, then it is not a reason to accept the conclusion at all.

However, trying to evaluate a negative consequences argument can get more complicated. People who use this type of argument can modify the argument slightly to avoid the problem of proving their premise. For example, opponents of euthanasia can say that euthanasia *might* lead to the killing of handicapped people. It is *possible* that euthanasia will have terrible consequences. These consequences are so bad that we should avoid anything that even might produce them. So we should avoid euthanasia.

We could modify the smoking argument in the same way. If we did, the premise would be "It is possible that smoking leads to lung cancer," and the conclusion would still be "You should not smoke." The premise supports the conclusion because you want to keep the risk of getting lung cancer as low as possible. Now is this modified premise true? It is easier to find evidence that smoking *might* lead to lung cancer than it is to find evidence that smoking *does* lead to lung cancer. There are enough examples of people who smoke and who have lung cancer to make the modified premise believable.

What lessons can you learn from all this? Well, you should see that there is a structure common to many of the disputes and controversies you hear about. Philosophers and other people very often use a certain type of argument to convince you to believe them. (I called it the "negative consequences argument," but the name isn't important.) Second, you should see that judging the argument requires you to think carefully. It isn't so easy to decide whether or not the premises are true. And I hope you have learned that you can monitor your own thinking. Even though you encounter this type of argument all the time, you can improve your decisions and your judgment by becoming more aware of how you think. If you don't pay attention to your own thinking, it will be easy for you to make mistakes, keep bad habits, and be misled.

Understanding the Dilemma
BELIEVER OR QUESTIONER?

The essays in this section represent a fundamental contrast between two ways of thinking. The believer says his belief in God is not based on evidence; it is not rationally justified, as the beliefs in protons or dinosaurs are. The believer is acting on the general principle that we should accept some statements like "God exists" even though we have no evidence for them. Not everything is rational or explicable. In contrast, the questioner says that no one should accept beliefs on the basis of faith. That attitude will lead to very bad consequences. For example, people who believe without evidence could become overly obedient to authorities, could lose their ability to think for themselves, or could fall into stereotypical thinking because it makes them feel better. The questioner's principle is that a person should not believe something unless he or she has good evidence for it.

This is one big difference between believers and questioners: believers think that some things are beyond human comprehension. Questioners think that, sooner or later, we can find evidence to help us understand everything we can think about. But there is another difference. Let's suppose the believers are right when they say some things are beyond comprehension. Let's suppose that we have no reason whatsoever to accept either side in the debate about immortality; it is just unknowable. Then what do we do? A believer says we should *choose* the answer we want to believe. Since the two answers are equally acceptable, we can pick either one. But a questioner has a different view. If we have no good reason to accept one answer over another, then we should not accept *either* answer. We should suspend judgment until we understand the situation better.

Who is right, the believer or the questioner? Is faith a reasonable attempt to deal with a difficult, mysterious world? Does it answer questions and solve problems in the only way available? Or is faith a childish refusal to accept reality? Does faith lead to conformity, intolerance, and delusion?

Your answer to these questions depends on your confidence in human beings' abilities. If you believe we are capable of understanding the world and our place in it, through our own intellectual efforts, then you are a questioner. If you think human beings cannot understand ultimate matters by our own efforts, then you are a believer. Your answer also depends on how strongly you think we need answers. Believers want answers very badly, and in the face of conflicting evidence, they choose an answer. Questioners say that on some questions we must simply wait until we learn more. Until then, we do not have any answer.

BELIEVER

1. Faith is courageous and admirable.
2. Reality is more complex and deeper than the human mind can ever comprehend, and yet we can have opinions about things we do not understand.
3. I can separate the areas where I have faith from the areas where I look for evidence.
4. I *feel* that some things are true, and that is good enough for me.

QUESTIONER

5. The world is lawful and organized, and we can understand it.
6. Choosing beliefs for no reason is just prejudice and wishful thinking masquerading as philosophy.
7. A person who believes one thing on the basis of faith will soon believe other things on the basis of faith.
8. Hoping that something is true does not make it true, and my choices cannot make God exist.

FOR FURTHER STUDY

Historical Examples

BELIEVER: William James. "The Will to Believe." In *The Will to Believe and Other Essays*. Dover, 1956. Originally published in 1897. In this famous essay, James argues that if we cannot know the answer to an important question, and several answers are possible, then we should choose one answer and believe it.

QUESTIONER: Plato. *The Apology of Socrates*. Many editions. Fourth century B.C.E. Socrates said, "The unexamined life is not worth living." He tried to understand justice, courage, and wisdom, and refused to accept the conventional, superficial answers, even when his continual questioning endangered his life. He does not reject faith in exactly the same way as the questioner in the second essay, but he does defend a persistent and thorough reliance on reason.

OTHER SOURCES

Michael Peterson, et al. *Reason and Religious Belief: An Introduction to the Philosophy of Religion*. Oxford University Press, 1991. Clear, readable; argues for a compromise between believer and questioner.

John Hick. *The Philosophy of Religion*, 4th Edition. Prentice-Hall, 1990. Subtle, sophisticated responses to the questioner.

Baruch A. Brody. *Readings in the Philosophy of Religion: An Analytic Approach*, 2nd Edition. Prentice-Hall, 1990. Brody's book contains James' essay, as well as a famous contrary view: "The Ethics of Belief," by W.K. Clifford. Clifford is a questioner.

Hans Küng. *Does God Exist? An Answer for Today*. Trans. Edward Quinn. Crossroad Press, 1991 (1980). Chaps. 1–3 are a discussion of modern philosophers' ideas about faith.

David Cook. *Thinking About Faith: An Introductory Guide to Philosophy and Religion*. Zondervan, 1986. Simple discussion, from a Christian perspective.

Ian G. Barbour. *Issues in Science and Religion*. Prentice-Hall, 1966. Discusses the methods of science, the methods of religion, and the consequences for religion of the latest discoveries in physics and biology.

Patrick Sherry, ed. *Philosophers on Religion*. Geoffrey Chapman, 1987. Short selections by great philosophers, from ancient Greece to the twentieth century.

Michael Shermer. *How We Believe: Science, Skepticism, and the Search for God*. 2nd Edition. W.H. Freeman, 2003. Discusses anthropologists' and psychologists' investigations of religious belief, and argues for more skepticism.

1.6 IS BELIEVING IN GOD NECESSARY FOR A MEANINGFUL LIFE?

Meaning Theist or Existentialist?

Part of answering a question is figuring out what the question is really asking. One question many people associate with philosophy is "What is the meaning of life?" Before anyone can answer that question, he or she must try to understand what the question is asking. And that is not clear at all. It's not like the question "What does 'BLT' stand for?" Anyone who speaks English knows what this question is asking, even if he or she doesn't know the answer. People know what would count as an answer. But other questions are harder to interpret. "What is the meaning of life" is one of those. It's hard to know where one should begin looking for an answer, or even what would count as an answer.

One way to interpret the question is to see it as asking why things happen in life. Why do bad things happen to people? Why do some people get cancer and others do not? Why do two people fall in love? Was it destiny? Was it karma? Do people create their own lives, or is everything the result of fate?

Another way to interpret the question is to ask what pattern or structure a life has. Does every life have a beginning, a middle, and an end, like a good story? Does everyone go through certain stages? In a famous passage in *As You Like It*, Shakespeare says

> And one man in his time plays many parts,
> His acts being seven ages. At first the infant,
> Mewling and puking in the nurse's arms.
> Then, the whining schoolboy with his satchel
> And shining morning face, creeping like snail
> Unwillingly to school. And then the lover,
> Sighing like furnace, with a woeful ballad
> Made to his mistress' eyebrow. Then a soldier,
> Full of strange oaths, . . .

The psychologist Abraham Maslow says that people try to satisfy higher and higher levels of needs, until they reach the highest level, which is self-actualization. Other writers suggest other patterns that human life has.

The two writers in this section have a third interpretation of the question. They both interpret "What is the meaning of life?" as a question about goals and purposes. Why are we here? For what purpose? What should we be living *for?* They agree that an answer to the question would be a description of a goal, such as serving God or fulfilling one's potential, which would give one's life meaning. They agree on what the question is asking, but they disagree on the answer. The meaning theist argues that in order for anyone's life to be meaningful, it must be devoted to God. The existentialist claims that everyone wants to find an ultimate goal that will make life worthwhile, but there is no such goal. Nothing makes life meaningful.

YES: MEANING THEIST

"The Meaning of Life Is the Submission to God"

> The problem in my life and other people's lives is not the absence of
> knowing what to do, but the absence of doing it.
>
> —*Peter Drucker*

Peter Drucker was a management expert whose books guided a whole generation of business leaders. His statement sums up the point I want to make in this essay. We all know what the meaning of life is, but we don't want to face it. The meaning of life is the submission to God. I think a few simple observations can help us realize what we already know in the backs of our minds.

First we should think about meaning. To understand the meaning of life we have to know what meaning is. That may seem too abstract, but consider this: if we want to know what an unemployed life is we have to know what unemployment is. If we want to know what a courageous life is we have to know what courage is. The same applies to understanding a meaningful life. So what is meaning?

Meaning, in the first place, is a property of words. Words have meaning. "Shoe" is a meaningful word in English, "eohs" is not. By extension, we can say other things have meaning. "He gave her a meaningful look," "She didn't mean to startle her friend," "My high school ring means a lot to me." And we can say a life is meaningful. In all these extended cases, what we are saying is related in some way to the original, linguistic use of the word "meaning."

How is the meaning of life like the meaning of words? Well, everyone agrees that a meaningful life is a life with a purpose. A person with a meaningful life has a long-term goal she believes in and pursues with energy and confidence. For many people raising a family is their life-goal. Everything they do is organized around that purpose. For example, they search for a mate, fall in love, have children, build a home, earn money to pay for it, and so on. For others their careers are the main focus of their efforts. They define themselves by their work, and feel good about themselves because of their competence at work. They try to learn from experience, improve their skill, take on more responsibility, and earn more respect. Ordinary daily activities lead to something larger. Artists make creating art their purpose. Health care workers try to relieve suffering and give people hope.

Meaningful lives are purposeful lives. We see these lives as meaningful because they are like meaningful words. To be meaningful a word has to point to something beyond itself. A word, by itself, apart from its meaning, is just a sound. "Shoe" rhymes with "glue." It consists of a "sh" sound and an "oo" sound. It is written with four letters, which are only physical marks on paper. To be meaningful, the sound or the marks must point to the things people wear on their feet. You know the meaning of the word when you know what it signifies, beyond the physical word itself. The same is true of lives. A meaningful life is dedicated to something beyond itself, beyond the little tasks of maintenance and immediate gratifications, like brushing your teeth or going to a new movie.

It's easier to see that a meaningful life aims at something if you consider the opposite: a meaningless life. The ancient Greeks had a myth to illustrate a meaningless life. A man named Sisyphus angered the gods, and as a punishment they condemned him to push a large boulder up a steep hill. It was hard work. But when he finally reached the top, the gods sent the boulder rolling back down to the bottom, and Sisyphus had to turn around, trudge down the hill, and start pushing all over again. Sisyphus' life is meaningless because he isn't getting anywhere. The terrible thing about his life isn't the hard work but the pointless repetition. He is doing the same thing over and over, with no progress, no goal. He knows that when he reaches the top of the hill the next time, the boulder will just roll back to the bottom again and he will be back where he started. His life isn't aimed at anything. It has no purpose. Unfortunately some people's lives today are similar to Sisyphus'. A meaningful life, in contrast, consists of activities and projects that take one forward, toward a worthy goal.

But that's not all. The second point to notice is that the purpose of a meaningful life has to be a worthwhile, valuable purpose. A friend of mine has a neighbor who spends most of his time reading about celebrities. His goal is to learn the birthdates of movie stars and singers, and for each day of the year—January 1, January 2, etc.—to find as many celebrities as possible who were born on that day. He spends a lot of time at it, he seems to enjoy it, and he doesn't take an interest in many other things. His life has a purpose, but it is a trivial, useless purpose. If making his list is all he accomplishes in his years on earth, his life will be wasted.

This may sound harsh, and some people will say "It's a free country. People can do whatever they like." I agree. The point is not that the birthday man should be prevented from doing what he wants. The point is that there is a concept of a meaningful life, and his life doesn't fit the concept. It's like asking what makes a person healthy. We all define "healthy" in terms of strength, flexibility, endurance, good digestion, sleep, and efficient bodily functions. Suppose someone said that he wanted to smoke and have breathing problems, feel aches and painful joints from lack of exercise, have a bad liver from drinking too much, but he wanted to call his condition "healthy." Well, it's a free country and he can say whatever he wants. But that doesn't make him healthy. Neither does the birthday man have a meaningful life.

I am saying that the goal a person pursues in her life has to be a valuable goal, not just any goal. In this way a "meaningful life" is actually different from a "meaningful word." A meaningful life points to something, just as a meaningful word points to something. But a word can refer to anything—good, bad, or ugly. However, a person cannot dedicate his or her life to just anything and make it meaningful. Collecting string, never stepping on cracks in the sidewalk, memorizing all the lyrics of all of Madonna's songs—these and similar trivial goals do not make a life meaningful. On the other hand, helping and loving others does make a life meaningful. Nurturing living things makes life meaningful. Adding to human knowledge makes life meaningful. We all understand this on some level, although we may be reluctant to admit it. The fact that a meaningful life must be dedicated to something that is valuable shows that when we talk about a "meaningful" life, we really are extending the word "meaning" beyond its normal, linguistic usage. We are adding this evaluative element. A life is not literally meaningful in exactly the same way a word is, although it is similar.

The idea that a person's goal in life must be valuable, not trivial, will be more convincing if we consider the next point. And in fact, this third point illustrates another similarity between the meaning of a life and the meaning of a word. The purpose of a person's life must be not only valuable, but objectively valuable. It must have a real value that other people can recognize. An individual can't simply decide for himself or herself that some goal has the kind of value that makes life meaningful. In this way a meaningful life is just like a meaningful word. A person cannot make words meaningful for himself alone. I cannot decide that the word "shoe" will mean shirt. I can try to say it, but I would soon get confused. Even if for some reason I wanted to make up a purely personal, private language, I would hear others using the words in the normal way and I would forget the special definitions I gave them. Other people wouldn't understand me, of course. But besides the practical impossibility, the word "shoe" means shoe, not shirt. That's an objective fact that remains a fact regardless of what I do. To say "The word 'shoe' means shirt for me, but shoe for everyone else" makes no sense. That's not how meaning works.

We cannot create our own personal language, and we cannot create our own personal value. This may surprise some people. Our selfish ego rebels at this idea, but another part of our mind recognizes it. When a person wonders if her life is meaningful, she is wondering if what she is aiming at is really significant. Is it important, and worth the effort? She may aim at something—making a large amount of money, for example—that is valuable to her, but she wonders if it is a meaningful goal. She wants a purpose in living that is objectively valuable, not just something no one else cares about. We can see this if we think about another example of a failed life. Some people in mental hospitals are psychotic, which means they do not perceive reality as it is. It is less common now, but in the past some people suffered from "delusions of grandeur." They believed they were Napoleon, or Cleopatra, or Jesus, and that the other inmates were their loyal subjects and followers. They interpreted every event and every conversation to fit their fantasy, and added hallucinations to make them complete. Some of these people were supremely happy. They were completely fulfilled and satisfied by their "work" in their "palace." But they were helpless people who deserved pity, not envy. The example shows that what makes a life meaningful is not contentment, or even happiness. The happiness must be based on reality, on something objectively valuable and worth seeking, not a personal fantasy.

So far I have claimed that a meaningful life must be devoted to some purpose, the purpose must be valuable, and it must be objectively valuable. The last point to see is that the basis for objective value is "God." "God" has absolute value, and everything else has value in relation to "Him." I put the word "God" in quotation marks to indicate that different people think of God in different ways. Some think of God as Jesus, others think of Allah, others of Krishna, others of a more abstract being. Some believe God is not a person, but a great creative force, a guide and source of law. But however one thinks of him or her or it, God is ultimately real. God existed before anything else existed, and he will continue to exist without end. He does not depend upon us; on the contrary, we depend upon him. So he is an objective reality.

Moreover, he is good and wise, helping and just. (I say "he" but that is only a habit.) All religions agree about this. It's hard for us to formulate a clear, precise idea of perfect love in our minds, or perfect goodness. That's why we fall back on incarnations and particular embodiments or examples. But when we try, we are trying to understand God. That's what God is—perfect goodness. When a person sees how wonderful a laughing child is, or feels moved by an act of great generosity, or appreciates the awesome beauty of the laws of nature, she is beginning to understand the goodness that can give life meaning. Therefore, when someone looks for some objective value as a life-goal, she is looking for God, even if she doesn't realize it.

Someone might say that we can devote ourselves to some objective good without necessarily believing in God. But that is a mistake. We must look outside ourselves, individually and as a species, to find meaning. Any cause or purpose powerful enough to give our lives an objective purpose must be larger than our own desires. It is a truism that a person who thinks only of himself or herself is missing the great potential of life and is usually unhappy. "A man wrapped up in himself makes a very small bundle," Ben Franklin said. The same is true for humanity as a whole. If we only serve human interests and human desires, we are still "wrapped up in ourselves." We need something larger than humanity—something outside of, or above, humanity, something glorious and transcendent—to give our lives objective value.

People look for ways to serve God, although they may not call their goal "God." What would happen if you asked people who have a purpose in life, such as nurturing a family, "Is nurturing a family good?" They would say "Of course it's good. It's the noblest and best and most perfect thing there is." It's completely selfless. In fact, it's godly. People are drawn to God by many routes, through sacrificing for a family, helping the poor and sick, taming violence with peace, or preserving the living earth. All are ways to try to get closer to perfect goodness. All are meaningful lives because they are dedicated to God.

Key Concepts

meaning	meaningless	purpose
valuable	objective	absolute good

Critical Questions

1. How is a meaningful life like a meaningful word, according to the meaning theist?
2. Why does the meaning theist say the life of the man who collects celebrities' birthdays is meaningless? Do you agree?
3. Can the meaning theist use the comparison with meaningful words to support his point about the birthday collector? Can he support his point in any way?
4. The meaning theist claims that a meaningful life must be aimed at something that is objectively valuable. Why aren't insane people's lives meaningful? If they are happy, doesn't that make their goals objectively valuable?

5. Jews, Christians, and Muslims have different beliefs about God. Does the meaning theist believe they can all have meaningful lives? Or are some religions "meaningless"?

6. If an atheist devotes her life to saving disaster victims, feeding starving people, and promoting economic development in underdeveloped regions, is her life meaningful or not, according to the meaning theist?

NO: EXISTENTIALIST

"The Myth of Ultimate Meaning"

The most famous first line of any book in philosophy is probably the first line of Albert Camus' "Myth of Sisyphus." He says "There is only one truly serious philosophical problem, and that is suicide." Why shouldn't I commit suicide? What makes my life worth living? All the other questions that philosophers discuss, about free will and genuine knowledge and natural rights, are secondary. If you don't have a good reason to live, Camus says, you don't need to worry about the other questions.

And it's not easy to find a good reason to live because life is "absurd." When Camus says absurd, he doesn't simply mean that the universe is purposeless, although it is. The universe itself is indifferent, neither good nor evil. When a tornado tears apart a town and kills people, the universe is not being cruel, and when the sun dries out the flood it isn't being generous. Wind and sun don't feel anything. Natural processes just roll forward without any regard for human wishes. But humans are not indifferent. People want to find meaning and purpose and value in the world. But it isn't there. That conflict, or disconnect, is why human lives are absurd. Absurdity is the "confrontation," as Camus says, between the irrational, blind universe, and the human "longing for clarity."

Other writers and philosophers have expressed similar points of view. David Hume, for example, says that actions are meaningful when they are aimed at some goal. Working hard in school is meaningful because it leads to a degree, which leads to a better job. Getting a better job is meaningful because it provides income to do what you enjoy, like going to the beach. But going to the beach doesn't lead to anything. It's just fun. If it doesn't lead to any goal, then it isn't meaningful in the way other actions are. There is no purpose for it. The two kinds of actions are different. There is a good reason to work hard in school—it leads to a desirable goal. But there is no reason like that to lie on the beach. Hume's point is that people's lives are meaningful and full of purpose as long as they are directed toward some goal. But what makes the ultimate goal meaningful? Nothing.

This is a significant fact. Ultimate goals are arbitrary and not justified. Going to school is not arbitrary. A person can give a good reason for doing it. But what reason can one give for seeking pleasure or avoiding pain? A man lies on the beach because he enjoys it. "But why do you do enjoyable things?" He has no answer to that question. A woman works to put food on the table because she doesn't want to starve. "But why don't you want to starve?" She can't give reasons for her ultimate values. She just wants them, for no reason. And if people's ultimate values are really arbitrary, or groundless, then all those things they do to accomplish the ultimate values are arbitrary too, because their value depends on the value of what they lead to. When you step back and look at your life as a whole, there is no reason for doing what you do.

Hume was analyzing the concepts of meaningful action and purpose in life. Leo Tolstoy, the Russian novelist, reached the same conclusions but in a more emotional way. He was married with children, wealthy, and famous. But he says he gradually began asking himself "why?" At first he could brush aside the question and his activities seemed worthwhile without an answer. But eventually the question became more pressing. One day "I suddenly said to myself: 'What is that to me?' Or, thinking of the fame which my works would get me, I said to myself: 'All right . . . What of it?' And I was absolutely unable to make any reply." He says he was paralyzed. He could continue eating and sleeping and getting dressed, mechanically, but without a reason to live, "there was no life."

The great majority of people today believe they have an answer for Tolstoy. The purpose of life is to worship God, they say. The ultimate reason for doing anything, according to this point of view, is that God requires obedience. Even if getting an education isn't directly worshiping God, it is developing one's mind so that one can directly worship him better in other ways. Some people say silent prayers all through the day. They continually make every action—such as waking from sleep, eating, seeing the sky, making a decision—part of worshiping God. So every part of life is an act of worship, directly or indirectly. Life as a whole has a purpose. In fact, Tolstoy himself accepted this answer and became a devout Christian in his later years.

But this takes us back to Hume's question about ultimate ends. If a life has meaning because it is devoted to God, what gives God meaning? Obeying God's laws is like obeying the rules in school. We do it to serve a higher purpose or reach a goal. In school the purpose is to get an education, graduate, and get a good job. What is the purpose of obeying God's rules? To get to heaven, some might say. All right, and what is the purpose of that? Well, being in heaven doesn't have a higher purpose or a reason. It's like lying on the beach.

Some believers have a different answer to the question of why we should obey God. People obey God not to reach bliss in paradise—which seems a little selfish and superficial—but because following God's plan makes everyone better. It gives people's lives structure: they know what is permitted and what isn't, what is good and what is evil, and they choose good because God commands it. Obedience gives people a moral center, and a direction in life—toward greater devotion and sacrifice for God. Following God's laws will make people happy, according to this point of view, but that's not why they do it. They aren't just planning for heaven either. They lead a righteous life because it's morally good, and doing the right thing—obeying God—is the highest goal anyone can imagine. All these things make a life meaningful, many people say.

Is this alternative answer better than the goal of getting to heaven? In this answer the reason to obey God is not a selfish reason, like achieving ultimate pleasure in an afterlife. But what is the reason? Because it's the right thing and it makes the obedient person moral. "Why be moral," one might ask. That's not a ridiculous question in this context. Following all of God's laws is not easy. For one thing, it's not easy to know what they are—does God forbid abortion, does he condemn homosexual love?—and even if we know the laws, it's difficult to obey them. How many people sell all they have and give it to the poor, as Jesus commands us to do? Few people are able to devote their lives entirely to worshiping God (even if they tell themselves they do). If we could obey the commands, why should we? Should we be moral because it will make us happy? It's possible that such a life would make a person happy, although that seems doubtful. But happiness is irrelevant, according to this answer. Obeying God is just something we ought to do, whether it makes us happy or not, for no further reason.

But then obeying God becomes an arbitrary choice. As Milton Steinberg says in *Basic Judaism*, religious people "vindicate their entire lives in one heroic decision." Such a person "makes a single but tremendous act of faith; he posits a lone but gigantic postulate." The postulate, or assumption, is that we ought to obey God. That chosen purpose makes everything else meaningful. But the choice is not meaningful itself, in the way that going to school or getting a job is meaningful. If a person wants to silence the inner demand for meaning, then perhaps the religious postulate will do the trick, as apparently it did for Tolstoy. But if a person wants to *understand* what makes life meaningful, the religious leap won't help.

Perhaps there is another way to answer Camus and Hume and explain how life can be meaningful. One of the classical Greek philosophers thought he had an answer. Aristotle, who was the student of Plato and the teacher of Alexander the Great, said the goal of life is happiness. The word he used was *eudaimonia*, which meant something like "well-being" or "fulfillment." But it's similar to the English word "happiness." People do things like go to school, look for work, get married, and so on for reasons. A person gets married so that he can spend more time with the person he loves, and he wants to spend time with her because it makes him happy. But people do not try to find happiness in order to reach something more. Happiness is everyone's ultimate, final goal.

It's true, as Hume says, that we have no reason to pursue happiness. Achieving happiness is our reason for everything else we do, and justifies getting married, for example. But we can't justify wanting to be happy. Trying to be happy is just something we do instinctively or automatically, without having a reason, so Hume says it is not meaningful. Aristotle knew this, but he believed being happy is enough to make a person's life meaningful anyway.

Was Aristotle right? Does doing something that makes me happy give my life meaning and make it worthwhile and valuable? Maybe not. Imagine a fictional person, whom we can call Pete. Pete lives for snowboarding. Literally. He works in the local video store during the week, rents a cheap studio apartment, and goes up into the mountains every weekend to snowboard. That's all he cares about, but it seems to be enough. He says he's happy. He has no ambitions. His life is simple, and in fact, he does seem rather carefree and untroubled at the moment. But what of the future? Will he ever get married? What happens if he's injured? What happens when he gets old? Shouldn't he make something of himself? He enjoys the brief thrill of boarding down the mountain, but it does not seem to be a meaningful life.

Or take another example. Pol Pot led an organization in Cambodia in the 1970s—the Khmer Rouge—that murdered millions of Cambodians. Not much is known about Pol Pot's personal feelings, but it's possible that he believed in what he was doing. It's even possible that he was happy. Maybe he achieved happiness through genocide. Maybe he believed the people he was killing were dangerous enemies of Cambodia. His beliefs were obviously false and crazy, but other people have beliefs that seem obviously false, and yet they also may be happy. (They may even be happy because of the false beliefs.) If Pol Pot was happy, was his life meaningful and valuable? Certainly not to his victims. Historians condemn Pol Pot as a deranged murderer whose life was a crime and a tragedy. So happiness may not be enough. These examples seem to show that a happy life is not necessarily a meaningful life.

Aristotle says happiness makes life worthwhile, but he would condemn Pol Pot because, he says, Pol Pot couldn't really be happy. Neither could Pete. To be happy, according to Aristotle, a person has to fulfill his or her true nature. We have to exercise our humanity. Otherwise we won't be happy. What is our true nature? For Aristotle, it's experiencing new things, learning, and understanding more and more. It's developing our minds—the unique human capacity to think—not just in school but throughout our lives. Using our minds is what makes us human, and different from animals. Pol Pot was behaving irrationally, so he couldn't really have a happy life (even if some actions gave him pleasure). While Pete may enjoy what he's doing for now, he isn't developing his human potential, so he can't be happy either, according to Aristotle.

But this response is not convincing. Aristotle was a philosopher, and naturally he assumed that his way of life—thinking and learning—was the best. What made him happy was using his mind, and he couldn't imagine that doing something else could make another person just as happy or happier. But in fact people are different. Learning to think rationally and reading more books isn't the ideal life for everyone. Some people find satisfaction in watching TV; some are devoted to their businesses; some serve their communities. If people can be fulfilled in other ways besides developing their intellects, then maybe people can achieve happiness in all sorts of ways, ways that wouldn't satisfy Aristotle, or me or you, but may satisfy them.

But that means people like Pete can be happy wasting their time seeking brief, temporary thrills, or people like Pol Pot can be happy murdering their neighbors. Those are not worthwhile, significant lives, and therefore happiness is not the answer to living a meaningful life. In fact, it's difficult to see how anyone could answer Hume and Camus. It seems that any goal one chooses is either ultimate, and therefore arbitrary, or based on personal, subjective happiness, and therefore distinct from significance and meaningfulness.

Perhaps the question "What makes life meaningful?" is one of those questions that seem to make sense, but actually do not. Maybe no one can answer the question because it's not a real question in the first place, like "What is the color of melancholy?" or "What happens when an irresistible force meets an immovable object?" These are pseudo-questions. On the other hand, people seem to agree that some lives are meaningless. So we all have some understanding of the idea after all. If we spent a lifetime trying to answer the question, would that be a meaningful life?

Key Concepts

purpose	arbitrary	worshiping God
a reason	happiness	human nature

Critical Questions

1. What is the important difference between going to school and lying on a beach, according to the existentialist?
2. Does the existentialist believe that a life devoted to worshiping God for the purpose of getting to heaven is meaningful, or meaningless?
3. What difficulties does the existentialist see in giving one's life meaning by being a moral, good person, in the sense of obeying God's commands?
4. Do you think Pete the snowboarder is living a meaningful life? Did Pol Pot live a meaningful life? Can you give a reason for your answer?
5. Why would Aristotle say that neither Pete nor Pol Pot was happy?
6. Do you think your ultimate goals in life are instinctive drives, like breathing and eating, or are they conscious, deliberate choices you have made?

Methods and Techniques
OBJECTIVITY

In both these essays the concepts of subjective and objective play a role, so it should be useful to examine those concepts. They are important because they come up again in discussions of several other philosophical questions.

Ordinarily the word "subjective" refers to something in someone's mind. "Objective" refers to something that exists independently of a person's mind. If I touch a hot stove and burn my finger, the pain is subjective. It exists in me, not in the stove (or in anyone else). The stove, on the other hand, is objective. It exists whether I touch it or see it or know about it.

Some subjective things are sudden sensations, like the pain of a burn. Or longer lasting feelings, like the excitement you feel at the end of a close game. Or a memory of something you did last week. Or the mental picture you have of your kitchen. Objective things are everything that exists outside our own minds—physical objects like chairs and rivers, events like the birth of a baby or a rain shower, and causal relations, like the relation between sunlight and photosynthesis in a green leaf.

People sometimes speak of an objective truth. An objective truth is a statement that is true independently of anyone's feelings or thoughts about the matter. For example, it is objectively true that Mount Everest is the tallest mountain on Earth. It doesn't matter how anyone feels about mountains or heights or Everest. It doesn't even matter if some people *believe* that Mount McKinley is the highest mountain. Their belief does not change the fact, which is independent of anyone's subjective mental states. It wouldn't even matter if everyone believed that Mount McKinley was taller than Mount Everest. Truth does not depend on a majority vote.

On the other hand, there are subjective truths as well. Sometimes people say "That's true for you but not for me." For example, consider the statement "Algebra is very easy." That may be true for you but not for me. Other examples are "The room feels hot," "Raw oysters are delicious," and "The children's singing was beautiful." The truth of these statements depends on what goes on in someone's mind. I may be feeling hot even if the temperature in the room is 68 degrees. You may feel cool in the same room, so "The room feels hot" is true for me but not for you. Feelings are subjective. (But "The temperature in the room is 68 degrees" is objective.) The height of Mount Everest does not depend on anyone's feelings or beliefs or mental experiences. It's an objective fact.

Another way to use these concepts is to describe people's attitudes, or their method of thinking. Objectivity is an attitude a person can have. The person can think about a topic objectively (or can at least try to consider it objectively). That means the person attempts to observe, analyze, or judge the situation as it actually is, without allowing his or her feelings, wishes, unrelated memories, or personal prejudices to influence his or her thinking. Only the objective facts of the case enter into her thinking. For example, an umpire in a baseball game attempts to observe a slide into home plate as accurately and carefully as he can, without allowing his friendship with the players to influence his perceptions. If a dispute arises between the two teams over one of the rules of the game, the umpire tries to make a decision that is fair and impartial. He tries to focus entirely on the facts of the case and set aside any feelings he has about the players or wishes about which side should win the game. It may be very difficult to achieve complete objectivity in such a situation, but that's what the term means. Perhaps it's an ideal that we can strive for, and may or may not reach.

While the meanings of "subjective" and "objective" are relatively clear, the things that are subjective and objective are matters for debate. The most contentious thing is moral values. Some people say that moral statements are objective truths like the statement about Mount Everest being the highest mountain. For example, some "moral objectivists" say that everyone has an inalienable right to freedom of expression, and the right is an objective fact, even if governments ignore the right or deny it. Others take the opposite view. They argue that morality is subjective, in the sense that moral statements express a person's or a group's subjective feelings. These "moral subjectivists" would argue that a statement like "everyone has an inalienable right to freedom of expression" can be true for Americans but not true for Iranians (to use a hypothetical example). That is, Americans feel approval for free expression, whereas Iranians do not. Having a right is not an objective fact, but a matter of feeling or preference that some people have. It's like Jones having an attractive personality. Some people may find Jones likable, and others may not. Regarding rights, some people may get very upset if the government suppresses a person's expression of his or her opinions, and others may not. And that's all we can say.

It's not easy to decide whether morality is objective or subjective. The problem comes up when people from different countries encounter each other or must work together in international organizations like the United Nations. Most Americans say that basic human rights are universal and objective. People from Iran and China disagree, and claim that Americans are simply trying to impose their attitudes and feelings on others who have different preferences. Everyone agrees on what the words "objective" and "subjective" mean, but they disagree on whether moral beliefs and statements are objective or subjective.

Why do many Americans insist that morality is objective—that people have rights, that torture is wrong, that all human beings deserve equal respect—when others clearly disagree? If these are objective facts, shouldn't everyone be able to see them? In other words, how do we decide that something is objective rather than subjective—a real, existing characteristic of the world rather than a personal feeling or mental experience that we project onto the world? Moral objectivists say that the sign of objectivity is absolute certainty. For example, you can be absolutely certain that $2 + 2 = 4$ or that squares have four sides. If you think about these statements, you realize that they must be true. They couldn't be false. You aren't just pretty sure or almost sure. If you think about the ideas, you can be absolutely sure that they are true. That's the mark of objectivity. Squares must have four sides, regardless of anyone's feelings or attitudes. Now consider this statement: "Torturing children is wrong." Moral objectivists say they are as certain of this statement as they are about squares having four sides. It couldn't possibly be false. It is true independently of what anyone feels or believes, they say.

Even if some people said they disagreed, and that sometimes torturing children was justified, that wouldn't show that morality is subjective. It would only show that something is interfering with those people's thinking. (If they said sometimes squares have five sides, and $2 + 2 = 3$, we wouldn't decide those statements were subjective.) We have already seen that objectivity doesn't depend on what people believe. If people believe that Mount McKinley is the tallest mountain, that doesn't make it the tallest mountain.

This is not the end of the debate, of course. It is only the beginning. But the question about morality illustrates some of the complications that arise when we apply the concepts of objective and subjective to various topics. Similar complications arise when we ask whether meaning in life is an objective fact, the same for everyone, or a subjective condition, dependent on someone's personal feelings or wishes. The moral theist claims it is objective, and the existentialist claims it is subjective.

Understanding the Dilemma
MEANING THEIST OR EXISTENTIALIST?

The meaning theist and the existentialist actually agree on two important points, but they disagree on a third issue, namely whether or not God is necessary for a meaningful life. In order to construct a personal philosophy of your own, you should decide whether you are closer to the first or the second essay on that important issue. That means you must look closely at the reasons they give to support their views. But you should also ask yourself if you can agree with them where they agree. You might see a problem with the principles they both believe are true.

One principle both writers accept is this: a meaningful life is a life that has a purpose. To live a meaningful life, a person must have some large goal, or something to live for. The meaning theist believes this principle because he says that a meaningful life is like a meaningful word. To be meaningful, a word must refer to something outside of itself. The same applies to a life: it must aim at something. The existentialist doesn't present an argument for this principle but simply takes it for granted.

Do you agree with the two writers on this point? Can you imagine a way of life that is "aimless," "purposeless," but nevertheless meaningful? Must you be pointed in a certain direction in order to be successful? Some people say we should "live for the day," be mindful, or be absorbed in the moment, without worrying about the past or the future. If a person accepted whatever happened, without an ultimate goal, would that be a meaningful life?

In thinking about this, you might ask yourself if a person without a life-goal could be happy. But both writers agree that that is the wrong question to ask. A person who lives for the moment might be happy, but being happy does not make life meaningful, according to both writers. The meaning theist says that happiness is not enough for two reasons. What makes a person happy might be trivial and senseless, like memorizing celebrities' birthdays. A life devoted to something trivial and senseless can't be meaningful. Or what makes a person happy might be a delusion, and not based on reality. Lives based on illusions are ridiculous (or tragic), not meaningful. The existentialist agrees with both these points, and adds a third. A person might find happiness in destroying other people, or in being a tyrant, or in some other harmful way, and we can't believe that cruelty and murder make life meaningful.

This second point that both writers accept may be more difficult to go along with. Many people say that their goal in life is to be happy, and they believe that if they reach their goal, their lives will be meaningful. In other words, for many people, living a meaningful life is the same as living a happy life. But both the meaning theist and the existentialist reject that connection. The two kinds of lives are not identical, they say, and they give several examples of people to support their claim. The people they describe are happy (they suppose), but their lives are not meaningful or valuable or worthwhile. The meaning theist adds that a person's belief that her life is meaningful is not enough to make it meaningful. A meaningful life is like a healthy life. You can't just call anything you like "healthy."

But even if a person can be happy living a meaningless life, can we turn the relationship around? Can a person be unhappy, but live a meaningful life? The writers didn't give an example of that. If happiness and meaningfulness are completely separate things, then they should be able to describe a person whose life is meaningful, but who is not happy. Could they? Is that possible?

So far I've only reminded you of the principles on which the two writers agree. But of course the dilemma of this section arises because the two writers also disagree. They disagree about God. Specifically, they disagree on whether or not devotion to God is necessary for having a meaningful life. The meaning theist claims that our concept of a meaningful life depends on our more basic concept of a meaningful word, and then draws out that comparison. A meaningful word points to something outside itself, and a person can't decide for herself what it points to. Word meaning is an objective fact, not a personal decision. The same applies to the meaning of a life, in the sense that a person can't simply decide that a life is meaningful when it isn't. The meaning theist also claims that a life must be directed at something valuable in order to be meaningful, and that is different from meaningful words. So the two kinds of meaning are similar but not exactly the same.

Finally, the meaning theist says that the only real, objective value that can give our lives meaning is "God." God is absolute goodness, and people struggle to understand that idea. But absolute goodness must be greater than merely man-made amusements or shifting human desires in order for it to be objective. Our lives (like words) must point to something outside themselves in order to be meaningful, and the kind of value that makes life good is not simply satisfying a desire, the meaning theist says.

The existentialist rejects this point of view, but it's important to understand why. It's not because the existentialist doesn't believe in God. Maybe there is a God or maybe there isn't. That's not the disagreement. Instead, the existentialist states that there is no good reason to devote one's life to God. That's the essential point. The existentialist bases the argument on what it means to have a reason to do something. A person has a good reason to do something when doing it leads to a desirable goal. For example, I have a good reason to jog in the afternoons because it leads to better health. I could spend an hour taking books off the shelf and then putting them back where they were. But why should I? If an action does not lead to any goal or serve any purpose, then it is meaningless and capricious, the existentialist says.

Now, why should a person devote her life to God? Is there a reason? That is, does it lead to a desirable goal? If the meaning theist says that doing so leads to happiness in heaven, then he or she is being selfish. Serving God is only a means to a higher end, which is to enjoy the pleasures of heaven. Should we obey God because God is very powerful and can destroy us? Submitting to power allows a person to survive, but that's another self-centered goal. Is it because following God's directions enables us to do good things, like heal the sick? But we can heal the sick and do other good things directly, without getting the idea from God. If healing the sick or comforting less fortunate people gives life meaning, then it isn't obeying God that makes life meaningful. On the other hand, if the meaning theist says there is no *reason* to devote our lives to God, then doing so is meaningless and capricious, like shuffling books for no reason.

This disagreement about God takes us back to the two principles I mentioned at the beginning: about having a purpose and happiness. All the different principles are interconnected, and what you believe about one influences what you believe about the others. The meaning theist says that a meaningful life is a life with a purpose (that was the first principle), and the only purpose that can give life meaning is to worship God. But worshiping and obeying God doesn't have a purpose or aim at anything. It is good and meaningful for its own sake. But this seems to be a problem. If serving God can be good and meaningful for itself, without leading to any further goal, then could other things be worthwhile, without leading to any further goal? Could lying on a beach be worthwhile and make life meaningful, even if it doesn't lead to anything? Both the meaning theist and the existentialist say no. But you might disagree. Are some things worthwhile in themselves, even if they don't lead to anything? The existentialist says nothing is. We must have a reason for doing anything, and that means a goal. The meaning theist says the only thing that is worthwhile in itself is serving God. But you might think of other things that are valuable for themselves.

For example, you might believe that happiness is valuable for its own sake and makes life meaningful, even if it doesn't lead to anything. Philosophers such as Aristotle and John Stuart Mill have said that happiness is the highest good, the *summum bonum*. The meaning theist disagrees, and claims that human beings must find a source of goodness above their own feelings. There is a higher good than human happiness. The existentialist says that happiness may or may not be good, but it is not enough to make life meaningful. So, what do you think? Is worshiping God necessary for a meaningful life? Or is that commitment an arbitrary decision? Can anything make life meaningful? Are you a meaning theist or an existentialist?

MEANING THEIST

1. Our idea of a meaningful life depends on the more basic idea of a meaningful word.

2. To be meaningful, a word—and a life—must aim at something outside itself.
3. A person's goal in life must be something really valuable and worthwhile; selfish, temporary satisfactions are not enough to make life meaningful.
4. Whenever people think of objective, absolute goodness, they are thinking of "God," even if they don't realize it.

EXISTENTIALIST

5. A meaningful life is a life with a purpose, a life directed toward some goal.
6. Being happy is not the same thing as living a meaningful life, because people can be happy in useless, absurd lives, and even in destructive, cruel lives.
7. If serving God does not lead to a worthy goal, then it is arbitrary and meaningless.
8. Having a reason to do X means doing X in order to reach some goal.

FOR FURTHER STUDY

Historical Examples

MEANING THEIST: Leo Tolstoy. *My Confession.* (Excerpts in Klemke, below.) By living and working with peasants, Tolstoy found that simple labor and absolute respect for people (pacifism) gave him a sense of meaning.

EXISTENTIALIST: Albert Camus. *The Myth of Sisyphus and Other Essays.* Vintage Books, 1955. Argues that life is absurd, but that consciously embracing the absurdity can give it a heroic quality.

OTHER SOURCES

Julian Baggini. *What's It All About: Philosophy and the Meaning of Life.* Oxford University Press, 2005. Survey of various approaches and solutions, written in an easy, engaging style.

Oswald Hanfling. *The Quest for Meaning.* Basil Blackwell, 1987. Covers the same topics as Baggini, but in a slightly more academic, philosophical style.

John Cottingham. *On the Meaning of Life.* Routledge, 2003. Argues that spiritual practices, performed sincerely, and with the hope that one might encounter transcendence, can give life meaning.

Julian Young. *The Death of God and the Meaning of Life.* Routledge, 2003. Discussion of philosophers' views, including Plato and Hegel, "before the death of God," and Nietzsche, Sartre, and Camus, "after the death of God."

E.D. Klemke, Steven M. Cahn, eds. *The Meaning of Life: A Reader.* 3rd Edition. Oxford University Press, 2008. A collection of excerpts and essays arranged under "The Theistic Answer," "The Nontheistic Alternative," and "Questioning the Question."

Thomas Nagel. *What Does It All Mean?* Oxford University Press, 1987. Chap. 10 argues that life is meaningless, since everyone and everything will eventually die, but that it might not matter that life is meaningless.

Current Controversy

1.7   IS BUDDHISM PHILOSOPHY?

Buddhist or Specialist?

Tablets from ancient Mesopotamia reveal that in Sumeria five thousand years ago people speculated about the nature of the universe, our place in it, and the best way of life. Probably in the very earliest human societies people asked profound questions and searched for answers. But around 600 B.C.E., in ancient Greece, some men began giving new kinds of answers to the age-old questions, and debating the merits of their different answers. The Greeks called the creation and analysis of these new answers "philosophy," the love of wisdom.

Before 600, people had proposed religious answers to their questions. The invention of philosophy marked a turning point in Western civilization. How were the new philosophical answers different from the old religious answers? That is an interesting question, but it isn't easy to answer. It is part of a larger question: what is the difference between religion and philosophy?

Are some ideas inherently religious ideas, and some philosophical? For example, the early religions used myths, or stories, to try to explain the nature of the world and our place in it. But stories aren't necessarily religious. Historians and even scientists tell stories as well. Religious myths are about supernatural beings who can cause storms with their breath or create living beings from mud. However, fairy tales are also stories about supernatural beings, but they aren't religious. Religious stories are about gods and goddesses, but philosophers talk about gods or God, and ask whether anyone can prove that God exists, among other things. While it isn't controversial to say that religion and philosophy are different, any attempt to explain the difference is controversial. Any attempt to explain what religion and philosophy are is controversial.

At about the same time that the Greeks were inventing philosophy, Siddhartha Gautama was proposing a new set of ideas and practices in India that grew into Buddhism. Buddhism is normally classified as a religion, but in some basic respects it is different from other religions and similar to philosophy. Examining the fundamental ideas of Buddhism forces us to ask whether it is a religion or a philosophy. Is philosophy a Western invention, like the symphony, geometry, and the assembly line? Or is it a universal human activity, like music, government, and agriculture? Even though "philosophy" is a Greek word, Asian societies could have invented their own versions of philosophy. But it is also possible that they never did, and produced only various types of religion. Could Buddhism be both? Or are religion and philosophy different from each other?

The first essay in this section argues that the Buddha's teachings are different from religious beliefs, and so Buddhism should be considered philosophy. The second essay claims that the difference between religion and philosophy is not a matter of beliefs but of attitudes. It is useful to keep the two outlooks separate, so the second writer could be called a specialist.

YES: BUDDHIST

"The Philosophy of Buddhism"

When I was in college I met an interesting woman in the cafeteria and we talked for a while. When she learned that I was thinking of majoring in philosophy, she said "I love philosophy! Alan Watts' *The Way of Zen* is one of my favorite books." At the time I smiled because I believed she had made a simple mistake. Zen Buddhism is religion, not philosophy, I thought. Since then I have changed my mind. I have learned more about Eastern thought and Buddhism in particular, and now I agree with my friend. Buddhism is philosophy, not religion.

It is impossible to summarize something as large and complex as Buddhism in a few words, but perhaps I can indicate some of the main ideas. Buddhism began with Siddhartha Gautama, who was born in the foothills of the Himalayas in Nepal in 563 B.C.E. Siddhartha's father was the ruler of the district, and by surrounding Siddhartha with servants and pleasant sights he hoped to shelter him from the pain and frustration of the world. But one day Siddhartha left the palace grounds to visit the nearby town, and he saw what Buddhists call the four signs: an old man, a sick man, a corpse, and a monk. He learned that people change and decline, that our bodies fail, and that everyone dies. He also learned how some try to reconcile themselves to these realities.

Siddhartha was so transformed by his experience that he decided to leave the comfortable life of the palace and seek wisdom wherever he could find it. He went to respected teachers and studied the ancient Hindu scriptures with them. But he decided that books and scholarship were not bringing him the wisdom he sought. He then turned to the path of the holy monks, who wandered from village to village with their begging bowl, and tried to rise above earthly pleasure and pain by fasting and disciplining the body. After the most rigorous self-denial, and at the point of starvation, Siddhartha decided he was no wiser than he had been, so he gave up the monks' way of life.

He sat under a tree and vowed that he would not move until he found genuine wisdom. After forty-nine days of profound meditation, according to the legend, he had penetrated through layer after layer of illusion to the deepest heart of reality. He had discovered the secret of our existence. The central truth of Buddhism is that *the self does not exist*. We have various perceptions, thoughts, feelings, and desires, but they change continually, and there is no "self" that holds them all together. The ego that everyone cares for so much is actually an illusion. All the working and striving and hopes and struggles for "myself" are completely futile and in vain. There is no satisfaction and peace in ordinary life because there is no stable self to satisfy.

Siddhartha discovered that no one is separate from reality. We are all integral parts of the world, and the world changes constantly, like the water in a river, or the colors of a sunset. But everyone wants to be separate and special, and everyone wants to be fixed and defined for all time. The conflict between those normal human desires and the fundamental nature of reality produces the basic quality of our lives: yearning, dissatisfaction, suffering. Siddhartha summed up his discovery in "the four noble truths."

1. Life is suffering and pain.
2. The cause of suffering is greed, or the desire to possess things, to enlarge and feed the self.
3. By understanding that the self is an illusion we can give up desire and escape from suffering and dissatisfaction.
4. The way to achieve a real, complete understanding is to follow the eight-fold path.

The eight-fold path describes the way a person should live to overcome the unhappiness of existence. The eight rules are

1. right understanding or view
2. right purpose or intention
3. right speech or conversation
4. right conduct or behavior
5. right livelihood or work
6. right effort or persistence
7. right awareness or mindfulness
8. right meditation or concentration

The first two rules concern the way one thinks, the next three concern the way one acts, and the last three concern the way one grows spiritually. By following these rules diligently, a person can understand the secret of existence fully, with more than mere intellectual comprehension. This deeper kind of understanding is called enlightenment, or "nirvana," which means "extinguished." By realizing that the self is an illusion, a person can extinguish the desire and egotism that cause dissatisfaction and achieve a state of calm, peaceful harmony with reality. When Siddhartha achieved enlightenment or nirvana, he became the Buddha, which means "the enlightened one."

Buddhism has developed and spread for thousands of years since the Buddha created it. It is practiced by millions of people all over the world, with the strongest representation in India and surrounding countries, Southeast Asia, China, and Japan. Different schools have emphasized different aspects, but the four noble truths and the goal of enlightenment are its core.

Traditionally people have called Buddhism a religion, but I believe it is really closer to philosophy for three main reasons. First, Buddhists do not believe in God or gods. The Tibetan Dalai Lama, one of the foremost teachers in Buddhism, says that Buddhists are atheists. Therefore Buddhism is in a category different from Christianity, Hinduism, tribal religions, Islam, or any other major religion, where worshiping God or the gods is the primary focus. The Buddha taught profound truths about the nature of reality, but they are different from the stories of creation or nature spirits taught by religions. (In fact, the Buddhist view of reality is closer to modern physicists' ideas; see Fritjof Capra, *The Tao of Physics*.)

It's true that many fantastic legends and stories have grown up among some followers about the Buddha and his life—stories of demons and miraculous events—but the Buddha himself did not teach such things, and they are not part of the essential core of Buddhism. Buddhism is not a religion because it does not include supernatural elements.

The second reason that Buddhism is a philosophy is that a Buddhist's goal is enlightenment, not salvation. Enlightenment means understanding self and world, and the change in one's feelings and behavior that comes from the deepest kind of understanding. The main obstacle to enlightenment is ignorance and illusion. Through learning and meditation, one can achieve enlightenment here and now. Contrast this view with religion's emphasis on salvation and sin. A Muslim's or Christian's goal is heaven and union with God after death. A Hindu's goal is release from the cycle of rebirth and union with Brahma. The primary means of achieving salvation is devotion, obedience to God, or loving kindness. That is, the greater emphasis is on the way one lives and acts, rather than on the way one thinks and understands. Indeed, many religions say that their truths cannot be understood by finite minds at all. Moreover, the main obstacle to salvation is sin and committing evil, not confusion as in Buddhism. Buddhism encompasses thinking, feeling, acting, and meditating, but the starting point is "right thinking." It is an intellectual philosophy, which extends to one's feelings and actions.

Of course religions value truth and belief, but the truths that religions propound are revealed, sacred truths. They are written in scriptures or uttered by holy prophets, and humbly believed by worshipers. They have an unquestionable authority. But Buddhism does not encourage obedience to authority, or faith.

When the Buddha died, his last words were "Work with diligence. Be lamps unto yourselves. Betake yourselves to no external refuge. Look not for refuge to anyone beside yourself. Hold fast to the Truth as to a lamp" (Ross, 1980, p. 36). Buddhists believe the four noble truths, not because the Buddha taught them, but because they have tested them and found them to be true in their own experience. Enlightenment comes from one's own efforts, not from faith or grace or authority.

The third major difference between Buddhism and religion is Buddhism's doctrine of no self. Buddhists say we are aware of ideas, emotions, wishes, and other conscious experiences, but not aware of any additional "self." The Buddha compared the self to a chariot. A chariot is a collection of parts in a certain arrangement: wheels, front and sides, beam, harness. "And just as no part of this aggregate can be separated off and called a 'chariot,' so no part of the human creature can be set apart and called 'I'" (ibid.; p. 29). If a person can fully grasp the meaning of this truth and take it to heart, then he or she can overcome the pain and suffering of existence and achieve nirvana. Religions, in contrast, preach the importance of the soul. The self or soul is the most important part of a person. Most religions teach that it is immortal, and will reside in some unearthly realm, or perhaps will be reborn in another body. The soul may need to be cleansed or purified, but it definitely exists. In ancient Egyptian religion, the gods weighed one's soul on a balance with a feather, and if the soul was heavy with sins, one would be denied entry into the afterlife. The Buddhist view is a sophisticated philosophical theory that runs counter to religion's emphasis on the soul.

In Asia people do not make a sharp distinction between religion and philosophy, so the claim that Buddhism is a philosophy doesn't surprise anyone there. But Western philosophers like to draw lines and put things in boxes. They object to classifying Buddhism as philosophy for several reasons. First, the Buddha taught that everyone will be reborn into a new life, and one's next life depends on the law of karma, that is, the law that goodness will lead to goodness and evil will lead to evil. To Westerners, this sounds like a mystical, religious belief. The doctrine raised questions even in the Buddha's own day. If the self is an illusion, people asked, how can one be reborn into a new life? What is reborn? Perhaps the best answer is that the Buddha was using the commonly accepted Hindu belief of his time and place to express his own metaphysical doctrine that a person is identical with all of reality. Since there is no "I" separate from everything else, a future person will be as much "I" as the person here and now that I call "I."

When confronted with questions like this the Buddha refused to answer. He said that if a man has been shot with a poisoned arrow, he shouldn't ask who shot the arrow or what it is made of or from where it was launched. If he tried to answer all those questions, he would die before he found the answers. It is more important to understand the basic truths than to worry about trivial details. Some Western philosophers conclude that Buddhism is anti-intellectual and closer to religion than philosophy. But Buddhists' reply is that the way to truth is not disputation but living and doing and meditating. In that they are similar to other Western philosophers such as the American pragmatists.

Of course Buddhists couldn't care less what label people put on their ideas. And the issue of "philosophy" or "religion," in the narrow sense, is merely a verbal issue. But from a broader perspective, more is at stake. By labeling Buddhism a religion many people dismiss it and do not take it seriously. They see it as another quaint custom or exotic belief from the East. But the term "philosophy" carries prestige in Western society. If people acknowledge that Buddhism is a philosophy, then they might be willing to study it more carefully and recognize its philosophical sophistication and depth. Labeling Buddhism as philosophy may be one more small step toward breaking down barriers and fostering respect among all peoples.

Key Concepts

suffering	no self	eight-fold path
enlightenment	atheism	authority

Critical Questions

1. In your opinion, is it possible to believe that the self does not exist? Is it possible for you to believe that your body is not yours?
2. Why do Buddhists believe that life is full of suffering? Can happiness outweigh suffering in a person's life, according to Buddhists?
3. If a person reads the four noble truths and believes them, is that person enlightened?
4. In your opinion, could Buddhism be a religion even if it does not involve belief in gods? Or is belief in some kind of divinity essential to religion?
5. How is enlightenment different from salvation, according to the Buddhist?
6. Why did the Buddha refuse to answer questions from his disciples about doctrines?

NO: SPECIALIST

"The Difference Between Religion and Philosophy"

What is the difference between religion and philosophy? This is an important question because universities and governments and ordinary people treat the two as if they are completely different, and yet at first glance they seem very similar. Religion is concerned with God or the gods, the soul, good and evil, salvation, and belief. But philosophy is concerned with the same things: philosophers think about God and the ultimate nature of reality. They think about the relation between body and mind (or soul), right and wrong, the best way to live, and belief and reasons for believing things. Is there any difference between religion and philosophy?

Religion involves more than ideas. Many religions are based on scriptures or founding prophets. But philosophers study their "sacred" texts, such as Plato's *Republic* or Descartes' *Meditations,* just as carefully as religious people study theirs. Religions are normally organized in communities of like-minded people, such as Roman Catholics or Muslims. But philosophers organize societies devoted to the study of some great thinker, or devoted to the study of some system of ideas. The American Philosophical Association meets regularly, and many smaller societies provide opportunities for like-minded philosophers to share ideas. At these meetings philosophers even perform their "rituals" of reading scholarly papers, and examining "acolytes" (job seekers) to determine their worthiness to enter the profession.

Is Marxism a philosophy or a religion? In his *History of Western Philosophy,* Bertrand Russell points out that Marxism has its founding prophet (Marx), its sacred text (Marx's works), its future paradise (the classless society), its Satan (capitalists), its Church (the International), and even its schisms (the Soviet Union vs. China).

In spite of these similarities, which are more playful than serious, there is a fundamental and important difference between religion and philosophy. But the difference is not easy to describe because it is a difference in attitudes. Religion is based on commitment, whereas philosophy is based on criticism. Religion rests on worship and praise, whereas philosophy requires skepticism, doubt, and scrutiny. Religion begins with powerful emotions of awe, love, humility, and fear, whereas philosophy aims at the clearest possible thought and reasoning, unhindered by personal feelings. Perhaps few people reach perfection in religion or in philosophy, but the ideals are certainly different.

However, it is easy to say that philosophy and religion are very similar or that they are very different. How can one make a persuasive case for one point of view or the other? How can one support a claim about such broad, complex phenomena as religion and philosophy? That question is just as important as the original question about similarities and differences.

Before we can compare two things, we need to have a clear perception of what we are comparing. To show that religion is different from philosophy, one must first explain what religion is and what philosophy is. Probably the best place to begin is the dictionary. Dictionaries give us a general idea of what people mean when they use the words. Some definitions of "religion" are

1. belief in and worship of God or gods;
2. the expression of humankind's belief in and reverence for a superhuman power recognized as the creator and governor of the universe;
3. outward acts or practices of life by which people indicate their recognition of and faith in God or gods;
4. any system of belief and worship based on revelation and faith.

These definitions are very general, but they are a start. They emphasize some kind of divinity as the object of religion, faith or revelation as the means of knowing about the divinity, worship and reverence as the response to the divinity, and certain practices as the expression of the response. Religious practices include ceremonies, which are "sets of formal acts proper to special occasions, and behavior that follows rigid etiquette," such as christenings and funerals. And religious practices normally include adherence to moral rules.

Some definitions of "philosophy" are

1. study of principles underlying conduct, thought, and the nature of the universe;
2. study and knowledge of the principles that cause, control, or explain facts or events;
3. study of the basic principles of a particular field of knowledge;
4. critique and analysis of fundamental beliefs as they come to be conceptualized and formulated.

As broad and vague as these definitions are, they do suggest that philosophy is very different from religion. The objects of philosophy are basic principles and beliefs, or the assumptions underlying thought and conduct, not divinities. Philosophers study these principles, and even critique and analyze them; they do not accept them on faith. These definitions do not mention any emotional responses or expressions of reverence in ceremonies or philosophical practices.

The words "religion" and "philosophy" can also be used as adjectives, "religious" and "philosophical." A religious person is "devout, pious, conscientiously exact, scrupulous." "Devout" means "reverent, earnest, sincere." "Pious" means "reverently observant of religion, dutiful, godly, virtuous." A "philosophical" person is one who is "sensibly composed or calm," or "rational and serene under any circumstances." These additional definitions bring out the difference between commitment and criticism. Being religious, in other words, is a matter of being committed, or dedicated, or loyal. Being philosophical means putting aside one's feelings and thinking clearly.

Where else can we find information about the nature of religion and philosophy? We can read encyclopedias and general books to get more details than definitions provide. Encyclopedia articles on religion usually include information about particular religions, their histories, beliefs, and practices. So we can read that Judaism was one of the first religions to emphasize ethical monotheism, the belief in a single God who is just and benevolent; that the word "Islam" means peace through submission to God; that Hindus believe one's soul must be reborn again and again until it is purified; that Jainism forbids its followers to kill any living creature; and so on with other religions. Looking at articles on philosophy, we find descriptions of philosophers and their ideas, as well as accounts of areas and problems of philosophy. One area is metaphysics, the study of the nature of the universe. In metaphysics philosophers ask "What is the world made of, material objects alone, or do immaterial minds exist? Do properties of things, such as redness, exist? Numbers? Gods?" Another area is ethics, the attempt to understand the good life. Philosophers ask "What is the highest good for human beings: happiness, love, duty to the moral law, or something else? How can we know what is good or evil, right or wrong?"

The examples described in encyclopedias reinforce the conclusion that religion and philosophy promote different attitudes. Religion is oriented toward the supernatural, faith, and worship. Philosophy also deals with the nature of reality, the mind, and conduct, but the attitude is inquisitive and critical. Religious people want to believe, whereas philosophers are very reluctant to believe. They ask questions and look for problems.

Another source of information may be even better than dictionaries and encyclopedias. You can go to religious services, talk to devotees of particular religions, and try to enter into the frame of mind of religious people. If you go to a Roman Catholic service, for example, you will probably enter a large cathedral with towering columns, hear somber music, see beautiful stained glass windows and men in magnificent robes, people kneeling in prayer, and perhaps a sculpture of Christ suffering on the cross. If you participate in the service with an open mind and heart, you will begin to appreciate the real nature of religion. The images, stories, prayers, and people will create certain feelings and attitudes within yourself, and those attitudes will give you a better understanding of words like "God," "worship," and "reverence" than any dictionaries or encyclopedias can.

You can do the same with philosophy. If you take classes in a university, or attend a meeting of a philosophical society, you will hear highly abstract arguments for or against some claim. For example, a teacher might discuss the view that all our actions are determined by prior causes, and so we do not have free will. And you might see students or members of the audience raising questions or criticizing the speaker's position. It is all very theoretical and dispassionate. Philosophers have a strong desire to understand, and their disputes might even grow heated, but generally philosophers are "philosophical," i.e., calm and rational. By entering into the discussion, you can understand the desire for clarity and logical reasons that define philosophy. You will grasp philosophy's sense of critical skepticism and perhaps its sense of adventure and the unlimited possibilities opened up by fearless speculation. The attitude is almost exactly the opposite of the religious attitude.

How can we be sure that we have understood the real nature of religion and philosophy, so that we can compare them? It would probably take years of study in both areas, and even then some people may feel more affinity for one or the other. Some people might be biased toward or against religion or philosophy. For example, atheists might say the difference between religion and philosophy is the difference between soft-headed, wishful thinking and mature, objective reason. Or a religious person might say the difference is between a realistic search for answers in a mysterious universe and arrogant, sterile wordplay. Or people might have biased reasons for denying that any differences between religion and philosophy exist. But a sound comparison should be based on an objective view of the two things compared.

The fact that religion is different from philosophy doesn't imply that one is "better" than the other. Everyone needs to be committed to something, and everyone needs to be critical at times. In fact, the real mistake is to overlook the difference and to think that one attitude or the other is enough. Ironically, recognizing the difference between religion and philosophy allows us to practice both, at different times and toward different objects. But failing to recognize the difference and trying to combine the two attitudes would make it difficult for a person to practice either religion or philosophy very well.

Key Concepts

religion	attitude	commitment	worship
philosophy	criticism	skepticism	bias

Critical Questions

1. What are some ways in which religion and philosophy are similar?
2. What is the difference between them, according to the specialist? Do you agree? Is it an important difference or a minor difference?
3. The definitions in the essay emphasize several aspects of religion. Are any aspects more important than others, in your opinion?
4. Do encyclopedias add anything important to dictionary definitions, or do they only provide illustrations of what we already know from definitions?
5. Do you think the majority of people who attended several religious services would come away with similar beliefs about the nature of religion? Would it make any difference if different people attended services of different religions?
6. The specialist claims that a philosopher can be a religious person. Do you agree? Wouldn't the attitudes come into conflict within himself or herself?

Methods and Techniques
DEFINITIONS

Philosophers are interested in definitions because they want to be as clear and precise as possible. A standard definition is an explanation of the meaning of a word. Definitions are based on usage within a linguistic community. In other words, a definition simply reports what most average speakers mean when they use a word. So writing a dictionary is like taking a sociological survey. The experts who write dictionaries base their definitions on surveys of actual usage, in books, magazines, and newspapers.

Sometimes the meanings of words change, or a word will acquire an additional meaning. For example, the word "gay" is defined as "joyous and lively, light-hearted; or bright and brilliant, as in 'gay colors.'" For centuries when English speakers used the word "gay," that's what they meant. But recently the word has also come to mean "homosexual," and dictionaries have to be revised to report this new, additional meaning.

There are different types of definitions, and the specialist's essay illustrates some of them. A report of the ordinary meaning of a word is called a "lexical definition." A *synonymous* lexical definition simply gives us one or more synonyms for the word defined. For example, "booze" means "liquor." "Genuine" means "authentic, real, not counterfeit." "Bother" means "annoy, pester." In the essay, "religious" is defined as "devout, pious, conscientiously exact, scrupulous."

An *analytic* lexical definition goes further and breaks down the meaning into parts. It gives us the defining properties of something. The word "glower" means "to stare with sullen anger." The definition breaks down the meaning into three parts: to stare, but with anger, and not furious anger, but sullen anger. "Soul" means "an entity without material reality, regarded as the spiritual part of a person; the moral or emotional nature of man." Thus a soul is a part of a person; it is the spiritual, moral part; and it is immaterial. The specialist in the essay tries to analyze the meaning of the word "religion" into a set of attitudes and feelings toward a divinity, expressed through certain practices. "Philosophy" is analyzed into different attitudes as well.

Another way to define a word is to give examples. If someone asks me what the word "philosopher" means, I might say "Plato, Aristotle, Descartes, Hume, or a person like that." Or if someone asks what "cathedral" means, I might point to pictures of Notre Dame in Paris, Saint Paul's in London, Saint Peter's in Rome, and others. Definitions by example are called "ostensive definitions." They may be more specific and concrete than lexical definitions since they give specific examples, but there is a danger that the learner will not understand the correct meaning of a word. The person looking at pictures of Notre Dame and Saint Peter's might think that "cathedral" means "large, stone building." But in conjunction with lexical definitions, ostensive definitions are useful. The specialist refers to examples described in encyclopedia articles on religion and philosophy to supplement the lexical definitions.

In the next part of the essay, the specialist recommends going to a religious service or a philosophical lecture to understand what the words mean. This involves more than looking at examples. It requires one to do something, to go through certain steps, and see what an activity is like. A definition based on an action one performs is called an "operational definition." Scientists sometimes use operational definitions to define certain concepts. For example, the word "weight" might be defined as "the number you get when you put an object on a standard scale." "Intelligence quotient" means "one's score on a Stanford-Binet test, or another intelligence test." An operational definition does not attempt to isolate defining properties, but says the meaning of a word is whatever results from a certain procedure, so long as the procedure is performed correctly. The specialist claims that "religion" means a set of attitudes, and one way to understand the attitudes is to perform a certain operation (attend a service) and notice the resulting attitudes within oneself.

Definitions usually attempt to explain the meaning of a word on the basis of a survey of ordinary usage. The purpose is to report objectively what people mean when they use the word. But sometimes the person defining a word has strong feelings about whatever the word refers to. For example, someone might define "intelligence quotient" as "an arbitrary number used to exclude people from certain schools and jobs." People may ignore the objective meaning and insert their own positive or negative feelings into their definitions of "Communist," "conservative," "housewife," "Third World country," "technology," and so on. For example, does "technology" mean "the rampant development of machinery and electronics to further isolate people from nature," or is it "the use of science and industry to make our lives better"? When a definition is not an objective report of meaning, but is slanted to influence people's feelings about something, it is called a "persuasive definition."

It's important to distinguish persuasive definitions from emotive words. Some words include positive or negative feelings in the objective meaning of the word. "Harridan" means "a disreputable, shrewish old woman." "Crook" means "dishonest person." These are analytic, lexical definitions, not persuasive definitions. The specialist mentions persuasive definitions of "religion" and "philosophy" near the end of the essay.

Persuasive definitions do not report meanings but create new meanings in an attempt to influence people. Another type of definition that does not report meanings is called a "stipulative definition." Someone can stipulate a meaning for a word used in a special context. Thomas Hobbes was an English philosopher who wrote a book on government called *Leviathan* in 1651. There he said he would use the word "justice" to mean "the performance of covenants," that is, keeping one's agreements. This implies that when people have not made agreements, there is no justice or injustice. Hobbes didn't claim that he was reporting how people normally used the word "justice." He was stipulating a new meaning in the context of his theory of government.

The meanings of words are very important. But philosophers must not only think about the meanings of words. They must also think about the different ways of explaining the meanings of words.

Understanding the Dilemma
BUDDHIST OR SPECIALIST?

The issue in this section is the scope of philosophy. What is philosophy and what isn't? Are Eastern systems like Buddhism philosophy?

The Buddhist in this section claims that Buddhism is closer to philosophy than to religion for three reasons: Buddhists do not believe in God or gods, they seek enlightenment rather than salvation, and they do not believe in an immortal soul. Like philosophers, Buddhists value understanding more than anything, they try to live according to certain principles, and they have profound ideas about reality and human nature.

The specialist in the second essay doesn't explicitly discuss Buddhism, but argues that religion is different from philosophy because religion involves attitudes of commitment, worship, and faith, whereas philosophy requires attitudes of skepticism, questioning, and precision. The specialist would probably claim that Buddhism is closer to religion than to philosophy. So which view is more accurate, the Buddhist's or the specialist's? Is Buddhism philosophy or religion?

The issue is complex because it depends on two difficult questions: what is the essential nature of Buddhism, and what are the essential natures of religion and philosophy? The Buddhist doesn't say there is no difference between religion and philosophy. He or she only says Buddhism is more like philosophy than religion. The Buddhist is assuming that religion involves belief in God or gods, among other things. The specialist does not discuss Buddhism directly. Therefore you have to take the definitions of religion and philosophy in that essay and apply them to Buddhism yourself to see which one fits. The two points of view are connected not so much by what they say explicitly, but by what they imply.

Buddhism is normally classified as a religion, perhaps because Buddhists often behave like followers of other religions. For example, monks and monastic communities are an important part of Buddhism. Buddhist monks lead austere, pure lives, like the monks and nuns of other religions. Buddhists build temples and statues of the Buddha, and go to these holy places to worship and pray. They believe in reincarnation. And while Buddhist scholars develop and extend their ideas, Buddhists are generally not interested in "theological" sophistication or philosophical debates. Indeed, one version of Buddhism—Zen Buddhism—regards rationality and theory as obstacles to enlightenment.

The brief essay on Buddhism could not discuss every aspect of this large movement. And these "religious" practices of Buddhists lead us back to one of our central questions: what is the real nature of Buddhism? The question is difficult partly because of the difference between the Buddha's original teaching and his followers' practices. The Buddha himself did not build statues or pray to them, although later Buddhists have done so. The essay concentrates on the Buddha's original ideas rather than popular practices and beliefs of later followers, and assumes that the founder's ideas define Buddhism.

The specialist, on the other hand, in distinguishing religion and philosophy emphasizes practices and attitudes rather than ideas. Religion and philosophy deal with many of the same ideas, so the difference must lie in the attitudes toward those ideas. Religious people are devout, pious, scrupulously correct, and so on, whereas philosophers are critical, argumentative, and speculative. The actual behavior of Buddhists seems to manifest the religious attitudes rather than the philosophical attitudes.

But Buddhists do not believe in God or the soul. Can Buddhism really be a religion without those ideas? By placing so much emphasis on attitudes, the specialist runs the risk of turning everything into a religion. A person can watch football "religiously" if attitudes are sufficient: he is devoted, scrupulously correct, feels very strongly about it, practices weekly rituals, and so on. But obviously saying a person watches football "religiously" is extending the word "religion" metaphorically. It is not literally a religion. There is no God or afterlife. But there is no God or afterlife in Buddhism either.

Could Buddhism be both religion and philosophy? Could one say the ideas are philosophical but the attitudes are religious? Perhaps, but the specialist concludes by suggesting that philosophy and religion are like oil and water: they do not mix. It is impossible to be worshipful and critical at the same time about the same things. A person can be a religious scientist, for example, but she reserves her religious attitudes for God, the soul, and salvation, and applies her scientific, critical attitudes to chemistry or biology or some science. She can't have a religious attitude toward her test tubes or a scientific attitude toward the soul.

One of the deep, underlying disagreements between the Buddhist and the specialist concerns the nature of understanding or enlightenment. The Buddhist argues that Buddhism is closer to philosophy because Buddhists seek understanding. And the specialist claims that philosophers attempt to understand basic concepts and broad issues. But the two positions seem to disagree about the nature of philosophical understanding. The Buddhist believes a person achieves enlightenment through meditation and examining consciousness itself. One comes to realize that the self is an illusion, and that realization affects one's whole life. But the specialist points to examples of philosophers asking questions, formulating theories, and engaging in debates with others. Understanding comes through collaborative dialogue and explanation, not through solitary introspection. Moreover, philosophical understanding is theoretical. The effects of an explanation on one's emotions or treatment of others is irrelevant to its truth or falsity. The Buddhist and the specialist are making different assumptions about understanding.

This section is about religion and philosophy, two broad, complex phenomena. The differences in perspective between Buddhists and specialists are- so numerous and so basic that it is difficult to compare the two. And yet, developing a worldview involves deciding what you think about religion and philosophy. So, do you find yourself agreeing with the Buddhist or with the specialist?

BUDDHIST

1. The essence of Buddhism is the four noble truths and the eight-fold path.
2. Buddhism is not a religion because it does not involve a belief in God or gods, the soul, or faith.
3. Buddhists value understanding achieved through one's own efforts, not submission to authority.
4. Eastern philosophy may be different from Western philosophy in some ways, but the two traditions can gain valuable insights from each other.

SPECIALIST

1. While religion and philosophy deal with many of the same topics, the attitudes they promote toward those topics are completely different.
2. Religion involves commitment, worship, faith, and ceremonies, whereas philosophy involves skepticism, questions, criticism, and wonder.
3. We can understand religion and philosophy by studying definitions and examples, and by participating in their activities.
4. Attempting to combine such different outlooks as religion and philosophy will lead only to confusion.

HISTORICAL SOURCES

BUDDHIST. E.A. Burtt, ed. *The Teachings of the Compassionate Buddha.* NAL, 1955. Wide range of brief selections from various sources.

SPECIALIST. A.J. Ayer. *Language, Truth, and Logic.* Gollancz, 1936. Distinguishes between scientific philosophy and soft-headed emotionalism, on the grounds that all meaningful statements must be empirically verifiable.

OTHER SOURCES

Nancy Wilson Ross. *Buddhism: A Way of Life and Thought.* Vintage, 1980. A clear, well-written account of history, doctrines, and current practice.

Ray Billington. *Understanding Eastern Philosophy.* Routledge, 1997. Survey of Hinduism, Buddhism, Taoism, and Confucianism, and in the second half, a comparison of key Eastern ideas with Western counterparts.

David J. Kalupahana. *Buddhist Philosophy: A Historical Analysis.* University Press of Hawaii, 1976. An examination of the concepts of knowledge, causality, morality, and others, as expressed in certain ancient Buddhist texts.

Eliot Deutsch, Ron Bontekoe, eds. *Companion to World Philosophy.* Blackwell, 1997. Includes brief articles on "Buddhist reality and divinity," "The Buddhist concept of self," and "Rationality in Buddhist thought," among others.

Ninian Smart. *World Philosophies.* Routledge, 1999. Broad survey of many different regions, religions, and schools of thought, describing the context, origins, and diversification of Buddhism.

Joel J. Kupperman. *Learning from Asian Philosophy.* Oxford University Press, 1999. Challenging essays on the nature of the self, and ethical choice.

Steven Collins. *Selfless Persons*. Cambridge University Press, 1982. Detailed discussion of many different aspects and interpretations of the Buddhist doctrine of "not-self" for advanced students.

Jean-Francois Revel, Matthieu Ricard. *The Monk and the Philosopher: A Father and Son Discuss the Meaning of Life*. Schocken, 1999. Wide-ranging debate/discussion on science and religion, consciousness, reality, and politics, between a secular French political philosopher and his son, a scientist who converted to Buddhism.

CONNECTIONS

TRANSCENDENTALIST OR NATURALIST?

Chapter 1 raises six very important questions and the contrasting answers that philosophers have given to them. To build your own worldview you should try to decide which answers are the most convincing. They cannot all be correct, and different people might be persuaded by different answers. The answers to these fundamental questions that you can accept will make up your worldview.

Deciding what you believe about these deep issues is not a simple matter. It takes time, reflection, and talks with other people. The answers are all yes or no, but they include more complicated ideas, too. You should think about what an answer means before you decide that you believe it. One helpful way to understand an answer is to look at the alternatives. For example, if you think that you believe God exists, you should understand what it means to believe that there is no God, and vice versa. Knowing what you do *not* believe is part of knowing what you do believe. The opposing essays should help you see the contrasts among possible answers to these questions.

Another way to understand what the answers mean is to think about how you would put them into practice. What difference would it make in your life if you are a theist or an atheist? An abstractionist or a personalist? It would make some difference in how you think about events, about your future, about religion and religious people, and about the natural world. Your choice of an answer might also affect your behavior. For example, a personalist might talk to God, but an abstractionist probably would not.

Many people know what they believe, but they don't know *why* they believe it. They have a flat, simplistic worldview. They have memorized short answers to some questions, but they cannot go further than reciting their formulaic answers. If you want to build a solid, intricate worldview—a worldview adequate to your own complex experience and intelligence—then you should know why you accept some answers and reject others. You should be able to explain your beliefs and answer questions about them. Developing a wellgrounded set of answers is like building a sturdy boat: you have chosen the best design, you have learned how to put the keel, the hull, the rudder, and other parts together, you have attended to all the little details, and now you are confident that the boat will carry you over the waves wherever you want to go. If you don't know why you hold certain beliefs you are like a person desperately clutching a few pieces of driftwood.

The image of building a boat brings us to the point of this section. If you want to build a boat you must fit the pieces together in a way that works. If the boards making the hull do not fit together exactly right, the boat will leak. If the rudder doesn't fit to the stern in the right way, you will go around in circles or zigzag like a drunken sailor. The same applies to your worldview. The different answers you accept must fit together. Otherwise your worldview won't help you, and in fact it will be a constant source of confusion, frustration, and worry for you.

Therefore you should try to understand the *connections* among the answers to the questions in Chapter 1. Some answers fit together better than others. If you are persuaded by one answer to one question, that may be a reason to accept another answer to another question.

In Section 1.1, "Does God Exist?," you read about theism and atheism. Which of the answers in the later sections fit together with theism, and which are more compatible with atheism? Probably the clearest connection is between theism and the survivor, represented in Section 1.4, "Is the Soul Immortal?" Theists believe in a transcendent being, God, who is eternal and all-powerful. Survivors believe that they will survive the death of the body and will continue to exist in a realm beyond the ever-changing natural world. The similarity between these two positions is the belief in a transcendent level of reality. The theist and the survivor both believe in a *supernatural* world, beyond the natural world. The prefix "super" means above, or over, and both God and the afterlife are above or beyond the natural world.

In contrast, atheists believe that the natural world is all there is. Reality is the world of plants and animals, men and women, buildings and machines. It is what we can see, touch, and understand. As we understand more and more, we have no reason to believe in God or the afterlife or any supernatural phenomena. An atheist is similar to a mortalist because both deny that there is a transcendent level of reality, above our ordinary experience.

Let's call a person who believes in a supernatural level of reality a "transcendentalist" (because he or she believes there is a reality that "transcends" the everyday world). And we can call a person who believes that reality is what we observe and understand through ordinary experience a "naturalist." With those categories in mind, we can look at the other positions in Chapter 1 to see if they are closer to transcendentalism or naturalism. In other words, the two categories will help us look for connections, similarities and differences, among the different answers. To find connections, we should ask, "Is this answer committed to belief in a supernatural level of reality?" All the answers that say yes come from transcendentalists, and those that say no are naturalists' answers.

In Section 1.3, "Can God Allow Innocent Suffering?," you read about reconcilers and contradictors. Reconcilers believe that a loving, all-powerful God could make his creatures suffer—innocent suffering is compatible with such a God—whereas contradictors believe that a loving God would not make his creatures suffer. If there were a God who loved us and who could prevent innocent suffering, he would do it. It is clear that a reconciler is more sympathetic with belief in God. A reconciler wants to explain how we can continue to believe in God even in the face of the terrible catastrophes we see all around us. On the other hand, most contradictors say that the fact of suffering should lead us to give up any belief in God. We know suffering occurs, and there is no way to explain how a loving God could allow it. Thus a contradictor is similar to an atheist and a mortalist. They are all naturalists. But a reconciler is similar to a theist and a survivor. They are all transcendentalists.

However, these relationships can get complicated. It would be possible to believe in God, but also to accept the contradictor's argument. The way to accept the two beliefs is to deny that innocent suffering ever occurs. It may sound absurd to say that no innocent people ever suffer, but if a person believes the Christian doctrine of original sin, the person may believe that no one is completely innocent. We are all sinners in God's eyes, some people might say. We all deserve the punishments we receive. This person could agree that innocent suffering would contradict the existence of God, if it ever occurred, but it doesn't. But it is probably more common for contradictors to be atheists.

In answer to the question of Section 1.2, "Is God Like Human Beings?," an abstractionist says no, and a personalist says yes. An abstractionist believes that the word "God" refers to the abstract power of love, which courses through all things and creates harmony and unity among all things. A personalist, on the other hand, believes that God is like a parent, with a mind, with thoughts and plans and feelings, except that God is infinitely wiser, stronger, and better than a mortal parent. Both theories are about God, so both are closer to transcendentalism than naturalism.

This is clearer for the personalist than the abstractionist. A personalist says that God has human traits, but magnified far beyond anything we can grasp. God is intelligent, for example, but infinitely intelligent. God is powerful, but vastly more powerful than any natural force. God is both like, and unlike, human beings, and that is one of the mysteries surrounding God's nature.

However, an abstractionist could, just possibly, be a naturalist. It depends on how a person thinks about love. Is love a perfectly natural force, like other human emotions? Is it just gravity (mutual attraction), a force studied by physicists? If so, then an abstractionist is not saying anything that a naturalist would reject, although a naturalist would not call love "God." Or is love a supernatural force, more than merely human, more than merely natural, maybe beyond our comprehension? The essay "God Is Love" says that love is eternal, a moral guide, and all-powerful, and these characteristics go beyond purely natural forces. Its version of abstractionism, therefore, is closer to transcendentalism than naturalism.

The fifth question in Chapter 1, in Section 1.5, is "Is Faith an Answer?" A believer says that no one can know whether or not there is a God, and therefore one answer is just as good as another. The believer chooses the theist's answer. A questioner, on the other hand, argues that choosing answers that we want to believe, or that authorities tell us to believe, leads to terrible consequences. We should base all our beliefs on evidence and good reasons.

Since a believer believes in God, he or she is a transcendentalist. A questioner's demand for evidence is similar to a naturalist's. Naturalists believe we can observe the world and reach conclusions about it, based on our observations, i.e., evidence. But notice that while a believer is a transcendentalist, not all transcendentalists are believers. The two theists in Section 1.1, for example, give plausible reasons for their belief in God. Their belief is not based on faith but on evidence, and so they are both questioners, not believers. The same is true for the survivor and the reconciler. A survivor can be a questioner, and vice versa.

How do meaning theists and existentialists fit into this comparison between transcendentalists and naturalists? Since meaning theists believe in God, they are transcendentalists. In order for your life to have meaning, they say, it must be devoted to something higher than mere survival or personal pleasure. It must be devoted to God, who is perfect goodness.

This way of thinking about God makes the meaning theist similar to the abstractionist: God is love. I said above that an abstractionist might be a naturalist if she thinks that love is a natural force that we can study rationally. But the meaning theist claims that absolute love, or perfect goodness, cannot be a merely human, natural quality. It cannot be known through ordinary experience. It is precisely God's transcendental nature that gives our lives meaning. Our lives must point to something outside themselves, as meaningful words do, if they are to be meaningful. God is outside the natural world, and serving him is what gives our lives meaning.

An existentialist is a naturalist. The existentialist in Section 1.6 rejects the idea that belief in God makes life meaningful. The writer does not argue that there is no God (as the atheist and the contradictor do), or even that we shouldn't have faith that God exists (as the questioner does). The existentialist's point is that the existence of God or faith in God wouldn't help us live meaningful lives. If God exists and we obey him, that doesn't make our lives meaningful unless we have a reason to do so. Getting to heaven is not a reason that makes life meaningful, according to the existentialist, because it's selfish and superficial. Obeying God does not lead to any goal, so it is an arbitrary, meaningless decision. An existentialist is a naturalist because he or she rejects the supernatural, transcendental God as a source of meaning. Actually, existentialists believe there no source of meaning—life is meaningless—but that belief is not what makes existentialists naturalists, and it isn't necessarily a part of naturalism. Thus all existentialists are naturalists, but not all naturalists are existentialists. (Remember, too, that I have made up these labels to give us a convenient way to talk about ideas and beliefs. You will see the word "existentialist" in other places, and it might not mean exactly what it means here.)

The current controversy in Section 1.7 is about Buddhism and philosophy, or religion and philosophy in general. The Buddhist in this section maintains that Buddhism is closer to philosophy than to religion, because Buddhists do not believe in God, they hold a philosophical view of the person, and they do not rely on faith. The contrasting essay by the specialist doesn't discuss Buddhism specifically, but tries to show that religious attitudes are different from philosophical attitudes.

The specialist is not closer to transcendentalism or to naturalism, but could go either way. The specialist is discussing the nature of religion and philosophy in general, but is not taking a stand on any of the particular beliefs that religious people or philosophers hold. Perhaps a transcendental realm exists, or perhaps it doesn't. The specialist is only discussing differences in the ways people think about reality—transcendent or natural.

The Buddhist in this section, on the other hand, is a naturalist. (Like all major religions, Buddhism consists of many different divisions and groups, who disagree on various points among themselves, and some groups would reject the version of Buddhism presented here.)The Buddhist does not believe in a transcendent God or an immortal soul, and does not rely on faith in mysteries that are beyond our comprehension. According to this interpretation, Buddhism is primarily a moral doctrine. The spiritual aspect is in the development of deeper and clearer levels of consciousness. But spiritual growth for a Buddhist is not a supernatural process dependent upon aid from a transcendent source.

While the connections among different answers are sometimes complicated, it is safe to say that some of the answers in Chapter 1 are similar and fit together easily, while others are mismatched. We can represent the results with a chart.

Transcendentalist	Naturalist
theist	atheist
abstractionist	contradictor
personalist	mortalist
reconciler	questioner
survivor	existentialist
believer	Buddhist
meaning theist	specialist
specialist	

TRANSCENDENTALIST

1. The world is too vast, complex, and mysterious for us to understand completely.
2. There are many reasons for us to believe in a divine Creator, who is eternal, all-powerful, and good.
3. Human beings have a kinship with the Creator; essentially we are not animals but embodied spirits.

4. There are many ways to reach an understanding of reality, the mind, and truth; science shows us only one limited aspect of truth.

NATURALIST

5. The spectacular progress of science during the past four hundred years shows that science is the best way to understand the world.
6. To anyone who is willing to think, the existence of evil proves that there is no God.
7. Human beings are intelligent animals, biological systems that are born and that cease to function.
8. Believing things on the basis of faith is a dangerous practice, harmful to the individual believer and to society.

3.1 IS PLEASURE THE ONLY VALUE?

Hedonist or Pluralist?

Earlier (in Section 1.3) I said that the question "Can God allow innocent suffering?" probably draws more people to philosophy than any other question. But the topic of this section—"Is pleasure the only value?" or "What goals should we have?"—may be in second place. Many people assume that philosophers think a lot about how one should live, or what kind of life one should lead. So they come to philosophy looking for advice about the best way of life. Everyone would like to know what goals he or she should have, what is most important, what is less important, and what isn't important at all. We all need some guidelines to help us make important decisions, about career, marriage, friends, self-development, money, sex, children, and other concerns. And we need some sense of where it is all leading, or what it all adds up to. Everyone would like to know how to give his or her life as a whole significance, worth, and value.

The question about goals is just another way of asking what values I should have. A person's goals are the same things as the person's values. If one of your goals is to have a lot of good friends, then you value friendship. You enjoy it, you approve of it, you work to develop and keep friendships. If one of your goals is to be healthy, then you value health.

Philosophers' discussions of goals are not like psychotherapists' or counselors' discussions. People go to a psychotherapist with a specific problem. Perhaps they feel lonely, or they are unhappy with their jobs, or they get angry too easily. They want advice on how to change their lives to solve the problem. The therapist must try to discover the particular circumstances of the person's life that cause the bad feelings. Then the therapist may make some suggestions tailored to this particular client's problem.

Philosophers work differently. Philosophers think about goals that all human beings should have. Human beings are all similar in many ways. We are biologically similar, and have similar biological needs. We all grow up with families, we are all socialized by our societies, we all probably have similar psychological needs, such as self-esteem, challenging work, companionship, and perhaps others. Philosophers search for the proper goals of human life *as such*, not solutions to particular psychological problems. One can say that philosophers think about values—things that are good—and not just certain people's desires.

The first essay that follows argues that the highest goal we can have is pleasure. In fact, it is the only worthwhile goal. This view is called "hedonism." The second essay describes a wide variety of values, or goals, and rejects hedonism. Since it argues for the conclusion that there are many good things to strive for, we can call the point of view of the second essay "pluralist."

YES: HEDONIST

"Hedonism"

What makes life worthwhile? How should we live? These are the most important questions one can ask, and the most pressing questions. Before we can turn our efforts to anything—going to school, going to work, going to a movie—we should know why we are doing it, and whether we shouldn't be doing something else.

Different people propose different answers, but the most persuasive answer was put forward long ago by a school of philosophers called Epicureans (from the Greek philosopher Epicurus) or hedonists (from the Greek word for pleasure, *hedone*). They taught that the highest good is pleasure (and the absence of pain). Pleasure is what makes life worthwhile, and everyone should attempt to achieve as much pleasure as he or she can. Not only is pleasure the highest good, it is the only good.

This is not the same as "eat, drink, and be merry." Eating too much or drinking too much will result in indigestion and hangovers, or other discomfort and pain. Immediate, short-term pleasures often lead to long-term pain, so hedonism requires some restraint and self-control. A sober, disciplined person probably experiences more pleasure and less pain over a longer time than a party animal.

Some philosophers prefer the word "happiness" to "pleasure." But what is happiness? Happiness is nothing more than the experience of pleasure, or the anticipation of pleasure, or the memory of pleasure. If you will recall a time when you were happy, you will notice that you were doing something that you enjoyed. Maybe you thought of your satisfying work in the garden. Or you were anticipating some future pleasure, perhaps an evening with your special friend after you finish working. Or you were remembering the great time you had last weekend at the beach. Happiness is necessarily connected with pleasure, although the pleasure can be past, present, or future.

Critics condemn hedonism as "a pig's philosophy," suggesting that hedonists value only physical pleasures. But there are various kinds of pleasure. There is the pleasure of resting after hard work, of being loved, of interesting conversation, of learning something new, and other "mental" pleasures.

The pursuit of pleasure can take many forms. One person may find pleasure in being with her family and providing for them. Reading bedtime stories to her children makes her feel warm and delighted. Another person may derive satisfaction from fame or approval or social reputation, and pursue that. Some people enjoy art, music, or literature, and say that aesthetic appreciation is the purest pleasure. Sex is definitely pleasurable, and so are the rituals of flirting, pursuing, choosing clothes, daydreaming, and exchanging secrets that go with it. The term "pleasure" encompasses many things, but they all have that special, pleasing experience in common.

Hedonism rests on two main beliefs. First, pleasure is good. And second, pleasure is the *only* good. Are these beliefs true? Well, let's look at the first one, pleasure is good. Virtually everyone accepts this belief as true. If you have to wait at the airport for a delayed flight, is it better to stand or to sit down? Is it better to be bored or to read an interesting novel? Of course, the pleasant ways of passing the time are better than the unpleasant ways, everything else being equal.

There are some unfortunate people who will stand, or spend the whole time worrying needlessly. Some people punish themselves for no good reason. Pleasure makes some people feel guilty. It is possible to renounce and shun pleasure voluntarily, just because one has been taught that pleasure is bad. But is it wise? Is that a good way to live? If you examine your own feelings in an unprejudiced way, you will say no.

Thus virtually everyone believes that pleasure is a good thing. Such universal assent means something. But, in addition, hedonists *know* that pleasure is good. Their belief is not just a "personal value," and not just a biological instinct. They know pleasure is good in the same way they know most other things: They perceive it with their senses. For example, how do you know that the sun shines during the day, or that grass is green? You see it, obviously. How do you know that it is cold in Chicago in February? You feel it. If you haven't felt it yourself, then you believe someone who has felt it. How do you know that lemons are sour? You taste it.

Now, how do you know that a hot bath after a hard day's work is good? You feel it. As you settle into the tub and your muscles relax, you say, "This is great." You feel that pleasure is good. Or after a delightful dinner and a long talk with good friends, you say, "What a nice evening. We should do this again." The pleasure of companionship is good. It is as obvious as the fact that grass is green, and we know both facts in the same way. We feel that pleasure is good just as directly as we see, taste, and feel the other facts.

While most people will accept the first hedonist belief, that pleasure is good, few will accept the second belief, that pleasure is the *only* good. Many say that selfless love is the most wonderful experience we can have, but it is not the same thing as pleasure. And loyalty to one's community, or performing one's duty, are surely valuable, even if they require pain and sacrifice. Some say pure virtue itself makes life worthwhile. Knowledge, creativity and art, the natural world, personal growth, and many other things have been held up as valuable goals. To these people hedonists seem to have a very narrow-minded outlook. They have a one-track mind and ignore many important values in life.

Or do they? Many of the things that seem to be alternatives to pleasure in reality are not. They are valuable because they *lead to* pleasure in the long run. Hedonists can say this because they make a distinction between means and ends. They admit that some things, like hard physical exercise, are valuable, but are not enjoyable at all. But exercise is a means to achieving something else, like winning a race or looking attractive. And those things *are* pleasurable. Some people exercise so they can be healthy and live longer. Why do people want to be healthy and live longer? Because health helps one enjoy life, and a longer life means more pleasure.

Moreover, the exercise is valuable *only* because it helps a person achieve the other things. If exercising, or dieting, or going to the dentist, or studying engineering, or working to make money, did *not* lead to pleasure of some kind (or the absence of pain), no one would do them. What would be the point? Would a young woman work in a boring job if she weren't paid? No. The reason for working hard and making sacrifices is to achieve pleasure in the long run. On the other hand, pleasure is its own reward. It is an end, not a means. If something is pleasurable, people do it for its own sake. No one has to explain why she wants it.

The means we use to achieve pleasure can be complicated. Many people are devoted to their family, their community, and their country. And loyalty to the group, sacrifice for the good of the whole, public service, are good. But they are all *means*, not ends. They are ultimately means to one's own pleasure. They benefit the group by making it more stable, or secure, or prosperous. And since the person making the sacrifice is a member of the group, he or she benefits as well. Human beings are social animals. We depend on each other in countless ways. That means that often the best way for us to benefit ourselves is to help others, because they can return the favor and help us in ways that we cannot help ourselves.

Like public service, most of the other goals in life, such as knowledge, art, and conservation of nature, are valuable as means to one's own pleasure. Even obedience to God's commandments is a means of gaining the pleasures of heaven, or avoiding the pains of hell.

Pleasure is the only good. The enlightened pursuit of pleasure is the only realistic morality.

Key Concepts

pleasure	happiness	senses
highest good	mental pleasure	means and ends

Critical Questions

1. The first essay says hedonism consists of two main beliefs. What are they? In your opinion, must those two beliefs go together, or could a person accept one but not the other?
2. Why should you believe that pleasure is good, according to the essay?
3. Does a hedonist believe that individuals always do what they think will produce pleasure for themselves?
4. The hedonist makes a distinction between means and ends. Can you think of some other examples of means and ends?
5. Why are people devoted to their families and communities, according to the essay? Do you agree?
6. In your opinion, are there any things that are morally good, but do not produce any pleasure for anyone? (For example, kindness, work, knowledge, respect, love?)

NO: PLURALIST

"A World of Values"

Philosophers try to make sense of human experience. They often do this by proposing a theory to explain how diverse aspects of our lives fit together. For example, Freud claimed that all of a person's actions were, in one way or another, the expressions of the drive for sexual satisfaction. Some political philosophers have claimed that all political events—laws, elections, taxes, revolutions, ideologies, and so on—are results of a struggle for power. These kinds of theories often help us see an underlying reality, and relations among events, that we would not have seen without them. They give unity and coherence to our outlook on life.

The danger in such theories is oversimplification. We all want to understand the confusing, conflicting events in our lives so badly that sometimes we ignore facts, or distort them, to preserve a simple, familiar picture of the world. We produce "Procrustean" theories. Procrustes was a figure in Greek mythology who forced visitors to fit his bed by stretching them if they were too short or cutting off their legs if they were too long. I suspect that many people, including philosophers, act like Procrustes when they think about values.

The topic of values is complicated. But some philosophers oversimplify the issue by suggesting that there is really only one value, and that all the good things in life are somehow reflections of the one true value. Different philosophers have proposed different ultimate values. Some say it is survival, or "life," or continued existence. Some say it is devotion to God. Some say love, loyalty to loved ones, or community. Some say pleasure, or happiness.

But philosophers should not only try to find unifying themes in human experience. Above all they should seek the truth. And to remain true to experience they should sometimes remind us just how complicated and multifarious life can be. In fact, human beings have always recognized many different values, which cannot be redefined or collapsed into each other. A survey of the main values will show just how different they are. There are personal values, which concern oneself and do not involve other people. And there are social values, which essentially involve other people. Let us begin with personal values.

Personal Values

Most personal values have to do with the preservation and development of the self, while some depend on other kinds of personal experiences. Probably the most basic and universal personal value is *survival*. Humans are living organisms, and therefore we have a drive to preserve ourselves. We want to live; we are afraid of death. Many people express this value as a desire for money. They organize their lives around the pursuit of money—for example, they seek a high-paying job—because they want to guarantee that they will always have food, clothing, and shelter. They value security.

Other people value *health*. They read and learn about proper diet, vitamins, cholesterol, fiber, and so on, and they feel that eating right is very important. Health is not exactly the same as survival. Those who value health might actually take serious risks, such as skydiving or kayaking. What they fear is not death but illness and loss of vitality.

Of course many people value other things besides survival and health. They take these for granted and look further to see what life has to offer. They may value *personal growth*. That is, they may want new experiences, opportunities to meet different kinds of people, successes, and also failures, to feel what they are like. They may travel, change jobs, go to school, have an affair. They want to expand themselves, to add dimensions, skills, and memories to their lives.

Others think of personal development as *creativity*. People who value creativity feel that they are already full of ideas and experiences, and they want to express them. They may be inspired by creative work in the arts—film, music, novels, dance—or by creative problem solving in business or science, and they want to express their own unique talent. They want to make something new.

Another personal value is *excellence*. Excellence simply means doing something in the best way possible. For example, one house painter may slap on the paint as quickly as possible so that he or she can go on to the next job, whereas another painter will take the time to avoid painting the glass in the windows, to see that every corner is covered, and to make the coat of paint smooth and even. The two painters receive the same payment, but one values excellence. Many people admire excellence in others, such as the excellence of athletes.

However, much of the time people do not think about preserving themselves, or enlarging themselves. They just want to have *fun*. They do not worry about necessities, health, being creative, or striving for excellence. When these goals are taken for granted, or ignored, then people want to enjoy life. Enjoyment is certainly an important value. Most people watch several hours of TV every day, go to several movies every month, play games on their computers, read gossip magazines, go to restaurants, and engage in sex. People do these things because they are enjoyable. They have no other purpose. After our needs are satisfied and we feel secure, then we want some pleasant stimulation.

It's true that some people never aim higher. They think that pleasant stimulation is the ultimate goal in life, perhaps because they have never learned about other values. But I think most people have a broader outlook. After they have gained some security, and after they have had fun with movies or backyard barbecues (or sex or drugs), they look for something they think is important, not merely enjoyable. They understand that there are other values in the world, values that may be more important than pleasure, and maybe even more important than oneself.

We will turn to social values momentarily, but for now we should consider other personal values. One is *beauty*. Some people are very sensitive to their environment. They go to great lengths to surround themselves with beautiful things. They go to galleries to see paintings and sculptures, they listen to music, or they take photographs on the weekends.

People who value beauty enjoy seeing and hearing beautiful things, and therefore one could argue that beauty is really the same as enjoyment, that they are not two values but one. But that is just the kind of oversimplification that distorts experience. TV, movies, games, and magazines are not beautiful. They are too simple and superficial to be beautiful. The experience of beauty requires some effort; it takes some attentiveness, practice, and the exercise of the mind as well as the senses. Thus beautiful objects are different from entertainments, and the experience of beauty is different from the experience of having fun. For some people, it is far more valuable than simply having fun. To lump them together is to ignore important possibilities of experience.

Another important dimension of human experience is *freedom*. Many people place a great value on freedom and self-reliance. They want to lead their lives with the fewest restrictions possible. The important thing is not to have many paths open to them (as the term "freedom" might suggest), but to have *their* paths. They want to live as they think they should rather than as others think they should.

The last personal value to consider is *knowledge*, or understanding, or intelligence. Scientists, professors, counselors, economists, and many others place a great value on knowledge and understanding. They are curious about the world, they want to learn new things, to solve mysteries, and see how things work. They value knowledge itself, not the power or profits knowledge can produce. They admire others who can understand problems or who have acquired wisdom through experience.

Social Values

All the values I have mentioned so far belong in one category because they involve personal growth and development, or relaxation. They can be achieved by a single individual. But our relations with other people bring out a whole different dimension of value: the social values.

The most common social value is *love*. The word "love" encompasses many different feelings, relationships, and ideas, so when people say that love is the most important thing in their lives, they can mean different things. Some value an intimate, sharing relation with another person. Some include the warmth and trust of family relations. Some live mainly for the give and take they enjoy with their close friends. Love is not a personal value because when one person loves another, the person values the *other*. He may even value the other more than himself. At the very least, he values the relationshipóthe togetherness, communication, and interdependence. All the personal values are applied to the other as well as to himself.

Related to love is *compassion*. Everyone knows of people who help others. Religious groups organize soup kitchens, volunteers go to less developed countries to help build houses, executives act as big brothers to inner city children, secretaries teach illiterate people how to read. They see people who need help, and they want to help. A life that includes service is better than one that does not.

Another social value is *leadership*, or organization. Some people want to take charge, to make decisions, and to get others moving toward a common goal. Social interaction is extremely important to them, but it is a different interaction from love or service. It is interaction with groups rather than individuals. It is a kind of responsibility. However, a person who is too egotistical may mistake this value for power and control over people.

Many people value *esteem*. They want others to think well of them. They may conceive of this value in various ways, as respect, popularity, reputation, status, approval, or fame. The common factor in all these words is other people's good opinion of oneself. People have very different beliefs about how to gain esteem. Some pursue excellence, not because they value excellence itself, but because they think it will make other people think highly of them. Some try to make large amounts of money, gain knowledge, or cultivate friends for the same reason.

One of the most important social values is *justice*. Like love, justice is difficult to define. But most of us know when people are treated fairly and when they are not, and we are upset when they are not. Some people work very hard to bring about a more just society, where people's efforts and talents are rewarded, and where race, gender, and ethnic background neither help nor harm individuals in their pursuit of their values.

Justice is not exactly the same thing as *harmony*. Justice, or respect for basic rights, is perhaps the minimal condition for a good society. But many people want to go beyond justice; they want a society in which people cooperate, compromise, and enjoy each others' company. They envisage a society in which people are not only just, but even friendly and loving. Others conceive of harmony as cooperative effort, in which everyone in a community pitches in and works together for a common goal.

Another social value is *devotion to God*. All religions are founded on the cultivation of this relation. For religious people, the supreme value is God, the source of all goodness, beauty, wisdom, justice, and all other values. They value the spiritual dimension of existence—the communion with God—above everything else. The relation with God is something like the relation with another person, but much more, and the love and honor that apply to relations with people also apply to the relation with God, but in greater degree.

The last social value to consider is *nature*. Nature is not a person, but it is something outside the individual, and recognizing its value means entering into a relationship. The earth, the unspoiled forests, the streams, the massive mountains, and all the animals and plants in the natural world possess a kind of majesty that is unique. The more we experience nature firsthand, the more wonderful and inspiring—and precious—it appears. It isn't only beauty, or our own need for clean air and water. Nature itself is worthy of respect.

Nature and God are probably the broadest, most inclusive values. And there may be other values that aren't included in this brief survey. In particular, we must include morality, or *moral values*. Moral values used to be called "virtues," although that word sounds old-fashioned these days. Moral values, such as courage, honesty, perseverance, and loyalty, have to do with regulating one's own behavior and being a certain kind of person. They are ideals of conduct and character. Those who value morality want to behave in certain ways—to tell the truth and to stand by their friends, for example—and want to have these traits, or virtues (honest, loyal, brave, etc.).

I have put moral values at the end of the survey because they do not fit easily into the personal or social categories. As ideals of conduct and character, they are similar to personal growth. If we value morality we try to mold ourselves into the kind of person we think we should be. Self-discipline, self-reliance, curiosity, courage, and perseverance are all "self-regarding" moral values. We can achieve them on our own. At the same time, however, some of the most important moral values essentially involve relations with other people. Honesty, trustworthiness, tolerance, compassion, and justice are ideals guiding the ways we treat others. In a way, all the values—personal and social—are moral values, since they guide our behavior. They are the bases of the choices we make.

Pleasure

These descriptions of values are far too brief, but they should make the point that there are many different values. However, some philosophers try to reduce all of them to pleasure, so I want to emphasize several ways in which this view is mistaken. The word "pleasure" refers to a physical sensation or reaction to stimuli. But some people expand the word to include personal growth, excellence, love, justice, and every other value there is. They are determined to simplify human values, but in doing so they stretch the word beyond all recognition. The word "pleasure" no longer means anything if it applies to watching TV, striving for excellence, promoting justice, and so many other things as well. A person does not feel the same ways when she or he is engaged in these activities.

Not only are people's feelings different, but feelings are not values. The philosopher who reduces all values to pleasure is mistaking personal reactions for features in the world. Pleasure is a subjective feeling in a particular person. But beauty, justice, excellence, and other values are objective qualities in the world. Many people can recognize them, describe and analyze them, reach agreement about them, and prize them. My feelings do not make an action just or unjust, or a performance excellent or average. But one individual's pleasure is that person's alone, private and personal. It is subjective, not objective, as value is.

If enjoyment were the only value, then why do people disagree on the best goals in life, or the best society, or right and wrong? We are all very similar physically, and similar stimuli produce pleasure in us. But we disagree over values. Therefore values are not the same thing as pleasure.

But even if none of these things were true, and even if philosophers could show that on some basic level pleasure was the only value, they would still face the important question: what is the best way of life? Should individuals develop their abilities or devote time to others? Should they focus on doing the best work they can, or on achieving independence, or love? The philosopher's grand theory doesn't answer any of the real questions.

Which is the highest value? Personal growth? Love? Freedom? Justice? How can we rank the different values? What happens when values come into conflict? These are some of the questions that arise when we must choose a course of action. Making choices is difficult. But it is better to wrestle with these questions, and recognize that we do have choices, than it is to ignore all the different values and try to reduce them to one or two. Health is not the same thing as justice, excellence is not the same thing as love, and none of the values can be reduced to any other. The philosophers' attempt to simplify the world is understandable, and even excusable. But we should remember that, in the end, truth is more valuable than a false simplicity.

Key Concepts

personal values   oversimplify   pleasure
social values   morality   objective quality

Critical Questions

1. Is creativity different from excellence? Isn't being creative the same as being excellent?
2. Suppose I value health and freedom because both give me pleasure. Does that show that they are the same value? Or are they still different values?
3. In your opinion, does it make sense to say that nature is valuable in itself, apart from its usefulness or beauty to mankind?
4. How does the pluralist define "moral value"? Are all values moral values, according to the pluralist?
5. The pluralist says the hedonist cannot define pleasure. Suppose the hedonist defined it in terms of *behavior*: it is "whatever leads a person to continue or repeat an experience." Is that an adequate definition, in your opinion?
6. Are the values that the essay describes objective qualities of the world? Is health objective or subjective? Creativity, excellence, compassion, justice, etc.?
7. Can you suggest a way to rank the values the essay describes? Is there any way to show that one value is more important, more valuable, than another value? By what standard is one value more important than another?

Methods and Techniques
FACTS AND VALUES

The essays in this section are about morality. Both discuss the goals we should have. I said in the introduction that your goals are the same as your values. Moral philosophy, or ethics, is concerned with values. Both essays also try to base their recommendations on certain facts, like the fact that many people sacrifice some pleasure now in order to achieve greater pleasure in the future, or the fact that people say they value many different things. So ethics is concerned with facts, too, especially the facts that may help us decide what is the best way of life.

Everyone talks about "facts and values." They are common, basic ideas, and so philosophers try to understand what they mean and clarify them, since philosophers look at all our most basic beliefs and ideas. The concepts of God, self, knowledge, freedom, and some others are the subject of philosophy. But the concepts of fact and value are not very easy to understand, just as all the basic ideas turn out to be slippery and elusive when we try to pin them down.

What is a fact and what is a value? Well, roughly speaking, we can say that a fact is something that is established as true. It is an actual state of affairs, or a real condition in the world. For example, it is a fact that Boston is north of New York. It is a fact that Socrates died in 399 B.C.E. Those are both states of affairs, or circumstances, that have been established as true. It is not a fact that Los Angeles is the capital of California. Notice that facts are complex situations, not objects. Socrates himself is not a fact, nor is the city of Boston. But Socrates' death in 399 is a fact, and Boston's location relative to New York is a fact. When we say something about something else (and our statement is true), then we are reporting facts.

How do we know that Boston is north of New York? How do we "establish" something as true? The most common way is through observation. If you travel from New York to Boston, and look at a compass along the way, you will observe that you are going north. Or if you cannot observe it yourself, you can rely on the testimony of someone else who has observed it. We often rely on other people's observations. For example, it is a fact that a mammal's heart is divided into four chambers. Most people have not cut open mammals and observed their hearts. But it is still an established fact because some qualified experts have dissected mammals and made the observation. On the other hand, I might say "The planet Pluto has a core of iron." But no one—not even an expert—has observed the interior of Pluto, and so I cannot say it is a fact that Pluto has a core of iron. It is a hypothesis, or a theory, but not a fact. Even though Socrates died twenty-four hundred years ago, that fact is established in the same way. Many people observed the event and wrote about it, and we accept their testimony.

What is a value? A value is also a state of affairs or condition, just as a fact is. But it is a state of affairs that people approve of. It is something that people desire, or pursue, or try to preserve. For example, tolerance is a value. People approve of tolerance, they try to promote it, and they admire it when they see it. They have positive feelings about it. Values arise out of our human ability to imagine a situation that is different from the actual, present situation. For example, if I am hungry, I can imagine getting food. I want food, and can try to get it. If I do this regularly over a period of time, then you could say that I value food. I can also imagine people being tolerant of each other's differences, even if they are not tolerant now. If I want tolerance and try to promote it, then I value tolerance. Tolerance is a value for me.

I can also look at a past situation, like a war, and feel regret and remorse about it. I can wish that it never happened. I can imagine what things would have been like if it had not happened, and I feel sorry about it. Then I value peace. Or I can look back on my own behavior and feel guilt or shame. For example, perhaps I remember telling a lie and I feel badly about it. If I want to be an honest person, and try to be more honest, then I value honesty.

Values are related to facts in the same way that the ideal is related to the actual. The way people actually behave is not necessarily the way they *ought* to behave. It is a fact that some people hate others; we value people respecting each other. The actual condition of our society is not necessarily the *ideal* condition. We can look at people and society and imagine a better way. Values are the better way, whether it is honesty, or tolerance, or peace, or liberty, or whatever. On the other hand, sometimes the actual *is* ideal. Sometimes we read about a cab driver who returns a wallet he found with a thousand dollars in it. The ideal is not always imaginary. What makes something a value is that people approve of it, not that it does not exist.

This preliminary analysis of facts and values is only a beginning. The concepts are central to ethics, so philosophers want to understand them as fully as possible. But many questions remain. For example, are values objective or subjective? Values are states of affairs that people approve of, but does the approval make them valuable, or do we approve of them because they are valuable in themselves? Is honesty valuable and right because we approve of it, or is it valuable whether we approve of it or not? The same question arises about facts. Do we call something a fact just because most of the people in our culture believe it? People establish facts by making observations, but observations can be mistaken. (Do we say tolerance is a value just because most people in our society value it? Can we "observe" that intolerance is evil and wrong?) You will read about some of the further questions that remain in the following sections concerning moral philosophy.

Understanding the Dilemma
HEDONIST OR PLURALIST?

The choice in this section is between hedonism and pluralism. Which is more appealing to you? Are you a hedonist or a pluralist? Is your goal in life to enjoy yourself as much as possible, or do you have other goals and values besides pleasure? Are your other goals just pleasure in disguise?

Perhaps the most important point to understand is that the hedonist and the pluralist are not arguing about psychology. The first essay, representing hedonism, does *not* say that everyone is motivated by a desire for pleasure. In fact, it says the opposite: some people deliberately do things that do not make them happy. And the second essay presents the issue in terms of values, objective qualities in the world, not motives or feelings.

The question in this section is an ethical question, not a psychological question. Philosophers distinguish between "psychological egoism" and "ethical egoism." Psychological egoism is the view that everyone always tries to benefit himself or herself. It is claimed to be a psychological fact about people. Some people accept psychological egoism and some people do not. In contrast, ethical egoism is the view that people *ought* to act in a way that benefits themselves. It is a theory about what is valuable, however people actually behave. In this section the two essays are concerned with ethical issues, not psychological issues. (You will read about psychological egoism in Section 4.5.) Note, too, that egoism—benefitting oneself—is not the same thing as hedonism—valuing pleasure. I can be an egoist but not a hedonist if, for example, I value power or knowledge for myself over pleasure. And I can be a hedonist but not an egoist if I try to promote pleasure among all people equally and not just for myself.

What does make life worthwhile after all? What kind of life do you believe you ought to live? If you live to be 70 or 80 years old, and you look back over all those years and activities, will you respect yourself and feel proud? If you spent most of your time figuring out ways to please yourself, will you respect yourself? If you spent most of your time figuring out ways to help other people, will you believe that you have missed the most valuable part of life?

The decision you must make is not about organizing your day, but about organizing your life. You are searching for an organizing principle for your life as a whole. Of course everyone needs food, clothing, and shelter. Everyone must spend some time arranging for his or her own needs to be met, usually working at a job. But how much time is enough? Do you acquire the necessities, and then go on to try to achieve something, make yourself a better person, or make the world a better place, which takes most of your time and energy? Or do you spend all of your time trying to be comfortable, to gain security, to improve your circumstances, to be entertained, to enjoy life?

How do you decide between hedonism and pluralism? Is it a "personal" choice, like your brand of clothing or hair style? Both the hedonist and the pluralist say no. They both give reasons to back up their views. They both think that their reasons are sound, convincing reasons that should persuade an open-minded reader. To decide which view you hold, you should look back at the two essays, and find the reasons the authors give to support their conclusions. Why is the first a hedonist? Why is the second a pluralist? What persuaded them? And which of their reasons are more persuasive to you?

Hedonists claim that their theory is easy to understand. They say they can explain why anything is valuable. "It gives me pleasure," they say. What's so great about health, freedom, love, or justice? They give us pleasure. And that is a good reason. If something is pleasurable, then, other things being equal, it is desirable and good. It is valuable unless some other consideration outweighs the pleasure. But pluralists do not explain why things are valuable. Pluralists say many things are valuable besides pleasure, so it is not their production of pleasure that makes them valuable. But then what is it? Why is freedom a good thing? Pluralists might say that their value is basic and ultimate. It just is good. After all, hedonists cannot explain why pleasure is valuable. It just is valuable, they say.

Hedonism is therefore a simpler theory. There is one basic principle in the theory (pleasure is valuable), and everything else is explained by reference to that basic principle. Moreover, it is a plausible principle. Pleasure is valuable, and it makes other things valuable. Pluralism is a much more complicated point of view. Pluralists make many assumptions. That is, pluralists say there are many basic, unexplained values. Another complication is the relationship among these values. What do we do when they come into conflict? How do we decide which of two basic values is *more* valuable? Pluralism has no answer.

However, pluralists say that the simplicity of hedonism is a false simplicity. Hedonists make everything depend on pleasure, but consequently they *over*simplify matters. It is a mistake, according to pluralists, to think that all the experiences we have when we pursue all the different sorts of value are the same, namely "pleasure." Hedonists' explanation is an illusion. Pluralism remains true to our real, everyday experience.

Thus the basic issue in this section is simplicity vs. complexity, and theoretical sophistication vs. common sense. Do you want a worldview that is rigorously logical, clearly organized, and made up of a few simple axioms? Or do you think it is more important to remain close to ordinary experience, even if that means your outlook is complex, leaves loose ends dangling, and is not so easy to understand?

HEDONIST

1. The ultimate reason (and, finally, the only reason) for living is to achieve happiness, which is the same as pleasure.
2. "Pleasure" is a broad term, which includes intellectual, social, and moral activities.
3. What makes anything *good* is that it helps someone, and that means it gives someone pleasure.
4. It is good to help others, but it is good because it is enjoyable, or because not helping others leads to guilt.

PLURALIST

5. Many people who think about values oversimplify matters.
6. Ordinary people recognize both personal and social values and obviously believe many things besides pleasure are good.
7. Values are objective features of the world that we pursue, not subjective feelings.
8. Values are basic and ultimate; they cannot be explained, or reduced, to something more basic (such as pleasure).

FOR FURTHER STUDY

Historical Examples

HEDONIST: Epicurus. *The Essential Epicurus*. Prometheus, 1993. Third century B.C.E. The original version of hedonism.

PLURALIST: Ralph B. Perry. *Realms of Value*. Harvard University Press, 1954. Perry develops a concept of value as "interest," and explains personal, moral, aesthetic, social, and other values.

OTHER SOURCES

William DeWitt Hyde. *The Five Great Philosophies of Life*. Macmillan, 1926. Elementary discussion of Epicurus (hedonism), the Stoics, Plato, Aristotle, and Christianity.

John Hospers. *Human Conduct: Problems of Ethics*. Shorter Edition. Harcourt Brace Jovanovich, 1972. Part 2, "Ideals of Life," surveys four ideals: epicureanism, stoicism, self-realization, and following nature.

Yi-Fu Tuan. *The Good Life*. University of Wisconsin Press, 1986. Compares different ideals from various cultures, in the context of defending a theory of happiness.

David P. Gauthier, ed. *Morality and Rational Self-Interest*. Prentice-Hall, 1970. Classical and modern writers ask "Is self-interest rational?" "Is moral motivation based on interest?" and "Is morality advantageous?"

Abraham Maslow. *Toward a Psychology of Being*. 2nd Edition. Van Nostrand Reinhold, 1982. Maslow describes a hierarchy of values, at the top of which is self-actualization.

Nell Noddings. *Caring: A Feminine Approach to Ethics and Moral Education*. University of California Press, 1984. An extensive description and analysis of caring rather than a defense.

Risieri Frondizi. *What Is Value?* 2nd Edition. Open Court, 1971. A brief, simple discussion of issues, including the objectivity/subjectivity of values.

Peter Caws. *Science and the Theory of Value*. Random House, 1967. Caws presents his definition of value in chap. 5, "Fact and Value."

M.S. Everett. *Ideals of Life: An Introduction to Ethics and the Humanities*. John Wiley and Sons, 1954. Includes chapters on basic human wants, the pursuit of happiness, traits of character, the ethics of democracy, etc.

Hunter Lewis. *A Question of Values*. HarperSanFrancisco, 1990. Lewis claims
that one's method of making choices determines one's values, and discusses six methods: authority, logic, sense experience, emotion, intuition,
and "science."

The books by Russell, MacIver, and Maurois listed in Section 3.2 also describe
various ideals and goals in life.

3.2   CAN WE UNDERSTAND HAPPINESS?

Definer or Skeptic?

In Section 1.2, "Is God Like Human Beings," I raised the question of whether
one can believe God exists when he or she has a very sketchy, vague (or
empty) concept of God. Now we come to happiness. Can you wish for happiness if you have no clear idea of what happiness is? Can you look for something
if you don't know what you are looking for? Where would you begin your
search? In what direction would you look? You would be wandering aimlessly.
And suppose you stumbled across your goal accidentally: how would you recognize it or realize you had found it? If you say that you are happy, how can
you be sure? How do you know?

Many people will probably say that they *do* know what happiness is. "For
me happiness is seeing the Giants win the Superbowl," someone will say. Or
"Happiness is lying on a beach in the Virgin Islands." Is this enough? Does this
person know what happiness is? It might be enough for ordinary, practical living. But some people want to step out of the day-to-day routine and try to *understand* their lives. For those who are curious about deeper questions, and
who want to have a coherent worldview, it is not enough.

This kind of answer to the question "What is happiness?" faces two problems. First, different people enjoy different things. What makes one person
happy will have no effect on another person. So what is happiness? The person
watching the game is happy, *and* the person lying on the beach is also happy.
They must have something in common, since the word "happy" applies to
both. What is it? Can we understand happiness?

There is a second problem. When you say happiness is lying on a beach,
you have only mentioned an activity that makes you happy. The activity is not
the same thing as happiness. For example, no one would want to watch the
Giants win the Superbowl three times a day, seven days a week, or lie on a

beach continuously, until one dies. But one does want to be happy for the rest of one's life. Therefore happiness is not the same thing as an activity or even a set of activities. If not, then what is it?

If you want to take control of your life, you must have a clear idea of your chief goal. If you want to understand where you are going and why, you must have a concept of what you are seeking. Most people say their goal is happiness. So it makes sense to think about the nature of happiness.

The first essay below insists on the difference between the various causes of happiness and happiness itself, but it argues that we can understand and define happiness. If you agree with this essay you are a definer. In contrast, the second essay takes the skeptical view that we cannot know what happiness is. It claims that we muddle through life without understanding what goal we think we are pursuing. If you agree with the second essay you are a skeptic.

YES: DEFINER

"Happiness"

Philosophers are a quarrelsome bunch. They seem to argue for the sake of arguing. But, surprisingly, they all agree on one point. They all agree on what people want. People want to be happy. Happiness is the ultimate goal of everyone's life.

Of course people try to be happy in different ways. Many want to be rich. Others pursue fame and popularity, others excitement, or security, physical vitality, and so on for different types of people. But if you asked these various people why they want these things, you would hear one answer over and over: I want to be happy. These things are all means to one end—happiness.

Maybe we should leave it at that, and enjoy the rare concord among philosophers. But at the risk of stirring up more arguments, I would like to ask a simple question. What *is* happiness? What is it that all men and women, young and old, rich and poor, seek so persistently throughout their lives? It isn't easy to say, although I believe happiness can be defined.

Happiness is not the same thing as money, no matter how many yuppies think otherwise. Obviously it's not, because many people with large amounts of money are bitterly unhappy. I am tempted to say that rich people—with their divorces, their suicides, their alcoholism—are even less happy than poor people. But it isn't true. It seems that way only because *People* magazine writes about their troubles, while no one wants to read about poor people's misery. Both rich and poor are unhappy.

Happiness is not fame. It's not a stable family life. How many housewives living quietly in suburbia with their average families are unhappy? Many. At least many say they are. Wealth, fame, and family may make some people happy, but they do not make everyone who has them happy. Therefore, we cannot *define* happiness as these things. If we defined happiness as having money, then everyone with money would be happy, by definition. There could not be a single rich person who was unhappy, if happiness were defined as having money. But it is easy to find counterexamples to that definition. The same applies to fame, stable families, or what have you.

Most books pretending to explain happiness make this mistake. They all have quite a bit to say about the *causes* of happiness, but little to say about happiness itself. One expert declares that the secret of happiness is satisfying work. A PhD in psychology takes two hundred pages to say that the secret of happiness is love. Another guru says it is health. But these are causes of happiness (so they say). What do these things cause? What is happiness itself? How do I know if I am happy or not?

We will never understand happiness itself by studying external conditions and causes. A person wouldn't get the slightest appreciation of a good meal by looking at the stove. Happiness itself is an *inner condition*, or a state of mind, not the external circumstances of one's life.

Now we are making progress. We are on the right track, although we haven't arrived yet. What sort of inner state is happiness? Some have said it is simply pleasure. Happiness, they say, is the sensation one has when one relaxes in the pool on a hot day, tastes a favorite drink, or cuddles in bed with one's partner.

But I'm afraid we just took a wrong turn again. Pleasurable sensations last only a short time. It sounds very strange to say my friend was happy for thirty seconds last week, and for five minutes yesterday. Happiness lasts longer than that. It is a condition, not just a sensation. It cannot be defined as pleasure, because even if a person is in pain, from the temporary hunger of a diet, or muscle aches from tennis, we can still say he is a happy man. An exhausted jogger can be happy precisely because she is in pain. "No pain, no gain," she thinks.

Happiness is an inner state, but not a short-term sensation or emotion. It lasts a long time. So, we have returned to the right track from the dead end of pleasure, but now the way ahead is obscure again. People can be happy in so many different ways, and their inner mental states must be very different. Both the race car driver and the homemaker can be very happy, but their mental states must be just about opposites. One thrives on danger, risks, physical exertion, noise, and grime (I mean the race car driver, not the homemaker), and the other finds happiness in security, children's laughter and miniature accomplishments, neatness, and meals together. How is the inner state of the movie buff, escaping to a fantasy world, like the inner state of the tax accountant, or the emergency room nurse?

In spite of the differences in the emotions and thoughts, crises and victories that these people must experience, I believe a single thread runs through all their lives. The thread that ties them together is that they are *achieving most of their goals*. The goals are different, just as the people are different. But they are all successful in what they are trying to do.

Happiness itself is not a matter of learning what to strive for—love, health, work, self-acceptance, or any other goal. Happiness depends upon *reaching* your goals, whatever they are. The goals can be different, but happiness is the same in each person. Happiness is dynamic, not static. It involves change, not immobility. Happy people feel that they are taking steps that bring them closer to their ultimate goals.

How wrong it is to think that happiness is pleasure, or leisure, or having drinks handed to you on your yacht. Achieving your goals will require work, and planning, and sacrifice, whatever your goals are. Human beings are active. We build things, search for answers, care for others, improve the world. Unlike amoebas, we are not happy if we are only passively absorbing food or drink, or soap operas.

I was careful to say happiness "depends upon" reaching one's goals, not "is" reaching one's goals. I did not want to make the same old mistake of confusing the cause with the thing itself. We already decided that happiness is an inner state of mind. In spite of the differences among happy people, they are all reaching their goals. They have that in common. Does that mean they have some inner mental condition in common as well?

I think it does. Everyone who reaches his or her goals must have similar feelings. A successful woman must feel satisfaction when she recalls her past accomplishments, and she must feel confidence, optimism, and a sense of competence when she looks forward to goals still to be reached. Together, these add up to self-esteem, self-respect, and calm assurance, based on objective achievements.

Happiness is this mental state. It is the feeling of accomplishment, of success, of confidence. Different people will have different goals, but all happy people will have these feelings and this perception of themselves and their place in the world. That is what it means to be happy.

Key Concepts

definition	successful	cause
counterexample	inner condition	self-esteem

Critical Questions

1. If every rich person were happy, except one, could we define happiness as being rich? Could we say the one unhappy rich person is just an abnormal exception?
2. What kind of thing is happiness, according to the essay?
3. Why can't we define happiness as pleasure, in the definer's view?
4. What external condition do all happy people have in common? What *is* happiness?
5. What would a person have to show to prove that the definer's definition is wrong? (How does the definer show that other definitions are wrong?)
6. Does the definer think that the particular goal one pursues is crucial to one's happiness, or is achieving one's goal the only requirement? Suppose my goal is to rob banks, or be a dictator of a South American country. Can I be happy by achieving those goals, in the definer's view? Do you agree or disagree?

NO: SKEPTIC

"The Elusive Dream"

Writers like me stand apart from ordinary life so we can observe it. That is both good and bad. It's bad because it makes us feel different, and sometimes lonely. It's good because people's posturings and obsessions are so hilarious that once you step aside and look at them dispassionately you are endlessly entertained.

Take happiness for example. How many books have been written about it? How many fortunes made, and lost, in its name? It's even enshrined in our sacred Declaration of Independence. Americans have a legal right to it.

But the idea of happiness is an illusion. Happiness itself is real enough, but no one knows what it is. The idea is an illusion, a mere will-o'-the-wisp, impossible to pin down. Just try to define this all-important concept.

Is anything absolutely essential to happiness? It would be natural to think that health is essential. But health isn't absolutely necessary, since many people have endured illness, blindness, paralysis, and other physical problems, but have still been happy. Epicurus, the Greek philosopher, suffered poor health all his life, but his letters reveal a cheerful, curious, serene man.

If not health, then perhaps love is absolutely necessary for happiness. But the stubborn fact is that many great artists and philosophers never married. They were devoted to their work, and human relationships were simply less important to them. Who is to say that none of them was happy?

It is impossible to name anything that is absolutely essential to happiness. People are just too complex and variable. Early Christians were tortured in horrible ways, but they died singing praises to God, happy in their martyrdom.

Perhaps we should approach the idea from the opposite direction. Does anything guarantee happiness? Many people say to themselves, "If only I had a million dollars, then I would be happy!" But money is no guarantee of happiness. Some rich people are happy, but others aren't.

If you put four of five male friends together for an hour, the conversation *invariably* turns to one subject: sex. (I'm not sure what women talk about.) Men fantasize about numerous partners, exotic locales, different styles and techniques. If their fantasies were realized, would they be happy? I don't think it's a sure thing. In fact, some therapists report that playboys who actually live that way feel a hollowness and lack of meaning in their lives. On the other hand, being tied to one partner is no guarantee of happiness either.

There are no guarantees. No possessions, no activities, no set of beliefs, separately or together, are sufficient for happiness. The reason is that people are too complicated, contradictory, even perverse (which is why life is so interesting).

Just think about the different things that make people happy. Some can be happy only if they are free and independent. Others are devoted to someone, incomplete by themselves, people who need people. The Roman poet Lucretius said happiness is standing on the shore watching others drown at sea. In other words, happiness is relative; it means being better off than one's neighbors, at whatever level one's neighbors live. But watching others drown, or starve, or live under tyranny, upsets many people, and makes them unhappy, not happy. There are as many kinds of happiness as there are people. Each person is happy in his or her own way.

An exasperated psychologist might step in at this point and make the following suggestion: "Instead of searching for definitions and analyzing concepts, like a philosopher, why don't you take a scientific approach? If you want to know what happiness is, just pick an example and study it. After all, if you want to know what an aardvark is you don't discuss the idea of an aardvark, you look at examples. Leave the definitions and concepts to the philosophers."

How refreshing and direct! No wonder psychology has made such great strides in this century. No wonder it is universally admired and revered. Unfortunately, in this case, the suggestion won't work. How can we pick an example of happiness if we have no idea of what it is? How can we recognize it when we see it, if we have no definition of it and can't say what it is? Can you go and study an aardvark if you don't know what it is? The psychologist's suggestion is useless without a clearer concept of happiness.

One author made an exhaustive study, and concluded that happiness is having more satisfied desires than unsatisfied desires. In other words, happiness is getting most, or many, of the things one wants. The problem with this definition is that people can want things that are bad for them. Kids want drugs; graduates want high-powered, stressful, heart-attacking jobs; women want a decisive, macho man, or a sensitive wimp, and so forth. Getting what they want makes them unhappier than they were.

Maybe we can save the definition by saying that happiness is getting most of the things one *ought* to desire, or things it is reasonable to desire, not getting the things one does desire that may be harmful. If one knows what one ought to desire—what is really important—and one satisfies those desires, then one will inevitably be happy.

But this modification of the definition only takes us around in a circle. What desires *ought* one to have? What is really important? Well, one ought to desire the things that make one happy. What is important is what leads to real happiness. That is the only way to separate beneficial desires from harmful ones.

But now the definition is circular. It defines happiness as whatever leads to happiness. We can see the circularity if we spell out each step of the proposal. The first definition was

(*a*) happiness = satisfying desires.

But we desire things that are bad for us. So we modify the definition:

(*b*) happiness = satisfying desires we *ought* to have.

How do we know which desires we ought to have?

(*c*) desires we ought to have = desires that lead to happiness.

Therefore,

> (d) happiness = satisfying desires that lead to *happiness*.

Definition (d) is circular because the concept we do not understand—happiness—is itself used in the explanation of the concept. That is no help at all.

Happiness cannot be defined. People who say they are searching for happiness do not understand what they are saying. They have no idea of happiness. If people aren't driven by a desire for happiness, then why do they do what they do—work hard, take vacations, have kids? There are many explanations, of course. They do it because their parents did it, or the TV tells them they ought to do it, or they can think of nothing else to do. Or it may be sheer accident. They stumble into some job or relationship, it makes them feel a little better, so they continue. But there is no grand scheme, no ultimate goal.

If you are still caught up in the race, then you think it is all very important and you have big plans. But if you stand apart for a moment, you will see that people don't know where they are going.

Key Concepts

concept	guarantee	ultimate goal
essential condition	desires	circular

Critical Questions

1. How does the essay show that nothing is essential for happiness?
2. How does the essay show that nothing guarantees happiness?
3. Why can't we look at an example of a happy person and define happiness on the basis of that example?
4. What is wrong with the idea that happiness is having more satisfied desires than unsatisfied desires?
5. Is this idea the same as the definer's theory of happiness, or is it different? Do the skeptic's criticisms invalidate the definer's theory, in your opinion?
6. The skeptic says that the definition of happiness as getting most of the things one ought to desire is circular. How is the definition like a circle?

Methods and Techniques
ESSENTIAL PROPERTIES

These two writers are trying to understand the nature of happiness. They do that by trying to formulate an adequate *definition* of happiness. What is a definition? A definition is an explanation of the meaning of a term. But how do you explain the meaning of a term? For example, how do you explain the meaning of the word "owl"? You can look it up in a dictionary, of course, but how do the dictionary makers explain the meaning? Generally a definition of a word like "owl" gives the *essential characteristics* of an owl. It tries to state the properties that something has that allow people to recognize it or classify it as an owl. The dictionary definition of "owl" is "a nocturnal bird of prey (order Strigiformes) with a large head, large eyes, and a short, hooked beak." These are all characteristics of owls. If you find something with these characteristics, then you know it is an owl. And if you want to tell someone what an owl is, you can give her or him this list of characteristics.

If this definition is a good one, then these characteristics are essential. That means that all owls *must* possess these characteristics. All owls are nocturnal; there are no owls that hunt in the daytime, by definition. If we found a bird that looked like an owl but was active during the day instead of at night, we would put it in a separate category, because being nocturnal is an *essential*, defining characteristic of owls. It is just as essential as having wings or being a bird. An animal that hunts at night but is not a bird would not be an owl, because being a bird is part of the definition of "owl." It is essential.

Owls have other characteristics besides the ones in the definition. Maybe owls have four toes on their feet, three in front and one in back. But that is not an essential characteristic. If we found a bird with two toes in front and two in back, it could still be an owl, so long as it has the essential characteristics. These other traits are called *accidental* characteristics.

It is even possible that we could discover some obscure trait that *all* owls have. For example, maybe their spleens are always larger than their kidneys. But that is still an accidental characteristic, because it is not part of our *concept* of an owl, not part of our definition. A person can understand what an owl is without knowing about its spleen. But a person cannot understand what an owl is without knowing that it is a bird, or that it is nocturnal, and so on. Anyone who really understands what an owl is must know its essential properties.

Philosophers try to formulate definitions of very general terms, like "happiness," "God," "person," "liberty," "morally wrong," and so on. For example, is goodness an essential property of God?If someone says that God is evil, should we reply that she hasn't really understood what the word "God" means? Or suppose a baby is born with massive brain damage. Is it a person? Is self-consciousness or potential self-consciousness an essential property of persons? In other words, they try to determine the essential properties of these things. It is not so simple as looking in a dictionary, because different dictionaries give different lists of essential properties. And sometimes dictionaries are not perfectly accurate expressions of our concepts.

The first essay proposes a definition of "happiness." That is, it explains what the definer believes is the essential characteristic of a happy person. It is the inner state resulting from reaching most of one's goals. Is that trait really essential? Or is it accidental? Is it possible to find a person, who most people would agree is happy, but who does not have that inner state? Or is it possible to find a person who has the inner state, but who is not happy?

Definitions are not arbitrary. We cannot define words in just any way we like. Some definitions accurately state our concepts, and others do not. We test definitions by looking at examples (of owls, or happy people) to see if they really have the characteristics the definitions say they must have.

Understanding the Dilemma
DEFINER OR SKEPTIC?

The first essay in this section offers a definition of happiness, and the second essay says happiness cannot be defined. So on one level, the issue is "Is the definer's definition of happiness correct?" The definer says that happiness is reaching most of your goals (whatever they are), and more precisely, it is the feelings of confidence and pride that result from accomplishing things. But the skeptic claims that many people want things that are bad for them, and they are not happy when they reach their goals, so happiness cannot be defined that way.

Is the definer's definition correct? How can we decide? Well, a true definition of something picks out the property or properties that all those things have in common, and that nothing else has. For example, we can define "hemophiliac" as a person whose blood lacks the clotting factor. All hemophiliacs have that property (i.e., if they are cut they bleed without forming clots), and no one else has that property. Now, do all happy people have something in common? Do they have the properties the essay describes in common? And do no unhappy people have those properties? The definer says yes, and the sketpic says no. What do you think?

You can think about this conflict between the definer and the skeptic on a higher level as well. That is, you can ask whether or not other important concepts, like virtue, knowledge, justice, person, or love, can be defined. The essays in this section are about happiness, but a definer would probably say we can define the other general ideas, too. We need to find clear examples of something like knowledge, and then try to isolate the properties that all the examples have in common. That should not be so difficult, the definer says. And it is very important. We need a clear definition of knowledge if we are going to pursue knowledge as a goal, or give people college degrees on the grounds that they are "educated," i.e., have knowledge. We need a clear definition of justice if we are going to apply justice in our courts. How can we know if we are in love without a definition of love? Folk wisdom says "You will know it when you feel it." But that is no answer. Suppose you feel something strong and deep. Is it love or not? You cannot know without an adequate definition.

But a skeptic takes the opposite point of view. Words like "knowledge" and "justice" are applied to so many different situations that we can never find something they all have in common. Different people follow different rules in applying the words. One person looks at a situation and says, "This is just," while another person says, "This is unjust." We can define "hemophiliac" because that is a specific, physical condition. But justice and knowledge are things that human beings create. They are too abstract, too vague, and too value-laden to be defined. The same is true of the other concepts. A major obstacle is our emotions. Everyone cares too much about these things. We can construct a definition, but everyone's definition will serve his or her own purposes. For example, everyone will define virtue as "the way I behave." We will use other words and examples, but that is what our definition will amount to. We will define justice in a way that proves our own claims are just, and so on. Therefore we can never formulate a correct definition. We must continue to muddle through, without knowing where we are going, or what we are doing.

Who is right? Can we formulate clear, acceptable definitions of important terms like "happiness" and "justice"? Or is all our thinking about these large abstractions confused and subjective? Are you a definer or a skeptic?

DEFINER

1. Happiness is a definite inner state, which we can understand and pursue in an intelligent way.
2. The essence of happiness is the feelings of confidence, pride, and so on that result from achieving most of one's goals.
3. Understanding the nature of happiness and other key concepts is absolutely essential for social harmony and a meaningful life.
4. To define something like happiness or justice, one needs experience of a broad range of examples, and an ability to find what all the examples have in common.

SKEPTIC

5. There may be such a thing as happiness, but we have no idea what it is.
6. Happiness cannot be the feelings resulting from achieving one's goals, because many people have self-destructive goals.
7. For better or worse, everyone muddles through each day, solving immediate problems, without understanding large abstractions like happiness, justice, or knowledge.
8. People use abstract words in so many different circumstances that there is no factor common to all the instances.

FOR FURTHER STUDY

Historical Examples

DEFINER: Aristotle. *Nicomachean Ethics*. Many editions. Fourth century B.C.E. In Book 1 Aristotle methodically explains his conception of happiness, and shows how it is based on human nature.

SKEPTIC: Arthur Schopenhauer. "On the Suffering of the World," and "On the Vanity of Existence." In *Essays and Aphorisms*. Penguin, 1970. Originally published in 1850. Schopenhauer claims that we swing back and forth between desire and boredom, and can never achieve happiness.

OTHER SOURCES

Darrin McMahon. *Happiness: A History*. Atlantic Monthly Press, 2005. Wide-ranging history of many people's ideas about happiness, emphaszing the obstacles.

Jonathan Haidt. *The Happiness Hypothesis: Finding Modern Truth in Ancient Wisdom*. Basic Books, 2006. Assesses various ancient and modern philosophical theories in the light of contemporary psychological research.

P. Richard Layard. *Happiness: Lessons from a New Science*. Penguin, 2005. Emphasizes the social context necessary for happiness, by an economist.

V.J. McGill. *The Idea of Happiness*. Praeger, 1967. Historical survey followed by discussion of four issues: self-realization, happiness vs. duty, fulfillment vs. prudence, and happiness vs. pleasure.

Bertrand Russell. *The Conquest of Happiness*. Bantam, 1968. Originally published in 1930. Analysis of the causes of unhappiness and happiness, including (for happiness) zest, love, family, work, and impersonal interests.

R.M. MacIver. *The Pursuit of Happiness*. Simon & Schuster, 1955. Reflections on the Golden Rule, art, knowledge, love, and death, among other parts of a happy life.

Robert Nozick. *The Examined Life*. Simon & Schuster, 1989. In chap. 10 Nozick discusses various conceptions of happiness, and argues that pleasure is not the only good.

3.3   IS MORALITY RELATIVE?

Relativist or Absolutist?

Americans have some peculiar attitudes toward America and other countries. For one thing, most Americans pride themselves on being tolerant. We say we will welcome immigrants from any other place, regardless of race, creed, or color. We say that people in America are free to do as they please. They can practice any religion, live any lifestyle, and promote any political cause. Because who is to say that one religion or lifestyle is *better* than another?

At the same time, however, Americans seem to think that the ideals of the Bill of Rights and the Constitution—freedom of speech, the right to a fair trial, a government accountable to the people, tolerance itself—are universal. They are ideals and values that *everyone* should accept, even people in foreign countries. If some dictator tyrannizes his people, we condemn him for violating basic human rights, and we might even send in the marines.

This split shows that Americans are ambivalent about values. Some say values are *relative*. That is, each society creates its own values, based on its own history, traditions, geography, and needs. And each society's values are legitimate for that society, but not necessarily legitimate for other societies. One society cannot judge another.

Other people have a different view. They say that some values are *absolute*. They are basic and universal, binding on all human beings. Americans, fortunately, have discovered these absolute values, and we have enshrined them in our political system. If another society has different values, then they are simply wrong.

Which side is correct, the absolutists or the relativists? Are there any actions that are absolutely wrong, in every society at every time? Or are human beings so diverse and flexible that no single standard can apply to all of us? This is the problem of relativism. The first essay in this section presents the relativist view. It tries to show that morality is an inextricable part of culture, and cultures are different in different societies. The second essay attacks the relativist position, and claims that it leads to logical absurdities.

YES: RELATIVIST

"Moral Relativism"

In the nineteenth century, when European missionaries and explorers encountered primitive tribes in Africa, they sometimes required the women of the tribe to dress "properly," like a Victorian lady. The women had to put on corsets and long skirts.

Today we smile at such blatant ethnocentrism. Proper attire in London is not proper in the tropics. But many people think that, when it comes to moral rules, what is proper in London *is* proper in the tropics and everywhere else. This is *moral absolutism*—the belief that some moral rules are binding on everyone, regardless of cultural differences.

The attitude supported by modern social science is *moral relativism*—the belief that morality is part of the complex web of beliefs, traditions, feelings, and practices we call "culture." One people's culture is different from another's. So their morality is different as well. People in one society might place a great value on the family and respect for ancestors. People in another society might value individuality and independence to a much greater degree.

Some tribes in New Guinea and Australia practiced cannibalism, and boasted about it. Many other cultures condemn cannibalism with the greatest vehemence. Among Bedouin tribes in Arabia, adultery on the part of a wife was grounds for execution. (They had different standards for men and women.) Among the Ituri pygmies of central Africa, marital fidelity was not highly valued, and Eskimo wives slept with visitors as an act of hospitality. In the American Southwest, the Hopi ideal of behavior was sharing, avoiding conflict, and subordinating oneself for the sake of peace. Their neighbors, the Apache, expected young men to prove themselves in war.

But absolutists know about this variety in moral values and are still not convinced. They claim that some societies are more "advanced" or "civilized" than others. To make the case for relativism, we must go beyond these scattered cases and examine the nature of morality itself. If we look at some basic facts about morality, we can see that it is a part of culture. I want to emphasize three important facts. Morality is a set of rules, it is learned from cultural authorities, and it requires some standard of judgment.

1. Morality Is a Set of Rules. When an average person thinks of morality, he or she probably thinks of rules. "Thou shalt not kill." "Honesty is the best policy." "This above all: to thine own self be true." For most people, "a highly moral person" is a person who always obeys the rules. All societies have rules, although different societies have different rules.

Once we recognize that morality is a set of rules, we should acknowledge another fact. All rules—whether moral, legal, social, or the rules of games—are created, not discovered. They are invented by people as a means to coordinate their interactions with each other. They are invented, and they can be changed if people decide they are no longer useful. The rules of basketball, for example, didn't exist before human beings invented them.

Moral rules are a lot like legal rules, i.e., civil laws. Laws tell us what is permitted and what is forbidden. And no one would claim that laws are discovered or universal. They are invented, and relative to a particular society. The only difference between laws and moral rules is that moral rules are not normally written down officially and publicly by a society, as laws are. And moral rules are enforced informally by social pressure, rather than formally by the police. But they are still rules, and rules are devised, not natural.

Since all rules are artificially created, and morality is a set of rules, it follows that morality is artificially created. Moral rules are prescribed by a society to keep order and to encourage certain forms of behavior. There is nothing "absolute" or "natural" about them.

Moral rules and civil laws are very different from scientific laws. Scientific laws are descriptions of the way the natural world works. For example, Boyle's law says "Gases expand when they are heated under constant pressure." An interesting fact about this law is that we cannot violate it, even if we want to. We have no choice. If we heat a gas, it will expand. But people can and do violate moral rules all too often. One common moral rule is "Tell the truth." But people frequently violate that rule. Another interesting fact about scientific laws is that they are the same for everyone. In every society, Boyle's law holds true. In Asia, Africa, South America, and everywhere else, gases expand when they are heated. Cultural differences are irrelevant to scientific laws.

2. Each Person Is Taught a Set of Moral Rules. The second thing we should notice is how we *know* moral rules. Why do we honor a particular set of rules? The answer is that we learn them unconsciously as we are growing up. An important part of any culture is the method of rearing children. And a large part of the supervision of small children consists of teaching them right and wrong. By the time they are grown, these basic feelings and values have become part of their personalities. Children are told "Do not hit" so often that it becomes second nature to them. They learn that hitting creates a situation in which everyone is very upset, including adults, who are their main sources of stability and security. The feeling that hitting is wrong becomes so deeply ingrained that it may even seem to be inborn.

Where else do we learn right from wrong, if not from parents and authority figures? Someone may say we rely on our conscience to know right and wrong. But people's consciences tell them what their parents and teachers taught them years earlier. Certainly small children, say 3- or 4-year-olds, do not have much of a conscience. They can be cruel, violent, deceptive, and utterly selfish. They only acquire a conscience as they grow older and are molded by the people around them.

It may be true that every adult, in every society, has a conscience. That is to be expected, since morality is an important part of every culture. All people are taught to have a conscience. But different people's consciences tell them different things about right and wrong. A Hopi's conscience said very different things from an Apache's conscience. And who is to say that one society's conscience is more authoritative than another's?

3. No One Can Step Outside All Moral Systems. The question of which conscience is more authoritative leads to the third point. Someone might say that one society's rules are objectively "better" than another's. But that judgment implies that a person can stand outside the two societies and evaluate them on the basis of some independent standard. For example, I might say England's way of producing goods is better than China's. I am making an objective judgment because I am not involved in either society. I can look at them from outside. Of course the English would say their system is better, and the Chinese would say theirs is better, but they are both biased, because they are involved in their systems.

However, even if I am outside of their societies, I must still use *some* standard in evaluating the two economic systems. I say England's system is better than China's. That is a value judgment. But the word "better" depends on some *standard*. In fact, I am evaluating England and China by the standards of *my* culture. By "better" Americans mean more efficient. Others might use a different standard. The Chinese may define "better" as ensuring full employment, and by that definition China's way is better than England's. But everyone must have *some* standard, or else we cannot make any value judgments at all.

The important point to see is that no one can stand outside *all* cultures and decide whose morality is objectively the best. I do not want to say that a person cannot escape the strong psychological influences of his or her society. Actually people do move from one culture to another; they forget their old values, or standards, and completely adopt the different values and attitudes of their new society. Some people emigrate from one society to another, and assimilate to their new society. These transformations are psychologically possible. Rather, I want to make a logical point. No one can rise above all societies and make moral judgments about them, because every moral judgment is based on some system of values. And value systems are created by societies. If a person judges something to be good or evil, that judgment must be based on some society's moral values. Therefore it is biased, not objective. Every evaluation, every assessment, is based on *some* standard. That isn't a fact about psychology. It is a logical requirement.

We might use one set of values one day, and a different set of values on another day, but if we make moral judgments at all, then we must use some values. Values are invented by societies. So we must operate *within* some society's moral code. We cannot objectively judge *all* codes, because we always have the limited point of view of one particular code.

We can make the point by using an analogy. Culture is like language, and particular cultures are like particular languages. If we want to talk, then we have to use a language. We might move from one language to another, but we cannot talk without using some language. We cannot step outside of all language, so long as we want to talk. Just as talking requires some language, so making value judgments requires some values. If we want to make value judgments, then we must use the standards of some culture. Moral standards (like languages) are invented by societies. Therefore, it makes no sense to say some systems of morality are objectively better than others. No one can be objective in this matter, not because of psychology, but because of logic.

These three facts show that morality and our moral feelings are part of culture. Even moral absolutists admit that societies create culture, and cultures are different in different societies. These basic facts show that morality is relative to the society that creates it.

Key Concepts

moral relativism	rules	scientific law
moral absolutism	civil law	conscience
culture	biased	

Critical Questions

1. A relativist says morality is a set of rules. How does that show that morality is relative? Relative to what?
2. What are the differences between moral rules and scientific laws?
3. According to the essay, how does anyone know what is right or wrong?
4. You probably believe that cheating in school, or stealing, or taking unfair advantage of people generally, is morally wrong. Do you believe it because your parents or grandparents or someone taught you? Is that the only reason you believe it?
5. A relativist says an objective evaluation of a society is impossible. Why? Do you agree?
6. Is the relativist right? Are the moral values of a theocratic state like Iran (censorship, subordination of women, assassination of foreign critics, etc.) just as valid, just as true, as the moral values of America (the Bill of Rights, etc.)?

NO: ABSOLUTIST

"Right for You, Wrong for Me?"

In discussions of moral issues, someone always says that what is right for one person is not right for another person. I want to examine this claim, and I will begin by describing a specific case.

In many countries in Africa and Asia people practice female circumcision. The custom involves "cutting off all or part of a young girl's clitoris and labia, and in some cases stitching her vagina closed until marriage" (*New York Times*, Nov. 23, 1993). The United Nations reports that millions of women, mostly Muslim, are affected. People in these countries have followed the custom for centuries, and feel strongly about it. They say that it keeps a girl chaste and virginal. One father stated that he had his daughter circumcised "so that later she will behave herself" (ibid.). (The procedure often makes sexual intercourse joyless or painful, according to Western doctors.) Women also defend the custom. One mother said she did it for the good of the child, "to make her like the other girls so that she could find a husband" (ibid.).

Is female circumcision morally right? It is an honored tradition of long standing in these countries. The parents are doing what they believe is best for their daughters. The parents, including women who have had the operation, certainly believe it is right. On the other hand, the procedure is usually performed without anesthesia in unsanitary conditions. The girls often develop "hard scars, cysts, swellings or infections," and it may cause lifelong health problems. A French lawyer, Linda Weil-Curiel, is emphatic: "This is butchery invented to control women," she says. "It's a form of violence we would never allow here against white girls" (ibid.). She has no doubt that the custom is morally wrong. So some say it is right and some say it is wrong.

But I am more interested in a third answer. Some people say it is morally right for the Africans and Asians, but it is wrong for us in America or Europe. These people say that the Muslims have decided that circumcision is morally proper, and so it *is* proper, for Muslims. But the same Americans or Europeans would never dream of treating their own daughters the same way. In general, some say that every person must decide what moral principles to adopt. It is a personal decision, and no one can judge another, or say another's principles are wrong. What is right for you may not be right for me, some say.

This third answer is called "moral relativism." It is a fairly popular point of view these days, but I don't think it makes sense. The problem isn't that moral relativists approve of actions that offend me (although they do). The problem is that they cannot explain what they believe in a clear, coherent way. Let's see how it applies in practice. Suppose a woman in Mali (in West Africa) named Mrs. Diarra helps circumcise her 3-month-old baby. Her moral principle is that she should help her daughter abstain from sexual intercourse until marriage, and even then realize it is not a source of pleasure. In addition, imagine that a Frenchwoman named Mrs. Robert learns of the operation. Mrs. Robert is a moral relativist, so she says Diarra did the right thing, for Diarra, although it would not be right for Robert. Robert's conscience tells her that she should not mutilate her daughter's genitals, with or without anesthesia, no matter what the traditions are. So Robert's view is that the very same action—female circumcision—was morally right for the woman in Mali, but would be morally wrong for herself in France. In fact, Diarra was admirable for doing what she believed was right. But the idea of doing the same thing to her own daughter she feels is repugnant and horrifying. She has different values and moral standards.

While this sounds reasonable, it leaves an important question unanswered. The question is "What is the crucial *difference* between Mrs. Diarra and Mrs. Robert that makes the same action right for Diarra and wrong for Robert?" There must be some very significant difference, since the very same action is right for one person but wrong for the other.

One obvious difference is that Diarra lives in Mali whereas Robert is a Frenchwoman. They live thousands of miles apart. But why is that important? Right and wrong do not depend on geography. If you want to convince someone that an action is wrong, you will not say, "It is wrong because we are located north of 20 degrees of latitude." That isn't a reason. It's irrelevant. Mali has a hot and dry climate, very different from France. But surely the different weather or geography is not a crucial moral difference. No one would say circumcision is morally right in Mali because the average temperature there is 90 degrees.

Perhaps the crucial difference between Mrs. Diarra and Mrs. Robert is simply that their values are different. They have chosen different principles. Or they were taught different principles by their parents or their cultures. That is why it is right for Diarra to circumcise her daughter, but it would be wrong for Robert to do the same.

This is probably the difference that moral relativists have in mind. But consider the consequences of this explanation. If it is right for Diarra to circumcise her daughter because she *believes* it is right, then it is right for a child molester to abuse children, so long as he *believes* it is right. In other words, the relativist says that the crucial difference between Diarra and Robert is a difference in their beliefs about what they should do. And that difference is enough to make an action right for Diarra but wrong for Robert. But then the relativist is saying that a person's *belief* that he should do something is enough to make it morally *right* that he should do it.

That makes no sense. No one thinks that it is morally right for the child molester to molest children, even if the molester, in his perverted way, does believe he ought to do it. Some societies teach their children that slavery is morally right, that people who practice a different religion aren't fit to live, that women who try to achieve equality with men are evil witches, or that criticizing the government is morally wrong. But teaching something doesn't make it right. It doesn't matter how old a custom is, because age isn't enough to make it right either. Fortunately these hateful attitudes are disappearing as literacy and education spread throughout the world. But a relativist believes all attitudes—all moral values—are equal, and so it could be just as fortunate if racism or violence gained popularity.

Thus there is *no* difference between Diarra and Robert that is important enough to justify the relativists' view. Different climates, different diets, different beliefs, different educations are not enough to make an action right in one place and wrong in another.

The idea that what is right for one person may be wrong for another person (in the same situation) is an idea that sounds attractive. It sounds very tolerant. And it would be nice if we never had to judge anyone else. But the idea makes no sense. If you believe that something is right for you, then you have to believe that it is right for anyone else in similar circumstances. Relativists cannot point to any crucial differences that make an action right for one person but wrong for another.

Relativism has another flaw. It does not recognize that people with different principles come into contact. To see how that happens, let's go back to Mrs. Diarra again. Mrs. Diarra is a real person, and in fact she was born in Mali but was living in France when she circumcised her baby. Imagine (hypothetically) that Mrs. Diarra was baby-sitting for Mrs. Robert, the French relativist, and she decided to circumcise Mrs. Robert's daughter, "for her own good." (In African countries friends and family, not only the child's mother, often perform the operation.) What would the relativist say about that?

If she follows her own principle, she will have to try to prevent Diarra from circumcising her own daughter, or have her arrested for doing so. She will tell Diarra that she should stop, that what she is doing is *wrong*. But Robert also believes that Diarra is admirable for believing in her principles. It is *right* for Diarra to circumcise girls, since that is what her principles tell her to do. She has done the same thing for her friends in Mali. Therefore in this case, the relativist must say female circumcision is right *and* wrong at the same time. Mrs. Diarra did something that was right and wrong. But that statement makes no sense. It is like saying someone is, and is not, pregnant, or the entire line is straight and also curved. The relativists' conclusion that the circumcision is both right and wrong shows that relativism is a confused and contradictory doctrine.

It doesn't help to say the action is "right from Diarra's point of view but wrong from Robert's point of view." Robert, the relativist, has to make a decision: will she applaud as Diarra applies the razor blade, will she continue to feel warmly toward Diarra, or will she protest, try to stop Diarra, and get angry at her for committing a moral evil? She cannot have it both ways. Moral relativism sounds reasonable, until two groups with different values come into contact, and an action by a person in one group affects a person in another group. When that happens, relativism collapses. The relativist who says that the action is both right and wrong isn't saying anything. It is like saying that the door is open but also closed at the same time. That is empty and uninformative.

Imagine another example. In the American South before the Civil War many people believed slavery was legitimate and even beneficial. Many people in the North believed slavery was abhorrent. Suppose a relativist says slavery was right for people in the South, but wrong in the North. But now imagine that a black man from the North crossed the border into the South and was enslaved. What does the relativist say? Was the enslavement right or wrong? The relativist should not condemn the slave owner, because slavery is morally right in the South, he says. On the other hand, the black man was not originally from the South. Where he grew up slavery was wrong, according to the relativist. In fact, the relativist has no answer. He cannot say anything about the morality of the action. His theory breaks down when two cultures come into contact.

And cultures are coming into contact more and more as the world shrinks through travel and communication. If a relativist like Mrs. Robert really believes that circumcising her own daughter would be a brutal, inhuman, domineering act, then she should tell Mrs. Diarra that what she did to her daughter was brutal and wrong. Period. Not wrong for Robert but right for Diarra. Just wrong. In fact, Diarra's daughter spent three weeks in the hospital and almost died. The mother was charged with violating French laws against harming children.

It is very difficult to tell someone that his or her action is morally wrong. But the arguments about irrelevant differences between people, and about contact between cultures, leave no alternative. If you are going to have any moral principles at all, then you are going to have to say everyone else should have the same principles. That isn't arrogant. In fact it is humbling. It means that you must work very hard and think very carefully before you adopt any beliefs about right and wrong, because those beliefs will require you to judge others.

Key Concepts

moral belief   cultural contact   tolerance
cultural differences   contradiction   universal principle

Critical Questions

1. What is the position that the essay wants to criticize? Does the moral relativist believe female circumcision is right, or that it is wrong?
2. The absolutist says the moral relativist must believe there is a big difference between Mrs. Diarra and Mrs. Robert. Why must the relativist believe this?
3. The fact that Diarra and Robert were taught different values is not enough of a difference, in the absolutist's view. Why not?
4. Do you think it is morally wrong for people in Africa to circumcise their daughters?
5. How would a relativist respond to the absolutist's example of the northern black man enslaved in the American South? Would he say the enslavement was morally right or wrong? Would it make any difference if the relativist himself or herself were the person enslaved?
6. Why is relativism attractive to many people?
7. Suppose Sue's most sacred moral principle is tolerance. In the absolutist's view, must she say that intolerant people living in an intolerant society are morally wicked? Or is that intolerance on her part?

Methods and Techniques
AD HOMINEM

Both the relativist and the absolutist present interesting arguments for their views. Both are thoughtful and balanced; both have plausible reasons to support their conclusions. But discussions of relativism are not always so cool and objective. Relativism is a sensitive issue. Often in introductory philosophy classes, when the topic of relativism comes up, the discussion degenerates into personal accusations, raised voices, hurt feelings, and stony silence.

The problem lies in the two sides' perceptions of each other. Relativists sometimes see *absolutists* as reactionaries: arrogant, self-righteous fanatics who want to impose their own narrow-minded values on everyone else, cultural imperialists, whose real goal is domination and power. Or they see absolutists as straight-laced, unhappy people living under terribly restrictive rules, who think that if they can't have any fun then no one else should either. But relativists see *themselves* as tolerant, open-minded, aware of people's basic freedoms and differences. They think that they enjoy and respect people in all their manifold diversity.

On the other side, the perceptions are entirely different. Absolutists see *relativists* as spoiled, self-indulgent egotists who only want an excuse to follow their whims and reject all standards: perpetual adolescents who cannot tolerate any rules or self-restraint. Or they see relativists as permissive, timid people who condone horrible crimes under the cloak of tolerance. Actually they are merely cowards. But absolutists see *themselves* as mature, responsible people, defending the pillars of civilization—family, civic pride, law, hard work, higher standards of literature and art, etc.—against the anarchic, degrading effects of relativism, which means no standards and no rules of any kind.

Obviously with such different images of each other, the two sides will not be able to understand each other. Nor will anyone else who wants to learn about relativism be able to get a clear picture of the real issue. The accusations are too emotional, the disputants are too involved.

Arguments like these between relativists and absolutists exemplify an important mistake that philosophers sometimes make. The mistake is called an "ad hominem." The words *ad hominem* are Latin and mean "to the man." An ad hominem is an attack on a *person* rather than a criticism of the person's *belief*. For example, suppose a Senator proposes a tax cut to stimulate the economy. One of his opponents then says, "We should not vote for the Senator's tax cut. I happen to know that he got the idea from his rich banker friends. And besides, he is a notorious womanizer." While these comments may be typical of the debates in Congress, they are completely worthless as arguments. The opponent is attacking the Senator, not the idea of a tax cut. Even if the Senator does cheat on his wife, that fact is irrelevant to the tax cut. It is no reason to believe the tax cut is a bad idea. To criticize the tax cut itself, the opponent would have to show that the government cannot afford to cut taxes, or that it would only benefit a small minority of people, or that it is undesirable for some other reason. Attacking the person who proposes it is an illogical mistake.

The opponent's other point is also an ad hominem, though perhaps it isn't so glaring. In saying the Senator got the idea from his rich banker friends, the opponent is trying to undermine the Senator's reputation, or criticize his motives. But those attacks are also irrelevant to the question of whether a tax cut would improve the economy. It may be true that the Senator is only trying to help his friends, or trying to get reelected, or that he has no idea of how the economy works. Nevertheless, pointing out these facts would be an ad hominem. They are not reasons to believe a tax cut is a bad idea. They are criticisms of the person, not the belief. (Of course criticisms of the person might be appropriate and relevant in another context, such as a reelection campaign.)

When relativists say that absolutists are intolerant bigots, the relativists are guilty of committing an ad hominem. They are criticizing people, not beliefs. It is possible that absolutists *are* bigots, but that absolutism is still true. The same goes for absolutists who say relativists are spineless cowards. Whether they are or are not is completely irrelevant to the truth of relativism. In order to decide whether relativism or absolutism is true, we must look at something besides the character or background of the people who hold those views.

Understanding the Dilemma
RELATIVIST OR ABSOLUTIST?

Everyone believes that some things are morally right and some things are morally wrong. Even the most hard-boiled cynic will become angry if his wallet is stolen. Assuming that people have beliefs about right and wrong, we can ask many questions about those beliefs. The question in this section is "Can morality be *different* in different societies?" In other words, can an action be right in one culture, but (the very same action) wrong in another culture? This is not the same as asking whether people in different societies can have different *beliefs* about right and wrong. The question is about right and wrong itself. Can an action really be right in one place and really be wrong in another? The relativist says yes, and the absolutist says no.

For example, probably everyone in the United States would say slavery is wrong. If one person tried to sell another, everyone would be outraged. But could slavery be morally right in another society, in Asia or South America or Africa? Can we say child abuse is horrible and intolerable here, but perfectly OK and maybe even a good thing in another society? The relativist says yes, and the absolutist says no. Who is right? Are you a relativist or an absolutist?

The relativist makes certain assumptions about the nature of morality and its place in society, and the absolutist makes different assumptions. According to the relativist, when we say something is morally wrong (e.g., "child abuse is wrong"), we are reporting the beliefs of our society. We are playing the role we have learned and internalized, and if we had grown up in another society, we would feel differently. But according to the absolutist, when we say something is wrong, we are talking about something in the world, something objective, like facts.

One way to look at the difference between relativists and absolutists is to focus on facts. What are facts and how do we know them? To an absolutist, it seems like an undeniable fact that beating a child is wrong. It is like seeing clearly that one line is longer than another, or that a figure is square and not round. If someone says, "Yes, it is wrong here, but in another society it is OK," the absolutist decides that the person is just ignoring the plain facts. The person has embraced a *theory* about morality and cultures, and clings to it so desperately that he can look at coal and call it white.

However, a relativist might say exactly the same thing about an absolutist. To a relativist, moral judgments are based on feelings that we all learn from our society. The words "right" and "wrong" are like the words "beautiful" and "ugly": they mean different things to different groups. They are expressions of cultural attitudes, not descriptions of objective facts. Thus if someone says beating a child is absolutely wrong for everyone, in any society, the person is expressing *his society's theory* of morality without realizing it. He is in the grip of a theory that prevents him from seeing the facts, and prevents him from seeing events the way other people see them.

Which person, the relativist or the absolutist, is most influenced by his theory? Which one is incapable of seeing the facts as they really are? Which has a more accurate perception of reality? Are you a relativist or an absolutist?

RELATIVIST

1. An action may be right in one society and wrong in another society.
2. Moral rules and moral values are invented by a society, like the customs regulating clothing, meals, and property.
3. Different societies can have different, irreconcilable values regarding basic aspects of life, such as preserving life, sexual relations, raising children, owning property, etc.
4. There is no difference between what a society *believes* is right and what *is* right.

ABSOLUTIST

5. The moral relativist cannot explain her or his position in a clear, coherent way.
6. If you believe an action is morally wrong, then you should have the courage of your convictions and say the same action is wrong everywhere.
7. The similarities among people around the world outweigh the differences; all people agree on basic moral judgments, even if they disagree about superficial styles and customs.
8. A group cannot make an action morally right or wrong simply by saying it is right or wrong.

FOR FURTHER STUDY

Historical Examples

RELATIVIST: Plato. *The Republic.* Books 1 and 2. Many editions. Fourth century B.C.E. Plato was an absolutist, but at the beginning of *The Republic* he presents the position that he wants to reject, and his presentation is one of the clearest, most striking discussions of moral relativism in the history of philosophy.

ABSOLUTIST: Cicero. *On Law.* Book 1. Harvard University Press (Loeb Classical Library). First century B.C.E. Cicero defends his belief in Natural Law largely by criticizing the relativist alternative. He points to the ways in which we are all similar, and to the similar values we all share, such as enjoyment of pleasure and fear of death.

OTHER SOURCES

Randolph M. Feezell, Curtis L. Hancock. *How Should I Live? Philosophical Conversations about Moral Life*. Paragon House, 1991. Imaginary conversations among a philosopher, Unitarian minister, environmentalist, religious fundamentalist, businessman, and others.

James Rachels. *The Elements of Moral Philosophy*. Random House, 1986. Chap. 2 is a critical examination of the factual basis of relativism and the implications of the theory by an absolutist.

John Hospers. *Human Conduct: Problems of Ethics*. Harcourt Brace Jovanovich, 1972. Brief discussion.

John Ladd, ed. *Ethical Relativism*. Wadsworth, 1973. A small anthology with a good selection, including several anthropologists.

David Wong, "Relativism." In Peter Singer, ed. *A Companion to Ethics*. Blackwell, 1991. A defense of relativism.

Abraham Edel. *Ethical Judgment: The Use of Science in Ethics*. Free Press, 1955. Chap. 1 is a discussion of the sources of relativism. Edel believes growing knowledge in social science will undermine relativism.

Shia Moser. *Absolutism and Relativism in Ethics*. Charles C Thomas, 1968. A critique of relativism, with interesting data from various cultures.

Gilbert Harman, Judith Jarvis Thomson. *Moral Relativism and Moral Objectivity*. Blackwell, 1996. The philosophers present their views and then reply to each other.

John Gray. *Isaiah Berlin*. Princeton University Press, 1996. Sympathetic presentation of Berlin's "pluralism"—his belief that there are many goods and good ways to live, some incompatible, and there is no way to justify one in preference to another.

3.4   IS HAPPINESS THE STANDARD OF MORALITY?

Utilitarian or Formalist?

Everyone has to make moral decisions at one time or another. Some women get pregnant without intending to, and then they must decide whether or not to have an abortion. Americans in 2003 had to decide whether or not to support the war against Iraq. Students sometimes have opportunities to cheat and must decide whether or not they will be honest. People who are comfortable must decide how much of their income, if any, they should give to the poor, and so on.

One way to make these tough decisions is to go to some authority, like a priest, or perhaps a more experienced friend, and ask him or her. Or one can try to imagine what some hero or heroine would do in a certain situation. What would Gary Cooper in *High Noon* do? Or Florence Nightingale? Or your grandmother? Or one can just flip a coin.

But for many independent, reflective people none of these strategies is very satisfying. They seem too haphazard or capricious. Some people want a more systematic, methodical way of making moral decisions. Philosophers are like that. They want to sleep soundly at night with clear consciences like everyone else, so they want to make correct decisions. But they also want to understand *why* a particular decision is right. They want to see the *pattern* in moral decisions. They want to understand what unifies right actions, and sets them apart from wrong actions. In other words, they want a moral *theory*.

Having a moral theory that you can believe in is a very comforting thing. If you understand why some actions are right and others are wrong, you will feel much more confident that your decisions are right. After all, without a theory, you might misinterpret Gary Cooper. And who is to say that Cooper is the best role model anyway? Furthermore, if you have a moral theory, then you can justify and defend your decisions if anyone challenges you. You can explain yourself in a reasoned, intelligent way to others. Finally, once you step back and see the general features of moral decisions, you will be prepared for any future problems that arise. You will feel secure knowing that you will be able to make the right decision.

Moral issues are fascinating problems to think about, simply from an intellectual point of view. But philosophers are also human. The moral theories they construct not only satisfy their intellectual curiosity, but they also satisfy the need for a clear conscience and the need to feel justified.

In the following essays, you will read defenses of two famous theories of morality. The first essay argues for the utilitarian theory, and the second defends the formalist theory. Utilitarianism says that our pursuit of happiness is the basis of our moral judgments and feelings. Formalism says that a basic human characteristic is our ability to follow rules, and that unique human ability is the basis of morality.

YES: UTILITARIAN

"Utilitarianism"

"Utilitarianism" is a long, strange word, which stands for a simple, familiar idea. It is an idea about morality. Everyone must think about morality at least occasionally, because everyone must make moral decisions. "Should I volunteer down at the soup kitchen?" "Should I declare this money on my income tax form?" But utilitarianism is about morality in general. It is a theory about why we say some actions are morally right and others are morally wrong, in any context. The simple idea is that a morally right action is one that creates the greatest happiness for the greatest number of people. If you want to do the right thing in any situation, you should ask what would lead to the greatest happiness for all concerned, and do that. Wrong actions are ones that produce unhappiness. Utilitarianism, then, is a moral theory, and in fact, it is the best theory we have.

Thinking about moral theories is not exactly the same as thinking about a particular moral question. If you are wondering about volunteering at the soup kitchen, you might consider several factors: you are tired after work; but the homeless people feel worse than you do. Many of them are drug addicts; but many others are not. Volunteering is not the best way for you to help; but you aren't doing anything to help now, and so on. Thinking about moral theories requires you to step up to a higher level. Instead of debating a particular decision, you should consider a wide range of right and wrong actions. You may not know whether volunteering is right or wrong, but you do know many examples of right and wrong actions. You should try to find out *why* certain actions are right, and why others are wrong. One theory will explain the morally good deeds in one way, and another theory will explain them differently.

But then how do we choose between different moral theories? Well, a moral theory is like a sorting machine. Suppose an inventor has a machine that he says will sort apples into two groups: those that are good for eating and cooking, and those that are spoiled, bruised, wormy, and not good for anything. He puts an apple into the machine, and if it is good, a green light comes on, but if it is bad, a red light comes on. But now another inventor comes along with another apple-sorting machine, and he says his is better. How would a grocer test the two machines? The grocer would try to see which machine produces the most *correct* sorting. That is, are all the apples that the first machine says are good really good, or are some of them actually bad apples? And are all the ones it says are bad really bad, or does it throw away some good apples? Which machine makes the fewest mistakes?

A moral theory is like the imaginary apple-sorting machine, except that a moral theory sorts actions into groups of right and wrong. Sometimes a theory will put a right action into the group of wrong actions, or vice versa. For example, we all know that helping a blind person across the street is right. If a moral theory implies that such an action is wrong, then the theory is faulty. Or if the theory tells us that rape is right, then it is a very poor theory. The best theory is the one that makes the fewest errors. It is the one that agrees with our ordinary moral judgments most often.

When we step back and look at a variety of right and wrong actions, we find that utilitarianism gives us the best explanation of why they are right or wrong. Utilitarianism is the theory that all morally right actions produce the greatest possible happiness for the greatest number of people. It is the best moral theory for two main reasons. First, utilitarianism is in agreement with our ordinary feelings and judgments about right and wrong. It explains why we say certain actions are right and others are wrong. Second, it is the broadest moral theory. It incorporates the best ideas in other moral theories, but avoids their mistakes and limitations.

Examples. To see why utilitarianism is the best moral theory, let's first survey some examples, and see how well the theory explains them. Everyone agrees that murder is wrong. But why is it wrong? Because it destroys a life, it takes away a person's chances to be happy. Why is cruelty wrong? Because it creates pain and unhappiness. Take another example. Suppose a terrible accident occurs and the hospital desperately needs blood. You are healthy so there is no good reason why you cannot give blood. Utilitarianism says giving blood in this situation is morally right, because it produces a large amount of happiness in the patients, and only a little inconvenience for you. Most people would also say giving blood is the right thing to do, although they might not be able to say why it is right. Utilitarianism explains why.

Almost everyone believes that adultery is wrong. Can utilitarianism explain that judgment? The man and the woman who commit adultery may be strongly attracted to each other, and may experience real bliss in their lovemaking. Doesn't that *increase* happiness, and so shouldn't utilitarianism say it is morally *right*?

But adultery also leads to unhappy partners who are deceived, the breakup of marriages, maybe unwanted children, and less respect for vows and honesty. If we consider *all* the consequences of adultery, we see that the amount of pain and heartbreak outweighs the amount of happiness, and therefore utilitarianism agrees with common moral feelings that it is wrong.

Here is another problem case. If a right action is one that makes the most people happy, then shouldn't I withdraw my money from the bank and hand it out to people on the street? That would make hundreds of people happy, so the utilitarian theory should say the action is morally right. But no one believes that I am morally obligated to bankrupt myself. Is the theory mistaken about this action?

Actually there is no conflict between utilitarianism and ordinary moral judgment here. Utilitarianism says that a right action is one that leads to the greatest happiness for everyone, *including me*. My own happiness is just as important as other people's happiness—not more important, but not less. If I gave away all of my money, I would be homeless and starving and very unhappy. In fact, my misery would outweigh the widespread but shallow happiness created by giving a lot of people a few dollars each. Therefore utilitarianism does not say that I should sacrifice everything for others, although it does say that some sacrifices are morally required.

Why is stealing wrong? Because it leads to unhappiness for the victim, and maybe more stealing by others who follow the example. But suppose a starving man steals bread for his family from a wealthy restaurant owner, who has plenty of food and won't miss the bread. The stolen bread makes the starving man very happy, and the loss does not upset the wealthy man very much. The starving man's happiness vastly outweighs the wealthy man's irritation. In this case, stealing may lead to greater happiness for all concerned than not stealing. Utilitarianism says that stealing may be justified in this particular case, so long as it does not lead to widespread stealing in other circumstances, for example, by people who are just lazy. (The fact that it might lead others to break the law is why breaking any law is almost always wrong.) I think most people would say the same thing about the starving man. Our moral sense tells us that this particular theft was justified. All these examples show that utilitarianism explains the underlying basis of our ordinary moral judgments. We all follow (more or less) the utilitarian guideline without realizing it.

Other Moral Theories. Not only does utilitarianism explain common moral judgments, it does not have the flaws that other theories have. Many philosophers and religious leaders have tried to explain why certain actions are right and others are wrong. For example, a very widespread theory says that right actions are those that you would want others to do if they were in your place. "Do unto others as you would have them do unto you." Or "Whatever you want people to do for you, you should do for them." This theory is called the Golden Rule. Not only Jesus, but Confucius, Zoroaster, and other ancient prophets said essentially the same thing. So, for example, should you give some change to a beggar on the street? If *you* were the beggar, what would you want the passerby to do? You would want him to give you some change. Therefore the Golden Rule says you should give some money to the beggar.

But this is almost exactly the same as saying that people should do whatever creates the most happiness. Everyone wants to be happy. You want others to do things for you that make you happy. That's what "you would have them do unto you." So if you should treat others the way you want them to treat you, then you should try to make them happy. It's the same as utilitarianism.

Actually utilitarianism is a better theory. The Golden Rule can lead to actions that most people would say are not right. For example, imagine that Smith and Jones are friends. Smith comes to Jones and asks for a loan so he can market his new product: alcoholic beverages for infants. He calls it "Baby Booze." Jones tries to convince Smith that the idea is crazy, but Smith's mind is made up. He thinks Jones does not understand the baby food market. Should Jones lend his friend the money? The Golden Rule says Jones should treat Smith the way he would want Smith to treat him if he asked for a loan. If Jones had an idea for a new product, he would want Smith to lend him the money, even if Smith disagreed about the wisdom of the investment. Therefore the Golden Rule says Jones should lend Smith the money.

But that would be foolish and wrong. He would be harming himself for no good reason. He would lose his money, and Smith would gain nothing. In other words, the Golden Rule sometimes requires people to make needless sacrifices.

It sometimes requires people to put others before themselves in a way that helps no one.

In contrast, utilitarianism says a person should do what creates the most happiness for all concerned, including himself. Everyone's happiness is equally important. The loan to Smith would give him a little temporary happiness, but it would make Jones unhappy for a long time. The unhappiness outweighs the happiness; therefore, it is wrong. It doesn't matter who is happy and who is unhappy. What matters is the total amount of happiness and unhappiness that results from an action.

The Golden Rule often requires one to make sacrifices, such as giving money to the poor. But there is nothing morally admirable about making oneself miserable. That is merely neurotic. There isn't even anything admirable about making oneself miserable for the sake of others, if the others benefit only a little. The only time we admire self-sacrifice is when it benefits others a lot, in fact, more than one's own loss. For instance, we admire a soldier who throws himself on a live grenade and dies to save the lives of many of his comrades. But if he did it only to protect their ears from the noise, then we would decide he had cracked up and was insane, not a hero. This shows that in making a moral judgment, we consider more than sacrifice or devotion to others. We weigh the happiness and unhappiness that results from an action, although we may not realize that we are doing so.

The Golden Rule can backfire in another way as well. Suppose Ben is a meek and timid bureaucrat. What he dislikes most is having to make a decision or take the initiative. He has always listened to his mother, and he likes his life that way. Recently he has developed an interest in Betty, his officemate, and he asks her out on a date. He respects her and wants to do the right thing. If he applied the Golden Rule, he would make all the decisions on the date, suggest what she should have in the restaurant, tell her what to think about the movie, and where they should go afterward. That is how *he* would like to be treated; so he would treat Betty that way. But dominating Betty is not morally right. It is arrogant and insensitive. And it is not likely that either of them would enjoy their date.

The Golden Rule is based on the assumption that people are all alike. It says I should treat others the way I want to be treated because what makes me happy will also make others happy. But people are different. In this case, it is morally wrong for Ben to treat Betty the way he wants to be treated. The Golden Rule theory holds that one rule can explain all right and wrong actions. But some philosophers believe that being a good person means obeying several rules, like "Keep your promises," "Help the needy," "Don't hurt anyone," "Don't steal," and so on. We might call this the "multiple rule" theory. Right actions are those that conform to the accepted rules, and wrong actions are violations of the rules. So if you have promised not to tell anyone about your friend's illness, it would be wrong to tell. And it would be wrong because the action breaks the rule that says "Keep your promises."

But what is the purpose of these rules? They are all designed to promote happiness. The reason for obeying them is to create the greatest happiness for all concerned. The theory of utilitarianism goes beneath the surface of our think-ing about morality. It explains *why* we feel the rules are important and we should obey them. Thus the multiple rule theory is just a more superficial and complicated version of utilitarianism.

There is nothing sacred about the rules themselves. In fact, as we noted above, stealing might be morally right in some circumstances. Moreover, the rules sometimes come into conflict. If a man promises to meet his wife at eight, but comes upon an automobile accident on the way, it would be better for him to stop and help than to keep his promise. Why? Not because of the rule that says "Help those in need"; another rule says "Keep your promises." It is better to stop because that action would lead to more happiness for everyone than keeping his promise. The rule theory says he should never break his promise, but most people would disagree. Thus utilitarianism is closer to our normal moral judgments.

If we want to understand morality, we must look at the feelings that most people have about right and wrong. Where else can we look? Philosophers are no better people than anyone else. They do not have a special authority on morality. Rather, they look at their own and other people's moral decisions, and try to make sense of them. They try to understand, not preach.

Utilitarianism provides the best explanation of the decisions most of us make. And it includes the correct parts of other moral theories, without mak-ing the mistakes they do. Since it explains the data, we should accept it as true.

Key Concepts

moral theory	consequences	Golden Rule
ordinary moral judgments	greatest happiness	moral rules

Critical Questions

1. What is the purpose (or purposes) of a moral theory? How can we evaluate different moral theories?
2. What does a utilitarian believe?
3. Has the utilitarian correctly interpreted the Golden Rule? In the example given, would the Golden Rule require Jones to lend Smith money? Would it require Ben to guide and control Betty?
4. Does utilitarianism ever require sacrifice, or require a person to do some-thing painful, or something that makes him unhappy?
5. If the enslavement of 10 percent of the population of ancient Athens in-creased the happiness of the other 90 percent, and also freed them from labor so they could produce their magnificent drama, architecture, science, and philosophy, would the enslavement be justified, in your opinion?

6. Suppose a hotel is on fire. You can run in and help your two parents in room A, or four strangers in room B, but you can make only one trip. Which people do you think you should help? What would a utilitarian say?

NO: FORMALIST

"The Principle of Morality"

Having children is the most rewarding thing I ever did. It is also the most challenging, especially today. What I worry about the most is not my children's physical health—although that is a constant concern—but their *moral* health. Will they be honest, caring, and mature? My wife and I want to bring them up to be good people. I feel that is the most important task I have in my life. After all, I (and my wife) brought them into the world; I am responsible for them.

But how can one teach a child to be good? That would be a difficult question even in the best of times. But today, it's urgent. I used to think that I would watch the news on TV with my children, to try to make them more aware of the world and its problems, and maybe more concerned. But I can't even watch the news myself any more. The violence is sickening and numbing. Children killing children, children having babies, babies being abandoned. I don't want my children exposed to such brutality until they are much older. But they will have to go to school, and what influences will work on them there?

How can a parent make sure a child learns to tell right from wrong? How can I make my children want to do the right thing? I've been thinking about the problem for some time now, and I have decided that the best way is to teach through example. Young children learn by imitating, not by indoctrination. Four- and 5-year-olds do not understand the broad and long-term consequences of their actions. They only understand that someone is taking care of them, and they want to be like that person.

This is not new. Everyone talks about "role models" nowadays, but I think the issue is more complicated than most people realize. Who is a good role model? Children have to see more than just a few good deeds. They have to see a dedicated, conscientious person. Children are able to sense a person's inner feelings and thoughts, even if they aren't capable of abstract reasoning. They know what's in your heart. A good role model must be a good person herself or himself. And being a good person is more than doing good deeds. External behavior is too superficial. You can't fool children with pretense.

I think that being a good person means having principles. It is a matter of doing things for the right reason. Let me explain what I mean with some examples. At the kindergarten in my neighborhood I have met some of the teachers and aides. One teacher is very good; she plays games with the children, tries to attend to each one, she is sensitive to any problems that come up, and is always cheerful. Her aide does the same things. But in talking to these two women at the parent–teacher meetings I discovered that they are different. Their behavior is the same, but their motives and intentions are different. The aide has been working at the kindergarten for about a year. She began because she enjoys being with children. She laughs and plays with them almost as if she were a 4-year-old herself. The teacher, however, laughs and plays because she decided that that is the best thing for the children. She does what she believes she ought to do. Externally, the aide's behavior and the teacher's behavior are the same. But internally, the teacher is acting on her principles, whereas the aide is just doing what she enjoys.

I think the teacher is a better model for the children to follow. From the aide they will learn to do whatever they enjoy. But from the teacher they will learn to do what they believe in, what helps others, what requires dedication. I trust the teacher and I know she will always do what is best for the children. The aide is wonderful with the children now, but she may lose interest next week. She is guided by her emotions, or interests, not by her principles. She isn't a bad person. Far from it. She simply isn't the best model of moral behavior for the children to follow.

Here's another example. Imagine two young mothers with newborn babies. The babies require almost constant attention and devotion, which the mothers give them. Both mothers make sacrifices involving careers, money, time with husbands and friends, their own rest and health, and so on. But imagine that one mother does all this because she feels that is the right thing; she would prefer to do less, or hire a nurse, but she thinks that would be shirking her duty. The other mother works just as hard, but she does it because she actually enjoys it. She feels tremendous satisfaction in seeing her child grow. And she knows that eventually the child will love her and help her in return.

There are mothers of both types. But now ask yourself which mother is more admirable. Which is acting with a greater degree of moral conscientiousness? I think the answer is the first mother, who acts from a sense of duty. The second mother isn't wrong; she simply isn't acting morally. That is, we shouldn't condemn her, but we should not hold her up as an example of highly moral behavior either. She is just doing what makes her happy. The first mother, however, is an example of a person acting for moral reasons.

Consider another example. Imagine that each of the new fathers has borrowed money from his parents to cover the expenses of raising the baby. And each promised to repay the loan after two years. Each one has to give up vacations and other things to scrape up the money. Suppose that each one does repay the loan, but, like the mothers, they have different motives. One father repays the money because he promised; he feels an unbreakable obligation. He repays because it is the right thing to do. The other repays because he would feel embarrassed if he didn't; he would look irresponsible in the eyes of his wife and parents. And failure to repay might make it difficult to borrow again in the future, should the need ever arise. Although the action is exactly the same (repaying the loan), one father is thinking morally and the other is not. One is highly admirable and the other is not.

These examples suggest that the difference between a morally good person and an indifferent, neutral person (neither good nor evil) lies in their motives or intentions. The key to acting morally is *adherence to principle*. The admirable teacher, mother, and father do what their principles tell them is right. And they do it because of their principles. The aide and the other mother and father do what they feel is in their interest or will benefit themselves. That is not necessarily wrong; it just isn't acting morally. Some actions are neither moral nor immoral. If I have chocolate ice cream rather than vanilla, is that moral or immoral? It's neither. Doing what we enjoy, in most cases, is neither right nor wrong.

I want my children to have examples of moral, decent people around them. But that means more than just people doing good deeds. It means people with principles. This way of thinking about morality is based on some fundamental facts about human beings.

We are all able to act for other reasons besides self-interest. In this respect human beings are different from animals. Animals always pursue their own welfare (safety, food, mating), or they are impelled by instinct. For example, a hen that defends her chicks against a snake isn't heroic. She isn't acting morally. She is only responding instinctively to certain stimuli. She would react the same way to a garden hose or a piece of thick rope. She does not know what a snake is. She does not know what would happen if a snake bit her. Her reaction is programmed. Every time she sees a "snake" she goes through the same sequence of responses.

People are animals, too. Everyone desires safety, companionship, happiness. Humans may or may not act instinctively in some circumstances. But humans are also rational. That means (among other things) that we can follow a rule. Anyone can learn a rule, like "Knock before you enter someone's room," and apply it in new situations. We can think about when the rule applies and when it doesn't. Is this someone's room or only a closet? Would a knock wake up the child who is sleeping? Or we can decide to ignore the rule and barge in.

Animals are different. Learning to follow a rule is not the same as learning to respond to a signal. In Pavlov's famous experiment, he always rang a bell before he gave his dogs their food. Soon the dogs learned that the bell was a signal for food. When they heard the bell they automatically began salivating, anticipating the food. They were not following a rule. They did not choose to respond to the bell. The response was automatic; they could not have refrained from salivating. When seals in a circus clap their flippers they are also simply responding to a signal from their trainer, anticipating food. They have no choice but to clap. But people choose to follow a rule. When a couple goes to a formal dinner party, there are many rules they must think about. And they must decide which rules they are going to follow, and which ones are old-fashioned or inappropriate. Animals can be trained to respond to cues, but they are not following a rule.

That capacity to understand a rule and apply it distinguishes people from animals, not only intellectually, but morally as well. That is what morality is all about. Acting morally means acting on principle, or living according to rules. Acting on principle is not the same as pursuing happiness. If a person believes, for example, that stealing is wrong, and she adheres to her principles, then she will not steal. It doesn't matter how happy the stolen money or clothing or car would make her, because when a person acts on principle, she doesn't consider benefits, or harmful effects, at all. She considers only the principle involved. "Would this action be dishonest, or selfish, or cruel, or a case of stealing?" she asks. Human beings are capable of disregarding benefits or consequences of actions and acting a certain way entirely because it is the right thing to do. And that is what it means to act morally.

Evidence from history supports the same conclusion. Who are the moral heroes in history? Everyone would agree that Dr. Martin Luther King was exemplary. Dr. King did not set out to achieve security or happiness. On the contrary, he risked life and limb to live by the principle of justice. He was arrested numerous times in the fifties and sixties, roughed up, ostracized, and threatened. In Memphis he finally made the ultimate sacrifice for his beliefs. But he never wavered in his commitment to the principles of nonviolence and social justice. His actions certainly brought benefits, after much suffering. But those consequences and calculations were not why he lived as he did, and not why we admire him. We admire him for his adherence to principle.

Contrast Dr. King with Booker T. Washington. There is no doubt that Washington provided great service to blacks and Native Americans. His educational efforts, particularly at the Tuskeegee Institute, gave thousands of young men and women the vocational skills they needed to become economically productive and self-reliant. He enjoyed helping people. He was a good man, but he is not the moral hero that King is. The difference, I think, is that Washington wanted to improve people's living standards and make them happier. King wanted to force people to behave decently, whether that made them more comfortable or not. Washington was aiming at greater happiness for people, and he did it because that felt natural to him. King was aiming at justice, and he did it because he knew it was right, however difficult and costly the task was.

Who are the villains in American history? One might point to Herbert Hoover because he presided over the beginning of the Great Depression and did little to prevent it. But historians do not condemn Hoover. He did what he thought was right; he was simply mistaken. Ulysses S. Grant was probably responsible for more American deaths (probably more Union than Confederate deaths) than anyone else. But he is actually held up as a hero because he was fighting for the principles of liberty and equality. He just did it in a particularly bloody way. One American who is widely condemned is Benedict Arnold, the traitor of the Revolutionary War. Why? Not because he brought misery to people. The actual effects of his plan to surrender West Point were negligible, because the plot was discovered. But he is still regarded as thoroughly evil because he violated his oath, he betrayed his country, and he scorned all his principles.

We also admire inventors, builders, and writers, like Thomas Edison, Theodore Roosevelt, and Dr. Seuss. They improve standards of living and bring happiness to people. But they are not *moral* heroes (unless, for example, a scientist makes a discovery because of his devotion to truth). We are glad that people like Edison and the others lived, but we do not respect them in the same way that we respect moral heroes. All these examples demonstrate that moral consciousness is a separate, autonomous area of life. It is distinct from the pursuit of happiness, whether for oneself or for others. It rests on our ability to live by principles.

In this essay I have argued that acting morally means acting in accordance with one's principles, but I have said nothing about which principles one should have. That is another topic and would require a whole essay for itself. I will only conclude this essay by saying that we know which principles to follow by listening to our consciences. Everyone agrees on basic moral principles: tell the truth, do not hurt people, keep your promises, and so on. Just as humans are all more or less rational, so all have a conscience that speaks more or less clearly. It is sometimes difficult to think rationally because our ego gets in the way. In order to think rationally we must put aside our self-interest. We must do the same in order to hear what our conscience tells us. If you are facing a moral decision (e.g., should I tell a lie?), you should ask what you would expect others to do if they were in your place. You should imagine that you are not involved in any way. Then your ego will not interfere with your moral judgment, and your conscience will guide you.

Everyone accepts the same basic moral principles. Where we disagree is on the *applications* of principles to complex situations. That requires careful reflection, and reasonable people may disagree. But we can apply principles and live by them, disregarding self-interest. That is what morality is all about. My children are too young to understand this essay now, but they are not too young to understand the difference between a moral person and a person who thinks only of happiness. I hope I can teach them to imitate moral people, and to become moral people themselves.

Key Concepts

moral principle	sense of duty	instinct
self-interest	following a rule	moral heroes

Critical Questions

1. What are some examples of acting from self-interest? Is the mother who enjoys caring for her child acting from self-interest?
2. What is an instinct? Do humans have any instincts, in your opinion? Do you think humans have a "maternal instinct," or a "territorial instinct"? A "moral instinct"?
3. Is there a fundamental difference between a circus animal that has been trained to do something and a human who is following a rule? What difference do you see?
4. Have Dr. King's actions in the struggle for civil rights increased the total amount of happiness in the United States? Would we admire him even if

his actions led to greater *unhappiness* among the (white) majority of Americans?

5. The essay claims that right and wrong depend on following or not follow-ing certain principles. What evidence does it present to support the claim?

6. Do you agree with the formalist that there is a sharp difference between peo-ple we admire as moral heroes and people we admire as benefactors?

7. How do we know what our duties are, according to the formalist?

Methods and Techniques
MORAL THEORIES

Both of the essays in this section are defending moral *theories*. A theory is simi-lar to a generalization, which you have encountered before. Remember that a generalization is a statement about all or most of the members of some class: "all insects have six legs," "most adults can read," etc. Theories are also about all the members of some class. The molecular theory of gases is about all gases. The germ theory of infectious diseases is about all infectious diseases.

But theories are different from generalizations in several ways. One differ-ence is that theories describe things that we cannot see. They propose the ex-istence of objects or processes that are too small to see, or that are hidden in some other way. For example, the germ theory of disease says that diseases, which we can see, are caused by tiny organisms in the body, which are too small to see. Freud's theory of the mind proposed that certain processes like repression and sublimation occur beneath the level of consciousness, so we cannot observe them. Since theories are about these hidden objects and processes, they are much more complex than generalizations. A generalization is one statement, but a theory consists of a number of statements describing the theoretical objects and their relationships.

Scientists (and philosophers) propose theories to explain generalizations. (In science generalizations are often called "laws.") The hidden objects explain why a generalization is true. For example, before Pasteur developed the germ theory, people knew that disease was associated with poor sanitation. They could state a generalization: many people who live in unsanitary conditions will get sick. But they didn't know why open sewers or untreated wounds were associated with illness. The germ theory explains the connection. Germs grow rapidly in unsanitary conditions. When that happens they are more likely to in-vade the body and multiply there as well. Since theories explain generaliza-tions, they are broader or more fundamental than generalizations.

Utilitarianism is a theory of morality. Utilitarians' starting point is a set of generalizations. "All cases of murder are wrong," "All cases of adultery are wrong," "Most cases of stealing are wrong." Utilitarians take these for granted. They think everyone agrees on these statements. They are similar to the gener-alizations people made about diseases before Pasteur's theory appeared. Every-one could see that they were true.

Taking these statements as their data, utilitarians then propose an underlying process to explain why the statements are true. The theory of utilitarianism says that wrong actions lead to unhappiness. Most people do not realize that they are following a standard of maximizing happiness. That is why it is an "underlying process." They do not see or think about that effect of murder, adultery, or stealing. But if utilitarians are right, then utilitarianism has explained a wide variety of moral facts.

Formalists also start with a set of generalizations. They say teachers who help their children out of a sense of duty are more admirable, more moral, than other teachers who do the same thing because they enjoy it. And they give other examples of admirable behavior, and assert that everyone agrees on the cases. But their theory is different from the utilitarians'. They say moral people are acting on principle. It is the motive of remaining true to one's principles that makes an action right. We may not realize it, but the person's motive is the key. Thus formalists, too, are proposing an unseen, or unrecognized, process to explain why we say some people are acting morally.

Finally, notice that both theories attempt to unify a wide variety of judgments. We make moral judgments about all sorts of actions, in all sorts of situations. And yet utilitarians and formalists both claim to have found a single process or concept that explains them all, and therefore brings them all together. That is an important characteristic of theories.

Understanding the Dilemma
UTILITARIAN OR FORMALIST?

A utilitarian believes that what we ought to do is try to make the most people happy. The standard or test of morality is the consequences of an action. When you face a choice, and you act in a way that leads to the greatest happiness for the greatest number of people, then you have done the right thing. If you act in a way that needlessly causes pain, or that does not produce the most happiness possible, then you have done something morally wrong.

A formalist believes that we ought to obey certain rules, like "Do not lie." An action is right if it is in accordance with the rules and wrong if it breaks a rule. A formalist believes that being moral, or doing the right thing, is not the same as producing happiness. Trying to make people happy is fine, but it is not the same as thinking morally.

Now, where do you stand? What do you think is the standard of morality: the consequences, or the rules? Do we judge a person by looking at how much happiness results from his action, or by looking at his intention to obey some principle?

In thinking about your decision, you should note that utilitarianism is similar to hedonism. Both the hedonist and the utilitarian say that our goal should be happiness (or pleasure). But there is an important difference. A hedonist believes everyone should pursue his or her own pleasure, whereas a utilitarian believes a person should try to create happiness in general. All happiness is equal, so to speak. Producing happiness for others is just as good as producing happiness for myself, the utilitarian believes. Formalism is a little like pluralism. A formalist believes that being a moral person is certainly valuable, and being moral is not the same as pursuing happiness. So there are important values besides happiness. But a formalist may or may not believe in the other values described by the pluralist.

Both views in this section have the same objective, which is to *explain* moral judgments. They are not so interested in *what* we ought to do as in *why* we ought to do it. They take for granted that some actions are right and some are wrong, and they assume that most people agree on these points. But they go on to ask what do all right actions have in common, and what do all wrong actions have in common? What makes an action morally right or morally wrong? What is the standard of morality? In deciding whether you are a utilitarian or a formalist, you should decide which theory gives the best explanation of common moral judgments. The choice is not between two goals, or two ways of life, but between two ways of thinking about morality.

How can you decide? Well, formalists emphasize the unique character of moral decisions. They say that deciding to act in accordance with a principle is different from other decisions based on desires, even desires to help others. Deciding to keep a promise because it is right is different from doing it because you want to make people happy or because you would feel bad if you didn't keep it. The experience of duty, of moral obligation, of dedication to principles, is unique. If you have had this special experience, then you may think of morality as the formalist does. If you haven't, then you may be a utilitarian.

The difference in experiences is related to a broader difference. Formalists believe that morality arises out of human beings' ability to obey rules, and that ability is the fundamental difference between human beings and animals. Humans can rise above instinct, desire, and the pursuit of goals. Unlike animals, we have a moral sense. We can choose to act on principle. Of course utilitarians believe human beings are different from animals in various ways too, but the differences are not the basis of their theory of morality. Like all animals, we want to be happy. Like social animals, we want all the members of our group to be happy. So while both utilitarians and formalists recognize differences between human beings and animals, for formalists the differences are absolutely crucial to morality.

Where do you stand? Which theory provides the best explanation of why specific actions are right or wrong? Is the feeling of solemn moral obligation reducible to the desire to make people happy? Do we have a moral sense that makes us radically different from animals? Are you a utilitarian or a formalist?

UTILITARIAN

1. Being a moral person means thinking about the consequences of one's actions, and trying to make people happy.

2. Fundamentally, the rule theory of morality says the same thing as utilitarianism: make people happy.
3. If we make a list of the things a person ought *not* to do, we find that they all deny or limit happiness in some way; that is the common denominator.
4. Happiness (my own and others') is the only goal worth pursuing.

FORMALIST

5. Being a moral person means obeying certain principles, no matter what.
6. People are different from animals in that people can deliberately decide to obey rules, without being pushed by desire or instinct or calculations of interest.
7. We admire people who stick by their principles more than we admire people who try to please everybody.
8. Honesty, integrity, and fair play are valuable independently of happiness.

FOR FURTHER STUDY

Historical Examples

UTILITARIAN: John Stuart Mill. *Utilitarianism.* Many editions. Originally published in 1863. Mill explains the greatest happiness principle, different types of pleasures, and the foundations of the theory.

FORMALIST: Immanuel Kant. *Foundations of the Metaphysics of Morals.* Many editions. Originally published in 1785. Kant claims that being moral depends on following rules that everyone could and should follow.

OTHER SOURCES

James Rachels. *The Elements of Moral Philosophy.* Random House, 1986. Chaps. 7 and 8 explain and evaluate utilitarianism, and chaps. 9 and 10 do the same for Kant's version of the rule theory.

John Hospers. *Human Conduct: Problems of Ethics.* Shorter Edition. Harcourt Brace Jovanovich, 1972. Part 7, "Rules and consequences," is a discussion of the rule theory, with Hospers' attempt to reconcile that theory with utilitarianism.

J.J.C. Smart, Bernard Williams. *Utilitarianism: For and Against.* Cambridge University Press, 1973. Each philosopher defends his outlook, and then replies to the other.

Bernard Gert. *The Moral Rules*. Harper & Row, 1970. Ten basic rules and why it is rational to obey them.

Michael D. Bayles. *Contemporary Utilitarianism*. Anchor, 1968. Critiques and defenses of utilitarianism by contemporary philosophers. Difficult.

Robert Bolt. *A Man for All Seasons*. Vintage, 1990. Originally published in 1960. Interesting play (and film) about Thomas More, Henry VIII's Lord Chancellor, who lived according to his principles.

Dale Jamieson. "Method and Moral Theory." In Peter Singer, ed. *A Companion to Ethics*. Blackwell, 1991. The nature of moral theories.

Brenda Almond. *Explaining Ethics: A Traveller's Tale*. Blackwell, 1998. A readable survey of the major issues.

3.5   IS SOCIETY THE SOURCE OF VALUES?

Functionalist or Moral Theist?

A lot of people wonder how they should live their lives, what goals they should pursue, or what makes life worth living. They wonder what values they should have. They may read some books in philosophy to find answers. Or they may get answers from psychologists, theologians, or novelists. In Section 3.1, one essay proposed pleasure, and the other proposed a variety of personal and social values, as the best goals to have.

But some people aren't satisfied with the answers they receive. They take the next step and ask *why* should anyone pursue a certain goal? Or what is the *basis* of this recommendation? These inquisitive people are not necessarily rejecting the answer. They might agree that love, or excellence, is the highest good. But they want to understand why one goal is higher than, or preferable to, another. They want to understand the sources of values, whatever values one has.

Actually, this general question about the source or basis of values is more typical of philosophy than the question of what particular values we should have. A person who recommends a way of life, or who lays down rules people should follow, is called a "moralist." A moralist tells you how you should live. Jesus and Mohammed are good examples of moralists. People who campaign against drugs are also moralists. A moral philosopher, in contrast, is a person who examines the *reasons* for adopting one way of life or another. A moral philosopher is more interested in the arguments that moralists use to back up their recommendations than in the particular values they propose. A moral philosopher might examine the assumptions a moralist makes, or the consequences of adopting the moralist's rules.

The essays in this section do include reasons to back up their claims. But they are not primarily aimed at persuading the reader to accept certain values. They are primarily interested in the sources of value. The first essay finds the source of value in society. It argues that morality has an essential function in any society, so it represents a functionalist point of view. The second essay finds the source of value in God. It represents the point of view of a moral theist.

YES: FUNCTIONALIST

"An Objective Basis for Morality"

Most people believe that they should not lie, cheat, or steal. They believe it is morally wrong to hurt others needlessly, and if they do abuse someone, they feel guilty about it. Why do people feel this way? Is there any rational basis for these moral beliefs? Or are they just personal preferences, or arbitrary, cultural traditions, with no objective foundation?

Morality has an objective basis. It is objectively true that a person ought to tell the truth, cooperate with others, and treat people fairly. But it takes a certain detachment to see the foundations of moral values. We may not know why we feel strongly about telling the truth, or respecting others' rights. Since we cannot explain the grounds for our beliefs, we may decide that there are no grounds, and that our beliefs are arbitrary.

But our perspective is too limited. We are like soldiers in the middle of a battle. To a soldier, a battle is nothing but chaos. He must run here and there, without understanding why. But to a general, a battle is highly organized, it moves according to plans, it follows a logic of warfare. Morality is like that, too. If we were to step back and look at our whole society, and other societies as well, we could see a pattern. We could see that every society operates according to certain rules. Three particular rules are absolutely essential for any society to exist at all. Those rules are what we call morality.

No society could exist if its members did not communicate with each other. Even a society as small as a family would disintegrate if its members could not tell each other what they wanted, or intended to do. If they could not communicate, they would not be of any help to each other, and would drift apart. Now if communication is essential, then *honesty* is essential, too. Communication means truthful communication. Lying is not communicating. Thus one rule that is absolutely essential for any society to exist is "Tell the truth."

Truthfulness is essential because members of a society must communicate. They communicate because they must cooperate. Human beings learned millions of years ago that their chances of survival are better when they work together than when they try to live alone. They could find food, build shelter, and defend themselves more effectively by cooperating. Cooperation means that one person cannot think of another person as a stick, or merely an animal. If two individuals are going to work together to build a shelter, each one has to realize that each is dependent on the other, that the other has value, and that the shelter would not exist without the other. Cooperation among individuals requires a certain minimal *Respect* for each other, so "Respect others" is a second essential rule.

Respecting others means recognizing their property and their freedom to do what they want, sharing things with them, and listening to their ideas. It means restraining one's natural impulses to be first in line, to take a larger portion, or to act regardless of what others think. It is often frustrating. Living in society is beneficial, of course, even with the frustrations. But individuals must *believe* that they benefit, or else they will not cooperate or will leave. They must be *motivated* to accept the restraints, and that means that their efforts must be rewarded. In other words, for any society to exist at all, the members must receive what they deserve. They must be treated fairly. The society must be just. Thus, "Treat people fairly"is the third essential rule.

Honesty, respect for others, and justice are the foundations of any society. They are also the core of morality. All the basic moral principles can be traced back to these three attitudes. For example, most people believe it is morally wrong to break a promise. That belief is an extension of the idea of being honest. If one person promises another to paint the fence and does not do it, then she or he has lied. Again, most people feel a moral obligation to help someone in trouble, such as a person in an auto accident. That is an extension of the idea of respecting the value of others.

These three basic rules must be obeyed before a society can exist. There are cases where one or more of them is temporarily broken. For example, societies with slavery break the second and third ones. But such societies inevitably break down. They cannot last. Violations like slavery lead to revolution and chaos because they are inconsistent with society itself. We have seen the gradual elimination of slavery over the course of history.

Another society may try to institutionalize lying. The citizens might be forced to lie to each other about the past, or their living standards, or their personal beliefs. But such pervasive dishonesty creates tensions and mistrust that eventually cause a breakdown.

If honesty, respect, and justice are essential for any society to exist, then every existing society must enforce these rules. Every society must make its members feel very strongly about them. They should feel more strongly about them than about inessential things, like the style of clothes people wear, or the kinds of foods they eat. Getting food is essential for society, but no particular way of getting it and no particular food is essential. That difference in seriousness, in importance, is the difference between moral rules and mere custom.

Not only must the essential rules be taken very seriously, but they must be universal as well if they really are essential. But do not societies have different values? For example, the Eskimos used to leave their grandparents out in the cold to freeze to death. Some people said that showed they did not respect their relatives the way Europeans did. But actually the Eskimos only had different *factual* beliefs. They believed that they were helping the old people reach heaven sooner, and helping the remaining people survive. Their *moral* principle—"help others"—was the same as the Europeans'. That is true for all societies. It is their factual beliefs that are different, not their values.

Honesty, respect, and justice are absolutely essential for society. That is an objective fact. Human beings are social animals, whether we want to be or not. Every individual must live in a society. And that is an objective fact. As a social being, every person ought to obey those rules. People can quibble over the details, but the basic moral rules are built into the nature of things. They are as objective as any other facts.

Key Concepts

limited perspective	communication	moral rule
society	cooperation	objective fact
necessary condition	fairness	

Critical Questions

1. What are the three basic rules of morality, according to the essay? Are those the only moral rules?
2. A functionalist says all societies enforce those three rules. Why do they enforce the rule "Respect others"?
3. What does the functionalist mean by "justice"? Why do societies require their members to be just?
4. The functionalist admits that some societies violate the basic moral rules (e.g., tolerate slavery). How is that possible, if the rules are essential for society to exist?
5. The functionalist also admits that societies are very different from each other (e.g., Eskimos and Europeans). How is that possible, if all societies enforce the three basic rules?
6. Can I grant that the rules the essay describes are essential for society to exist, but still say that that is no reason for me to obey them?

NO: MORAL THEIST

"The Current Crisis and Its Solution"

We are living in a crisis. The house is burning around us while we sit and dawdle. In the streets we see the most horrible and revolting crimes every day. In the schools our children wander from class to class, searching for something to believe in, and not finding it. About sixteen thousand attacks, robberies, and other crimes occur in our schools *every day*. One student in five reports carrying a weapon of some type (*Newsweek*, March 9, 1992, 25). The young people of our country no longer know what is right and wrong. But adults seem just as confused. Our elected leaders are convicted of lying and taking bribes. Of all the children born in this country in 1991, 25 percent were born to unmarried mothers (among teenagers, the figure is 66 percent) (*New York Times*, Dec. 4, 1991, A, 20).

We are in a moral crisis, drifting aimlessly at sea with no landmarks in sight. But people cannot live this way, with nothing to believe in. Some will embrace any kind of ridiculous philosophy, so long as it tells them something is morally right. They will cling to it desperately, and defend it with repeated slogans and shrill shouts, trying to convince themselves it is true. (When people become angry in an argument, it is a sure sign that they don't have good reasons for their opinion.) Others feel a kind of vague nausea, being tossed back and forth by events around them, not knowing which way to go.

We need an *authority* that we can trust and obey, an authority who will tell us what we should do and why we are here. The only way out of the crisis is to rediscover the God of our fathers. Only then will we have a sense of morality again.

The reason for all the violence and confusion today is that we have forgotten the true nature of morality. We have come to believe that we can discover right and wrong by studying human needs or by studying nature. It is a fact that every person needs food, clothing, and shelter. Some say that fact implies that we ought to help everyone satisfy those needs. Others say it is a fact that we are dependent on the fragile natural world around us. They think that implies that we have a moral obligation to respect nature.

But no *fact* creates a moral obligation. The fact that we have needs or that nature is fragile does not automatically prove that anything is morally right or wrong. Let us grant that the statement "People have needs" is true. What follows? What does that fact prove? Can we draw the conclusion "We ought to help people"? No. There is no logical connection between these two statements. A person could just as rationally draw the conclusion "People are weak and contemptible." I am not saying either conclusion is correct. I am saying that a person can go one way as easily (logically) as the other. Mere facts are not enough to believe in. Facts are not moral values. That confusion was one step toward the crisis.

Morality does not depend on facts but on *commands*. "Thou shalt not kill" is a moral principle. It tells us clearly and directly that killing is wrong. Anyone with authentic moral values has a firm commitment to obey certain commands: respect others, tell the truth, keep your promises, relieve suffering, and others. Of course we need to know the facts of a case before we can decide what we should do. We can investigate the facts; that is what trials and juries are all about. But after the facts are settled, we need a law or command in order to decide what we should do. A law has the form "Do this," or "Do not do that." No amount of facts can add up to a command.

Morality is a set of values that guides our lives. The only thing that can guide us in a principled way is commands that we are willing to obey. We are in a moral crisis because we are not willing to listen to commands anymore. We have no moral values at all.

Secular humanists tell us we can give *ourselves* commands. They admit that moral values, by their very nature, are rules to be followed, not whims or passing fancies. But they say we can decide for ourselves which rules we will follow, and which commands we will obey. The commands ultimately come from ourselves.

These humanists are deceiving themselves (and others who follow them). They see half of the truth but blindly miss the other half. Morality means commands. (They understand that.) But it makes no sense to say "a person commands himself or herself." Everyone agrees that there is a difference between obeying a command and doing whatever I want. But if I command myself, then I can also revoke the command at any time. I gave it, so I can take it back, or give another one. But if I can cancel a command whenever I want, then in what sense am I obeying commands? I am not. I am doing whatever I feel like doing at the time. That is not following rules. It is not obeying commands, and it is not morality.

We have lost sight of true moral consciousness. We have made ourselves as gods, thinking that goodness begins and ends with our own desires. But we are only gratifying our inflated self-image. We see the consequences of our arrogance all around us, in crime statistics, suicide rates, drug abuse, race relations, and the abysmal state of our society.

If morality requires commands, and if we cannot command ourselves, then where do the commands come from? The obvious answer is God. (Obvious but so hard to accept.) Only God has the authority to give commands that we can obey with confidence. Only God has the infinite wisdom, the love, the mercy, to give commands that we can trust completely. God can give us the strength to overcome our stubborn pride, submit, and do what we know is right. All we need to do is ask.

But some subtle reasoners refuse to accept the obvious. They say God cannot be the source of moral commands because that would put us in an insoluble dilemma. When God says, "Thou shalt not kill," either He has a reason for saying it, or He does not. Let's suppose He has a reason. Maybe He believes that people should not kill because all life is precious, these critics say. But then *that* is why we should not kill. God's command just reminds us of that principle—all life is precious. But He is not the source of the principle, because it is a reason for Him, too. If God has any reasons for His commands, then we can understand those reasons, and God becomes irrelevant.

On the other hand, let's suppose that God does not have reasons to justify His commands. Then He is arbitrary and capricious. If He has no reasons for giving us the commands He does, then He is just acting on impulse. But it would be insane to feel bound by commands issued that way, no matter who gave them. Therefore, whether God has reasons for His commands or does not, He is not the source of moral values.

Only certain types of people think this dilemma is a problem. Only people who have turned away from God and bowed down to Reason are disturbed.

They have put rationality and having reasons above God, and attempt to test God by a standard of reason. In fact, by the standard of their own personal comprehension. This is foolish arrogance. Reason is a wonderful gift but it is not absolutely limitless. Some truths are beyond and above reason.

It is only because these people worship reason that the second option above disturbs them. "How can we obey God's commands if He has no reasons to justify them?" What a foolish question! The fact that *He* wills it is the reason. That is more than enough of a reason to obey.

Morality depends on commands, and the only commands with sufficient authority are commands from God. But what if there is no God? Then there is no morality. That is the crisis we are in today. We should try to bring people back to faith in God, for their sake, and for ours.

Key Concepts

authority	facts and values	arbitrary
commands	dilemma	reason

Critical Questions

1. What kind of crisis are we in today, according to the essay? Do you agree or disagree?
2. What relation does a moral theist see between facts and morality, e.g., the fact that people have needs, and the moral obligation to help them meet their needs?
3. Can you give some examples of commands that are issued by some authority? What makes the person or organization an authority?
4. Suppose I make a New Year's resolution. I tell myself, "From now on, I must look for some good in every single person." Would that be a moral principle, according to a moral theist?
5. Humanists say that anyone who believes that God is the source of morality faces a dilemma. What are the two sides of the dilemma?
6. Does a moral theist think that God has reasons for the commands he gives?

Methods and Techniques
NECESSARY CONDITIONS

Both of the essays in this section depend on the idea of a *necessary condition*. A necessary condition is just what it sounds like. X is a necessary condition of Y if you cannot have Y without also having X. For example, people say, "If you want to make an omelet, you have to break some eggs." They mean that broken eggs are a necessary condition of an omelet. "Where there is smoke there is fire." Fire is a necessary condition of smoke. Now, if you know that X is a necessary condition of Y, and you know that Y exists, then you can infer that X exists as well. (If you smell smoke, and you know that fire is a necessary condition of smoke, then you can infer that a fire is burning.)

A related version of the same argument goes like this: if you really want to be a doctor, and going to medical school is a necessary condition of being a doctor, then you must want to go to medical school. The inference is about what you must want, or approve of, rather than about what must exist.

Philosophers often use this sort of necessary-condition argument, but they use it in cases where the connection between X and Y isn't so clear. One example is language. Young children learn language differently from the way they learn other subjects, like geography or science. They learn their native language very quickly, without effort or teaching, and in large amounts. All children do this, regardless of their other talents. How is this possible? Some people argue that it is possible *only* if human beings have an innate language faculty. They say that the human mind must be specially wired, or evolved, to learn language. An innate language faculty is a necessary condition of such learning.

Anarchists say that a necessary condition of genuine freedom is the abolition of all government. Governments enforce laws, they employ police to harass citizens, they confiscate our earnings, they restrict us in a thousand ways. Thus if you really want to be free, you must want to abolish government.

Another example is mathematical knowledge. Everyone knows that $7 + 5 = 12$. But we know it in a peculiar way. We are absolutely certain of it. Once we understand the equation, we realize that it could not possibly be false. Nor will it ever change. We also know that if you draw a straight line through the center of a circle, you get two equal parts. We are absolutely certain of that, too. And everyone agrees that it is true. There aren't many things that *everyone* agrees on. Some philosophers who reflect upon this sort of knowledge claim that it can exist only if there is another dimension of reality—a nonphysical, eternal, perfect realm, which we can grasp when we think about mathematics. In other words, they say this nonphysical realm is a necessary condition for the existence of mathematical knowledge.

In the first essay, the functionalist claims that moral rules are a necessary condition for society. Society could not exist without the three moral rules. And since we all value society, we must value the moral rules as well. But in the second essay the moral theist claims that God's commands are a necessary condition of morality. Morality could not exist if there were no authoritative God to lay down the rules. If we believe that some things are right and other things are wrong, then we must believe in God.

Understanding the Dilemma
FUNCTIONALIST OR MORAL THEIST?

A functionalist and a moral theist agree that morality is a set of *rules*. In this respect they are both formalists and not utilitarians. But they disagree on the basis or source of the rules. A functionalist believes that morality is an organic part of society. Society, its structure, its needs and operations are basic, and morality is a natural outgrowth of society, like law.

A moral theist, however, believes that society is not enough. Social pressures cannot explain the unique power of moral rules. The moral theist says that moral commands have a profound emotional force or weight. They are absolute. They are more important than laws made by a society. The very idea of breaking them fills people with anguish. A society cannot endow its rules with the same kind of force. The only possible source of moral commands is God.

The disagreement between a functionalist and a moral theist is not about which rules are binding on us. They might both agree that lying is wrong, that we ought to keep our promises, and that we should respect other people. The disagreement is about the basis of these rules. Where do the rules come from, and why are they obligatory? The functionalist answers "society," and the moral theist says "God."

The emphasis on society makes the functionalist sound like a moral relativist. But they are different. A functionalist believes certain basic moral rules are essential to the existence and functioning of society, and every society needs the *same* rules. The first essay in this section mentions honesty, respect, and justice. A relativist, on the other hand, believes societies create moral rules (like the functionalist), but he or she believes different societies create *different* moral rules. So a functionalist is more similar to a moral absolutist than to a moral relativist. (I say "similar to" and not "is a moral absolutist" because functionalists believe morality is created by people, and depends on people's needs and desires. It is not "objective" in the sense of being part of the world independent of humanity. Most absolutists believe morality is not created by people, but is part of objective reality in some way.) The moral theist is a moral absolutist in the full sense of the word.

Are you a functionalist or a moral theist? The choice is obviously related to your beliefs about God. If you are an atheist, then you cannot be a moral theist. On the other hand, if you are a theist, then you believe that God is the source of everything, including morality. But you might not believe that God gave explicit commands to us. You might believe, instead, that moral value is implicit in human nature, or in society, or in the natural world, and it is up to us to discover it. This example shows that the relations among the various answers, like theist and moral theist, are complex and subtle.

FUNCTIONALIST

1. Society molds and shapes people in many ways, including their moral values.
2. Being a morally good person means conforming to your society's demands.
3. Some rules are absolutely essential for society to survive at all, and naturally people will have very strong feelings about those rules.

4. Morality is a human invention; it does not exist outside of human desires, agreements, and intentions.

MORAL THEIST

5. Some moral rules have an *absolute* force, and their only possible source is God, not society.
6. The best guidelines on how to live are the rules and advice given by the world's great prophets, God's messengers.
7. Moral rules are more important and more sacred than social rules or laws.
8. God has spoken clearly, in all the world's religions, about what we ought to do and ought not to do.

FOR FURTHER STUDY

Historical Examples

FUNCTIONALIST: John Rawls. *A Theory of Justice*. Harvard University Press, 1972. In chap. 1 Rawls tries to show how moral ideas are related to the fundamental structures of society.

MORAL THEIST: Hastings Rashdall. *The Theory of Good and Evil*. Clarendon Press, 1907. In vol. 2, Book 3, chap. 1, Rashdall argues that the objectivity and strict obligation of moral duties strongly suggest that God is the source of the duties.

OTHER SOURCES

Arthur L. Caplan, Bruce Jennings, eds. *Darwin, Marx, and Freud: Their Influence on Moral Theory*. Plenum Press, 1984. Essays by biologists, historians, psychologists, and philosophers.

Daniel Callahan, H. Tristram Engelhardt, Jr., eds. *The Roots of Ethics: Science, Religion, and Values*. Plenum Press, 1981. Papers by contemporary philosophers, some including responses by other philosophers.

Walter Lippmann. *A Preface to Morals*. Macmillan, 1929. Mainly historical, surveying the decline of religion-based morality and analyzing the options facing the modern world. Very well written.

Hunter Lewis. *A Question of Values*. HarperSanFrancisco, 1990. Lewis describes six types of value systems, distinguished by their methods of making moral decisions, for a popular audience.

Gilbert Harman. *The Nature of Morality: An Introduction to Ethics*. Oxford University Press, 1977. Defends a "social custom theory of morality."

Mary Midgley. "The Origin of Ethics." In Peter Singer, ed. *A Companion to Ethics.* Blackwell, 1991. Looks for clues in the social lives of other animals.

George Silberbauer. "Ethics in Small-Scale Societies." In Singer. Examination of functionalism.

Jonathan Berg. "How Could Ethics Depend on Religion?" In Singer. Berg describes a variety of ways it could.

Current Controversy

3.6   SHOULD DOCTORS EVER END PEOPLE'S LIVES?

Protector or Euthanizer?

The word "euthanasia" comes from Greek words meaning "good death." That sounds like an oxymoron, i.e., a phrase made up of words with opposite meanings, such as "moderate extremist," or "wealthy beggar." How can death be good?

In this amazing age, many things are possible that have never been possible before. We have the technological means to keep people alive long after the heart attacks and pneumonias and accidents that would have killed them in earlier periods. We have the means to save infants born with defects that would have certainly ended their lives shortly after birth a hundred years ago.

But in the view of many people, this powerful technology is a mixed blessing. It can save lives, but it can also prolong a life beyond the point that the patient wants to live. It can keep a person alive, in the sense that the heart still beats, but the person might be permanently unconscious, completely dependent on machines for breathing, receiving nutrients, and eliminating wastes, and a demanding consumer of scarce medical resources. In cases such as these, some people argue that death can be good. A natural, peaceful passing from life's stage can be preferable to the continued pumping and draining of the organism for the sake of "life."

On the other hand, few people want to take the responsibility for killing another person. A patient may be old and sick, but would you be willing to inject the drug that stops her heart? Perhaps there is hope. Some patients recover in ways that their doctors can't explain. And if we allow doctors or others to begin killing people, where will it lead?

On its face, the act of taking an innocent life seems wrong; everyone knows it. The prohibition against killing another person—not in order to defend oneself or society—is so ancient and deeply ingrained in our moral consciousness that many people refuse to cross that line. It is the most basic moral law we know.

Nevertheless, the prospect of sinking into a confused, artificial twilight, tied to machines, severed from other people, and perhaps in great pain, makes many people approve of euthanasia. This may be a case, unusual in philosophy, where the new conditions we have created, i.e., our new power over life and death, raise fundamentally new philosophical problems. But the nature of the problem is also similar to others you have probably already encountered. We are torn between two inclinations and two ways of thinking: to respect life and preserve it, or to be merciful and rescue people from "a fate worse than death." This new philosophical dilemma is just as difficult as the oldest ones.

The first essay that follows takes the traditional view, opposing killing, and claims to be protecting innocent, vulnerable people. It can be called the protector's point of view. The second essay defends euthanasia, so it can be called the euthanizer's point of view.

NO: PROTECTOR

"Having Reasons for Moral Decisions"

In 1982 a baby boy was born in Bloomington, Indiana. Known in court documents as Infant Doe, he had Down's syndrome, which meant he would be mentally retarded and have a shorter-than-normal life span. He also had a blockage in the digestive system that prevented food from reaching the stomach. Relatively simple surgery could have solved that problem. But the parents refused to allow the surgery, or intravenous feeding, and the court supported the parents' right to make that decision. One doctor described the scene in the hospital:

> Baby Doe's shrunken, thin little body with dry cyanotic skin, extremely dehydrated, breathing shallowly and irregularly, lay passively on fresh hospital linens. Blood was running from a mouth too dry to close. Death by starvation was near. Too late for fluids. Too late for surgery. . . . (Bernards, ed., 1989, pp. 202–203)

The child died a few hours later. What was the right thing to do in this case? If you were the parent of a handicapped child, what would you do? If you were the doctor, what would you do?

Faced with such a heartbreaking image, many people feel that the child's life should have been saved and extended for as long as possible. The doctor describing the case was appealing to our feelings of pity.

But suppose the handicap is more severe. One expert in the treatment of spina bifida asks "Is it moral to encourage the survival of a child who will be a paraplegic, incontinent, and will require multiple surgical procedures for hydrocephalus, orthopedic deformity, and bladder dysfunction?" (ibid., p. 191). Besides the severe, painful, recurring physical problems, the child would have no personality and would barely be conscious during its short life. Wouldn't death be a merciful release in this case?

Another doctor describes a case of an infant born with "a skin condition similar to third degree burns over almost all of its body for which there was no cure." The slightest movement was intensely painful. "Providing basic nursing care caused tearing away of the skin. The infant could not be fed orally because of blistering in the mouth and throat." The child would live only a few days at best. "Wouldn't it have been reasonable, merciful, and justifiable," the doctor asks, "to have shortened the babydying by an intended direct action?" (Baird, Rosenbaum, eds., 1989, p. 121).

Descriptions such as these are very upsetting and emotional. In some cases, our feelings tell us that it is horrible to allow the child to die, and we should do whatever is necessary to save the life. But in other cases our sympathy and pity lead us to the drastic decision to end the suffering by ending the life. Unfortunately there are many cases, and so far I have described cases on both sides.

But now I want to suggest that we need to use more than our feelings. These wrenching cases do not help us make a *moral* decision. Being moral and doing the right thing requires more than feeling certain emotions, because our emotions whipsaw us in opposite directions. To be moral one must act for a good reason. A person can do the right thing accidentally, so to speak, without understanding why it is right. But to act deliberately and morally, one must have a good reason and a sound justification for one's action.

What is a good reason? For example, in the case of the child with the skin disease, what is the reason for favoring euthanasia? The doctor would say it is right to end the child's life because of the fact that the child is suffering terribly and has no chance to escape the suffering. In the case of Infant Doe, the attending physician might say it is right to save the child's life because of the fact that the surgery would be relatively easy to perform and chances of recovery are good. So when people think about moral problems, they offer relevant facts to support their decisions.

But facts aren't enough. The doctors in both these cases are also applying general principles. The first doctor is assuming a principle of mercy: one has a moral obligation to relieve pain and reduce suffering. The fact that the infant is in great pain, *together* with the principle that one should reduce suffering, leads to the decision to accelerate the end of the child's tragic life. Neither the fact by itself nor the principle by itself is enough to justify the decision. But together they are enough, in the doctor's opinion. There are exceptions, as when a doctor causes some discomfort in order to prevent greater discomfort later. But in general, reducing suffering is a basic moral principle that guides our thinking about particular cases.

The second doctor is also appealing to a general principle. The surgery to save Infant Doe is relatively simple, but that fact is relevant only because of the underlying principle: one should respect human life and never destroy it. Infant Doe may not be just like everyone else, but he is certainly human, and it is wrong to destroy human life. Therefore it is wrong to let him die, and the right thing to do is to operate and help him.

All moral reasoning depends upon determining the facts and applying principles. For example, people disagree about the morality of capital punishment. Is it morally right to execute a convicted murderer? Many people allow their feelings to guide their moral judgment. They feel pity for the victim and his or her family, and they feel anger at the criminal and want to make him or her suffer. But feelings are not good moral reasons, because they are inconsistent—we can also feel pity for the criminal whose hard life led him to commit a crime—they change from moment to moment, different people have very different feelings about things, and it is difficult to compare them or even know what we are feeling.

Making a moral decision about capital punishment means determining the facts and deciding what principles apply. That isn't easy. Some say it is a fact that capital punishment deters would-be murderers, and others say we do not know for sure if it does or doesn't. But most moral disagreements are about principles and their applications. Some say the principle of "an eye for an eye" requires execution of convicted murderers. Others say the principle of respecting human life requires the alternative sentence of life in prison. The basic disagreement is usually over the meaning and validity of certain principles, and their priority.

The issue of euthanasia is an issue of principles. Doctors try to save lives, and they try to reduce suffering. They might do other things as well, but in their role as doctors, those two principles are the most basic and fundamental commitments that guide their decisions. Normally, the two principles go hand in hand. Relieving the pain of a ruptured appendix also saves the patient's life. A heart bypass operation prevents a fatal heart attack, and also relieves chronic chest pain. But sometimes they come into conflict. Handicapped infants may face many challenges and even pain. If the pain is intense and cannot be treated—which is rare—then some people decide that the obligation to relieve suffering outweighs the obligation to respect human life. They decide to end the child's life to stop the suffering. Others believe the obligation to preserve life outweighs the duty to reduce suffering. Which principle takes priority?

A natural impulse is to reach for a compromise. One might think that sometimes respect for life takes precedence, and sometimes relieving suffering takes precedence, depending on circumstances. But this is a comforting illusion. The decision to elevate one principle over the other must be a thoughtful, reasoned decision, not a whim or momentary emotional response. But how can one justify the choice? These principles are the most basic ones doctors have. They cannot use a more basic principle to guide the decision about priority. In fact, switching from one to the other is simply relying on the strong feelings elicited by the particularities of a case, without having a principle. It is giving up on making a moral decision. One of the principles must be fundamental, if doctors are going to make moral decisions rather than respond arbitrarily.

In the rare cases when these basic obligations conflict, saving lives takes priority over relieving pain. The principle of respecting human life is the foundational principle of medicine, although it is not the only principle. Doctors can justify their decisions by using the principle of relieving pain, or the principle that medical students can learn only by practicing on real patients, and even the principle of cutting costs (by using generic drugs rather than name brands, for example). In most cases, all these principles can apply at the same time. But principles are not all equally important. Doctors agree that cutting costs never takes moral priority over saving lives. It doesn't make sense to let a person die rather than pay the cost of a prescription drug. Nor would a doctor risk a patient's life in order to let a medical student treat the patient, although if there is no risk to the patient, letting the student gain experience is morally justifiable.

While the priority of saving lives is clear in comparison with other principles, some people refuse to give it priority over the principle of reducing pain. But saving lives is more basic than this principle as well. For ending a life is final and irreversible. It destroys all hope. It ends all possibilities. So long as a person is alive, there is hope for improvement, even if the life is difficult and painful. The situation can change, and no one can be absolutely certain that it won't. But if a doctor ends a child's life, he or she can be absolutely certain that the child will never improve, and will never again experience the vital thrill of being alive.

Nancy Dubler describes the case of a college professor who learned that he had an inoperable cancer and had a short time to live. In long talks about his situation he grew even closer to his family, and he threw himself into his work with even greater intensity. He also gave his doctors clear instructions that he wanted them to do everything possible to prolong his life. Every day and even every minute was precious. Toward the end he was confined to bed and so weak he could barely speak. His heart stopped, but the medical team revived him. He had to be attached to a ventilator, which prevented him from talking to his wife at all. But on a pad of paper he was able to scrawl one word: "Hope." Ending a life is not only fundamentally wrong, it is cruel, because it deprives people of that powerful, sustaining emotion.

Another reason to give the principle of life priority is that the principle of reducing pain is so difficult to apply. How much suffering justifies the decision to end a life? What kind of suffering? No one believes that a small amount of pain justifies ending a patient's life. Amputating a leg mangled in an accident causes pain and suffering, in the recovery room, in rehabilitation, and in the frustrating adjustments to the new condition. But no one recommends letting the patient die instead of removing the leg. How much pain and frustration are enough to justify ending a life? There is no answer. There is no clear standard for deciding when relieving pain outweighs preserving life, and therefore the suggestion that the principle of relieving pain sometimes takes priority over preserving life makes no sense. When is "sometimes"? To think that it does take priority is to give up on moral thinking and to fall back on arbitrary, emotional responses to individual cases.

Doctors have always made saving lives their primary goal, and they have relieved suffering as well. Usually the two principles complement each other. But if doctors began subordinating the principle of respecting life to the goal of reducing suffering, it would be a fundamental change and would have serious, long-term consequences. It would create doubts in the public's mind about doctors. Patients have to trust their doctors. They have to provide doctors with detailed, personal information about their bodies and their lives. They have to cooperate fully, and even believe in the doctor's ability. Belief is a real factor in getting better. The foundation of their trust is the confidence that the doctor will do everything possible to save the patient. But if doctors began ending lives, even if it were only a few and in extraordinary circumstances, the seed of doubt would be planted and it would grow.

To say that respecting human life takes precedence over all of doctors' other duties is to say that the principle is an absolute. No consideration should make a doctor deliberately destroy an innocent person's life. Some people maintain that we should not have any absolute principles. The so-called postmodernists, as I understand them, reject absolute principles as unnecessary restrictions on people's freedom. It's true that absolutes are restrictions, but are they unnecessary or undesirable? There is nothing wrong with being absolutely just or absolutely good. Even postmodernists want to be absolutely free. It would be wonderful if people could be absolutely fair to each other, although we probably won't be. But saying that a principle is absolute is no criticism in itself. In fact, we must have some absolute principle as the basis for ranking and deciding among other principles.

In some circumstances, patients decide that they want to die. They may feel that they are a burden to their families, or that they have nothing to look forward to. But such depression is treatable. If patients are made to feel wanted and respected, they almost never ask for euthanasia. Most cases of physical pain are treatable as well. But if patients insist that they want to die, neither doctors nor nurses nor relatives are under any obligation to help them die. Doctors should counsel them and try to relieve their pain, but killing is wrong, and therefore helping someone kill himself or herself is also wrong. As a last resort, health professionals can withdraw from a case and let someone else take over.

The medical profession is a dignified and revered institution. Doctors have regulated themselves and made wise decisions for their patients for a long time. They handle highly emotional situations every day, and maintain their poise and clarity in very difficult circumstances. I am confident that they will continue to recognize the difference between moral decisions based on principles and emotional decisions driven by momentary pressures.

Key Concepts

feelings	principle	arbitrary
reason	hope	absolute

Critical Questions

1. According to the protector, why can't we rely on our feelings to decide whether euthanasia is right or wrong?
2. Suppose two patients need liver transplants, but we have only one liver available. I say patient A should get the liver because she is 24 years old, whereas patient B is 58 years old, and they are otherwise similar. Am I thinking morally, according to the essay?
3. Doctors save lives and they relieve suffering, but sometimes the two goals come into conflict: saving a life prolongs the suffering. Can doctors decide which goal is more important on a case-by-case basis, according to the essay? Why or why not?
4. Suppose a patient has condition XYZ, and 100 percent of the scores of patients with XYZ have died withing six months of being diagnosed. Should a doctor tell the patient he has no chance of living more than a year, according to the essay?
5. The essay says that the principle of relieving suffering cannot be applied in practice because there is no standard to follow. But suffering cannot be measured. Why can't doctors simply say that if a patient is suffering "greatly," or is in "intense pain," with no chance of recovery, then relieving pain outweighs saving lives?
6. Suppose a patient calmly and persistently wants to die. She is in pain, has only months to live, and depends on a kidney dialysis machine to stay alive. In your opinion, should her doctor grant her request, turn off the machine, and let her die? What would the protector say?

YES: EUTHANIZER

"The Complex Issue of Euthanasia"

The issue of euthanasia is complex, and the biggest mistake we can make is to oversimplify matters. That is exactly what opponents of euthanasia do. They rely on absolutes, black and white descriptions with no shades of gray, and aggressive condemnations of anyone who sees different sides. I would like to examine some of these extreme positions, and suggest more moderate alternatives. Nothing is more serious than decisions about life and death, and people have a moral obligation to save lives. But it is not an absolute obligation. We should try to save lives, but in some rare cases it is better to help a person die.

The term "euthanasia" covers many different things. First, there is a difference between voluntary and involuntary euthanasia. In voluntary euthanasia the patient asks the doctor or provider to help him or her die. The patient may request help directly when he or she is ill, or the patient may complete a "living will" at an earlier time, asking doctors not to take extraordinary measures to prolong life, or not to resuscitate after the heart stops. Involuntary euthanasia occurs with infants or comatose patients who are unable to make their wishes known. Parents or relatives decide what is best for the patient, and may decide that ending the suffering is best.

Another complication is the distinction between active and passive euthanasia. Active euthanasia occurs when a doctor or other care-giver acts to bring about death. For example, a doctor may administer a drug that suppresses breathing or stops the heart. Passive euthanasia occurs when the doctor withdraws or withholds treatment, knowing that the result will be death. If a patient is on a respirator, for example, and cannot breathe without it, a doctor might remove the respirator. The patient will die, but the main cause of death is the disease or accident that interfered with breathing, not the doctor. In active euthanasia, the doctor is the direct cause of death. (Some philosophers deny that any real difference exists between active and passive euthanasia, and that is another complication.)

A related concept is "doctor-assisted suicide." A doctor may prepare a lethal dose of drugs and make it available to the patient with an explanation of its effect, but the patient actually administers the drugs to himself or herself. All these different scenarios raise difficult moral questions about responsibility, intentions, compassion, and killing. Simple answers cannot do justice to the whole spectrum of cases.

And yet some people take the position that no form of euthanasia is ever justified. They believe that human life is sacred, and that our most basic moral duty is to preserve life and never destroy it. For example consider "Baby Boy Houle."

> The child was born on February 9, horribly deformed. His entire left side was malformed; he had no left eye, was practically without a left ear, had a deformed left hand; some of his vertebrae were not formed. Furthermore, he was affected with a tracheal esophageal fistula and could not be fed by mouth. Air leaked into his stomach instead of going to the lungs, and fluid from the stomach pushed up into the lungs. (Baird, Rosenbaum, eds., 1989, p. 8)

The child soon developed pneumonia, and brain damage was suspected because of poor circulation. Aggressive surgery and treatment could keep the child alive for a few days, but the parents decided against it. However, several doctors disagreed with the parents and took the case to court. Maine Superior Court Judge David G. Roberts ruled "At the moment of live birth there does exist a human being entitled to the fullest protection of the law. The most basic right enjoyed by every human being is a right to life itself" (ibid., p. 8). The doctors worked furiously, but in spite of their efforts Baby Boy Houle died after fifteen days.

It was morally wrong to keep that child alive. It accomplished nothing but to prolong the poor boy's desperate struggle and agony. Those who hold the rule "preserve human life" as an absolute cannot consider all the factors of the situation. Life is good, but it is good because of what it brings people—joy and growth and love and opportunities to share with others. Bare life itself, in the sense of a beating heart or expanding lungs, is not necessarily good, especially if it is accompanied by pain, dehumanizing dependence on machines, or a vegetative unconsciousness. In other words, it is the quality of life that people value, not simply life by itself. Unfortunately, in some cases, the quality of life is so horrible that it is wrong to extend it. Instead of thinking that "life" overrules every other factor, we should weigh the goods and the evils of each case, and recognize that sometimes the evils outweigh the goods, including life itself.

Many who oppose euthanasia do so on religious grounds, and say that "doctors cannot play God." That is, questions of life and death should be left to God, and once life exists, doctors should do whatever they can to preserve it. But who can know for sure what God wants? It is hard to believe that God wanted Baby Boy Houle to suffer for two weeks before he died. No one knows what God wants. Nevertheless, some religious leaders claim that they know, and since euthanasia is such a difficult issue, anyone who offers simple, absolute answers will attract a following. But we can find better answers if we apply our deepest moral feelings of sympathy and compassion, and think carefully about each case on its own merits.

Another absolute rule some people hold is that doctors should preserve lives and never end lives. In an article entitled "Doctors Must Not Kill," the authors say

> This issue [euthanasia] touches medicine at its very moral center; if the moral center collapses, if physicians become killers or are even merely licensed to kill, the profession—and, therewith, each physician—will never again be worthy of trust and respect as healer and comforter and protector of life in all its frailty. For if medicine's power of life may be used equally to heal or kill, the doctor is no more a moral professional but rather a morally neutral technician. (Gaylin, Kass, Pellegrino, Siegler, 1988, pp. 2139–2140)

Is "doctors must n ot kill" an absolute rule? I don't think it is, nor do I think the profession would collapse if doctors adopted a more flexible attitude. In fact, many doctors do discretely help suffering patients die. Patients know it, ask for help, and appreciate it. Doctors' duty is to *care* for people and do whatever they can to help them. Their duty is not simply to keep people alive without considering anything else. Doctors are capable of making good decisions, in collaboration with patients and their families. They have the experience and the intelligence to weigh all factors, and do what is best for the patient. Sometimes dying sooner rather than later is best.

Some opponents of euthanasia believe in another absolute rule: "never give up hope." No matter how ill a patient is, a miracle is always possible, they say. Doctors may discover a cure, or patients may spontaneously recover. We must always hope. But euthanasia destroys all hope. It removes the possibility of recovery because it welcomes death.

This attitude is not brave. It is simply unrealistic. An intelligent person will try to estimate the probabilities and weigh the costs. A heart weakened by eighty years of work and several heart attacks is not going to become strong and healthy. An advanced and uncontrollable cancer is not going to disappear. Medical predictions may not be 100-percent reliable, but some are close. To encourage hope for a miracle in the face of such odds is misleading, not moral. It is willfully narrow-minded. And there is the cost. Should we really ask a person in terrible anguish and desperate for release to "never give up hope," and to endure the horrible pain—for how long?—because there is a one-in-a- million chance that he or she will recover? No, we should consider all the factors and do what is best in each situation. In most cases, hope is appropriate, but in other cases it isn't.

The most common argument against euthanasia is the slippery slope argument. The claim is that if society approves of euthanasia in any case at all, it will soon extend euthanasia to all sorts of unconscionable cases. If doctors decide that the right thing to do in the Baby Boy Houle case is to let the baby die peacefully, then they will soon be killing healthy babies. One writer says

> Once any group of human beings is considered unworthy of living, what is to stop our society from extending this cruelty to other groups? If the mongoloid is to be deprived of his right to life, what of the blind and deaf? What of the cripple, the retarded and the senile? Or even the diabetic, or the obese individual? (Bernards, 1989, p. 28)

We must cling to our absolute rule with all the fervor of a true fanatic, this writer suggests, and resist compromise, reason, or discussion, because those will open the floodgates of moral anarchy. At this point opponents of euthanasia often describe the Nazis' policies of eliminating undesirables, and claim that we are only a short step from such depravity.

This position is more rhetoric than argument. It deliberately attempts to arouse powerful emotions of anger, fear, and indignation, and tries to substitute those responses for careful thinking. But if we put aside the strong-arm tactics, we see that the intellectual force of the argument is very weak. The argument assumes that people making decisions ten or twenty years from now will not be able to think for themselves. All they will be able to do is imitate their predecessors (us), and will even expand our policies in absurd directions. The people of the future will have no compassion, no sense of justice, no principles, unless we hold on to our absolute rule.

But this is not credible. It is hardly probable that people of the future will turn into moral monsters if we today consider different aspects of particular cases instead of sticking to a simple rule. The absolutists' mistake is to assume that everyone else is just like them. Without simple rules as guides, the world seems too overwhelming and confusing to absolutists. Without simple rules, people of the future will become monsters, they say. But other people are not so dependent on black and white absolutes. We often recognize degrees and multiple standards with different weights. We can weigh the pain and dependence against the chances for improvement. Sometimes hope will prevail, but sometimes the need for relief will take precedence. If a person is in terrible pain and will not get better, there is no reason to prolong the agony. We can balance the belief that doctors will never harm people with the belief that they will relieve suffering. We can expect both from doctors, and can trust them to make the best decision for the patient in light of all the relevant factors.

Some people seem to be afraid to use their own intelligence. The biggest danger related to euthanasia is not a slippery slope but simple-minded rigidity.

Key Concepts

voluntary	active	quality of life	trust
involuntary	passive	playing God	slippery slope

Critical Questions

1. What is the difference between voluntary and involuntary euthanasia? Between active and passive euthanasia?
2. What does the euthanizer mean by "quality of life"? In your opinion, can doctors or relatives judge the quality of life that a handicapped infant will have in the future? Can one person ever judge another's quality of life?
3. Some say we should not "play God." Does that view imply that radical new developments in medicine, such as heart transplants or in vitro fertilization, are morally wrong?
4. How does the euthanizer respond to those who say "doctors must not kill"? In your opinion, which would damage doctors' reputation more, their willingness to end people's lives or their unwillingness to relieve people's pain when euthanasia is the only possible relief?
5. The slippery slope argument claims that once we cross the line of killing innocent people, we will not be able to establish another clear line to restrain our killing. What is the euthanizer's response to this argument?
6. Janet Adkins, age 54, was the first person to die using Dr. Jack Kevorkian's suicide machine. She was diagnosed with Alzheimer's dis-

ease, but was in the earliest stages (if the diagnosis was correct) and was otherwise healthy. In your opinion, should a doctor have granted her request and helped her die?

Methods and Techniques
JUSTIFICATION

Imagine that your friend Jenny rushed up to you and said "There's been a terrible earthquake in California!" You would probably ask for details, but if you were a philosopher you might ask "How do you know?" Jenny says she heard it from Bob. "How does Bob know?" you ask. If Jenny is a true friend, she might explain that Bob watched the news on CNN and CNN had a reporter on the scene who saw walls sway and felt the earth move.

Philosophers and other people want to justify their beliefs, and this scenario is an example of how they might do that. Philosophers try to trace a belief back to its source, and if the source is reliable, then the belief based on it is justified. In this case, the belief depends upon an eyewitness (or several eyewitnesses), but also upon four subsequent links, from the witness to the news studio, to Bob, to Jenny, and to you. To say the belief is justified is to say one is right to believe it; it is very likely to be true.

This image or model of justification is very common. Many people think of justification as a kind of ranking of beliefs, or an arrangement of beliefs from the most reliable to less reliable ones. The eyewitness' belief is ranked first, the newsroom's report depends on the witness so it is ranked second, and so on.

Consider another scenario. You are having dinner at your favorite restaurant and you must decide what to order. You enjoy several dishes. After studying the menu, you decide that the sweet and sour pork is the dish you like more than any other, so you order that. But the waiter tells you they are out of sweet and sour pork. So you must decide which dish is second best. You choose egg foo yung, and after you order you try to rank your other favorites in case they are out of egg foo yung. This is a process of deciding on your priorities. If you know your priorities, then when you face a choice or conflict you will know what to do. This is the same kind of justification as the case of beliefs about an earthquake, except here you are ranking preferences rather than beliefs, and you are justifying your actions or decisions.

Now consider a third scenario. You have promised your friends to come over and play cards tonight, but on your way out of the office your boss asks you to give a presentation to the Board of Directors tomorrow. When you get home your spouse reminds you that tonight is your daughter's school concert. At about that time your mother calls to say your father isn't feeling well and could use a visit. What do you do? You have four obligations—keep your promise to your friends, prepare a presentation to get ahead in your career, support your daughter, and cheer up your parents.

Is it possible to rank moral obligations the way we rank preferences in food? Can we say that, as a general rule, family comes first, then work, then friends? And among family, children's needs take precedence over adult's needs? If so, then you would choose to attend your daughter's concert. The justification is the ranking of the types of obligations. But this model doesn't tell us how to produce our ranking in the first place. Does family really come before work? On the basis of what principle or obligation does one make that decision?

Or should we say the four obligations are all important and the particular facts of the situation will determine which obligation is most pressing? How ill is your father? Could you lose your job if you give a poor presentation? In the first essay above, the protector argues that if we are going to be moral, we have to rank our principles, with one at the top to supercede all others. But the euthanizer claims particular facts can justify a decision to fulfill one obligation or another.

Many people think of justification as a search for foundations. Ranking principles provides a kind of foundation, with the highest ranking principle as the solid base. You encountered another search for foundations in the moral theist's essay "The Current Crisis and Its Solution." It assumes that morality consists of commands, like "Do not kill." But the force of a command depends upon its source. If a salesperson says you cannot get a refund on the dress you bought (i.e., you must keep it, a command), then you can ask to speak to the supervisor. The salesperson's command is backed up by the supervisor's command. If the supervisor issues the same command, you can go to the manager, and perhaps the owner of the store. If the owner says you must keep the dress, then you have no choice but to obey. On the other hand, if the owner agrees to a refund, then the salesperson's command is invalidated. The lower level commands depend on the higher level commands.

A moral theist assumes that moral rules are like these commands. If they have any force, they must come from some ultimate authority that cannot be questioned. The only source that cannot be questioned is God, according to a moral theist. Thus God performs the same function in morality that certainty or eyewitnesses perform in knowledge. God is the unquestionable starting point, the unshakable foundation, and no moral rules are secure until we have traced the connection between them and this ultimate authority. The protector claims that the command "preserve human life" is an absolute, but does not say the command comes from God.

Other philosophers, like hedonists and utilitarians, think that happiness, not God, is the ultimate foundation of morality. They say that an action is morally right if it leads to happiness (or pleasure). It may not lead directly to happiness. Going to the dentist may not be enjoyable in itself, but in the long run it does lead to happiness. So for these philosophers, an action must be connected to happiness before it can be morally right. This way of thinking about morality is different from moral theists' way in several respects. For example, this way does not see morality as a matter of rules, but as a matter of goals. Moreover, it does not look back to the source of a command or an action, but it looks forward to the consequences or goal of an action. But this way, like the moral theist's approach, is an attempt to justify actions on the basis of some *foundation*. It proposes an ultimate moral justification of all actions (i.e., happiness), and the ultimate foundation, which justifies other actions, does not need further justification; it is self-justifying.

The search for foundations is probably a natural human tendency, but in Western philosophy it is also the result of the profound influence of Euclid, the Greek mathematician. Around 300 B.C.E. Euclid organized the science of geometry. He began with definitions and axioms. Axioms are basic statements that are self-evident and unquestionable. One axiom, for example, says "Two parallel lines never meet." If the lines are parallel, like railroad tracks, then no matter how long they are, they will never touch. Anyone who thinks about this statement will see that it must be true. Then, Euclid drew out the implications of these basic foundations, and proved a large number of additional truths about lines, squares, circles, angles, and so on. Each truth was shown to be based on the definitions and axioms. When you study geometry today, you are studying Euclid's ideas.

Euclid's system was so impressive that it was accepted as the perfect model of all science and indeed all knowledge. Even if you have never heard of Euclid, your way of thinking and your basic assumptions have been shaped by his book. That explains, in part, why philosophers often search for foundations.

Understanding the Dilemma
PROTECTOR OR EUTHANIZER?

The dilemma in this section is clear and urgent. If a person is suffering terribly with no real chance of relief, is it ever permissible to end the person's life? Should we stop the pain, but kill the innocent person, or should we preserve life, but allow the tormenting pain to continue? Everyone feels a strong reluctance or inability to take another person's life, but everyone also feels a strong desire or necessity to help people in terrible pain.

Our first impulse is probably to try to escape the dilemma by denying that it exists. We might say that if a person asks us for help in ending his or her life, then we are not really killing anyone. Or we might claim that pain is always manageable with the right drugs, and no one needs to suffer at the end of life. But neither of these attempts is successful. Helping a person who wants to die is not the same as other kinds of killing, but it is still killing. And unfortunately, drugs cannot work miracles on the human body. In some cases, people have to make a difficult decision about ending a life or allowing the agony to continue.

Both sides in this debate believe that they are taking the compassionate position. Both want to do what is best for people, especially people who need help the most. The protector believes that certain classes of people are particularly vulnerable: the handicapped, the very ill, unwanted infants, the elderly. Handicapped or physically challenged individuals make many healthy, busy people uncomfortable. Many don't want to take the time or make the effort to help, perhaps because they don't want to be reminded that they could easily be in the same position. But protectors believe that those who are in the greatest need deserve the most help. In addition to the physical problems, society's tendency to ignore or deny or hide the neediest people makes it even more important to preserve their basic rights. True compassion means protecting the innocent. Protectors believe that the euthanasia movement is just the latest and most extreme expression of American society's impatience with (or fear of) people who are not "successful."

However, from the point of view of euthanizers, protectors are hard and insensitive, and it is euthanizers who are taking the compassionate position. Euthanizers want to relieve pain and end suffering. They say they want to help people who need help, and sometimes patients dying of cancer need help. Stewart Alsop, the journalist, described a young man with whom he shared a hospital room when Alsop had cancer. The young man had a large, cancerous tumor in his stomach, and drugs could reduce the pain for a short time. But soon the man would begin to whimper, then moan "very low, as though he didn't want to wake me. Then he would begin to howl, like a dog" (Baird, Rosenbaum, eds., 1989, p. 7). Alsop said if the patient were an animal, he would mercifully be put to sleep. "No human being with a spark of pity could let a living thing suffer so, to no good end." Real compassion leads to euthanasia, supporters say. So protectors and euthanizers disagree over who needs help, and over the proper expression of compassion.

Another basic disagreement arises from the two sides' defenses of their views. The protector in this section argues that the duty to respect life takes priority over the duty to relieve pain. In fact, the principle of preserving human life is the highest moral principle. Since no other duty or principle can outweigh that one, it has the status of an absolute guide. Some principle has to be the most important one, and the protector says respecting human life is the best candidate for the position.

But the euthanizer in this section rejects absolutes. We all have many moral duties, including the duty to preserve human life and the duty to relieve pain. But it is a mistake to think that one always outweighs the other. In some situations one should preserve life at the cost of some pain, but in other situations the pain is so great and the time remaining is so short that the life should be ended. The decision depends on the wishes of the patient, the quality of life saved, the chances for improvement, and perhaps other factors. But life and death are too complicated to be governed by absolute rules.

Thus a protector tries to solve the dilemma by showing that the principle of respecting life should never be violated. A euthanizer tries to solve the dilemma by claiming that the particular facts of a case will indicate which side is the morally right choice. Therefore, a major disagreement between protectors and euthanizers is over absolute principles. Must we have some highest priority, or can we adapt our priorities to different circumstances?

The disagreement over absolute principles is a difficult, abstract issue. It isn't about euthanasia itself, but the nature of moral reasoning. The protector does not claim that the rule "preserve human life" is self-evident, like "the whole is greater than the part." Nor does this essay claim that the rule is a divine command and therefore absolutely binding. Rather, the claim is that if we want to think and behave in a rational, consistent way, we need some basic guiding principle that allows us to order all our other principles. Without some stable foundation, our responses to moral problems will be capricious and subjective, depending on our varying feelings of the moment. Even the euthanizer has an absolute principle. It is "Never allow a person to suffer terribly; always prevent extreme, relentless pain." The euthanizer will not violate that principle, even to save a life.

The euthanizer's response is that we should be guided by the facts of each case, and not by absolute rules. Suffering is a matter of degree, and therefore the euthanizer rejects the charge that he or she is following an absolute rule. No rule can indicate when the suffering is great enough to justify euthanasia. Only a compassionate, informed, experienced judgment can guide us.

A final basic disagreement concerns the consequences of legalizing or validating euthanasia. The protector predicts that if doctors begin practicing euthanasia, people's attitudes will change. They will regard doctors differently, and they may lose hope more easily. The basic idea is that having an absolute prohibition against destroying innocent human life gives us a clear, plausible boundary between what is morally permissible and what isn't. Once we eliminate that boundary, we cannot find another clear, plausible boundary to take its place. How much pain is necessary? Who decides? How do we define "consent"? Are financial considerations ever relevant?

These are difficult questions, the euthanizer says, but they are not impossible to answer. Of course the decisions are complex, but that just means we must gather as much information as possible and consider it carefully. It doesn't mean we should give up. People deal competently with other very complex matters without making one factor the only consideration. If euthanasia were legalized, it would lead to a whole network of laws, restrictions, clarifications, and guidelines to help us make decisions, just as divorce, adoption, organ transplants, and job termination have. Society would not collapse into anarchy, but would begin dealing with a difficult problem in a more humane way.

PROTECTOR

1. Thinking morally is not the same as feeling pity.
2. A wise moral decision must be based on a good reason, which means an acceptable principle.
3. Some principle must be paramount, and the best candidate for the ultimate principle is "respect human life."
4. The decision to euthanize patients who are in pain is not based on a workable principle, but is a return to acting arbitrarily on emotional impulses.

EUTHANIZER

5. The compassionate and right thing to do in some rare cases is to relieve a person's suffering by ending his or her life.

6. The world is too complicated for us to rely on absolute rules.
7. It isn't mere life that people value but the quality of life.
8. Allowing medical professionals to end some patients' lives will not lead to a wholesale disregard for patients' rights; to believe it will is to assume that future generations cannot think for themselves.

FOR FURTHER STUDY

Historical Examples

PROTECTOR: Albert Schweitzer. *Civilization and Ethics.* A. and C. Black, Ltd, 1923. Argues that reverence for life in all forms is the fundamental principle of morality.

EUTHANIZER: David Hume. "Of Suicide." In Stephen Copley and Andrew Edgar, eds. *David Hume: Selected Essays.* Oxford University Press, 1993. Originally written in 1757, published posthumously. Argues that suicide is natural and in no way contradicts the belief in a divine creator.

OTHER SOURCES

Neal Bernards, ed. *Euthanasia: Opposing Viewpoints.* Greenhaven, 1989. Variety of accessible articles on different aspects of euthanasia.

Robert M. Baird, Stuart E. Rosenbaum, eds. *Euthanasia: The Moral Issues.* Prometheus, 1989. Like Bernards, but slightly more advanced.

Tom L. Beauchamp, ed. *Intending Death: The Ethics of Assisted Suicide and Euthanasia.* Prentice-Hall, 1995. Sophisticated articles for more advanced students.

Gerald Dworkin, R.G. Frey, Sissela Bok. *Euthanasia and Physician-Assisted Suicide: For and Against.* Cambridge University Press, 1998. Dworkin and Frey present a variety of arguments in favor of euthanasia, Bok a variety against.

Willard Gaylin, Leon R. Kass, Edmund D. Pellegrino, Mark Siegler, "Doctors Must Not Kill." *Journal of the American Medical Association* 259, no. 14 (April 8, 1988): 2139–2140.

Nancy Dubler, David Nimmons. *Ethics on Call.* Vintage, 1993. Well-written chapters on various issues in bioethics.

Margaret Pabst Battin. *The Least Worst Death: Essays in Bioethics on the End of Life.* Oxford University Press, 1994. Defends euthanasia on the grounds of mercy and autonomy, and criticizes protector arguments.

Peter Singer. *Rethinking Life and Death: The Collapse of Our Traditional Ethics.* St. Martin's, 1995. Ambitious attempt to reinvent morality based on a notion of quality of life; defends some types of euthanasia (as well as abortion, infanticide, and respect for animals).

Herbert Hendin. *Seduced by Death: Doctors, Patients, and the Dutch Cure.* Norton, 1997. Critical report on euthanasia in the Netherlands, by a protector.

Edwin R. DuBose, Ronald P. Hamel, Laurence J. O'Connell, eds. *A Matter of Principles? Ferment in U.S. Bioethics.* Trinity Press International, 1994. Articles examining the roles of principles in reasoning about bioethics, with explorations of alternatives.

CONNECTIONS

HUMANIST OR OBJECTIVIST?

Your values are a very important part of your worldview. In this part of the book you have been reading about goals in life, obligations to others, happiness, rules, society's restraints, and other aspects of morality. One conclusion you have probably drawn is that the topic of values is complicated. But tangled areas like values are just the places you should try to find connections. In some cases, an individual's values are in conflict, and those tensions create not only confusion but often dissatisfaction on the job, anxiety over important decisions, and needless problems with others. Making connections among your values is simply unifying and integrating your character, and that benefits everyone.

What connections can we find among the positions in Chapter 3? Is there some basic issue that divides all the positions into two camps? We used that method to organize the positions in Chapters 1 and 2, where we found basic divisions between transcendentalists and naturalists, and between conservatives and liberals. Can we apply the same method here?

I think we can, so long as we remember that we are picking out only one thread in a densely woven piece of cloth. When we say in Chapter 1, for example, that atheists are similar to mortalists, and both are naturalists, we are focusing on only one aspect of the two positions. Both positions believe that the natural world described by science, including the physical body, is all there is. But we could find other relationships between these two positions, and between these two and the other views presented in Chapter 1. Classifying all the positions as transcendentalist or naturalist is only one way of organizing them. You can probably think of others.

The same applies to Chapter 3. I can suggest one basic division, but you might see others. The division I am thinking of is this: does morality depend upon human desires or upon something else? In other words, are right and wrong relative to human beings and their wishes, or are they more objective than that? Are all valuable things in some way dependent upon satisfying people's desires? Or are some things valuable independently of any human being's desires? Do all obligations ultimately boil down to the duty to increase people's happiness? Or do people have duties and obligations based on conscience, or God's will, or nature, which are binding without considering the promotion of human happiness?

If you believe that all right and wrong, or good and evil, *do* depend on human desires, then you are a "humanist." But if you think morality has an *objective* basis, independent of satisfying human desires, then you are an "objectivist." This is one way of organizing the positions in Chapter 3.

Probably the clearest examples of a humanist and an objectivist are in Section 3.4, "Is Happiness the Standard of Morality?" A utilitarian believes that all right actions are actions that create the greatest happiness for the greatest number of people. That is his or her theory of morality. And it clearly makes the utilitarian a humanist: the utilitarian believes morality depends on satisfying human desires, which is the same as doing whatever makes the most people happy. However, a formalist (the opposite of a utilitarian) claims that morality depends on the fundamental difference between humans and animals. Human beings can deliberately obey rules, but animals are merely conditioned, or trained. The ability to follow rules gives us a special, *moral* way of thinking, which is different from trying to satisfy our desires. Therefore, in the formalist's view, doing the right thing is always obeying the relevant moral rule, such as "Tell the truth" and "Repay your debts." Behaving morally has nothing to do with trying to satisfy people's desires. Thus, a formalist is an objectivist.

Another example of an objectivist is in Section 3.5, "Is Society the Source of Values?" In that section you encountered a moral theist, who believes that morality depends upon God's commands. We all feel the absolute obligation of moral rules, such as children is wrong." We are as certain about this rule as we are about anything. Many people say that they would rather die than break it. Now the only possible source of such a grave, supreme obligation is God, a perfectly wise, compassionate, all-powerful being. Only the authority of God can provide an adequate basis for such an absolute command. Thus right and wrong do not depend on human desires but on God's commands. Morality is more than merely satisfying our desires.

The opposing position in Section 3.5 is functionalism. Functionalists believe that being moral does mean obeying rules, but the rules are invented by society. They are the rules that are necessary for society to function at all, rules human beings invented to make life easier. For example, we all have a moral obligation to tell the truth. Why? Because if people did not normally tell the truth the whole fabric of society would collapse. Society depends on communication, and communication depends on trusting people to tell the truth. Society depends on other basic rules as well. But the rules are creations of human society; they exist to serve human society. Therefore functionalists are humanists. Right and wrong depend on the human desire to live together in groups. Morality is a human invention, according to functionalists.

Notice that functionalists are similar to utilitarians because both are humanists. But they are different, too, because functionalists believe being moral means obeying certain rules. Utilitarians believe being moral means calculating the amount of happiness that will result from an action, and then doing whatever produces the greatest happiness. Rules are irrelevant at best, they say, and harmful (i.e., immoral) at worst, if a person puts obeying the rules above producing happiness. The functionalist replies that obeying the rules will lead to happiness in the long run, but that is not for you to calculate; your moral duty is to obey the rules that society prescribes to you. Hence a functionalist is similar to a formalist.

This disagreement between functionalists and utilitarians illustrates the important point that two positions can be similar in one respect—being humanists, for example—and different in other respects. If we made obedience to rules the basis of our classification, then functionalists and utilitarians would have to go into opposite groups. But if we make human desires the basis, then they go into the same group, i.e., humanists.

Section 3.1, "Is Pleasure the Only Value?," contrasts hedonism with pluralism. A hedonist says pleasure is good, and it is the only good. Everything else that we value is a means to that ultimate goal. A pluralist claims that there are many different values, some personal and some social.

A hedonist is clearly a humanist: an action is right if it produces pleasure, and wrong if it produces pain. Pleasure and pain are human feelings, and so good and evil depend on human nature and human desires, according to the hedonist. On the other hand, a pluralist believes there are other values besides pleasure. Pleasure is good, but it isn't the only good. Creativity, excellence, love, compassion, and justice are only a few of the many values we all recognize. However, all these values depend on people. They do not depend on *one* person, or on pleasure, but they do depend on human beings. That suggests that a pluralist is also a humanist.

But this conclusion would be too hasty. Pluralists also believe that beauty, nature, and God are important values. Beauty, they say, is an objective quality of things in the world, not a subjective experience. Nature, of course, is independent of human desires and goals. It is an objective value. And the same applies to God. Therefore, a pluralist is an objectivist. Not all values depend on human beings or arise out of human desires, even if some do.

Another section in Chapter 3 is Section 3.3, "Is Morality Relative?" A relativist says yes and an absolutist says no. Relativists believe that every society invents its own moral laws, and the laws are different in different societies. It is impossible to make an objective judgment of the various moral codes around the world. This position is similar to humanism. It sees morality as a human invention, based on human desires. Societies invent their own morality, according to a relativist, and one society's morality is just as legitimate as another's.

Absolutists argue that none of the differences between two societies can make an action right in one but wrong in another. If child abuse is wrong in one society, it must be wrong in every other society, because there is no basis for the difference in right and wrong. Furthermore, the theory of relativism breaks down when two societies come into contact. It cannot tell us whether an action is right or wrong. It is an untenable theory.

Most absolutists are, as a matter of fact, objectivists. They believe that morality is not based on human desires, but is a matter of obeying certain rules. The rules are universal and binding on everyone. We know the rules through our consciences. And most objectivists are absolutists. If morality is based on God's commands, or on nature, or something more objective than our desires, then it is universal and absolute. Or if it is based on our rationality—which makes us different from animals—then it is absolute, because all human beings everywhere are rational.

However, an absolutist *could* be a humanist, and vice versa. An absolutist could believe that morality depends on human desires, and that the most basic human desires are the same in all societies. Everyone wants freedom from fear, freedom from hunger, and freedom of thought, she or he might say. For example, the functionalist represented in Section 3.5 is an absolutist: moral rules are the same everywhere, but also a humanist: moral rules are human inventions. Nevertheless, it is probably easier for an absolutist to be an objectivist than a humanist. The diversity in different societies' actual moral values is hard to deny. It seems that people in different societies do have different desires and values, although it is difficult to say whether or not these are "basic" desires. The conclusion is that there is no logical barrier to an absolutist being a humanist, but the factual evidence seems to suggest that absolutism is closer to objectivism.

The idea that morality depends on human desires is also relevant to Section 3.2, "Can We Understand Happiness?" A definer says that we can define happiness, and goes on to claim that happiness is an inner state of mind. It is the feelings of confidence, self-respect, and optimism that people have when they are achieving most of their goals. That is what all happy people have in common. A skeptic, on the other hand, maintains that we cannot define happiness. No state of mind is common to all the people who are happy, because people are too complex and diverse. What makes some people happy makes others unhappy. We have no clear concept or definition of happiness.

Neither the definer nor the skeptic represented here is talking directly about morality. They are discussing happiness, not right and wrong. The definer says that we can define happiness, but does not say happiness is the basis of morality. It may be, or it may not be. A definer could believe that morality depends on objective facts in nature, or on God's commands, or on something else. So a definer could be an objectivist or a humanist.

But a skeptic would probably be an objectivist. Although the skeptic is not discussing morality, he or she does say that we cannot define happiness. So it is unlikely that the skeptic would go on to say that happiness is the basis of morality. If happiness is undefinable, but it is also the basis of morality, then we would not know what is right or wrong. We could not be sure that torturing babies is wrong. (The skeptic argues that we cannot define happiness as pleasure or the absence of pain.) But most people *are* sure that torturing babies is wrong.

We can know that some things are right and some wrong. Even a relativist admits that. Therefore, either happiness is definable, or happiness is not the basis of morality. Since the skeptic rejects the first of these implications, he or she must accept the second.

In the current controversy section, "Should Doctors Ever End People's Lives?," the protector says no and the euthanizer says yes. The protector argues that we should try to base our decision on principles rather than feelings. Moreover, we need a highest principle, or else we will go back and forth between contrasting duties, which is no better than shifting between emotional moods. The most reasonable candidate for our highest principle is "respect for life" because it allows for hope, and the principle "relieve suffering" is more vague and difficult to apply.

The opposing point of view, favoring euthanasia, claims that matters of life and death are too complicated to be reduced to a single principle. Many factors are relevant to each case, and we cannot say ahead of time which consideration will carry the most weight in a particular case. It depends on the specific circumstances. The euthanizer trusts our reasonableness and feelings of compassion.

While the two positions are clearly different, they do not fit the humanist–objectivist contrast very closely. A protector could be either a humanist or an objectivist. That is, a protector could regard the principle "respect life" as an expression of respect for humanity and human desires. We ought to abide by the principle because it is such a fundamental human drive. If that's what "respect life" means, and if that is why it is an absolute moral principle, then the protector is a humanist.

But "respect life" might mean we should respect all life, not just human life, because life itself is greater and more important than humanity. With that interpretation, the protector would be an objectivist because the basis of morality is something beyond human desires. Of course anyone who thinks the principle is a command from God is an objectivist. And protectors' emphasis on rules makes them similar to formalists, another kind of objectivist.

The euthanizer is closer to the humanist outlook, although he or she is not a perfect fit. The euthanizer says that there are no absolutes to guide our decisions about life and death, and that is different from objectivists' beliefs. Furthermore, the most important consideration for doctors and patients is the quality of life, including the joys, feelings, plans, and relationships people have. The emphasis on human experiences is similar to utilitarians' view that promoting human happiness is the foundation of moral thinking. So euthanizers are closer to humanism than objectivism. One should remember, however, that these connections are based only on selected aspects of the different positions. Emphasizing different aspects might lead to different connections.

The connections among the positions in Chapter 3 are perhaps more complicated than the ones in Chapters 1 and 2. In fact, tracing out the connections is one of the most challenging aspects of building your worldview. In practical terms it means that before you can *finally* decide on one position you must consider several other positions that are connected. For example, before you decide on utilitarianism over formalism, you should think about the definer and the muddler. If you are leaning toward utilitarianism, then you should accept the definer's view over the skeptic's. (If you believe that a right action is one that increases happiness, then you should be able to explain what happiness is.) And there are other connections to keep in mind as well.

Humanist	Objectivist
utilitarian	formalist
functionalist	moral theist
hedonist	pluralist
relativist	absolutist
definer	definer
euthanizer	skeptic
	protector

HUMANIST

1. Morality depends on human aims and desires; if people did not exist, nothing would be right or wrong.
2. Being moral means promoting happiness, one's own and others'.
3. Moral beliefs and rules seem very serious and obligatory, but that is because they are backed up by the most solemn institutions of society.
4. There is no doubt that morality is dependent upon society and its requirements; but it is difficult to determine whether all societies have the same requirements or different requirements.

OBJECTIVIST

5. Moral values are part of the objective world, built into the nature of things.
6. Being moral means following unshakable principles, which are not just guidelines for achieving happiness.
7. Human beings have a moral sense, or conscience, which makes us different from animals.
8. The concept of happiness is so broad and vague that it cannot be the foundation of morality.

CHAPTER FOUR

FREE WILL, MIND, AND HUMAN NATURE

4.1 ARE WE FREE?

Hard Determinist, Metaphysical Libertarian, or Soft Determinist?

The word "free" has several different meanings. When people talk about freedom they are usually talking about political freedom. We all understand what it means to be politically free, or to lack political freedom. If you are not in jail, then you are free, or freer than people who are in jail. If you can vote for government representatives, in an open and fair election, then you are free. If you can choose your own occupation, your place of residence, the ways to spend your money, then you are free. And there are other aspects of political freedom.

Philosophers discuss political freedom, but they also think about a more basic kind of freedom called "metaphysical freedom." Metaphysical freedom means freedom of choice, or the freedom to choose as you wish. The opposite of metaphysical freedom is having your choices determined. You make a choice, and no one forces you, but your choice is predetermined before you make it, perhaps by your past history, your environment, events in your brain, or something else.

Metaphysical freedom does not depend on having a wide array of options from which to choose. Some people say the North Koreans are not free because there is nothing in their stores to buy. But that is political freedom, or the lack of it. Even if you have sixteen brands of deodorant to choose from, is the choice you finally make really free, or is it determined by something (such as advertising)? That is the question of metaphysical freedom. This kind of freedom does not depend on elections, or a Bill of Rights. It depends on the basic nature of decisions and actions themselves.

The first essay in this section argues that all our actions are determined, and the second defends the view that we are free, in the metaphysical sense. The third tries to find a middle ground, and claims that we have a special kind of freedom.

NO: HARD DETERMINIST

"One World, Not Two"

According to the Judeo-Christian tradition, the natural world was created for humankind, for our nourishment and pleasure. People were made in God's image, and so we are fundamentally different from stones, plants, and animals. That difference is the basis of our self-respect and feelings of worth, so we insist on the difference adamantly. We go so far as to say that we are exempt from the laws that govern the natural world. We have free will.

But it is possible to think of ourselves as an integral part of the natural world. We feel a wonder and awe for the natural world, and so we could still respect ourselves as a part of it. In any case, we *are* part of the natural world, whether that makes us feel good or bad. Therefore we are governed by the same laws that govern everything else. Our thoughts and actions are determined, rather than free. They are caused by prior events and follow regular laws, just like everything else. We know that our thoughts and actions are determined because we know that all events are causally determined.

In every subject of inquiry scientists have discovered laws that explain why things happen the way they do. When we look at the sky, we see a vast mechanism of stars and planets whose movements we can predict to within seconds, over periods of thousands of years. Astronomers know exactly when the next solar eclipse will occur, and the one after that. On earth, chemists now play with the elements the way children play with building blocks. They put molecules together to create synthetic materials, such as nylon. Biologists have broken the genetic code, and with their artificially created organisms, they are beginning to rewrite it. They can make new crops that resist insects. In every domain, we continue to discover regular laws of cause and effect.

With regard to people, we understand how we are created at conception, and how we grow and change through the years. We use hundreds of different drugs to affect the body in dozens of different ways. The same is true of our minds: psychologists prescribe tranquilizers, stimulants, mood-elevating drugs. Alcohol affects the will. Many drugs affect perception and even consciousness itself. We also understand the stages in the growth of the personality and mind. We know what conditions in childhood will make a person shy as an adult, or outgoing, or competitive, ambitious, and so on.

Whether we look high or low, near or far, we find that everything is lawful and proceeds by cause and effect. The inevitable conclusion is that *all* events are causally determined. We have looked in such a variety of places—in the sky, in the earth, among living things, in the human body, even in the human mind. And the conclusion is always the same: nothing happens by chance. Everything is caused.

It is true, as some people point out, that there are events for which we have not yet found causes. One example is mutations. Sometimes two organisms produce an offspring that has a new property, unlike either parent. The genes in the two cells from the male and female simply change, and no one knows why. Another example is radio signals from several places in outer space. No one knows what is producing them. On earth, no one knows what caused the ice ages over the past half a million years. The earth became much colder, then it thawed, then it grew colder again, and so on four times. No one knows for sure why.

What are we to make of these mysteries? Should we decide that they are probably not caused at all, and no one will ever find the causes? Or should we decide that we will probably find the cause in the future? We don't want to decide blindly, without thinking. Which is the most probable statement? Two factors lead to the second belief, that we will find causes in the future. First, these unexplained events are highly unusual. There are so many events whose causes we do understand, and only a few that seem to be uncaused. In fact, it is difficult to think of examples of events that appear to be uncaused. The fact that they are so rare suggests that they are, at bottom, like all the other events. They really are causally determined. We simply haven't found the causes yet.

Second, scientists have a long record of finding the causes of events. In the past, we didn't know what caused earthquakes. Some people might even have decided they were uncaused. But now we know that movements of the huge plates covering the earth cause earthquakes. People didn't know why some elderly individuals became senile. Now we know that the loss of function is caused in many cases by Alzheimer's disease. In the twenties, some people exhibited strange symptoms like loss of hair and teeth, and brittle bones. No one knew what caused the problems. But then scientists discovered vitamins, added them to the patients' diets, and the problems disappeared. The problems were caused by vitamin deficiency.

In other words, there are many cases where we did not know the cause of something, and then we found it. It is reasonable to believe that the same process of discovering causes of things will continue in the future. Therefore, even if there are areas where events happen that we cannot explain, all the evidence suggests that those events are causally determined, and some day we will discover the causes. It is virtually certain, then, that our own thinking and behavior are causally determined.

It's true, we do not know the causes of people's actions or decisions. We cannot predict what a person will think or say at any particular time. But our ignorance shouldn't mislead us. It is still extremely likely that something—some combination of environmental influences, memories, bodily states, or past experiences—causes a person's decisions. The combination of factors brings about the person's thought; given those preceeding events, the person had to make that particular decision.

How could it be otherwise? If we recognize lawful regularities in every aspect of the universe, then we would be irrational to claim that one small area—human willóis utterly different, and not determined by prior events. It would be like saying that scientists have understood why earthquakes occur, why machines work, why blue-eyed parents have blue-eyed children, and so on and so on, except on a little island in the Pacific Ocean. There none of the laws apply. Everything that happens is a miracle.

A ridiculous attitude, to be sure. And yet when the little island is our own minds, we assume we are different, and above laws. We should be more mature, as well as more logical.

Key Concepts

part of nature	self-respect	determined
governed by law	mechanism	generalization

Critical Questions

1. What does the hard determinist mean by "determined"?
2. Suppose that the idea that all actions are determined is very upsetting. Suppose it makes some people think they can commit crimes without being responsible. What do those reactions tell us about the truth or falsity of the theory? Do they show that the theory must be false?
3. How are the hard determinist's statements about the sky and the elements relevant to the conclusion that all our thoughts and behavior are causally determined? How do they support the conclusion?
4. Suppose you want to buy a new car. You like Fords, but you also want a reliable car. So you ask ten people who already own Fords if they are reliable. They all say that they never had any trouble with their Fords, though some are as much as eight years old. Does that make it *probable* that the Ford you buy will be trouble-free? Is it possible that the Ford you buy will break down after a week? How is this argument about Fords similar to the essay's argument about determinism?
5. The essay says that people who believe in free will think that the human mind is like a small island. How is it like an island? What does the writer mean?
6. Do you think that you are part of the natural world? Does that mean that all your actions are caused and governed by natural laws?

YES: METAPHYSICAL LIBERTARIAN

"Free Will and Common Sense"

The strongest argument supporting the belief in freedom of the will is plain, old common sense. If you simply look at what is evident right under your nose, you will see that you are free. Only a person in the grip of a powerful ideology could deny the obvious facts, and assert that he or she is really merely a puppet.

By free action I mean an action that is not coerced or constrained by anything. Free actions are those that are up to you. You choose them, and you could have chosen differently, because you were not forced to choose as you did. In contrast, determinism is the belief that the world is one huge, interlocking mechanism. Your actions are the necessary results of changes in your environment. Determinism says that we are like robots, whose movements are determined by their "input," or perhaps by stored instructions, but not by their own choice.

Such a theory is false, and you can see that it is false if you observe the contents of your own mind as you deliberate. Imagine that you are considering two alternatives, like having a cheese sandwich or a tuna sandwich for lunch. And then you decide to have cheese. You begin to make your sandwich. If you recall such an incident in your own life, and *observe* the thoughts and feelings that go through your mind as you deliberate and then choose, you will see that nothing determined your choice. You can see this as clearly as you see your own hand.

You probably thought about one possibility, and then the other. You thought about the taste, the ingredients, the preparation, and some of these made you feel better than the others. After a few seconds of this kind of deliberation, you decided on cheese. But it was a free choice. The feelings didn't force you. You could just as easily have chosen tuna.

Of course this sort of observation is different from observing an external object, since in this case you are looking within your own mind. But that is something people do all the time, for example, when they say, "I just had a strange thought," or "I feel a strong craving for applesauce." Such statements are not odd or questionable. In fact, a person's reports of the contents of his own mind are extremely reliable. It might be easier for you to observe your own mind than it is for you to observe the physical world around you.

So if you do look within your self as you make a decision, and you do not see anything forcing you to go one way rather than another, that should be very reliable evidence that you are free. Moreover, I know what it is like when I am *not* free. For example, if a mugger says, "Give me your money or I'll shoot you," I know that I am being coerced. When I look within myself, I recognize the fear, and I see how it determines my behavior. In that case I am not free. But most of the time, when I observe my own deliberations, I do not find any such coercion. I can choose one thing or another.

Determinists will not admit this because they are impressed by science. Scientists look for determining causes of things, and sometimes they find them. (Actually their failures to find causes are far more numerous than their successes.) But the determinist's thinking is muddled. Science is based on observations of objects and events, as the determinist acknowledges. But the scientists' knowledge of the objects and events begins with their knowledge of their own experience, the contents of their own minds. First come observations of the way things look to them, in their own inner experience, and then, on the basis of those, they make judgments about the objects themselves, outside their mind.

Think about an example from everyday life. If you are driving on a hot, flat road with your friends, you might say, "We should slow down for that water on the road ahead." Your friends reply that there is no water on the road. It is only an illusion, a mirage, and they turn out to be right. Then you say, "Well it looked to me like there was water on the road," and you are right; it did *look* like that to you, even though there was no water. You first know how things seem to you. Then you decide whether you are right or not. "How things seem to you" refers to your inner experience, which may or may not correspond to reality. The inner experience comes first, and then you decide the world is really like that (or you decide that you were mistaken).

Every scientific observation should be prefaced with the words "It seems to me that. . . ." When a scientist conducts an experiment and checks the results, he or she should say, "It seems to me that the litmus paper is red," or "It seems to me that the scale says 368 grams," or "It seems to me that the rat has stopped." Every observation is, at the most basic level, a report of what is in one's mind. If others agree that the scale says 368 grams, then the scientist can conclude that his perception is correct. But first comes his knowledge of his own mind, or his own experience.

Our experience is an experience of freedom. The results of science tell us that everything is determined. But we should trust our experience. Determinists put the cart before the horse. They ignore the inner observation of freedom, and accept only the outer observation of a mechanical world. But inner observations are more trustworthy than outer, because inner observations are the basis of outer observations.

Key Concepts

free action	deliberation	coerce
introspection	choice	mechanism

Critical Questions

1. How does the metaphysical libertarian define "free action"?
2. According to the essay, what can we observe to know that we are free? Does the metaphysical libertarian believe that nothing causes the choices he or she makes?
3. Do you agree with the essay that the person who gives money to a mugger with a gun is *not* making a free choice? If I see a pastry in a shop window and feel a very strong desire for it, and then go in and buy it, am I acting freely?
4. Do you think I should trust my observations of myself? Is it possible that something (a fear, a desire) could influence my deliberations, and cause my choice, even if I am not aware of it?
5. A metaphysical libertarian says a person knows one of the following statements, and then knows the other on the basis of the first. Which is dependent on which?
   (*a*) The tomato is red. (*b*) The tomato looks red to me.
   (*a*) The room feels hot. (*b*) The room is hot.
   (*a*) The soup tastes salty to me. (*b*) The soup has salt in it.
6. (*a*) Suppose you listen to the horn on Joe's car and the horn on Mike's car, and Joe's is clearly louder. But several of your friends all say Mike's is louder. Would you decide Mike's is louder?
   (*b*) Suppose you trip and fall, but you aren't hurt, and you feel fine. But your friends say that you must have a headache. Would you decide that you have a headache?

YES: SOFT DETERMINIST

"Verbal Disputes, Facts, and Free Will"

The problem of free will and determinism is always confusing to people who encounter it for the first time. I think that is because they do not realize that there are actually two problems: deciding what the facts are, and deciding what the words "free will" and "determinism" mean. The words are as important as the facts. It is necessary to understand the two sides of the problem before we can answer the question "Do people have free will?"

To an outsider, philosophers often seem to be obsessed with words. They take a short statement and tease out five different interpretations of it. Or they do not give a straight answer to a simple question, but say, "Well, it depends on what you mean by _____."

But they have a good reason for putting language under a microscope. We think with words. We describe the world and our experiences with words. There are no ideas except ones expressed in particular words. There are no facts that we can know about except ones described in particular words.

Words are like rows and rows of glass jars in our heads that hold experiences or facts. Some jars are big, some small, some short and fat, some with irregular shapes, some tinted green, brown, or blue, in hundreds of different combinations. But no experiences or facts can exist for us except in those jars, i.e., words. So if we want to understand our human experience of the world, then we must examine the "containers" very carefully.

Philosophers understand the importance of language as well as poets do. Even so, philosophers sometimes do not pay as much attention to words as they should. If that happens, they can fall into a verbal dispute. A verbal dispute is a disagreement that occurs because two people use the same word but attach *different* meanings to it without realizing it.

For example, is Hamlet real? People can argue about this all day without reaching any conclusion. For one person, "real" means something you can touch, or see, something material. In this sense, Hamlet is not real. For the other, "real" means something we all know about, or something that has properties we all agree upon. For this person, Hamlet is real. One person will offer evidence and arguments that seem perfectly convincing to him. But the other person rejects them, because to her they seem to be irrelevant.

Are erotic movies art? One person will say yes, another will say no, even if they agree on all the facts. One may use the word "art" to mean an entertaining representation of some aspect of life. Paintings are art, and so is TV. To the other, the word " may mean something that is thought provoking, continually interesting, and beautiful. TV and erotic movies do not qualify. But if they do not realize that they mean different things by "art," they will talk past each other and argue forever.

Some disputes about free will may be merely verbal disputes. People may define "free will" in different ways. To avoid that fruitless debate, it is essential to be perfectly clear about the meaning of the term "free will." In fact, people have used the term in two different ways. I think one way is correct. That is, it is closer to what ordinary people mean when they use the word "free." But we must understand both definitions if we want to avoid confusion.

One way to define "free will" is to say a person is free so long as her choices are *not caused*. That means that nothing whatever forces her to make one choice or another. Suppose that Helen looked at two blouses and decided to buy the green blouse rather than the red one, for no particular reason. She was in a hurry, she had to choose, and she chose green. It wasn't important; she could have chosen red just as easily. Now if it really is true that she could have chosen red, then her choice must not have been caused. If it *was* caused (by a fleeting memory of a green skirt she had at home, for example), then she could not have chosen the red blouse in the same situation (with the same memories). Many people say that their choices are free, in the sense that they could have made different choices in the same situations. When they say "free," they mean uncaused, or could have been different. We can call this the *uncaused* definition of "free will."

The other definition says that a person is free so long as her choices are *caused by herself*. That means that her own thoughts or wishes cause her to choose green rather than red. She is free because she is doing what she wants, and that is what "free" means. In our example, we can imagine that Helen's brief memory of her green skirt caused her to choose the green blouse. It wasn't a salesperson, or a loud commercial on TV, or a "Sale" sign, or anything outside of herself. She made a free decision because she did what she wanted to do, not what others wanted her to do, or what some external factor forced her to do. If some external power forces her to go against her wishes and values, then she is not free. But so long as no external forces compel her, and her choices are caused by her own thoughts and values, then she is free. We can call this the *self-caused* definition of "free will."

It is necessary to decide which definition best expresses what we usually have in mind when we think of being free. If we do not decide on one definition, then we may argue endlessly because we are talking about two different things without realizing it. It seems to me that the self-caused definition is correct. When we say we are free, we mean that nothing prevents us from doing what we want. We *also* mean that we could have acted differently and made a different choice, as the uncaused definition emphasizes. But when we say that, we do not mean that we could have acted differently with the *same* thoughts and wishes. When we say we could have acted differently, we mean that we could have if our thoughts and feelings had been different. The uncaused definition ignores this point.

But choosing one definition of "free" does not end the debate. Even if people agree on the meaning of the word, they can still disagree on the facts. Is everything that happens caused, or are some events uncaused? ("Cause" means make to happen; if *A* causes *B*, then when *A* occurs, *B* must follow.) Some people believe that all events, including all our choices and decisions, are the necessary results of prior causes. Given a person's desires and thoughts and beliefs, the person *had* to choose green over red. She could not have chosen red, so long as she had the personality and tastes she had. A person who believes that everything is caused is a determinist.

Other people believe that choices are not causally determined. A person is different from the material world, according to this position. A person is not just a machine, in which one gear moves another. We have some free play in our choices. A person's desires and thoughts do not *cause* her to choose green. She could have the very same desires and thoughts, but decide on a whim to take red instead. In the human mind, prior events do not absolutely require one outcome or another. Even in physics, the old determinist view is breaking down. In the twentieth century, physicists have said that the movements of the tiniest particles in an atom may not be strictly determined. The world is unpredictable, and that is specially true of the human mind. Let's call a person who believes this a libertarian.

Here the dispute is over facts, not just words. A determinist believes the facts are one way, and a libertarian believes they are another way. Now we have two issues, about the meaning of "free," and about the extent to which events are caused. On the first issue, we distinguished the uncaused definition of "free" and the self-caused definition. I believe the self-caused definition is correct. On the second issue, we distinguished the determinist and the libertarian. I believe the determinist is right about the facts. In my opinion, it is simply inconceivable that events could be uncaused. We cannot grasp the idea. We cannot sincerely believe that it rained on Tuesday, for example, but for no reason. Or that the lamp fell, but nothing caused it to fall. Of course we often do not *know* the cause. But that is different. I think libertarians are confusing the idea that *there is no* cause with the idea that we do not know the cause.

However, I realize that some people disagree with me. Everyone must decide which definition of "free" is best, and which description of the world is best. That leads to four possible positions.

All determinists (1 and 2) agree on the fact that everything is caused. But they define "free" differently, so they disagree on free will. Hard determinists say determinism proves that we are *not* free. Soft determinists say we can be

FACT		
	DETERMINIST	LIBERTARIAN
MEANING UNCAUSED	1. Hard Determinist (not free)	3. Free Libertarian (free)
SELF-CAUSED	2. Soft Determinist (free)	4. Random Libertarian (not free)

free, so long as our choices are caused by ourselves rather than by external forces. I believe the soft determinist position is the most reasonable one.

All libertarians (3 and 4) agree on the fact that some events are not caused. But again, they define "free" differently, so they disagree on free will. Free libertarians say we are free, since our choices are uncaused. But random libertarians say that our choices are uncaused, and therefore what we do is unpredictable, random, and accidental. Our choices are not caused by our own desires and plans. That is not doing what we want to do, so we are *not* free.

These four possibilities show that, while the problem of free will seems simple on the surface, it is actually very complicated. The complications cause misunderstandings among people. The average person who has not studied philosophy believes that we are free. And I think that is right; we are free. But I also believe it is important to understand exactly what that statement means. If we think carefully about the meanings of words, and about the facts, we can avoid verbal disputes and misunderstandings. More importantly, we can understand the complexities of our own beliefs.

Key Concepts

verbal dispute	self-caused	free libertarian
cause	hard determinist	random libertarian
uncaused	soft determinist	

Critical Questions

1. According to the soft determinist, why do philosophers pay close attention to words?
2. What is a verbal dispute?
3. What are the two ways in which the word "free" is usually defined?
4. How can people argue about definitions? Can't a person define a word in any way she or he pleases? What is the soft determinist's opinion on the correct meaning of "free"? Is the opinion supported?
5. What is the factual issue in the free will problem? What is the soft determinist's position on the factual question, and why does he or she hold it?
6. Suppose every part of my personality is strictly determined by my environment (e.g., smothering parents, sheltered childhood, conformist peers). My personality determines my choices later in life. Am I acting freely, according to the soft determinist? What do you think?

Methods and Techniques
INTROSPECTION

If you take a psychology course, the teacher might show you a labyrinth, with a lot of turns and dead ends, and ask you to draw an unbroken line from the outer edge to the center. After you have solved the puzzle, she or he might show you another one, and say, "This time, as you work on the puzzle, pay attention to what you are thinking and feeling *as you work*." You start, and you might talk to yourself like this: "Let's see, now I am looking at the center and at the outer edges. Should I begin with the entrance on the right, or should I begin in the center and work my way back to the edge? How to choose? Now I am being distracted by those people talking." And so on. After you finished, you could tell the teacher what went on in your mind as you worked.

The act of noticing or observing the processes of your own mind is called introspection. We can observe flowers and trees, listen to a lecture, and enjoy a meal, but we can also observe ourselves doing these things. I do not mean in a mirror—that would be observing our bodies—but directly, or inwardly. We observe our own thoughts, feelings, hopes, fantasies, doubts, and so on.

Introspection is an important and puzzling ability, so we should be careful in describing it. It is not the same as one of the five senses. For example, if the psychology teacher presses a cut-out letter of the alphabet on your back, you can probably identify the letter without seeing it. But you are using your sense of touch to acquire information about that physical object; you are not introspecting your own mind. Or if you taste a fine wine, and try to discover the "fresh, clear, and crisp" flavor the expert says it has, then you are using your sense of taste to acquire information about that wine. That is not introspection either.

Introspection means observing things about yourself, not objects in the world. That means your inner self, not your body. When you observe your face in a mirror, you are not introspecting. On the other hand, if you close your eyes, raise your eyebrows, and try to notice how it *feels* to raise your eyebrows, then you are using introspection. As you taste the wine, you pay close attention to the wine and try to describe it. But you can also try to notice how you search for the right words. Attending to the wine is just observation; attending to your own search for words is introspection.

In introspection you observe something that no one else could ever possibly observe. For example, suppose you have a backache from sitting and typing too long. It's a dull, constant muscle ache right in the middle of your back. If you watch TV or do something else you can almost forget about it, but if you turn your attention entirely to the soreness, it can almost fill your mind. But no one else can feel your backache. Your friend can notice that you have a backache, because you walk stiffly and hold your back. But she cannot observe it directly, as you can. She cannot feel it, or introspect it. In fact, everything that you introspect is completely beyond the reach of other people. And whatever other people can observe, like your face, you do not know through introspection. You know them through observation, like everyone else.

Our ability to introspect our own minds raises numerous philosophical questions. One is about free will: if introspection tells you that you are free, but observation tells you that everything is determined, which do you believe?

Understanding the Dilemma
HARD DETERMINIST, METAPHYSICAL LIBERTARIAN, OR SOFT DETERMINIST?

Section 4.1 is about free will. People care very much about freedom, and your image of yourself depends in part on whether or not you believe you are free. A libertarian is a person who believes we are free to make our own choices, and a hard determinist is a person who believes we aren't. A soft determinist claims that we are determined and free at the same time.

In the introduction to this section, I said that the issue is about metaphysical freedom, not political freedom. In other words, the issue is whether or not any choice or decision you make is really free. Political freedom was the topic of Section 2.2. Political freedom concerns the range of choices you have, or the variety of alternatives before you, such as the variety of news sources you may read, the range of occupations you may pursue, political candidates you may vote for, and so on. Metaphysical freedom concerns your choice of one particular alternative: was your choice free, or was it causally determined? And what do we mean by "freedom" anyway? Those are the questions these three essays consider.

They are fascinating questions. Do you think that everything you do is determined beforehand, before you do it? Is your future already fixed and set, but you just don't know what it is? Was it determined long ago that you would read this page at just this time? Was it determined by your childhood, the things you enjoyed and the things you didn't, your high school career, your parents' decisions, their income, your college counselor, other friends' remarks, the things you heard about job opportunities, interesting courses, your schedule this week, the conversation you had a half hour ago, and so on? Did all these causes lead inevitably to your actions at this moment?

Or are your choices not determined by previous events? You might believe that all these sorts of events influence you, and you may be aware of many facts and conditions, but that at the moment of choice, you decide which way to go. The previous events do not determine which choice you will make. If you believe your choice is not determined, then you are a metaphysical libertarian. Your view is similar to the view presented in the second essay.

A hard determinist believes that everything is caused and determined. Not only are your actions determined, but your thoughts, feelings, moods, and imaginings are also strictly determined. When you wish for something, like a cold Coke, or when you suddenly remember something, like a remark your friend made this morning, something caused that wish and that memory. There was a reason you had that wish at exactly that time, instead of a different wish. And if you decide to buy a Coke, something caused your decision. No one knows what caused your decision. A hard determinist does not claim that he or she *knows* all the causes of people's actions and choices, but says there must *be* some causes. There must be some causes for everything that happens. And therefore everything is determined.

Libertarians and determinists have different basic conceptions of the world and of people. (On the basic view of the world, hard and soft determinists line up together against libertarians.) Libertarians see the world as extremely complicated, so complicated that something completely new might happen at any time. Things are unpredictable and sometimes chaotic. Determinists see the world as orderly and governed by laws. Everything has its place, and remains in the proper relation to everything else. As for people, libertarians trust their own perceptions. They are suspicious of experts and the established "truth." They know what they see, and if scientists tell them they are mistaken, then they can go fly a kite. Determinists believe that their own perceptions are sometimes wrong, and always limited. A large group of people will probably have a better understanding of a situation than the determinist will, especially if the group is made up of trained, skillful scientists.

That is the basic issue in this section. But as you reflect on the problem you will probably soon realize that it has two dimensions, a factual dimension and a verbal dimension. That is, in deciding between determinism and libertarianism you should think about the meaning of the word "free." That is the point the third essay makes. If you are a libertarian, then you must believe that, in fact, we are free, *and* you must be able to explain what that means. It means that nothing causes your actions. We can observe our freedom within our own minds.

A hard determinist defines "free" the same way as a libertarian, but says that everything is caused, and so we are not free. A soft determinist defines "free" in a different way. He or she says free actions are caused, but they are caused by oneself. A soft determinist believes that everything is determined, but that some actions are free and some are not. The free actions are those that are caused (determined) by *oneself* rather than by something outside of oneself. A soft determinist tries to find a middle way between determinism and libertarianism, and does this by defining "free" in a special way. "Free" means self-caused. In general, to decide between libertarianism and determinism, you must make two decisions: you must decide what the words "free" and "determined" *mean*, and you must decide what the facts are. The third essay describes the basic options you have.

So, what is your view? Are you a hard determinist, a libertarian, or a soft determinist? Your decision on the issue of free will and determinism is an important part of your worldview. It is one of the most fundamental questions. Your belief will affect the way you think about human nature, social policies, other people, and yourself.

DETERMINIST

1. I am a product of many factors that have made me what I am, and which continue to shape all of my behavior.
2. The natural world is basically uniform and lawful, and I am part of the natural world.
3. My own personal impressions can be misleading, and if they conflict with the careful observations of many scientists, I should believe the scientists.

4. A belief in determinism will lead us to search for the causes of behavior, which eventually will enable us to help people in many ways.

METAPHYSICAL LIBERTARIAN

5. I am in control of my own life.
6. Human beings are not part of the natural world, but are different, set apart, precisely because we can choose how to live.
7. My inner experience of making a choice is proof enough that I am free, regardless of what scientists say happens elsewhere in the world.
8. If people believe all their actions are determined, they will become irresponsible, or lose all their initiative, or sink into despair.

SOFT DETERMINIST

9. The issue of free will depends on questions of meaning as much as it depends on questions of fact.
10. We should distinguish four possibilities, not two, based on different definitions of "free" and different beliefs about causation.
11. All the determinist's beliefs are correct, except for a mistaken definition of the term "free."
12. Since free actions are those that are caused by one's own thoughts and desires, rather than by external forces, we are normally free.

FOR FURTHER STUDY

Historical Examples

DETERMINIST: Thomas Hobbes. *Concerning Body*. In *The English Works of Thomas Hobbes*, translated by Sir William Molesworth. Vol. 1. John Bohn, 1839. Originally published in 1651. Chap. 9, "Of Cause and Effect," and chap. 25, "Of Sense and Animal Motion." Hobbes argues that every event is caused, including events in our minds, such as choices and decisions.

METAPHYSICAL LIBERTARIAN: Jean-Paul Sartre. *Being and Nothingness*. Pocket Books, 1993. Originally published in 1943. Part 4, chap. 1, "Freedom: The First Condition of Action." Sartre argues that a careful analysis of our own consciousness reveals that we are radically free.

OTHER SOURCES

Mark Thornton. *Do We Have Free Will?* St. Martin's, 1989. A clear presentation of numerous arguments for and against.

D.J. O'Connor. *Free Will*. Anchor, 1971. More complex discussion, more emphasis on science, than Thornton.

Richard Taylor. *Metaphysics*. 3rd Edition. Prentice-Hall, 1983. Defends fatalism.

Corliss Lamont. *Freedom of Choice Affirmed*. Continuum, 1990. Emphasizes the unacceptable consequences of adopting the determinist position.

Ted Honderich. *How Free Are You?* Oxford University Press, 1993. Discusses implications of modern physics, and the attitudes we should have if determinism is true.

Gerald Dworkin, ed. *Determinism, Free Will, and Moral Responsibility*. Prentice-Hall, 1970. Contemporary and historical selections, including David Hume's famous defense of a kind of soft determinism.

Richard Kane, *The Significance of Free Will*. Oxford University Press, 1996. Excellent analysis of the context of the problem, specific issues, and a defense of a libertarian position.

Daniel Dennett. *Freedom Evolves*. Viking, 2003. Argues that people are free because we learn about our environment and prepare ourselves for future events, so we are not at their mercy.

4.2   ARE WE RESPONSIBLE
FOR OUR ACTIONS?

Excuser or Judge?

Responsibility is very important to us. The whole justice system, with its courts, its highly trained and highly paid lawyers, the extremely elaborate procedures of a trial, the right to a jury of one's peers, even the traditions going back to Magna Carta, are all aimed at determining responsibility. Our society devotes almost as much time and energy and careful investigation to assessing blame as it does to making money. We also care very much about rewarding praise. The U.S. Patent Office determines who gets credit for ideas and inventions. Often people engage in long court battles over patents and responsibility for inventions.

On a more personal level, some of the strongest emotions we ever experience are guilt, or shame. We take responsibility very seriously. Some people are even driven to end their own lives if they feel responsible for some terrible action.

And on the other side, pride and self-esteem are extremely important to people. We work for years to acquire the feeling of being responsible for something good and worthwhile. Some spend years with a psychiatrist trying to develop that sense of accomplishment.

If the idea of responsibility is so important to us, then obviously we want to understand it as fully as possible. However, it is not so easy to understand. The concept is puzzling in some ways that the two essays in this section bring out. The first claims that the concept is not only puzzling, but actually senseless. It says the idea is a relict from a time when people believed in magic. If you agree that the idea is senseless, then you will excuse people who do undesirable things. You are an excuser. The second essay tries to analyze the way we actually use the concept, and argues that it is perfectly adequate, until something better appears. It says we may and should judge people, so if you agree with the second essay you are a judge.

NO: EXCUSER

"Rejecting Responsibility"

The dustbin of history is filled with beliefs and concepts that modern man has discarded. Some, like the belief in dragons and fairies, were dropped because we learned more about the world we live in. Others, like the belief that the universe is enclosed in a solid sphere, were dropped because people eventually realized they didn't make sense. (The whole universe can't be inside a sphere, because there must be an outer side of the sphere.)

People still accept unfounded, meaningless ideas. The concept of "moral responsibility" is such an idea. We want to blame someone when things go wrong, or praise someone for actions we like. But if we think carefully about how the idea of responsibility is supposed to work, we will discover that, in fact, it doesn't work at all. The whole idea is meaningless.

People who believe in moral responsibility face a dilemma. That is, they face two undesirable choices. One of them must be true; there are no other possibilities. But each one is incompatible with responsibility. No matter which they choose, they must give up their belief in responsibility.

The two possibilities are that human behavior is causally determined, or that it is not causally determined, i.e., it is free. If your action is causally determined, then you are not responsible for it. For example, if a strong man takes your hand and forces you to pull the switch of a fire alarm when there is no fire, then you are not responsible for the false alarm. Or if a dictatorship imprisons you and deprives you of food, you are not responsible for your failures due to weakness.

Nor must all causes be physical. If a doctor tells a nurse that certain pills are good medicine, when actually they are harmful, then the nurse isn't responsible for the harm done by giving the pills to patients. The nurse's actions are determined by the false belief, and ultimately by the doctor.

So if we take this side of the dilemma—human actions are causally determined—then we must conclude that people are not responsible for their actions. Now let's try the other side, and assume that your actions are *not* caused. But if your actions are *not* caused, then you aren't responsible either. If they are not caused, then they are unpredictable, random accidents, like a sudden twitch, or lurch. If your hand twitched for no reason, you would not be responsible for it. It is hard to imagine actions that aren't caused, but suppose a person could do something—hit someone, for example—that was not caused. Then the action would just happen, for no reason. The person is no more responsible for it than for other unpredictable accidents, like a sudden rain shower, or a hiccup. (When we say the action is uncaused, then we are ruling out the person's own wishes as causes. One cannot say the person wanted to hit someone, or else the desire to hit would be the cause.) Now surely a person is not responsible for random occurrences that happen for no reason. In sum, after looking at both possibilities, we can see the dilemma. Whether actions are causally determined, or free, a person is not responsible for them.

At this point, the believer in moral responsibility will claim that there is a middle way. You are responsible, the believer will say, when your actions are caused *by yourself*, although not when they are caused by events outside of yourself. For example, if a strong desire for money causes people to steal, then their action is causally determined, but it is determined by a part of them, i.e., their desire. No one forced them to steal, or misinformed them, so they alone are responsible. In general, then, according to this way of thinking, people are responsible for actions that are caused by themselves.

But this attempt to avoid the dilemma fails. It merely pushes the dilemma back one step, from actions to the values, or desires, or the self, that are the sources of actions. Now the dilemma applies to this inner self (instead of to actions). The two possibilities are that the *self* or values are causally determined, or they are not. Either way, the person is not responsible.

Take the example of the person who steals. If the thief's values and desires were caused by a poverty-ridden childhood, a neglectful, cruel father, and a greedy, grasping mother, then the thief would not be responsible for the kind of person he became. He didn't choose to have the desires and characteristics he has. He didn't choose to be born into that situation, he could not escape from it, and he should not be blamed for the results. On the other hand, if his personality and values are not caused at all, then he is not responsible for them. If they are not caused at all, then they are a kind of freak accident, or a so-called act of God, like a tornado, for which no one is responsible. Either way, caused or uncaused, the concept of responsibility does not apply to the self.

Believers in responsibility will try to escape this dilemma in the same way they tried to escape the dilemma about actions. They will say that people can choose the desires they have, and the traits that make up their personality. People are responsible for their own personality, because it is caused by themselves, according to this theory.

But this response makes no sense at all. It says we choose our personality, or the kind of self we want to be. But who chooses? We must have a personality and desires *already*, if we are able to make a choice. We must be a self, because only a self with certain desires can make choices. It makes no sense to say we choose to become a person. If we choose, then we are already a person. It makes no sense to say we choose all our desires. We must have some basic desires already, desires that guide our choices.

This shows that a person cannot choose, or cause, the basic desires that make up the core of his or her being. So the dilemma applies to this central core, or inner self. Either it is caused (by something external to the person), or it is not. In either case, we are not responsible for the self we are. Whether we look at actions, or at the selves and values behind the actions, we find that the concept of responsibility does not apply. The whole concept of responsibility is meaningless, and should be discarded.

Our modern criminal justice system has already abandoned the archaic "eye for an eye, tooth for a tooth" concept of justice. In mental health care, we used to treat the insane as if they were criminals, but fortunately those days are past. We should now move beyond this magical belief in responsibility. When we do, we will be able to treat offenders in a more effective, humane way, by changing the causes of their destructive behavior. It is only ignorance that makes us label them as undesirables and subhuman.

Key Concepts

actions	causally determined	choices
dilemma	uncaused	self

Critical Questions

1. What are the two sides of the dilemma that the essay discusses?
2. If our actions are not caused, doesn't that mean they are free? And aren't we responsible for what we do freely?
3. If our actions are not caused, then could we have prevented them, or avoided them?
4. The excuser says that the same dilemma that applies to one's actions also applies to one's self. How is this relevant? Does it show that we are not responsible for our actions?
5. Do you agree with the excuser that a person's self (i.e., personality, values) guides his or her choices?
6. Do you think you can choose your own personality? If so, what guides your choice?

YES: JUDGE

"No Excuse"

A cop is shot and dies. Who is responsible? Who should be charged with the crime? Obviously the person who pulled the trigger. But suppose someone said that there is no difference between the perpetrator and anyone else. That the shooter is no more responsible than a bystander, or someone in another state. Anyone who said such a thing would be laughed out of town. It's absurd.

But don't laugh. Some philosophers have actually said it. They said that there is no such thing as responsibility. No one is responsible for his or her actions, so there is no moral difference between the cop's murderer and his mother.

The "no responsibility theory" may be interesting, as a theory, but it is irrelevant to the real world. In the real world we often decide that a person is responsible for something, or that she or he isn't. Our decisions are based on several factors, and if we are careful, and we consider the relevant facts, then the decisions are justified. Some people *are* responsible for their actions and the consequences.

Four main factors determine the decision that a person is responsible for something. Actually we can best understand the four if we turn the matter around and look at situations in which a person is *not* responsible for something. In other words, let's consider the *excuses* people offer when they say they are not responsible. In the case of the cop murder, a person who was in another state and was not connected with the event in any way is obviously not responsible for it. If a person shows that he did not cause an event, then he has a good excuse. That shows that a person must *cause* an event before he or she can be responsible for it.

But causing it isn't enough. People can use a different excuse, and say it was an accident. It sometimes happens that two cops enter an apartment, they are fired at, they return the fire, and in the confusion one cop accidentally shoots his partner. No one blames the cop or says he is responsible for the death. He didn't intend to shoot his partner. It was an accident. So only a person who causes an event and *intends* to cause it is responsible for it.

Another excuse comes up in court, when a person pleads insanity. If the police catch the killer, and he is positively identified by witnesses, then he or his lawyer might claim that he is insane. If he is out of his mind and doesn't know what he is doing, then he is not responsible.

Finally, a person can say he had no choice. When a bank robber points a gun at a teller and demands money, no one thinks the teller is responsible for the robber getting the money. It is true that the teller caused him to get the money, gave it to him intentionally, and knew what he was doing. But the teller was forced to do it. Therefore, in order to be responsible for something, a person must do it freely, without being forced.

These are the four standard excuses people use. If any one of these four factors (cause, intention, sanity, free choice) is *missing*, then the person is not responsible. By the same token, if all four are present, then the person is re-sponsible. In other words, if a person's action causes something to happen, and he has *no excuse*, then he is responsible. He must take responsibility for his action.

It may be difficult to know whether or not the factors are present. It is noto-riously difficult to decide when a person is insane. Psychiatrists for the defense and the prosecution usually disagree. But if people do agree that the four factors are present—and they often do—then they also agree that the agent is responsible.

The intention excuse is complicated in cases of negligence. Sometimes peo-ple are held responsible for something because they could have prevented it but didn't. For example, if a parked car rolls down a hill and hits another car, the owner of the rolling car will say he didn't intend for his car to roll. It was an ac-cident. But a judge will say that he *should* have paid more attention, and could have prevented it from happening, if he had used his parking brake or parked more carefully. So even if he didn't intend for his car to roll, he is still responsible for the damage done.

The factor that philosophers have discussed the most is the last one, free choice. Sometimes a person does something intentionally, but is forced to do it, like the bank teller. That person is not responsible. But what else besides a seri-ous threat could force someone? Could a person's environment or upbringing or education force him to do something?

Some philosophers say that the robber who robs the bank does it intention-ally, but his *personality* causes him to steal. It is true that he chooses to steal, but his values and beliefs (his personality) cause him to choose that way. Even though he chooses to steal, he does not choose his personality. That is produced by his parents, his childhood experiences, his friends, his neighborhood, in short, his environment. His personality forces him to choose robbery, and he is not responsible for his personality.

Since the theft of the money is ultimately caused by things completely out of the robber's control (his environment), he is no more responsible for it than the teller. He did not choose to be the kind of person he is, and he couldn't avoid it. So he is not responsible, some philosophers say. In fact, everyone is a product of his or her environment, and therefore no one is responsible for the choices he makes and the actions he performs.

This is a common point of view among philosophers, social workers, sociologists, and others. But it is wrong. It is wrong because pointing to the robber's environment is *no excuse*. There is not a single, established law con-necting a person's environment with his personality. There are scientific laws connecting a person's diet with his health. For example, if a child does not get enough calcium, he will develop rickets. But philosophers cannot say that poverty causes someone to be the kind of person who wants to steal, because most people who grow up in poverty are *not* criminal types and do not steal. On the other side, rich people steal, too. Therefore it isn't poverty that causes people to become thieves. Do children grow up to be just like their parents?

Some do and some don't. So where is the reliable connection between environment and personality?

In fact, it is just an *assumption* that environment determines personality. No one really knows why some people have certain values, habits, and beliefs. Maybe it is the environment, maybe it is something else. Most likely it is a combination of dozens of things. No one knows.

What is the robber's excuse? He can't say he steals because he was deprived of toys as a child. Others were deprived, but do not have a thief's personality. It is undoubtedly true that *something* caused the thief to have the personality he has. Everything is caused. But "something" is not an excuse. Imagine a child who tells his teacher that he decided not to do his homework, but that he is not responsible for the failure, because "something" caused his decision. He doesn't know what caused him to decide not to do it, neither does his teacher nor anyone else. But everything has a cause. So he is not responsible. None of *my* teachers would have listened to such baloney, and they shouldn't have.

The robber causes the money to be given to him. He does it intentionally, and he is sane. Did he choose freely, or was he forced? The philosopher says he was forced because something—we don't know what—made him the kind of person he is. But that is not an excuse. He did cause the crime by his choice. He was not forced the way the teller was. There is no question about that. Without a more specific prior cause that made him choose the way he did (more specific than "something"), he is the obvious cause of the crime, and therefore he is responsible.

Suppose a scientist knows that gravity causes the tides, but he has no idea what causes gravity. Of course he knows that something causes gravity, since everything is caused, but he doesn't know what. The scientist does not decide that gravity is *not* the cause of the tides, just because something causes gravity.

In the same way, the philosopher knows that the robber caused the crime, but he doesn't know what caused the robber (i.e., what caused his personality). The philosopher should not decide that the robber is *not* responsible for the crime, just because something causes the robber's choice. "Something" is not an excuse. It may be true that if psychologists discovered the causes of the robber's personality, and knew for sure that they determined his choices, then we would say he was not responsible. Then he would have an excuse. But until that day arrives—and it may never arrive—the thief is responsible for his action.

Key Concepts

excuse	intention	personality
responsible	insane	environment
cause	free choice	

Critical Questions

1. According to the essay, what must we know if we know that Jones is responsible for the murder of a police officer?
2. What is the "no responsibility theory" that the judge in this essay criticizes? Does the no responsibility philosopher believe that the robber freely robbed the bank?
3. Why is the "no responsibility theory" mistaken, according to the judge? Does the judge say that the robber's personality does not cause his choices? Does the judge say nothing causes the robber's personality?
4. Do you think the school boy who decides not to do his homework is analogous to the bank robber? Should the school boy be excused?
5. If the robber is not responsible, does that mean that generous, heroic, or mature people are not responsible for their good deeds? Does it imply that we should not admire them or reward them?
6. If the judge admits that something causes the thief's decision to steal, then how is the thief different from the bank teller who hands over the money? Why is the thief responsible while the teller isn't?

Methods and Techniques
INFINITE REGRESS

The first essay uses several types of arguments in criticizing the concept of responsibility. One is to say that the concept leads to an *infinite regress*. "Regress" means to go backward, so "infinite regress" means to go backward forever. If a principle or explanation leads to an infinite regress, then it can never get started, or never get off the ground. It is not a real explanation.

For example, in one primitive religion the devotees believed that the earth rested on the back of a giant elephant. The elephant stood on the back of a giant tortoise. They were assuming that "everything must be held up by something." This principle seems reasonable and in conformity with everyday experience. If you stop supporting the book you are holding, it will fall. If you remove part of the foundation of a building, it will collapse. The believers simply generalized from these common observations, and extended the generalization to the world as a whole. Something must be holding it up.

The problem is that the principle leads to an infinite regress. If everything must be held up by something, then the elephant that holds up the earth must itself be supported by something. The believers decided a giant tortoise could do that. But their principle requires them to ask what holds up the tortoise. Even if their shamans and wise men could propose something to answer that question, they would have to ask what holds up *that*, and so on, ad infinitum (to infinity). There is no end to the "explanations," and therefore there is no real explanation. The principle itself is defective.

Here is another example. Some people have said that when you understand a language, you translate it into a language you already know. For example, when you take a course in French, and you understand the sentence *Il pleut*, you translate it into English: "It is raining." But if this principle is correct, then how do young children learn and understand their *native* language? Well, these philosophers say, the toddlers translate the sentences they hear into an innate, mental language, which the philosophers call "mentalese." But this is no explanation. How do the children understand "mentalese"? According to the principle, they must translate it into some other, deeper language they already know. There is no end to the process. The principle leads to an infinite regress, and so it must be mistaken.

In the previous section you read about introspection, and one principle concerning introspection leads to an infinite regress. Some philosophers have said consciousness is just an awareness of your own experiences. When you look at a tree, for example, you are aware of the tree, but you are also aware of your observation, or your experience, of the tree. When you remember your vacation, you are thinking about the beach, the restaurant, etc., but you are also aware that you are remembering. In general, these philosophers say, when you are aware of something, then you are also aware that you are aware. You are aware of your own mental experience. That is what it means to be conscious.

But this principle also leads to an infinite regress. It says that if I am aware of a tree, then I am also at the same time conscious of my own awareness of the tree. This consciousness is a second state of awareness. Its object is the first state of awareness (whose object is the tree). But the principle says that when a person is aware of something, then he or she must also be aware of that mental experience, that state of awareness. So I must be aware of the *second* state of awareness, too. That would be a third state, and I must be aware of that third state, which implies a fourth, and so on. There is no end of the process. But the mind cannot contain an infinite series of reflective states of consciousness, like a mirror held up before another mirror. The principle must be mistaken.

It is not always easy to see that a principle leads to an infinite regress. The example of the religious principle "everything has to be held up by something" is more obvious than the introspection principle "when you are aware of something then you are also aware that you are aware." To find an infinite regress, you should ask whether or not an explanation applies to itself. That is, when a principle says *A* is explained by *B* (e.g., the earth is held up by an elephant), then you should ask if the principle also applies to *B*. Is *B* explained by *C*, and *C* by *D*, and so on?

The excuser in the first essay claims that the idea of responsibility leads to an infinite regress. Responsibility is based on the principle "we are responsible for the things we freely choose." The excuser says we do not freely choose our actions because our desires and personalities determine our actions. So the defender of responsibility says we must freely choose those desires and personality. But the excuser says that won't work either. Even if we assume it is possible, the basic core self that selects values must also be freely chosen. And who makes that choice? And if something does make that choice, who chooses that something? And so on ad infinitum.

Understanding the Dilemma
EXCUSER OR JUDGE?

The two positions in this section do not have standard names. The question is fairly straightforward—Are people sometimes responsible for their actions?—but the two sides on the issue might be called different things. The view stated in the essay "No Excuse" could be called "responsibilist," or "accounter," because it says people are accountable for their actions. The opposite view, represented by "Rejecting Responsibility," could be called "antiresponsibilist," or "antiblamer," or perhaps other things. I have chosen the terms "judge" and "excuser" for the two positions because they are relatively simple and descriptive. Anyone who agrees with the second essay believes that you can judge people for their actions, and a person who agrees with the first essay wants to excuse people for their actions. The names are not important. The important thing is your beliefs. Do you believe people are sometimes responsible for their actions, or is no one ever responsible for what happens? Are you a judge or an excuser?

One way to think about this issue is to picture a line with two extreme points at each end. The point at the left end of the line represents the view that a person is responsible for everything he does, and the point at the right end represents the view that a person is not responsible for anything he does. The point in the middle represents the view that a person is responsible for about half of what he does, and the point between the middle and the left end represents the view that a person is responsible for about 75 percent of what he does, and so on. Where do you stand on that line?

The excuser stands at the right extreme: he rejects the whole idea of responsibility. Probably no one stands at the left extreme. No one says we are responsible for everything we do. Everyone accepts some excuses. The judge in the second essay even describes some excuses that relieve people of responsibility for what they do. For example, an insane person is not responsible. So the judge is not at the left extreme. He or she says we are responsible for some things we do, and not responsible for other things we do.

But *why* are we not responsible in some cases? An excuser argues that once you admit that people are not responsible in some cases, you must recognize that other cases are actually similar to those. That is, you must admit that their actions or choices were caused by something outside of their control. And you will gradually move closer and closer to the right side of the line until you reject all responsibility.

The question of responsibility is obviously related to the issue of free will and determinism, but it is not the same. In fact, both the excuser and the judge in this section are determinists, at least in the sense that both say all our actions are caused. But the judge maintains that we are still responsible for some of the things we do, even if they are caused. Apparently the way in which actions are caused is the important thing for responsibility, according to a judge. The excuser says simply that if all our actions are caused, then we are not responsible for them.

The excuser is proposing a radical point of view. Very few people have been consistent excusers. The position is not part of "common sense." It is very different from people's ordinary way of thinking. But that is not to say it is wrong. Every great idea was different from common sense at first.

When you consider your decision on this question, you might reflect on what others think and what people have usually said in the past. But that is not the real basis of your decision. The issue is not "What do most people think?" or "What have people thought in the past?" or even "What have I always believed up until now?" You have very likely believed that people are responsible for their actions. But now the issue is "Do you have good grounds for that belief?" Do you believe it just because others do, and because you are in the habit of thinking this way? Or is your belief sensible and based on good evidence?

Are you an excuser or a judge? Your decision will have far-reaching effects on your attitudes toward other people's actions and your own. This issue is especially important in determining your political outlook. It will influence your beliefs about wealth and poverty, about education and government aid, and particularly about crime and punishment.

EXCUSER

1. Punishing people for being born into a particular family and neighborhood is barbaric and cruel.
2. To explain all is to forgive all.
3. Many people accept the foundations of the scientific worldview, but do not think about all its implications.
4. People can change their habits and some of their values, but they cannot change the innermost core of their personality.

JUDGE

5. An individual's surroundings do not force the individual to do anything.
6. Putting the blame on parents or neighborhoods after doing something wrong is just an immature attempt to avoid taking responsibility for one's self-indulgent actions.
7. Belief in cause and effect is compatible with belief in responsibility, because individuals cause their actions and are responsible for what they cause.
8. You can be the kind of person you want to be, although it may take discipline and time to change.

FOR FURTHER STUDY

Historical Examples

EXCUSER: Clarence Darrow. *Crime: Its Causes and Treatment.* Crowell, 1922. The famous lawyer for the defense argues that people who are victims of circumstances should not be held responsible for their actions.

JUDGE: Jean-Paul Sartre. *Being and Nothingness.* Pocket Books, 1993. Originally published in 1943. Part 4, chap. 1, section 3, entitled "Freedom and Responsibility." Sartre believes that human beings have no essence, but choose what they are, and therefore are responsible for what they do.

OTHER SOURCES

Gerald Dworkin, ed. *Determinism, Free Will, and Moral Responsibility.* Prentice-Hall, 1970. Collection of classic and contemporary pieces presenting the standard positions.

Kenneth Bock. *Human Nature Mythology.* University of Illinois Press, 1994. Critical discussion of four types of determinism, based on God's will, forces of history, human instincts, and social conditioning.

Karl Menninger. *The Crime of Punishment.* Viking, 1968. A plea for a more scientific approach to the problem of crime, and a critique of the present criminal justice system.

Gertrude Ezorsky, ed. *Philosophical Perspectives on Punishment.* State University of New York Press, 1972. A large collection of classic and contemporary writings on reasons to punish someone, alternatives to punishment, and the death penalty.

Milton Goldinger, ed. *Punishment and Human Rights.* Schenkman, 1974. A collection of articles by contemporary philosophers on the justice of punishment and the various excuses that make punishment itself immoral.

Jonathan Glover. *Responsibility.* Humanities, 1970. Clear but challenging.

Herbert Fingarette. *On Responsibility.* Basic Books, 1967. Discusses what it means to live responsibly, and related concepts of self-realization and guilt.

Jennifer Trusted. *Free Will and Responsibility.* Oxford University Press, 1984. Broad survey for "readers who come fresh to philosophy," discussing many historical figures and topics.

4.3　IS THE MIND NOTHING BUT THE BRAIN?

Materialist or Dualist?

Everyone knows what the brain is. The brain is a mass of nerve tissue weighing about three pounds, protected by the skull, and attached to the spinal cord. It is divided into left and right hemispheres, each of which is further divided into "lobes," such as the frontal lobes, the temporal lobes, and the occipital lobes. Most of the surface is covered by "gray matter," which is enfolded upon itself to create "fissures." The nerve tissue of the brain consists of cells called "neurons." Each neuron is connected to many other neurons around it. Thus, much of the brain is literally a neural net. But while scientists understand the anatomy, or components, of the brain, they do not yet understand the physiology, or functioning, very well.

The mind is even more problematical. What is a mind? It's hard to say. When we think, remember, imagine, and decide, we *use* our minds. If an accident or disease makes it impossible for someone to do these things efficiently, then we say he has "lost his mind." But what *is* a mind? What is a thought, a memory, or an image? We all have thoughts and memories, so in some sense we know what they are. But it is very difficult to describe them or categorize them. Some activities require thought, and others do not. Some memories are pleasant, and some are not. Some things we can remember easily, while we must make an effort and dig deeply to remember other things. But none of this tells us what *kind* of thing a thought, or a mind, is.

In a way, we have opposite problems in understanding the brain and the mind. We know what the mind does—it thinks, remembers, etc.—but we do not know what it is. In contrast, we know what the brain is—it is a mass of neurons, arranged in lobes, etc.—but we do not know what it does, or how it functions.

This situation, together with other considerations, has led many philosophers to decide that, in all probability, the brain *is* the mind and the mind is the brain. We do not have two organs but only one. Now, is this a plausible theory? Does this suggestion help us understand the brain, or the mind? Is there any concrete reason to say the mind is the same thing as the brain? Is there any reason to say it is not?

These are the central questions in "the mind–body problem." The first essay that follows argues that the mind and the brain are identical. It says a human being is made up entirely of matter, so it presents the point of view of a materialist. The second essay argues that the mind has some peculiar, unique properties utterly unlike any physical object. Therefore the mind cannot be the same thing as any physical object, including the brain. One who believes that the mind and the brain are two utterly different kinds of things is called a dualist.

YES: MATERIALIST

"Body and Soul"

At the present time there are two basic ways of looking at human nature. One way sees human beings as parts of the natural world, fundamentally no different from animals and even plants, except that humans are vastly more complicated. The other way sees humans as composed of two parts, a body and a soul. The body is a physical object, like animals and plants, but the soul is a different *kind* of thing, not physical, but mental, or spiritual.

The second picture, called "dualism," has prevailed throughout history and in most cultures. But now the evidence supports the first picture, called "materialism." In this view, the mind is exactly the same thing as the brain. Experiences, like thoughts, emotions, memories, and decisions, are all tiny changes in the cells that make up the brain. No nonphysical soul is required.

Several recent discoveries support materialism. For example, scientists can measure the brain's electrical activity, or brain waves, at different times. The waves are different when a person sees a familiar object and when he or she sees a strange, unfamiliar object. They are different when a person listens to someone and when he or she answers a question. This shows that different states of consciousness are closely correlated with different states of the brain. It suggests that consciousness *is* an activity of the brain.

Another dramatic piece of evidence is that changes in the brain cause changes in a person's mind. In the 1940s Wilder Penfield, a Canadian neurosurgeon, operated on the brains of patients with epilepsy. The brain has no feeling, so Penfield performed the surgery with local anesthetic, while the patients were conscious. When he touched a place in a woman's brain with a small electrode, she said she could suddenly hear a piano. Later, when he touched the same place again, she said she could hear the piano again, although this time it sounded like a phonograph record. Other patients said the probing made them relive events in their past. Clearly memory is affected by stimulating the brain. The best explanation of these facts is the theory that the mind is identical with the brain, and experiences are events in the brain.

This "identity theory" (i.e., materialism) fits in well with other discoveries and with the main trends of modern science. One trend is toward consolidation and reduction. Reduction means that physics can explain chemistry, chemistry explains biology, biology explains psychology, and psychology explains sociology. In other words, sociology is "reduced" to psychology, psychology is reduced to biology, and so on.

For example, chemists know that sodium atoms and chlorine atoms join together to form salt. They have discovered many laws governing such reactions among elements and compounds. But what *explains* the combination? For an explanation of the laws of chemistry, we must look to physics. The atoms bind together because of the electrical forces among their electrons. And electricity is a part of physics. Physics explains chemistry.

Another example is the reduction of biology to chemistry. At the turn of the century some biologists claimed that life is a unique "vital force," and fiercely resisted the idea that life is just a matter of combining the right chemicals. But then chemists artificially created amino acids—the building blocks of all living things—in a laboratory. Later they discovered DNA, the chemical code that guides every living thing. They demonstrated that chemistry explains biology.

Materialism rests on the belief that some day scientists will understand the brain well enough to explain psychology in terms of biology, i.e., the brain. Penfield's discoveries are a first step in that direction. So materialism is part of the trend of reduction.

Another trend in modern science is toward simplicity. If one basic law will explain a set of facts, then there is no reason to have two or three laws. Or if one kind of object will explain the facts, then there is no need to believe in two or three kinds of objects. The most famous example of the drive for simplicity is Newton's law of gravity. Newton studied three apparently unconnected phenomena: the orbits of the planets, the path of a cannonball, and the tides. People had gathered quite a bit of information about these things from observation, but they seemed unrelated. Newton proved that all the various rules and laws that applied to these things could be derived from one broad, fundamental law, the law of gravity.

Another example is UFOs. We could say that people see airplanes, blimps, clouds of gas, and occasionally alien space ships in the night sky. But it is simpler to say that when they think they are seeing UFOs, they are actually seeing one of the other things. That enables us to eliminate one kind of thing we have to think about, and gives us a simpler picture of the world.

Or we could say there are normal women, insane women, and there are also witches. Then we would have three basic categories of women. But it is simpler to believe that the people who are called witches are actually just insane women. There are no witches. There are only normal women and insane women. These two categories still explain all the facts. But if we take that point of view, then we have eliminated one category, and our picture of the world is much simpler. We can do the same thing with thoughts, feelings, and sensations. They are actually chemical or electrical changes in the cells of the brain, not an additional, nonphysical kind of thing.

We must be careful here. Materialism does not say that the word "sensation" *means* "brain event," or that the idea of the mind is the same as the idea of the brain. The ideas may be very different. It only says that the mind actually *is* the brain, even if we do not realize it. The situation is parallel with the witch example. Our idea of a witch includes supernatural powers, the ability to fly on a broomstick, change people into animals, and so on. That is very different from our idea of an insane woman. Nevertheless, the so-called witches were actually just insane women. People just had a lot of groundless beliefs about some of the insane women.

Materialism is in harmony with the outlook of modern science, and that is a strong reason to accept it. Another reason is that the *alternative* is so strange.

Dualism says that a different kind of thing exists—a soul—and it is somehow connected very closely to a human body. What kind of thing is a soul? A spiritual thing? What does that mean? No one has ever described a soul or mind in specific terms. No one has ever defined the terms precisely. In fact, no one has a clear idea of these things.

Furthermore, how can this nonphysical soul cause my physical body to move? If the soul is nonphysical, then it is not located in space. But if it isn't, then how can my soul zero in on *my* body, but not affect another body? If it is nonphysical, how can it affect my physical nervous system? Actually, only physical things can affect other physical things.

Another problem with the alternative is that it violates the principle of the conservation of matter and energy. The principle states that the total amount of matter and energy in the universe is constant. Matter and energy are neither created nor destroyed. But if a nonphysical soul causes changes in my body, then energy has been added to the physical universe from outside. Or if I step on a tack, and my body causes big changes in my mind, then it seems that energy has flowed out of the physical world into the nonphysical realm of the soul. But a great deal of evidence proves that that is impossible.

Dualism is a strange and confusing theory. Materialism, on the other hand, is consistent with modern science, and is supported by recent discoveries. Clearly we should accept the theory that the mind is identical with the brain.

Key Concepts

materialism	correlation	simplicity
dualism	reduction	interaction

Critical Questions

1. What is materialism? What is dualism?
2. The materialist in this essay says mental events, like memories, are correlated with brain events, like stimulations of certain brain cells. What does "correlated" mean in this context? Does a materialist believe that the fact of correlation proves that mental events are the same thing as brain events?
3. According to the essay, how is the science of biology "reduced" to chemistry? How is reduction relevant to materialism?
4. The materialist says it is simpler to believe that so-called witches are just insane women. Why is it simpler?
5. The dictionary definition of "witch" is not "insane woman." When people talk about witches they do not mean insane women. Doesn't that prove that witches are not insane women?
6. How are witches relevant to memories, thoughts, and other mental events?
7. According to the materialist, why is dualism difficult to understand?

NO: DUALIST

"The Inner Life"

"Know thyself." That was the command carved in stone over the door of the temple at Delphi in ancient Greece. That was the beginning of wisdom, the Greeks believed. Do you know yourself? Are you a beast or a god? Or neither? Or both? How do you discover what you are?

It would be foolish for me to attempt to answer such large questions. All of history and literature are part of the answer. But I can say that one simplistic answer is wrong: You are not the same thing as your body. And if you want to find the correct answer, you must look within yourself. Of that I am certain.

If you set out to discover yourself, you can explore your individual personality, your quirks, preferences, habits, and all the traits that make you different from your friends. But to understand yourself, you should also ask a deeper question. You should ask what kind of being a *person* is. You are a person, a human being. What makes you and everyone else different from other things, like horses or automobiles? Since you are a human being, you will not know yourself until you know what a human being is. (When you understand that, then you can find out what particular sort of human being you are.)

One theory holds that humans are nothing more than living bodies. We understand ourselves by understanding how our bodies and brains work, according to this theory. Of course, people are different from simple objects like tables and chairs, but we are not a different *kind* of thing. We are not like ghosts, or spirits—nonmaterial beings—according to this theory.

The theory is mistaken. I am not just a living body. I *am* a different kind, or category, of thing. I am not the same as my body because I can imagine switching bodies with another person, but remaining who I am. For example, I can imagine waking up tomorrow in George Bush's body, but remaining the same person I am now, with the same memories and personality. That sort of thing frequently happens in movies and fairy tales, and it strikes us as entirely possible. If I woke up in Bush's body, and Bush woke up in mine, there would be a lot of confusion at first, but it wouldn't take too long for people around us to realize what had happened. Therefore, I am not the same thing as my body. If I were the same thing as my body, then I could not have a different body. A different body would be a different person.

If I am not a physical body, then what am I? I believe that I am the unique set of thoughts, emotions, desires, and memories that I find within myself. A human being is a being who has such an *inner* life, a being who is not only aware of tables and chairs out in the world, but who is also aware of inner events, like suddenly having an idea, and inner states like feeling confident and optimistic. I know about these events and states through introspection. They are states that others cannot know unless I tell them. The whole, rich stream of consciousness, with its inner dialogue, its colorful images, its subtle, shifting moods, its sudden joys and pangs of regret, make up the inner life.

Why do I say that I am these inner events instead of my body? The reason is that the inner events are *mine* in a special way that my body is not. As I said, my body could change, and even change radically, while I remained exactly the same person. But my inner life could not. If my inner life changes, then I change. Suppose I woke up tomorrow with completely different desires for the future. Instead of wanting to get married, I now want to join the French Foreign Legion. After the initial shock, my friends would say that I was not the same person I used to be. This shows that the person I am depends more on my inner life than on my body.

Suppose I woke up with a different set of *memories*. Instead of remembering working at the university for the past few years, I remembered living in the Amazon rain forest capturing rare birds. Suppose I did not recognize any of the people around me. Suppose I no longer understood English, but spoke only Portuguese. Even if my body were the same, people would say that there was a different person in it.

My inner life is mine (and yours is yours) in another way as well. It is private, in the sense that no one else can know it in the way I can. If I have a toothache, I know it immediately, directly, without any doubt. You may decide that I have a toothache, if you see me grimacing and holding my jaw, but you do not know it the way I do. You do not *feel* it. You *cannot* feel my joy or anger; you cannot have my memories or thoughts. Of course, you may have a toothache, but then it is *your* toothache, not mine. You may think exactly the same thing as I, but your thought is yours, mine is mine. You cannot know what my feelings and thoughts are like, except what I tell you about them. Nor can I know what yours are like. The inner life is private.

In contrast, no parts of my body are private in this strong sense. You can know my toes as well as I can, you may know my back even better than I. But what about my brain? Are events in my brain private? You cannot see what happens in my brain, so maybe that is why you cannot know my inner life. Maybe when I have a toothache, all that is happening is that my tooth is sending a signal to my brain, and something like a red light is flashing in my brain. Of course, I do not mean a real light, but some brain event, like one special neuron is vibrating, the "toothache neuron." Maybe when I think of Bermuda a certain set of neurons begins to vibrate. When I feel angry, maybe all that happens is that a gland secretes some chemical in my brain. Being angry may be having that chemical in one's brain. Is this possible?

It sounds very scientific, but scientific theories have been wrong in the past. Thoughts and feelings are private in a stronger sense than events in my brain. Anyone can, in principle, cut into my head and observe the neurons in my brain. But no one, in principle, can feel my toothache.

Physical objects and events *cannot* be private in the way that the inner life is. Physical events are in space, so theoretically they can be perceived from different points of view, by different people. Even if only one person can perceive the event (because it occurs under a microscope with one viewer, or something like that), still *any* one person could observe it. But I am the only person in the world who could ever have my toothache. Neurons and chemicals in the brain are physical objects, and cannot be private.

On the other hand, the inner life is private and *cannot* be public, in the way physical objects are. If your inner life were public, then I should be able to feel your toothache, just as I can see your toes as well as you can. But how could I feel your toothache? Even if a brain scientist hooked me up to your brain, how would I know it was *your* toothache and not *mine*? If *I* feel it, then it is my pain. There is no difference between a pain that I have that is mine, and a pain I have that the scientist tells me is yours.

There is another problem with the hypothesis that one person might be able to feel another's toothache. If the pain I feel is really yours, then I shouldn't mind it. I shouldn't care about it. It's your problem, not mine. But if I feel it, then I do mind it. So it must be mine. Only you can experience your inner life, only I can experience mine. The idea that parts of my inner life can be experienced by anyone, as physical objects can, is incomprehensible. It's nonsense.

All events and states in the inner life are private. No events in the body are private in the same sense. Therefore, the inner life is not the same as events in my body. I have not attempted to explain what the inner life—the self—actually *is*. And it is very difficult to do so. How is the inner life related to the body? When does it begin? If a thought is not physical, what is it? I don't know the answers to these questions. I still have not fulfilled the Delphic command. But is it better to have no answer to a question, or to believe an answer that is clearly wrong? I think it is better to be aware of one's ignorance, because only then will one continue the quest for the true answer.

Key Concepts

inner life	private	brain event
a different person	public	impossible

Critical Questions

1. Does a dualist think it is really possible for a person to be transferred from one body to another?
2. Do you agree with the essay that if your desires and memories changed, then you would be a different person? Don't people often change their minds?
3. Suppose a person has a special room in his house, and he never lets anyone else in. No one but he knows what is in the room. Is the room private in the dualist's sense?
4. Why can't a person's thoughts and feelings be the same things as events in his brain?
5. I can imagine that scientists locate the emotion center of the brain, connect my brain to yours like a cordless telephone, and when something happens that makes you feel joy or sadness, the signal is amplified and

routed over to my brain. Then I feel *your* emotions. Do you think this is possible?

6. The essay gives two reasons for believing that if I feel pain, then it must be mine, not yours. What are they?

Methods and Techniques
POSSIBLE AND IMPOSSIBLE

By now you have probably realized that many philosophical problems arise from simple words. Words like "God," "justice," "happiness," "right," "selfish," and "free" seem simple and straightforward but are actually very complex and hard to pin down. People disagree over the meanings of these words. Another such word is "possible." We all use the word every day, and yet it leads to several controversies.

Both essays in this section use the ideas of possible and impossible in trying to persuade you to accept their views. But what does it mean to say something is possible or impossible? It is difficult to get people to agree about what is possible or impossible. For example, look at the following list. Do you think each one is possible or impossible? Are some "more impossible" than others?

1. It rains Oreo cookies.
2. A woman is pregnant and not pregnant at the same time.
3. You find a dog that can fly.
4. You find a round rectangle.
5. You find a one hundred dollar bill in the street.
6. It rains continuously for three weeks.
7. A spaceship travels faster than the speed of light.
8. You draw a straight line between *A* and *B* that is longer than a curved line between *A* and *B*.
9. You live to be 130 years old.
10. You experience time as moving backward instead of forward.

Could it rain cookies? Some say yes, some say no. Could a woman be pregnant and not pregnant at the same time? Almost everyone agrees that this is impossible. Flying dogs? Here people disagree again. Round rectangles? People agree on this one; it's impossible. Everyone agrees that 5 and 6 *are* possible, though unlikely. But traveling faster than the speed of light is problematic. People will argue about it. They will agree that 8 is impossible. (We will return to 9 and 10 later.)

Why do many people disagree about some of these, and agree about the others? Is it because possibility is a matter of degree? I don't think so. Is it because some people are more imaginative, more open to possibilities, than others? Probably not. That may lead to disagreements on other cases, but the problem here is different. People disagree about Oreo cookies and flying dogs because the word "possible" is *ambiguous*; that is, it has two different meanings. Some use the word to mean one thing, and others use it to mean something else. For some people, when they say something is possible, they mean it is imaginable. They can picture it in their minds. There is nothing inherently contradictory or meaningless about the situation. In this sense, it is possible that a dog could fly and that it could rain cookies. We can imagine it happening. And in the same sense, if something is impossible, that means we cannot even imagine it. The words describing the situation do not make sense. They do not fit together, like "round" and "rectangle."

Other people use the words differently. When they say something is possible, they mean it does not break any scientific laws. It conforms to nature. We could actually see it someday, or perhaps it has already happened. If that is what "possible" means, then flying dogs and raining cookies are *not* possible. They violate known laws of nature (even if we can imagine them). Thus two people often disagree about what is possible because they are using the word with two different meanings.

Philosophers make a distinction between these two meanings. They call the first "logically possible" and the second "physically possible." Flying dogs are logically possible but not physically possible. We can imagine a flying dog, but such an animal is incompatible with laws about evolution, wings, and gravity. It is logically possible that cookies could fall to the earth out of clouds, but it is physically impossible. What is physically possible depends on what we know about the way the world works. What is logically possible depends on the meanings of words, or the concepts we use to describe the world.

While people disagree about some of these cases, they usually agree about others. For example, almost everyone agrees that a woman cannot be pregnant and not pregnant at the same time, that you cannot find a round rectangle, or a straight line between A and B that is longer than a curved line between A and B. These are all impossible. But if the word "impossible" means different things to different people, how can they agree on these cases? The answer is that logical impossibility *includes* physical impossibility. Whatever is logically impossible is also physically impossible. So if people who use the word in the logical sense say something is impossible, then people who use it in the physical sense will agree with them. However, if something is logically possible, then it may or may not be physically possible. We can also turn the relation around, and say that if something is physically possible, then it must be logically possible as well. That is why almost everyone agrees on 5 and 6.

Finally, 9 and 10 are strange cases. I'm not sure if 9 is, or is not, physically possible. And I'm not sure if 10 is, or is not, logically possible. What do you think?

Understanding the Dilemma
MATERIALIST OR DUALIST?

Is there more to you than your body and brain? Are you a soul, a mind, which inhabits your body, or dwells within your body, but is not the same thing as your body? Or are your body and brain all there is? Are you a very complex organism that can react to the environment in many different ways?

The first essay, which represents the materialist view, says that the mind is really the same thing as the brain. The second essay rejects materialism and tries to convince you that the mind is not the same as the brain, or the same as any physical object. The mind is a different kind of thing altogether. Thus the second essay represents the dualist view. A dualist believes the world is made up of *two* basic types of things: physical objects and minds. They are very different from each other.

When materialists talk about "the mind" they usually mean the whole collection of mental events and processes that we observe in ourselves and, indirectly, in others. A mind is made up of cognitive things like thoughts and ideas, memories, plans for the future, imagined scenes and events, and other parts of the stream of consciousness. It also includes emotional things like feelings of joy or regret, fear, desire, pride and shame, and so on. Materialists believe that each of these is actually some event in your brain, probably a very complicated event, but still just a physico-chemical event, not very different from electrical signals moving around in a television set. A brain is much more complex than a television set, but they are both physical objects. There is no need to believe that a brain is occupied by a spiritual "self" or nonphysical consciousness.

How can materialists prove that our minds are the same things as our brains? Well, they cannot prove their view. They simply offer it as a theory, and claim it is more reasonable in light of the evidence than dualism. The first essay summarizes the evidence supporting the theory.

The second essay does not offer evidence supporting dualism. Dualists do not say materialism is a possible theory, and dualism is another possible theory, and we must decide whether the evidence supports one or the other. That is not how dualists see the issue. Instead, dualists assert that materialism is *impossible*. It cannot be true. They point to some ordinary, commonsense facts that we can all see in our own minds, and say they prove that the mind cannot be physical. The second essay describes these facts, mainly about privacy. Dualists believe they can prove that dualism is true, because they can prove that materialism is false. So dualism must be true, since it is the only alternative.

The different ways of approaching the issue point to a basic difference between materialism and dualism. A materialist believes that science gives us the best understanding of the world. If you want to know what is real, what exists, and what the world is made of, ask the scientists. And if you ask them, they will tell you that the world is made of physical objects (including organisms).

Dualists do not reject science, or refuse to believe its discoveries, but they say we also have another way of knowing about the world. At least we have another way of knowing about one part of the world. The part is ourselves. And the way of knowing is introspection. We can look within ourselves at our own thoughts and feelings. For some people, this is a whole world to be explored, not by looking with your eyes, but by looking with "the inner eye of the mind."

But introspection is not science. Others cannot see into our own minds. Not even the most brilliant psychologist can know what you are thinking at any particular moment. Introspection is a different way of knowing.

MATERIALIST

1. The world is made up of physical objects, bodies in motion, and human beings are part of the world.
2. There are no such things as ghosts, spirits, goblins, or "out of body" experiences.
3. Science tells us what the world is made of, and science depends on observation and experimentation.
4. The physical brain is complicated enough to think, feel, plan, imagine, remember, and do all the things a soul is supposed to do.

DUALIST

5. Materialism is too simple; there is more to reality than physical objects.
6. I am not the same thing as my body or brain; I am a spiritual being.
7. I can know my own mind and self better than any external observer can.
8. My thoughts, sensations, and emotions cannot be physical events inside of me; they are too different from physical events.

FOR FURTHER STUDY

Historical Examples

MATERIALIST: Julien La Mettrie. *Man a Machine.* Excerpt in Lester G. Crocker, ed. *The Age of Enlightenment.* Walker and Company, 1969. Originally published in 1748. La Mettrie supports his view that the mind is the same as the brain by pointing to numerous examples of correspondence between bodily events and mental events.

DUALIST: René Descartes. *Meditations.* Many editions. Originally published in 1641. In Meditation 6 Descartes tries to prove that the mind is distinct from the body.

OTHER SOURCES

George Graham. *Philosophy of Mind: An Introduction.* Blackwell, 1993. Graham discusses a number of topics, including mind and body, computers' minds, and animals' minds, in nontechnical language, and provides many thought-provoking examples.

Colin McGinn. *The Mysterious Flame: Conscious Minds in a Material World.* Basic Books, 1999. Rejects reductionist materialism and dualism, and argues that the conscious mind can never be explained scientifically.

John Horgan. *The Undiscovered Mind.* Free Press, 1999. Skeptical survey of contemporary attempts by scientists to understand the mind, critical of neuroscience.

E.R. Valentine. *Conceptual Issues in Psychology.* Allen and Unwin, 1982. Chap. 5 is good discussion of introspection and its place in a scientific psychology.

Peter Carruthers. *Introducing Persons.* Croom Helm, Ltd., 1986. Chap. 2 makes a strong case for dualism, but in chap. 5 Carruthers comes down on the side of materialism.

William H. Halverson. *A Concise Introduction to Philosophy.* Random House, 1967. Part 6 presents both sides, but Halverson thinks the arguments for dualism are stronger.

P. Smith, O.R. Jones. *The Philosophy of Mind.* Cambridge University Press, 1986. Clear discussion of contemporary approaches.

P.M.S. Hacker. *Wittgenstein.* Routledge, 1999. Very brief survey, focusing on Wittgenstein's criticisms of the idea that mental events are private.

4.4 CAN COMPUTERS THINK?

Mechanist or Mentalist?

This may sound like a silly question. How could computers think? How could anyone think that computers could think? Computers are nothing more than machines, pieces of metal and electric wires, maybe with a glowing screen or a printer attached. Thought, on the other hand, is the glory of mankind, the noblest and most characteristic of our human activities. "Man is but a reed," says Pascal, "the weakest thing in nature. But he is a thinking reed." Thinking makes human beings admirable. But what is admirable about a clanking machine?

Not only does thinking make us worthy of respect, but it also makes us different. Many writers throughout history have agreed that what sets human beings apart from everything else is our ability to think. Horses may be faster than us and gorillas may be stronger, birds can fly and fish can swim, but we humans are smarter than they are. It is our intelligence and thought that has made us masters of the planet and rulers over the natural world. Thinking is our specialty, our particular talent, and we are very reluctant to admit that we are not so special after all.

But if thinking is so important, then we should think about thinking. We should use our intelligence to understand intelligence. And if we can find forms of intelligence in other places, then we should investigate those forms. It would be unintelligent to do otherwise.

People have always thought that they were special, and superior to others. And they have always found, as they learned more about the others, that the differences aren't so great. In biology, investigators have been chipping away at the barrier between humans and other species. They have discovered many examples of intelligent behavior among "lower" animals. Some accomplishments, like the spider's web, may appear to be intelligent but are actually due to instinct. But others can only be described as genuinely intelligent.

As we learn more about animals' mental abilities and consciousness, our attitudes toward them change. We begin to feel more sympathy and respect for them. If animals are intelligent, then we cannot treat them as mere objects. Many people today feel very strongly that animals have basic rights, perhaps not the same rights as human beings, but some rights nevertheless.

Could the same changes occur in our attitudes toward machines? It seems preposterous, but it seemed just as preposterous to the ancient Greek that an Egyptian could be his equal, or to an American slave owner that his slave should vote and serve in Congress. What seemed preposterous to them back then does not seem preposterous to us today, because we know more about people. But still, machines aren't even alive; they are inert and constructed. But then the Greeks said barbarians did not even speak Greek or wear civilized clothes. We now see that those characteristics were irrelevant to being human. Is being alive relevant to being intelligent? Could something that isn't alive be intelligent? That is only one of the questions we must answer.

The first essay in this section points out many similarities between computers and people, and concludes that computers can think. It represents the mechanist view because it claims that thinking is basically a mechanical process, whether it occurs in machines or people. The second essay, on the other hand, claims that there are some fundamental differences between machines and people, and says thinking is not mechanical. It represents the mentalist view.

YES: MECHANIST

"Can Computers Think?"

Dear _____:

Due to the skyrocketing costs of labor, and breakthroughs in miniaturization, you will be replaced by an IBM 88XR. Pick up your check at the Payroll Office.

Dear _____:

I'm sorry, but I've met someone else. He's witty, reliable, always says the right thing, and *so* intelligent. He's a Hewlett Packard Model 1000. No hard feelings?

Could people be replaced by computers? That may be going a little too far, but it isn't far-fetched to say that one day computers may be more intelligent than people.

Most people aren't aware of what computers can do now. In the 1970s computer scientists developed "expert systems." An expert system is a computer program that can make decisions like a human expert in some field, such as medicine. One of the most successful, called "MYCIN," can take in information about the symptoms a patient has, make a diagnosis of what disease is causing the symptoms, and prescribe the best medicine for treatment. In one test, a group of doctors' answers about several cases were from 42.5 percent to 62.5 percent correct, while MYCIN's answers were 65 percent correct.

Computers can also learn and improve their performance. For example, computers play chess (and other games) extremely well. They simply follow the same rules as human players. And like human players, they have certain strategies to win, like "Try to control the center of the board," and "If you must sacrifice a knight or a bishop, sacrifice the knight." But unlike humans, computers can remember every move of every game they ever played. So they can check their strategies to see how successful they are. If a strategy is helpful only 30 percent of the time, the computer can modify it and try something new in the next game. Over time, it gets better and better.

Computers interpret complex information, learn from their mistakes, calculate, store information and retrieve it, and so forth. This evidence suggests that they are intelligent. We say they are intelligent because their performance is very similar to what *people* do, and people are intelligent. In other words, computers' output (interpretations, calculations, learning, etc.) is very similar to human output. And humans produce such things by using their intelligence, by thinking. Therefore, computers probably produce their output by thinking, too.

We make this kind of inference very frequently. For example, when you plug in your coffee pot, it produces heat to heat the water. How does it do it? Well, if you take it apart you will find a coil attached to a resistor. When an electric current passes through them, they produce heat. Now, when you plug in your electric blanket, it also produces heat, just as the coffee pot does. How does it do it? A reasonable inference is to say that, probably, there is something like a coil and a resistor in the blanket, and when electricity passes through them, they produce heat, just as they do in the coffee pot. The two items are similar in their behavior (heat), so they are probably similar in their operation (resistor) as well. The same kind of inference leads to the conclusion that computers can think.

But of course computers and people are also very different. Computers are made of wires, whereas people are made of flesh and blood. They can't talk as people can, nor can they walk, or shake hands.

But computers' wires are similar to human nerves in that they carry signals. Computers can't talk, but they can print out messages, which is similar to talking. They can't walk, perhaps, but in the form of robots they move about on wheels, and can even extend an arm in greeting. It appears that every difference can be countered by another similarity.

Some people point to deeper differences. Computers are programmed. Everything they do is planned and put into them by humans. When asked "What is 2+2?" a computer can be programmed to reply "5" as easily as it can be programmed to say "4." It doesn't know the difference. So it seems that any intelligence computers exhibit is the intelligence of the programmer, not their own. They are merely complicated tools that can be used intelligently (by people).

But is this fact about computers fundamentally different from humans? People must be "programmed" too, although we prefer to say "educated." We must learn a language, learn to think, to add and subtract, to solve problems. We do these things in the ways we have been taught. In fact, everything that makes us human and intelligent must be learned. Many people balk at this comparison. They feel that there is something dehumanizing about the idea of "programming" people. But it is the word that has bad connotations. If we can put our self-centered emotions aside for a moment, and look at the facts, we will see that children must be taught to talk, to read, to interact with others, to experiment, and to think. We get children to follow certain rules by rewarding some behavior and punishing other behavior, until the rules are virtually automatic, whereas we can simply type in the rules to a computer. But both people and computers must be "taught." (The basic process is the same, whether we use the word "programmed," or "taught," or "conditioned.")

Once we learn enough, we can experiment and modify what we have learned in the light of new experiences. But so can computers. The chess-playing computers can modify the rules they follow if they aren't working well. Many people think that they are not programmed, and that they can learn and change completely independently of anyone else's instructions, whereas everything in a computer was put there by the programmer. But these people are simply ignoring how much they were taught at the beginning of their lives. Later, they did inform themselves and change their behavior. But so do computers.

Perhaps the difference between people and computers is that people are creative. We are unpredictable. We write poems and paint pictures. We act in ways no one ever thought of before. But computers can surprise us, too. The chess-playing computers invent new strategies that are sometimes brilliant. They can take apart and recombine elements of different rules in ways no one ever thought of before. They can write poems that sound as interesting as much of the modern poetry one reads in journals these days. Any computer could "invent new words" by randomly selecting letters of the alphabet, combining them, and assigning meanings to the results. Isn't that creative?

But surely one difference between people and computers is clear. Computers cannot enjoy a joke, or have a good cry, or feel emotions of any kind. They might print out something a person would say, like "I'm so sad," or "I've never been happier." But a person manifests emotions with his or her eyes, tone of voice, heart rate, posture, and a hundred other subtle signs. There aren't enough similarities between people's emotional behavior and computers' output to justify the claim that computers have feelings.

So computers are different from people in that they do not have emotions. But that difference is irrelevant to the point at issue. The claim is that computers are intelligent, not that they are like people in every way. Being intelligent doesn't require emotions. Remember Mr. Spock from *Star Trek*? He was the most intelligent person on the USS *Enterprise*, but he didn't feel any emotions. One could also say that computers run on electricity, whereas humans run on calories. But that difference has no bearing on the question of their intelligence. Without some *relevant* difference, the similarities make the case: computers can think.

People still feel there *must* be some crucial difference. But none withstands careful scrutiny. Therefore, it is logical to conclude that computers can think. Now is that so bad? Actually it's exciting. It opens up a whole new world of possibilities.

Key Concepts

intelligent	creative	analogy
programmed	learn	relevant
expert system	emotions	

Critical Questions

1. The essay never defines "intelligence." On what grounds, then, can it say that computers are intelligent?
2. The essay considers several objections to the mechanist thesis. How do the critics attempt to prove that computers are *not* intelligent?
3. Computers are programmed. Why doesn't that show that they are not intelligent, according to the essay?
4. Do you agree with the mechanist that computers can be creative in the same sense that people can?
5. Do you think it would be possible to invent a machine that could take dictation, as a stenographer can? Suppose it could record someone's voice, and then type what it had recorded, the way a stenographer does. But it would never get impatient, or feel frustrated, or proud, as a real stenographer does. Would the lack of emotion show that it could not take dictation after all? How is this example relevant to the issue?
6. How do you know that your friends can think? Does your evidence *prove* that they can, or only make it very probable that they can?

NO: MENTALIST

"People vs. Machines"

One of the most popular themes in science fiction is robots. Robots are machines that have human characteristics. They are also called "androids," "cyborgs," and sometimes just "computers." Although "HAL" in Kubrick's film *2001: A Space Odyssey*, didn't move around, he had human characteristics.

But science fiction is, after all, fiction. How close to reality are these fantasies? Can we really create artificial minds, or mechanical people? I think the answer is no. Computers today do not have minds, they are not intelligent, and what's more, they never will be.

But I may be in the minority on this question. A whole industry today is based on the assumption that we can build artificial minds. Thousands of technicians and engineers spend millions of dollars and countless work-hours every year in the "artificial intelligence" industry. They are convinced that they can build machines that have minds and can think.

Their starting point was stated clearly in a research proposal written in 1956. It said:

> The study is to proceed on the basis of the conjecture that every aspect of learning or any other feature of intelligence can in principle be so precisely described that a machine can be made to simulate it.[1]

In other words, if we can describe a process, then we can build a machine that can carry it out. For example, if you watch workers assembling a car, you can describe everything they do or every move they make. Then you can build robots to take their places, according to computer scientists. The same approach applies to intelligence, they say. If you describe the steps someone takes in solving a problem or doing something intelligent, then you can build a computer that will go through the same steps, and then the computer will be intelligent.

I think this approach is much more limited than computer scientists realize. A computer cannot duplicate *every* process. Scientists can describe the steps that the atmosphere goes through to create a hurricane. But a computer cannot create a hurricane. The most it can do is "simulate" a hurricane. It goes through steps that correspond to the atmosphere's changes, and it creates something that corresponds to a hurricane, such as an image on a screen. But an image is only a weak imitation of a hurricane. As for artificial people, the most that computer scientists can do is *simulate* intelligence, or create weak imitations of minds, not real minds.

But the computer scientists will say that a mind is different from a hurricane. Minds are intangible, abstract sorts of things. Maybe a mind just *is* the process, so that when a computer goes through the process, it has a mind. Let's grant the computer scientists their assumption. Let's admit for now that if we can describe the processes of the mind, then a computer can duplicate them, and that if it duplicates them, it has a mind of its own. I do not think this assumption is true, but let's grant it for the sake of argument.

Even if we admit all of that, it is still wrong to say that computers are intelligent. The reason is that we cannot describe the processes of the mind. We do not know what intelligence consists of. So we have no steps for the computer to duplicate. We are a mystery to ourselves.

Some examples will prove this. Think of the first words of the pledge of allegiance. Remember? Now, how did you do that? You sorted through all the things you know, and hit upon those particular words, "I pledge allegiance to the flag . . ." What steps did you go through in remembering that bit of information? What is the process of remembering? No one knows. It seems that you decide to remember something, and bingo! It suddenly appears in your mind. We don't know how we do it.

What is consciousness? A tape recorder can play back the pledge of allegiance, but it isn't conscious of doing it. When you recite the pledge, you are conscious of it. What is the difference? What steps can the computer duplicate that will make it conscious, rather than just an information storage, like a tape recorder? No one knows.

You understand the meanings of words like "revolution," "marriage," and "mature." How do you do it? What makes those words meaningful to you, while "licard," "clution," and "sud" are not meaningful? What is the process of understanding the meanings for words? We don't know.

The new industry of artificial intelligence is not following its own program. Its goal was to build a computer that can duplicate the processes humans follow when they remember, understand, perceive, or do other intelligent things. But it cannot duplicate those processes because we don't know what those processes are.

If it isn't following its program, then what is it doing? It is building more complicated tape recorders. It is building machines that give the external appearance of having a mind, but that do not have the real, inner substance of intelligence.

Since we do not know how we do intelligent things, no machine can duplicate them. It may simulate intelligence by producing the same results as a human, but it does not duplicate the inner process, because we do not know what the inner process is. But that doesn't prove that we will never know. Could machines have minds in the future, if scientists discover how we remember, understand, perceive, and so forth?

Computer scientists say yes, because they view human beings one way, and I say no, because I view human beings a different way. Computer scientists think that humans and the mind are complex wholes that can be broken down into single parts, and the parts interact according to strict laws. We understand the mind the same way we understand machines.

But I believe humans are different from machines. What humans are depends in part on what they think and believe about themselves. Humans are not just cells and muscles and reflexes and habits. We have a self-image, we have knowledge about ourselves, and an ideal self. And those beliefs are more important for understanding a person than the simple, interchangeable parts.

Psychologists understand the importance of self-image, at least to some degree. If they set up an experiment with students to test, say, the ways men and women work together on common tasks, they will not tell the subjects what they are testing. Instead, they will tell them they are running an experiment on timing rats in mazes, or creativity, or something else. If they told the students the truth, the students would be self-conscious, and the men and women would not behave naturally. What people believe, especially about themselves, *changes* the way they feel and think.

Imagine that you are on a basketball team, and you are practicing shooting free throws. The coach tells you that you are bending your back, but you should keep it straight. This information about yourself will change the way you shoot the ball. Just thinking about your back as you shoot will affect the process. Eventually you will modify your technique. Whenever we think about what we are doing, or learn something about how we operate, that information changes the way we do things.

The same thing applies on a larger scale to people in general. Suppose psychologists discover something about the processes of intelligence and the ways people ordinarily think. And suppose it becomes generally known. When people learn about these processes, that knowledge will *change* them. Because what people are depends in part on what they believe about themselves.

For example, if psychologists say that memory depends on associating one thing with another (like "1492" and "Columbus sailed the ocean blue"), and if people learn about association, then they will become self-conscious about memory. Some may try to associate things, others may try to prove the psychologists wrong, others may practice more. But at any rate, the new information will *change* the way people normally remember things.

This fact about people has far-reaching implications. We cannot ever *finally* understand the processes of remembering, solving problems, or other aspects of intelligence, because as soon as we learn about them, they change. We will never be able to describe those processes so that a computer could duplicate them, and thus have a mind. As soon as we described them, and people learned about them, they would change. Then the computer would not be duplicating the processes of the human mind.

People are a mystery to themselves. They always will be. And that mystery is an essential part of our self-image. It makes us feel that we are not just machines, which are thoroughly understandable. Instead, we feel that we have within us a spark of the Divine, the ultimate mystery. We feel a kind of awe toward each human being, precisely because we cannot fully understand her or him. Most important, so long as human beings are beyond our comprehension, they are also beyond our control.

Key Concepts

simulate	computer model	blind experiment
intelligent process	self-image	mystery

Critical Questions

1. According to the essay, how do computer scientists attempt to build intelligent machines?
2. Does the mentalist believe computer scientists can build computer models of hurricanes?
3. Why can't computer scientists build computers that copy the steps people take when they remember, solve problems, and do other intelligent things?
4. In psychology experiments, why do psychologists *misinform* the people who are in the experiment?
5. Is the mentalist right to say that what we discover about ourselves changes our behavior? Have people learned anything about human nature in the past five thousand years? If so, has that knowledge had an effect on our behavior?
6. In your opinion, if we discovered that human beings are fundamentally no different from computers, would that change our self-image? Would it change the way we behave?

Methods and Techniques
ANALOGIES

The first essay is based on an *analogy* between computers and people. Philosophers often use analogies, so it is worthwhile to examine the way they work.

An analogy is a similarity between two things. *Webster* defines the word *analogy* this way: "1. similarity in some way; 2. the inference that certain resemblances imply further similarity." So whenever you say that one thing is like another thing, you are making an analogy. The most interesting analogies are between things that *seem* to be very different. For example, when the poet e.e. cummings wants to describe his lover, he says "nobody, not even the rain, has such small hands," comparing the feel of his lover's hands to the feel of rain.

While poets use analogies in the first sense (striking similarities), philosophers use them in the second sense. That is, they make *inferences* based on similarities. To make an inference is to draw a conclusion from some evidence. An analogy in this second sense begins with a similarity between two things. That is the evidence. But then it goes a step farther: it reaches a conclusion based on the similarity. This second kind of analogy is also called an analogical argument, because it is a set of reasons to believe something. It is an attempt to persuade people that some conclusion is true.

The first essay is a perfect example of this two-step process. It says that the performance, or output, of computers is very similar to the performance of people. Computers give answers to questions, give solutions to math problems, propose good moves in games, and so on, and the answers are just like the answers people give. It describes a similarity between computers' output and people's output. But then it takes the next step. We know that people produce their answers and solutions by *thinking*. Therefore, we can infer that computers probably produce their answers by thinking, too. The essay begins with the similarity in output, and then draws an inference about the *sources* of the output.

Analogical arguments are common in philosophy and elsewhere. You have already encountered one in "Design or Chance?" an essay that attempts to prove that God exists. That essay also began with a similarity (actually several similarities): it said the natural world was similar to a machine. It then took the second step and drew an inference: it said that, since all machines are created by intelligent designers, we can conclude that the natural world was probably created by an intelligent designer as well, namely God. Like "Can Computers Think?," the earlier essay began with a set of observable similarities between two things, and on that basis, decided the two things are probably similar in *another* way (i.e., created by an intelligent designer).

How do you decide whether analogical arguments like these are strong or weak? How do you decide whether or not to accept the conclusion? There are three main things to consider: how many similarities are there, how many differences are there, and how relevant to the conclusion are the similarities and differences?

For example, the mechanist in this section tries to strengthen the argument by describing as many similarities as possible between computers' performance and people's performance. Of course the way to *refute* an analogical argument is to point out important differences between the two things compared. The essay considers several proposed differences (computers are programmed, people aren't, people are creative, computers aren't, etc.) and claims they are illusory. Or they are not *relevant* to the conclusion. For example, the mechanist admits that people have emotions and computers do not, but says that is not relevant to the conclusion that computers think.

Analogical arguments are not proofs. A mechanist does not claim to have proven that machines can be intelligent. But analogical arguments can still be good arguments. They can provide good reasons to believe something. If the similarities outweigh the differences, then it is logical to accept the conclusion.

Understanding the Dilemma
MECHANIST OR MENTALIST?

The question at the beginning of this section—Can computers think?—seems like a simple question, but actually it involves several complex questions. When mechanists or mentalists ask "Can machines think?" they are asking whether or not thinking is a mechanical process. Is the human mind like a machine: repetitive, simple, rigidly bound by rules, made of a few basic parts, and so on? Or is the process of thinking completely different from mechanical behavior: intuitive, unpredictable, unanalyzable, irreducibly mental?

One question concerns the uniqueness of humans. Thinking is a large part of what makes us human. We spend a lot of time thinking, it is essential to our survival, it is highly rewarding, and other animals do not think, at least not in the way we do. Thinking is one of the defining characteristics of being human. So if *thinking* is a mechanical process, then one might say that *people* are essentially like machines. One might say this. But there may be other human characteristics that make us different from machines. For example, the mechanist says machines can think, and human thinking is a mechanical process, but humans have emotions and machines do not. Thus our emotions make us different from machines.

Other questions concern facts and meanings. After reading the two essays, you should realize that you need as much information as you can get to answer this question. You need to know more about how people actually think and what happens when people think. And you need to know more about what machines do and what they will probably do in the future. Both essays in this section discuss interesting facts about psychology and artificial intelligence.

It is easy to get sidetracked by a semantic question. You might say, "Everything depends on what you mean by the word 'think.' If you define it one way, then machines can think, but if you define it a different way, then they cannot." But notice that the first essay does not define the word "think." The mechanist's argument does not depend on any particular definition. Neither does the second essay define the word. In fact, the mentalist says we do not know what happens when we think. So, while definitions are always useful, the issue here is not entirely about how we should define the word. It is more about what actually happens when we think, and what happens when machines process information, and how similar the two processes are. It is an issue about how the mind works, not about how we decide to define a word.

One interesting part of the issue concerns teaching. Can we teach people to think, or to think better? If thinking is a mechanical process, then it follows some basic rules. It is made up of simple, easy steps, which are combined into more complex, difficult processes. It is like an internal combustion engine. When you open the hood of your car and look at the engine, it looks complicated and confusing, and it is. But if a mechanic took it apart and explained what each part did, you would see that it is made up of simple pieces that do simple things. If thinking is a mechanical process, then we can teach people about the simplest parts and easiest steps, we can teach them to follow the rules and think more effectively. On the other hand, if thinking is a mysterious process that no one can understand, then we probably cannot teach people to improve their thinking. How could we teach them to think if we do not know how it is done?

This problem is related to the issue of freedom. Do we have free will? If thinking is a mechanical process, then it follows rules. That means it is subject to cause and effect. The way you think depends on the causes that produced your thinking. Your thinking is determined by prior conditions and inputs, just like a computer's "thinking." A mentalist rejects this idea. He or she claims that our thinking is free, and no one can control or condition us.

It is also related to the issue of nature. Is nature lawful and completely understandable, or is it too vast and complex for us to understand? In other words, is nature one huge machine, which obeys strict laws that we can discover? Or are some parts of the universe beyond our comprehension? Are we part of nature, subject to laws that we can discover? Or are we different and separate from the natural world? The mechanist says nature is mechanical and we are part of nature. We can understand how the world works, including our own minds. The mentalist says parts of nature are forever mysterious, and one of those parts is our own minds.

MECHANIST

1. The behavior (or output) of people and machines is actually very similar, if you look beyond superficial things like shape and color.
2. Human beings are made up of simple parts, and human activities like thinking are made up of simple steps, so there is no reason a machine cannot go through the same steps.
3. People believe their own thinking is different from machines' thinking because they believe they created themselves, and they ignore all the teaching and learning they had, which enabled them to think.
4. Many people let their feelings get in the way of their judgment when they ask, "Can machines think?"

MENTALIST

5. The differences between people and machines are infinitely more important than the similarities.
6. People react to the environment, but they are also conscious of *themselves,* and that quality makes them unique in the world.
7. There is a great deal about the mind that we do not understand, and will probably never understand.
8. If more knowledge means we begin to see people as machines, then we should *not* acquire more knowledge; some knowledge may be detrimental to human life.

FOR FURTHER STUDY

Historical Examples

MECHANIST: A.M. Turing. "Computing Machinery and Intelligence." *Mind* 59 (1950): 433–460. The principal inventor of the computer argues in a readable style that machines can think.

MENTALIST: Jacob Bronowski. *The Identity of Man.* Doubleday, 1972. Argues for the mentalist position on the grounds that human action cannot be reduced to a program of simple rules.

OTHER SOURCES

Keith Gunderson. *Mentality and Machines.* 2nd Edition. University of Minnesota Press, 1985. A generally skeptical survey of the issues; Gunderson points out mistakes on both sides.

Douglas R. Hofstadter, Daniel C. Dennett, eds. *The Mind's I.* Basic Books, 1981. A collection of stories, articles, personal essays, and excerpts from books on identity, the sense of self, computers, free will, and introspection.

William Barrett. *The Death of the Soul: From Descartes to the Computer.* Anchor, 1986. Historical survey of ideas about the mind since Descartes, and criticism of excessive reliance on technological images or models for understanding human nature.

John Searle. *Minds, Brains, and Science.* Harvard University Press, 1984. Using his famous "Chinese Room" thought experiment, Searle argues that machines cannot think, and (with qualifications) will never be able to think.

Richard Hanley. *Is Data Human?* Basic Books, 1997. Argues that machines can be persons, and explores other questions of identity raised by science fiction; informed, detailed, thoughtful.

Ray Kurzweil. *The Singularity Is Near: When Humans Transcend Biology.* Viking, 2005. Daring speculations, and some arguments, on the future development of computer intelligence, by a mechanist.

Note

1. Dorothy H. Patent, *The Quest for Artificial Intelligence* (Harcourt, Brace, Jovanovich, 1986), 1.

4.5   ARE WE ALWAYS SELFISH?

Psychological Egoist or Psychological Altruist?

Think about something you did that you believed was morally right. Maybe you returned a wallet that you found, or you visited a sick friend. Think about the experience from beginning to end. Now ask yourself this: didn't you feel good after you had done it? Didn't you feel proud, or relieved that you had resisted the temptation to sit back and do nothing? If you are like most people, the answer is yes. It does feel good to do what we know is right.

But that leads to another question. Isn't it possible that you did the good deed *because* you knew it would make you feel good afterward? Isn't it possible that you did it at least in part to benefit yourself, to make yourself feel good, or at least avoid a guilty conscience? Many people say it is not only possible, but is almost certain. We may help other people, or act in accordance with our principles, but the ultimate motive is to feel better ourselves.

They point out that a person is not always completely aware of his or her motives. You may have known someone who deceived himself, or did not fully understand herself. Maybe a man at work always laughs loudest at his employer's jokes. He says he is just being friendly and does not treat his boss any differently from anyone else. But it is obvious to you that he is trying to win his employer's approval. Or a woman wears a very short skirt. She says it is because these skirts are the fashion this year. But it is obvious to you that she likes to flirt with the men at her job.

So how can you be sure that you did the good deed for completely unselfish reasons? Isn't it possible that you can deceive yourself, just as other people deceive themselves? It is possible, and it is a problem that philosophers worry about. They worry about their understanding of themselves, since they are very concerned about their beliefs and values. They want to know what they really believe and really value. And they worry about the general problem: how can people be sure about their own motives? Is it possible that everyone's motive is always selfish?

The first essay in this section takes the view that people are always selfish. That view is called "psychological egoism." The opposite view is "psychological altruism," and it is defended in the second essay.

YES: PSYCHOLOGICAL EGOIST

"No Free Lunch"

A friend of mine told me about his grandfather's 80th birthday party. His grandfather had a fascinating life—sailed around the world in the merchant marine, sold insurance door to door, worked in vaudeville, ran his own import–export business, married three times. After the champagne, my friend asked the old man what was the most important lesson he had learned from all his varied adventures. He smiled and said, "That's easy. There is no free lunch."

My friend's grandfather may have become cynical in his old age. But he sincerely believed that everyone looks out for himself. In philosophical terms, he was a "psychological egoist." A psychological egoist believes that people are basically self-centered. He or she thinks that everything people do is designed to benefit themselves in some way.

The opposite point of view is psychological altruism. If you believe that, at least sometimes, a person will help someone else without wanting or expecting *any* reward, then you are a psychological altruist.

I have often wished that I could talk with my friend's grandfather. I wanted to ask him why he was so pessimistic. I never got the chance, but I tried to imagine what he would say. With his rich experience of people in all sorts of situations, I think he would point to examples. Look at the average businessperson, or the average shopper, he would say. Look at the lover pursuing his or her elusive prey. Look at the children playing. All around us we see people doing things to benefit themselves.

The examples are not completely convincing, however, because the altruist can point to many examples of people who want to help others. Look at the doctor who goes to the emergency room in the middle of the night. Look at the corporation president who gives to charity. Look at the woman who gives her friend flowers, just because her friend likes flowers. If these things happen—if just *one* person ever acts unselfishly—then the egoist is wrong.

But I have a feeling that my friend's grandfather would not give up so easily. An egoist can take the altruist's examples and *reinterpret* them, so they become examples of self-centered actions. The doctor who goes to the emergency room may do it for the money instead of for the love of humanity. Maybe the doctor does it for the admiration and respect he or she receives. Would the corporation president who gives to charity still make the donation if there was no tax break for it? Judging from the president's fierce pursuit of profits, I would say probably not.

An action that *seems* to be benevolent turns out to be self-centered. This kind of reinterpretation is a very powerful tool, but altruists may not realize how powerful it is. An egoist can point to cases where a person may not even be conscious of his or her own selfish desires, but acts on them nevertheless. The woman who gave her friend flowers may *subconsciously* want something in return—affection, loyalty—without knowing that is why she did it.

The egoist can also look for long-term benefits. A person can do things that are difficult, painful, and appear to be completely selfless. A mother works hard every day for her baby. But she may know, in the back of her mind, that when she grows old, she herself will need help, and her child is the person she can count on to help her. Her work may not produce benefits for her now, but it is a means to *future* benefits. Or the public-spirited man may have decided early in life that a person is happier if he is concerned for his neighbor. He may have decided that, in the long run, it pays to help others unselfishly.

There is another way to reinterpret actions that seem altruistic. The egoist says a person can try to benefit himself or herself by *avoiding pain.* In other words, even if an action does not produce any benefit, conscious or unconscious, short-term or long-term, it can still be self-centered, so long as it is better than the alternative. The altruist's trump card is the example of the soldier who gives up his life for his mates. Surely that man expects no benefits from his action, the altruist says. But it is possible that the soldier thought about the prospect of *not* doing it, and living with a guilty conscience, or with a reputation of being too cautious, or even cowardly. Never being able to look anyone in the eye. Maybe he wanted to avoid that pain and embarrassment, which would last his whole life. In a crisis, just the image of such a life, occurring in a split second, might be enough to cause him to act.

So, the egoist can reinterpret actions in several ways. That makes egoism much more plausible than altruism. After all, can the altruist reinterpret *any* actions that seem self-centered, and show that they are actually benevolent? Are there any cases where a person seems to be benefiting himself, but has an unconscious desire to help others, or thinks he is helping others in the long term? I cannot think of a single example.

It is possible that every action turns out to be a self-centered action, when we go beyond appearances. My friend's grandfather lived long enough and hard enough to understand people through and through. I have no doubt that he knew all about these reinterpretations, and more. He knew that often people's actions are not what they seem. The more I think about his lesson in life and how he might explain it, the more I feel that he may be right.

Key Concepts

psychological egoist   generalization   self-centered
altruist   motive   subconscious desire

Critical Questions

1. What is it about the grandfather that makes him believable, or an authority on the question of selfishness?
2. Does the psychological egoist believe that most people are selfish most of the time, or that all people are selfish all of the time? How would he or she define the term "selfish"?
3. Why does the psychological egoist say that the corporation president probably has a self-centered motive for giving money to charity? Would the same reasoning apply to an average doctor who goes to the emergency room?
4. "Help the needy without expecting any reward. If you live by this principle, you may expect to be rewarded." Can a person believe this? Is it a contradiction?
5. The essay says a person can give up his life for his friends, but his action still might be self-centered. How? How can a person expect any advantage for himself when he will be dead?
6. The essay says it is possible to reinterpret actions that appear to be unselfish, and find selfish motives behind them. Does that prove that the actions really are selfish?
7. What would psychological egoists have to know before they would admit that an action really is altruistic? What kind of example or evidence would convince them? Would anything?

NO: PSYCHOLOGICAL ALTRUIST

"Is Love Selfish?"

November 15, 20__. I thought this relationship would last. I thought this was it, the genuine article, real love. Now I'm not sure.

We had a fight. It wasn't too bad, no broken dishes. But something else broke. My image of her is shattered. I thought I knew her, knew her real feelings, knew how she thinks. But what she said sounded so different from the woman I thought I knew.

She said people in love are in the relationship just to please themselves. Nobody cares about anyone else!

No, that's not exactly what she said. I've got to concentrate and think through this if I'm going to put things back together. Let me think.

She said that when two people are in love, each one cares about the other, of course, but each one cares so much, and does all these crazy things, because doing them makes *himself* or *herself* happy, not because it makes the other person happy. Yes, that's it. That's how it started.

I asked her if *she* felt that way. Did she make my favorite casserole and laugh at my jokes because it made *her* feel good? She tried to change the subject, but I wouldn't let her. Finally she said she likes to cook for me because I enjoy it so much, I love the food and being together, and seeing me enjoy the meal makes *her* happy. And *that's* why she did it. For herself, really.

Then I asked her if she thought *I* was in the relationship for the same reason, for myself. She said yes. Oh God! You think you know a person, and then something like this happens.

Now wait a minute. I'm a mature person, I'm intelligent. I don't want to overreact and do something I'll regret later. So what happened next? We argued, it got out of control, I said some stupid things, she went to the bedroom and slammed the door. Now I need to think about what I want to say when she comes out again. Or tomorrow at breakfast if I'm sleeping on the couch tonight.

I'm not going to sweep everything under the rug. It will just come up again. So, is she right? Is love selfish? Am I in this for *myself*? No, dammit. I would do anything for her. She's so gentle and kind, and yet strong at the same time. Smarter than I am, to tell the truth. And great with her kids in school. I love it when she talks about her work. She can mimic her students and principal so well it makes me laugh till I cry. But she's a good person. I'm really proud of her volunteer work with "America Reads." And at night, when she snuggles beside me, I feel so warm and right and protective. I really do love her.

Hmmm. When I look at what I just wrote, I realize that it's all me, me, me. I say I love her because she makes me feel good. "I feel so warm." But that's how lovers talk. Could she be right? In fact, she said that when a woman falls in love, all she thinks about is her lover, seeing him, and doing things for him. Her excitement is so strong, and her joy so intense, that she almost forgets everything else. She can talk for hours with her friends about her new lover. She is much more tied up in her own feelings and her own happiness than a person who is *not* in love.

But she's wrong. There is more to love than that. That is more like infatuation than love. When a man falls head over heels for a woman (infatuated), he wants to please her, to bring her things, to look good for her, to take her places and be proud of her. He does things *for her*. But at the same time, those things make him feel terrific, like a man. He does things for her, *because* doing things for her makes *him* feel good. Pleasing her is a means to please himself.

But that is infatuation, not love. We have grown beyond that stage. Sure I want to please her. But she's part of my life now, a part of me. What I feel about her isn't joy so much as . . . well, *love*. It's deeper, a kind of rightness, or warmth, or being part of something that is better than myself alone.

What if she doesn't agree with me? Well so what? Who does she think she is anyway? What makes her the expert? Miss Know-it-all. How does *she* know what I feel? She can't get inside my skin. Maybe *she* is in this for herself, but she doesn't know what's going on inside of *me*, or anybody else for that matter. How can she say everybody always wants to please themselves? All she knows is herself. Maybe *she* does, the rat, but she can't know why other people do what they do. What an arrogant fool!

Oh no. I lost it again. I've got to control my temper or else we'll never get anywhere. Let's see, I was thinking about love and infatuation. They aren't the same. What's the difference? How can I convince Alice that they're different?

If I take her out for pizza and a movie, but she's in a bad mood, it doesn't bother me. In fact, I'm concerned about why she's in a bad mood. I found the movie times and the restaurant because I thought she would enjoy it. But I didn't consciously plan to do something to please her because I knew that pleasing her would give *me* a thrill. I didn't think of myself at all. I know that I didn't, because when she didn't respond, I wasn't hurt or dissatisfied, but instead I was concerned for her.

Although I must admit that, in the beginning, I did think about how much fun it would be, for me, to see her enjoying the great evening I had planned. And if she didn't, I would have been hurt. But that was two years ago.

I think that is the difference between infatuation and love, between selfishness and unselfishness. In both infatuation and love, one person does something for another, to make the other happy. But when a man is infatuated, he consciously thinks of the joy and happiness he will feel when he does it. He does something for his lover and for himself, in fact, ultimately for himself. And if it doesn't work, he feels hurt. But when a man is in love, he does things for his lover, and doesn't consciously think of himself at all. That is not selfish. Even if pleasing his lover does make him happy, he doesn't plan it that way, he doesn't think of his own happiness, so he is not selfish.

It can go farther. My father cared for my mother when she was dying of cancer. He had to make a lot of tough decisions, about his career, about having her at home, about being cheerful. He could have taken an easier path, she would have understood. But he loved her. He did things for her, and he knew that they would be more difficult, more painful for him, than other things he could have done. He wasn't doing it to make himself feel better. He wasn't afraid of a guilty conscience. He did think of himself, but what he thought was that he should give that part of his life to her. She needed it more than he did.

I hope I can be like my father. I hope I can love someone that much. I know it's possible, because he did it. Love is not selfish. Maybe Alice and I aren't there yet, but we can be. We can make it if we try hard enough.

Key Concepts

selfish	love	expectation
unselfish	infatuation	sacrifice

Critical Questions

1. What is the girlfriend's point of view (not the writer's)? Does she think a person can do something to make someone else happy?
2. The psychological altruist in this essay describes why he loves his girl-friend and what it feels like to be in love. Does that description show that he is unselfish?
3. What is the crucial difference between love and infatuation? Does a person who is infatuated want to do things for his or her lover?
4. What evidence does the essay mention that one can do things for others without expecting any benefits for oneself?
5. The psychological altruist says his girlfriend does not know what is going on in his mind. Why is that important? How is it relevant to their disagreement?
6. What do you think a psychological egoist would say about the altruist's examples?
7. Can you think of any possible example that would convince psychological egoists such as the girlfriend that they are mistaken? Would anything convince them?

Methods and Techniques
GENERALIZATIONS

A psychological egoist believes that everyone always tries to gain some benefit for himself or herself. Everything we do is intended to benefit us in some way. The egoist is making a very broad *generalization*. A generalization is a statement about some or all of the members of some class. The egoist is talking about the class of people and claims that they are all selfish. Actually, if we want to be precise, we should say the psychological egoist is talking about the class of people's actions. They are all motivated by a desire for personal gain, the egoist believes. But you can make generalizations about any class of things. The statement "Most firefighters are men" is a generalization about the class of fire-fighters. "Some birds cannot fly" is about the class of birds. "All the states in the United States have two Senators" is about the class of states. The opposite of a generalization is a particular statement. It is a statement about a particular object or event. For example, "Smith is a firefighter" is about the particular individual, Smith.

Since philosophers are trying to understand common human experiences, they make a lot of generalizations. From looking at the previous examples, you can see that generalizations vary in scope, or breadth. The broadest generalizations are about *all* the members of some class, and are called "universal" generalizations. "All the states in the United States have two Senators" is a universal generalization. "Every parking place was taken" is also a universal generalization because it is about all the parking places. Statements about *some* members of a class of things are called "limited" generalizations. The statements "Most firefighters are men," "Many people are allergic to pollen," and "A few volcanoes in Mexico are active" are all limited generalizations because they are about some, but not all, the members of different groups.

Generalizations are very common in writing and in conversation. We may use more generalizations than particular statements. Of course the obvious question about a generalization is "How do you know it's true?" For example, how does a person know that *most* firefighters are men? There are thousands of fire departments in the United States. It would take weeks or months to visit every one and count the men and women. If one has not visited every fire department, then should we say one cannot know that most firefighters are men? If a sociologist says "Sixty-five percent of women work outside the home," must every woman be asked about her work before the sociologist can make the generalization?

Fortunately there is a way to know that a generalization is probably true short of surveying an entire class of things. The method is to examine a *sample* of the class. A sample is simply a part of a class. For example, the government might write letters to two hundred fire departments around the country asking them how many firefighters are men and how many are women. The two hundred fire departments are a sample of the whole class of fire departments, which may include several thousand departments. If almost all of the firefighters in the *sample* are men, then the government will conclude that almost all of the firefighters in *all* the departments are men. The government makes an inference from the sample to the whole class, on the grounds that the makeup of the sample is like the makeup of the whole class. It makes a generalization about the whole class of fire departments, and says "Most firefighters in the United States are men."

All of us make generalizations based on samples every day. But some generalizations are sound and reliable, and some aren't. It all depends on the quality of the sample. A sample can be *representative* of the whole class, or it can be weighted, and a reliable generalization must be based on a representative sample. A representative sample is one whose makeup really is the same as the makeup of the whole class. But a weighted sample is one whose makeup is different from the whole class. For example, if you want to make a generalization about firefighters, but you only talk to men over the age of 50, then your sample is weighted. The best way to make a sample representative is to make it as large as possible. Or you can try to select a sample in a way that makes it similar to the whole class. Philosophers must examine generalizations, determine the samples they are based on, and then judge whether the sample is representative, and whether it supports the generalization.

Understanding the Dilemma
PSYCHOLOGICAL EGOIST OR PSYCHOLOGICAL ALTRUIST?

Is everyone always selfish? That is the question at issue in this section. A psychological egoist says yes, and a psychological altruist says no. Where do you stand? Are you a psychological egoist or a psychological altruist? This is not just a question about your own behavior (Do you ever help others without expecting any benefits whatever?), but is also a question about everyone's behavior. Does anyone ever help others without expecting any benefits?

In building this part of your worldview it is important to understand exactly what "selfish" means. A psychological egoist is not saying that everyone is selfish in the ordinary sense of the word "selfish." If you see a small child who has several toys, but who refuses to share them with any playmates, then you would say the child is being selfish. A psychological egoist does not believe that everyone always acts like the child. Obviously people sometimes share what they have and do things for others. But do they help others because they expect something in return? Do they share because they hope that others will share what they have in the future, or because they want to avoid being condemned? The egoist says yes. We all consider the costs and benefits of different actions, and do what we think will bring us the greatest rewards in the long run.

Is that true? Is that how human motivation works? The psychological altruist says no. Sometimes people are not selfish, even in this narrower sense of the word "selfish." It may be difficult, and it may be rare, but sometimes people make genuine sacrifices for others, without expecting any kind of benefits whatever. Maybe people are selfish most of the time, or much of the time, the altruist thinks, but not *all* the time.

The issue is about what motivates people and how people make decisions. It is similar to the issue of ethical egoism, which I mentioned in Section 3.1, but not the same. An ethical egoist says individuals *ought* to look out for themselves all the time and do what benefits themselves. An ethical altruist disagrees, and says people ought to help others. The two alternatives in this section are different. A psychological egoist says people *in fact* look out for themselves all the time. Maybe that is good or maybe it is bad; the psychological egoist doesn't say. He or she is just describing the way people actually behave. The ethical egoist, however, is prescribing the way people ought to behave, not the way they actually behave. Ethical altruism and psychological altruism are different in the same respect.

If you think about these two issues—how people do behave and how they ought to behave—you will see that they are necessarily connected. For example, if you are a psychological egoist then you cannot be an ethical altruist. In other words, if you believe that everyone is always selfish, then you cannot believe that people *ought* to be unselfish; because (you already believe) it is impossible to be unselfish. On the other hand, if you are a psychological altruist, then you can be an ethical altruist. Are the two issues connected in any other ways? Can a psychological altruist be an ethical egoist, for example? You should decide for yourself, and you should think about these kinds of connections in constructing your worldview.

Your beliefs about this issue are an important part of your worldview, but how can you decide who is right? You could flip a coin, but that would not satisfy you for very long. A more intelligent approach is to look at the two essays, and see how the authors decided. The first essay looks at a very wide range of experience, including the grandfather's observations over many years, and even people's unconscious desires. It examines many different kinds of cases. The egoist decides that the vast number of cases of selfishness show that everyone is selfish. In the second essay, the altruist talks about some cases, like the example of his father. And he also looks into his own mind and heart. His knowledge of his own motives seems to be what convinces him. Which method is more accurate? Which method do you trust, the egoist's or the altruist's? A wide range of examples, or your own inner experience? Remember that this is only a means of answering the main question of this section, which is, "Are you a psychological egoist or a psychological altruist?"

PSYCHOLOGICAL EGOIST

1. There is nothing "immoral," or horrible, about being selfish, since everyone is selfish in a basic sense.
2. If you didn't expect to benefit in *any* way from doing something, then you wouldn't have any reason to do it.
3. A person can do things for others and still be self-centered.
4. Since we are all members of the same species (*Homo sapiens*), we must all be psychologically similar in some ways.

PSYCHOLOGICAL ALTRUIST

5. If every individual thought only of himself or herself all the time, the world would be a dismal, terrifying place.
6. Many people are in love, many people value learning, a just society, a clean environment, and other things besides their own benefits or pleasures.
7. I know in my own case that I sometimes do things without expecting any rewards of any kind from anyone.

8. The fact that many people, or even most people, are selfish does not prove that all are.

FOR FURTHER STUDY

Historical Examples

PSYCHOLOGICAL EGOIST: Paul Henri Holbach. *The System of Nature.* Garland, 1984. Originally published in 1770. In chap. 11 of vol. 1, entitled "Of the System of Man's Free Agency," Holbach exhaustively analyzes people's motives and tries to show that they are always self-serving in some way.

PSYCHOLOGICAL ALTRUIST: Joseph Butler. *Fifteen Sermons Preached at the Rolls Chapel.* Lincoln-Rembrandt, 1986. Originally published in 1726. Butler is even more subtle and penetrating than Holbach; he paints a complex picture of human motivation, which includes altruism.

OTHER SOURCES

James Rachels. *The Elements of Moral Philosophy.* Random House, 1986. Chap. 5 is a careful, detailed critique of psychological egoism.

Alfred C. Ewing. *Ethics.* English Universities Press, 1953. Chap. 2 presents the arguments on both sides.

Michael A. Wallach. *Psychology's Sanction for Selfishness.* W.H. Freeman, 1983. A critique of egoism in contemporary psychology, emphasizing Freud and Maslow.

Paul Zweig. *The Heresy of Self-Love.* Basic Books, 1968. Historical survey of attitudes toward egoism, with an emphasis on literature.

Jane Mansbridge, ed. *Beyond Self-Interest.* University of Chicago Press, 1990. A collection of articles that defend psychological altruism and apply that view to various aspects of society and politics.

Robert Ardrey. *The Territorial Imperative.* Atheneum, 1968. An interpretation of some facts about animal behavior and evolution that suggest that mankind has a territorial instinct.

Alfie Kohn. *The Brighter Side of Human Nature.* Basic Books, 1990. See chap. 7, "Altruism Lost," and chap. 8, "Altruism Regained."

Peter Singer. *How Are We to Live: Ethics in an Age of Self-Interest.* Prometheus, 1995. Chap. 5 argues that biology supports altruism, and chap. 11 argues that our reasonableness and objectivity can override our selfish instincts.

4.6   DOES PERSONAL IDENTITY DEPEND ON MEMORY?

Lockean or Sartrean?

Americans may be more concerned with personal identity than people in other countries are. Originally the settlers and colonists came to the New World to start over and begin a new life. All through our history when things went badly people could pull up stakes, go west, and try a different way of life. Immigrants still come to America to find their true identity. America is the place where you can be whatever you want to be. Many of the classics of American literature are about people finding themselves, or deciding who they will be. Franklin's *Autobiography*, Emerson's "Self-Reliance," Whitman's *Song of Myself*, Twain's *Huckleberry Finn*, and Kerouac's *On the Road* are examples. Americans buy thousands of self-help books every year, trying to figure out their identity and how to live it. In other societies, where customs, social constraints, and family ties are stronger, the quest for individual identity may be less important.

Searching for one's identity means different things to different people. For some, the question is how the searcher is unique and different from everyone else. "What makes me special?" For others, the puzzle is to find out what is deep and defining about the person, in contrast to what is merely superficial and temporary: core vs. surface, reality vs. image. Some people wonder what determines the traits they have. Is it family inheritance, genes, the way one is born (and therefore unalterable)? Or do early environment, role models, or decisive experiences give one's personality the particular shape it has? Finally, the fact of change intrigues many people and raises questions about identity. Some people change dramatically. Some say their old self has "died" and they have been "born again." In Hermann Hesse's novel *Siddhartha*, a friend asks the protagonist who he is. He says "I do not know; I know as little as you. I am on the way. I was a rich man but I am no longer, and what I will be tomorrow I do not know. . . . Where is Siddhartha the Brahmin, where is Siddhartha the Samana [ascetic], where is Siddhartha the rich man?" (Hermann Hesse, *Siddhartha*, trans. Hilda Rosner, Bantam, 1971 [1922]). Siddhartha suggests that his identity has changed. These different questions—about uniqueness, a core self, causes, and change—show that the search for identity takes many different forms.

Many modern philosophers have focused on the last version of the search. In other words, they ask what makes me today the very same person I was twenty or forty years ago? If I am identical with the very different individual who existed forty years ago, what explains the identity? My body has certainly changed. Today it doesn't look at all like a small child's body. (Some people change their gender, from male to female or vice versa.) My personality has changed. If my personality is not the same, is there something inside me that persists through all these changes, maybe a soul or spirit that endures? That explanation appeals to some. But it's a strange "explanation," since we aren't aware of a continuous soul within ourselves, and it seems more mysterious than the problem of identity that it's supposed to explain. My consciousness does not endure: I go to sleep and lose consciousness every night. If absolutely nothing about me today is the same as it was forty years ago, how can I say I am the same person?

The ancient Greeks told a story to illustrate the dilemma of identity. A sea captain named Theseus sailed his old ship into the harbor for major repairs. The carpenters first replaced all the sails and masts and rigging. Then they tore up the battered deck and put in a shiny new deck. The bow was leaky and old, so they hauled the ship out of the water, took the bow apart plank by plank, and put in all new planks. Finally, the stern was sagging, so they did the same with it. At the end, every part had been replaced. Not a single board of the original ship remained. Was this Theseus' ship? Was it identical with the ship he had sailed into the harbor, or was it a different ship?

The same question applies to you and to each individual. If you have changed continuously, what makes you the same as the person who existed long ago? The English philosopher John Locke proposed an answer many years ago: he said you remember doing things and seeing things as a small child, so you are identical with the child, regardless of the changes that have occurred since then. The French philosopher Jean-Paul Sartre said you must choose the person you will be, and so your identity depends on your choices and values, not your memory. Which do you think is more important for your identity, your memories and the life you have lived, or your values and the things you feel are important? Are you a Lockean or a Sartrean?

YES: LOCKEAN

"The Binding Thread of Memory"

A recent item in the news illustrates an interesting philosophical issue. Terry Schiavo was a young woman in Florida in a "persistent vegetative state." A stroke had damaged her brain in a way that made her unresponsive to her surroundings. She was alive, but she couldn't stand, didn't talk, didn't focus her eyes on anything, didn't seem to be aware of people, didn't have any control over her body. She could breathe, but she had to receive nutrients through a tube in her stomach. And she remained in this vegetative state for years with no change.

The question that Schiavo's case raises is this: did Terry Schiavo still exist? Her body certainly existed, but her mind and personality seemed to be gone. The case made headlines because her parents and her husband disagreed on this question. Her parents said she was still there and deserved all the rights and protections as any injured patient. But her husband said she had died when the stroke destroyed her mind years earlier. He wanted to stop the feeding and let her body die as well. Her parents strongly protested, and went to court to force the hospital to continue the feeding. The governor of Florida and the state legislature got involved, and even members of the U.S. Congress offered their opinions. It was an emotional issue.

Ultimately the courts decided that Schiavo had no chance of ever recovering consciousness, and that when she was healthy she had indicated that she would not want to be kept alive in a persistent vegetative state. They also decided that her husband rather than her parents had the right to make life-and-death decisions for her when she couldn't make them herself. The food and water were withdrawn and she died thirteen days later.

Unfortunately, cases like this are not so rare. Brain injuries occur, and as people live longer, more of the elderly suffer from Alzheimer's disease and gradually lose their memories and cognitive abilities. So we have to ask what this gradual deterioration means. Cases like these raise many fascinating questions, but let's focus on one specific question. How do we decide whether the woman lying in the bed was the *same* woman as the woman who earlier led a normal, active life? Schiavo's husband said she was not the same person she was ten years earlier; she was not even a person at all any more. But the Schiavo case is only one example. It illustrates an important philosophical issue: what makes you the same person now that you were ten years ago? People change in many ways. What changes would make you a different individual—no longer Julia, or Richard, or whoever you are—and what changes would be less important? You could change your hair color, or your favorite food, your wife or husband, and many other things, but you would still be the same person. What would have to change in order for everyone to agree that you no longer exist and another person has taken your place? Another way to put the question is this: what is essential to your existence? You can change many things and remain the same person you are now. What is so intertwined with your self that any change would actually change your identity?

Some people accept a simple answer to this question, but it won't stand up to inspection. The simple answer is that you are the same person you were ten years ago because your body is the same. Same legs, same arms, same chest, and so on. And in fact that's how we normally decide the question. If you go to a high school reunion ten years after graduating, you might see a woman and wonder "Is that Kathy?" You recall the way she looked back in school, and compare the woman standing here now. "She's a little heavier, and her hair is different, but the height is right, and the eyes and mouth are the same. I guess it's Kathy." What we mean when we think like this is not that the body now is exactly *similar* to the earlier body, because it isn't. But it is the very same individual body. There is only one person continuing over that time, not two. In other words, the body is the criterion of personal identity.

This theory has fatal weaknesses, although at first glance it does seem to fit a number of situations. For example, imagine that you go up to Kathy and talk with her. But suppose she barely remembers you, even though you were good friends in school. And suppose her personality has changed. She use to be quiet and shy, and now she is laughing and talking loudly to everyone she sees. She no longer reads, but spends all her time with her real estate business showing houses to clients. You would probably say Kathy has changed, but you wouldn't say the person is not Kathy. It's still the same person as before—same face, same hands, same body—but she just behaves differently.

Let's push this theory and imagine a more unusual situation. Suppose Kathy's arms and hands are *not* the same; suppose she lost them in an accident and now has artificial arms. While we're imagining, let's imagine she also has a new heart, new kidneys, new liver, and plastic surgery. Last year, a woman in France had a face transplant, in reality, not in imagination. Suppose Kathy has a new face. Actually, everyone's body changes naturally at the cellular level all the time. Cells die and are replaced by new ones. After about seven years (scientists say), most of the cells in your body have been replaced. What all of this shows is that bodies change, sometimes drastically. Imagine that Kathy's body has changed drastically, completely. If the body is the criterion of personal identity, and virtually every part has been replaced, can Kathy be the very same person she was ten years ago?

People who accept the body criterion say this is not a problem for their theory. As long as the change is gradual, and the replaced parts function in the same way as the originals, it is natural to say the body is the same. Think of an automobile. We can change the tires, the lights, the upholstery, the fenders, even the engine, and if we do this gradually over a period of years, we say it's still our car, the same one we've always had. Think of a tree. In 2007 it is a little sapling, while ten years later it's tall and strong with long limbs. But it's the same tree, because the changes have been gradual, involving one small part at a time.

The main problem with the body criterion of identity is not change but omission. It leaves out the most important thing for identity, and that is memory. You are the same person you were ten years ago because you remember what you did ten years ago. Memory is a better test of identity than the body, and we use it in ordinary situations. Suppose Kathy approached you at your reunion, and you didn't recognize her. After all, she has new arms and a new face (literally). How could she convince you that she really was the same girl you knew in high school? She would show you that she remembers things she did ten years ago. She might say "Remember the time we sneaked into the basketball game without paying? You were so nervous you couldn't watch the game." If no one but Kathy knows about that, and she remembers other things that the original Kathy did, then you would decide this person really is Kathy, in spite of the different body. Memory is a stronger test of identity than the body.

We don't use this test very often because normally there is no question about whether a person now is identical to an earlier person. But on rare occasions we have to decide, and memory is our guide, not bodily continuity. Writers actually illustrate the importance of the memory criterion better than real-life cases.

Writers and film makers often present situations in which people "switch bodies." In one movie a daughter wakes up in the morning to find that she is in her mother's body, and vice versa. Funny mix-ups follow. How does the daughter, and the audience, know that she is now in her mother's body? Because she *remembers* being the daughter (events at school, dates, friends), even though when she looks in the mirror she sees her mother's body and the audience sees the mother's body. If the criterion of identity were the body, this situation wouldn't make any sense at all. We wouldn't even understand what we were suppose to think. "This (body) is the mother. Dark hair, 5 feet 7 inches tall. Why is she saying she is the daughter?" But the situation does make sense, even if it never actually happens. And that shows that our criterion for personal identity is memory of the earlier person's experiences, not identity of body.

It's true that in casual meetings we rely on physical appearances to decide whom we are with, that is, that "this Kathy" is really "my Kathy." But the physical body cannot be the criterion of identity, for the simple reason that the body can exist when the person does not. Everyone dies. But even if Kathy died, her body would continue to exist, at least for a while. Therefore, Kathy cannot be identical with her body.

We can use physical appearance as *evidence* of identity, even though memory is the *criterion* of identity. A criterion is the essential, defining quality of a thing, whereas evidence is a fact about something, but not essential. For example, I might see evidence that you are a medical doctor. You wear a white coat and a stethoscope, and you use medical terminology. But that is only evidence. You could be an actor, or an imposter. The criterion is earning a medical degree from an accredited medical school. If you have that, then I can be certain that you are a doctor. Without it, you aren't. Or I might see evidence that you are a mother. You have a playpen in the living room, kids' toys around, and you talk about your two children. But evidence isn't proof. You might be insane and delusional. But if I know that you gave birth (or legally adopted a child), then I know that you are a mother. One of those is essential. They are criteria of being a mother. The other facts are only evidence.

When we look at a person's physical traits like eyes and mouth, we are looking for evidence that she is the same person as an earlier person. But evidence is not necessarily a criterion. We can have good evidence and still be mistaken. Even if we are sure that the body is the same body, that is only evidence, not proof. But memory is a criterion. If the present person remembers the earlier person's experiences, then she really is the same person. We couldn't be mistaken about that. And here's another example to support the memory criterion. Imagine that you must undergo a dangerous brain operation. The doctor says you have a choice between two options. She can save your present body, but all your memories will be lost. Maybe you will have no memories or maybe you will have different ones when you awaken. Or, as a second option, she can save your memories but you will have a completely different body. Maybe she transplants your brain into the healthy body of a victim of brain cancer whose brain is removed. Which would you choose: same body, different memories, or same memories, different body? I believe this is a no-brainer (pardon the pun) for most people. They want to survive, and so they would choose the memories. The body is just a container, or a vehicle. This shows that what makes you the person that you are is your memories, not your body.

It's very unusual for the body and the memory to be separated, but sometimes they are, especially now with our advanced technology. And we can separate them in imagination. When we do, we see that the defining essence of an individual—the criterion of her identity—is her consciousness and memories, not her body.

Key Concepts

persistent vegetative state   same person   same body
switching bodies   evidence   criterion

Critical Questions

1. If Schiavo was in a persistent vegetative state, should we say that her personality was different but she was still the same person her husband married years earlier? Or should we say she was not the same person he married?
2. Why did the court decide to side with Schiavo's husband and order the hospital to stop giving Schiavo food and water?
3. Some people say being the same person depends on having the same body. But bodies can change completely—new heart, new legs, new face, all new cells. How do these people defend their theory in light of such changes?
4. The Lockean describes movies in which people "switch bodies." But that never happens in reality. Do you think the example of something that never happens provides any support for the Lockean's theory?
5. What is the difference between evidence and a criterion—for example, evidence that Great Britain is a monarchy, and the criterion for being a monarchy? How is this relevant to personal identity?
6. If you were the patient facing the brain operation, which option would you choose: preserving your body but losing your memories, or preserving your memories but getting a different body? Why?

NO: SARTREAN

"The Essential Self"

One of the oldest—and most interesting—questions in philosophy is "Who am I?" What makes me me? Everyone asks himself or herself this question, of course, but philosophers have devoted more attention to it than most people. They have interpreted the question in different ways. Many philosophers have tried to find the special quality that makes humans different from everything else. One said humans are the only animals that can think and reason. Another said humans use genuine language, whereas animals only signal each other with instinctive cries and gestures. Others said humans are the animals that laugh, or the animals that can feel shame. A popular theory was that what makes us human is the ability to use tools, but now we know that animals use sticks and rocks as simple tools.

The question all these philosophers are trying to answer is "What is *essential* to being human, and what is merely accidental or added on?" In other words, what do we have that, if it were taken away, would change us so much that we were no longer human? Of course humans have arms and legs and eyes, but those are not the essential things, because you can lose your legs and still be human. The other side of the question is "What quality or ability do animals *lack* that all humans have?" This is the same as asking what is essential, because if an animal had the quality, it would be human, not animal. Is it reason, as the philosopher said? But some people aren't very reasonable or rational and are still human. And on the other side, some animals are very intelligent. Is it language? Some disabled people cannot speak although they can learn to use sign language. Does that count? But then certain psychologists say chimps and dolphins can learn to use sign language. Obviously this is a difficult issue.

But there is a different interpretation of the question. When I ask myself "Who am I?," I'm not really asking what makes me different from animals. That may be part of the question, but it's not the important part. What I want to know is what is essential to me, as an individual, not what is essential to the human species. Even if philosophers made a convincing case that language, let's say, was the defining quality of human beings, and that no animal can learn a complex language, that would not answer my question. Yes, I can use language. But so can everyone else. I want to know what makes me the particular person I am. What would have to change in order for me to say that I am no longer the same person I was? And what quality do I have that no other person has? The form of the question is the same: what is essential to me? But I'm applying the question to myself, not to humanity in general.

Philosophers have discussed this question, too, and they have developed a plausible answer. I want to show that this popular answer is mistaken, and propose a different answer. The most popular answer is that a person is defined by his or her memories. You are the same person you were ten years ago because you remember the experiences you had then. If you had different memories, you would be a different person. Moreover, I cannot have your memories. I may remember the same events that you remember, but I experienced them differently from the way you experienced them, and I remember my experiences—my feelings, my point of view—not yours. So what is essential to a person, a specific individual, is his or her specific memories, according to this theory.

I believe this memory theory is mistaken. What is essential to a person is her values, in my view, not her memories. I am what I care about most. What is essential to me is my family, my friends, my work, my commitments, my pro-jects, my beliefs. And it isn't my memories of those things that are important; it's my hopes and intentions for the future that are essential. I would never give those up. If somehow I lost those, my life would be over. I would be a different person. It's hard to imagine such a case, but insofar as I can picture the person who had different values and beliefs, different goals and desires, that person would not be me.

It seems to me that values are more essential than memories for two main rea-sons. First, my memories are fixed, whereas the things that I want and admire are in the future. The future is full of possibilities. I can't change what happened in the past, but I feel that I *can* grow and change as a person. For example, a key part of my identity is being honest. That means I will try to be open and straight with people in the future. It's important to me. When I look back at the past, I remember being honest with people, and I remember a few times when I was not completely honest. But those times are gone and irrelevant to who I am now. When I held back or let people get the wrong idea about me (or even pre-tended to be something I wasn't), I wasn't really being myself. Now I can be more determined to be sincere and candid in the future, and that desire is what really makes me the person I am now. I know it is possible to be honest, and a good husband, and productive at work, and a helpful friend, and all the other things I want to be. I may not achieve those things perfectly, but I have the de-sires, and that's the defining thing. That set of desires, or values, is what I care about most.

Moreover, that future possibility is absolutely essential, not just an emotional attachment or a nice fringe benefit. It is essential that I make choices for myself. If I couldn't make choices, I wouldn't be the person I am. Values are different from memories because I can't make choices about my memories. What hap-pened happened. It cannot be changed, no matter what. But my identity is not written in stone like that. I have a future in which I can try to practice the things I believe in. Try to imagine that your future was like your past. Everything in your past is already determined. In theory, there could be a large book with a detailed description of everything you said and did for each hour of each day going all the way back to your birth. It would be an interesting book to read. But suppose there is a Volume II for the future. Everything you will do and say and even think is described in detail for every hour of every day in the future (until The End). In fact, I don't think I can even imagine that situation. If I looked on page 783 and saw "what I will do" next month, I would try to avoid it. Because a defining quality of my identity, and everyone's identity, is having an open future with many possibilities. Possibilities that *I* choose. That means having values and goals that I can try to implement in the future.

There is a second reason that values are more important than memories for personal identity (besides the fact that values are open to the future and mem-ories are closed and fixed). Getting to know a person means getting to know her values: what she enjoys doing, what she doesn't like, what she aspires to be, how she interacts with others, how she feels about herself. We can see this if we consider two people who get married. Ideally, the two will know each other very well, and each will know the kinds of things the other person will do and say and want in the future. It's true that they will also know something about the other's past and memories. But I believe that kind of knowledge is less important. I believe that because when marriages do not work out, it is often because one person did not understand the other person's values. One person may have different attitudes toward income and savings from the other, and that difference in values didn't become apparent until they were married and pooled their money. Or one person may be very ambitious and want to get a better job and be promoted, and is disappointed that the other person doesn't have that ambition. Maybe the husband is very close to his relatives, but his wife doesn't fit in and doesn't feel respected by them. When people discover these things about their partners, they are shocked and decide they really didn't know the other person after all. I know this happens because I've seen it, but I've never heard of a marriage breaking up because one person discovers a memory the partner has. The question "What is essential to me?" depends on my values more than my memories.

People whose marriages are in trouble often go to marriage counselors, or even psychoanalysts. A psychoanalyst would disagree with me and say that the most important key to understanding a person is her memories, especially her unconscious memories. Going through analysis means digging up long-lost memories. Those memories still affect our behavior and feelings in the present, psychoanalysts believe, even if we aren't conscious of them. For example, being scolded or rejected by a parent may make me feel worthless, or feel like a failure, even if all the external evidence tells me I am successful. The memories are really effective only if I have suppressed them and I'm not consciously aware of them. The psychoanalyst's job is to help me recover those suppressed memories that are influencing my present feelings. If I do, I see that they are childish and groundless, and the influence goes away. The psychoanalyst, then, says that getting to know yourself means exploring your memories, especially the ones that are hidden. They make you the person you are.

But I believe psychoanalysis actually supports my theory. My unconscious memories are important only because they influence my values and desires. If they do not, they are trivial and no one bothers with them. If a person's cold, demanding parents caused him to lack self-esteem, in spite of his accomplishments, that is an important fact about that person. He doesn't value himself, and even ignores reality to maintain the attitude. That is part of his identity. His unconscious memory isn't part of his identity, because he isn't aware of it. If he becomes aware of it, and it ceases to influence him, then it isn't important either. What is important for his identity is his values and feelings and actions, which may be influenced by memory or may not.

In fact, the memory theory of identity has serious problems, and the case of psychoanalysis illustrates one of them. I remember very little of my past. I can remember a few big events, but even they are sketchy, and getting more vague as time passes. I remember a conversation I had yesterday, or parts of it, but I will forget it by next week. Am I really such a fragmentary, inconstant, disjointed collection of images as my memory of the past? Surely I did many things, and many things happened to me, that I don't remember. Are they part of my identity? The memory theory has to say no. But then who did those things? I believe those forgotten experiences can be a part of me, if they influenced the values I hold now. What is essential to me is what I care about. My history (and certainly my memory of that history) is irrelevant unless it influences what I care about now. But if it does, then it is a part of me to that degree.

Not only do I forget much, but I sometimes "remember" things that never happened. It's quite amazing how differently two people can "remember" the same events. My wife and I have gone on vacations and if we tell friends about them, perhaps a year later, we tell completely different stories. We disagree about who said what, or what we saw, or which came first, and so on. The point is that everyone's memory is faulty. We all think we remember something, and we are mistaken. An elderly man "remembered" going to Australia. Actually he never made the trip, but he always wanted to go, and he eagerly watched programs on TV about Australia. Eventually, as he grew older, he believed he had been there, and he could describe places he "saw." If memory defines identity, then it seems we would have to identify this man as a person who traveled to Australia. But he was not a person who traveled to Australia. (If the false memory influences the man's current values—maybe he admires the Australian people—then the "memory" could be part of his identity in that way.)

Can a person change her identity? The memory theory says no, because you can't change the past. I believe the answer is yes. Consider the case of Karla Faye Tucker. Tucker participated in the murder of two people in 1983. She admitted that she killed the two. But in jail she changed completely. She converted to Christianity, and said she had been made into "a new creation" (Sister Helen Prejean, "Death in Texas," *New York Review of Books*, Jan. 13, 2005). She became kind and generous, reflective rather than impulsive, and worked tirelessly for the other prisoners. She came to feel terrible remorse for her earlier crime. She remembered it, but when she looked back, she seemed to be a stranger to herself. She could remember the acts, but they seemed senseless and repugnant, as if she were watching someone else. I believe she *was* remembering someone else. Her values had changed completely, and therefore her identity had changed.

However, society and the government insist that she was the same person and she should be punished for her crime. From an objective, external point of view, an unbroken chain of causes and effects linked the murderer with the later woman who was so loving and helpful. The causes and effects included Tucker's physical body and her memories. But from Tucker's inner, personal point of view, she was literally a different person. She admitted the continuity in the body and the memories, but to her, the changes in her values were so deep and pervasive that she could not even recognize herself in the earlier individual. When she asked "What is essential to me?," she saw that the answer was different from what it was earlier.

So the question becomes "Who decides what is essential to identity?" Does society decide who you really are, based on your past and your observable, physical acts? Or do you decide, based on your inner understanding of what is essential to you and your future? Society has to defend the memory theory because it has to hold people responsible for their actions. Society cannot exist without rules, and people must be held accountable when they break the rules. Every criminal could say "It wasn't me," and escape punishment. But that requirement for social order doesn't automatically imply that the memory theory is correct. It's just a social convention that society applies for efficiency.

Instead of believing that society can decide who you are, I believe that you are a better judge of what is essential for you. Each of us is the best judge of what is essential to us. I think I am a better judge because my ability to choose my future is bound up with my sense of being human. If I thought that something else determined my character and my identity, I would feel like a machine rather than a human being. I would be paralyzed, wondering what the external director has in store for me next. I would second-guess every decision, wondering what "really" made me choose one thing rather than another. (Whether the external determiner was social rules, or brain science, or my past.) Since my ability to choose is absolutely integral to my identity, I must be the one to decide who I am. Society or memory might tell me who I was, but not who I am. "Who decides what is essential to identity?" I do. And I decide that what I care about most is more essential to me than my memories. I am what I value.

Key Concepts

essential	values	future possibilities
knowing a person	psychoanalysis	false memories

Critical Questions

1. Why are values more important than memories for my identity, according to the Sartrean?
2. Does the Sartrean mean that certain values are "essential" to a person in the sense that the person cares intensely about them, or "essential" in the sense that the person couldn't exist without them? (I can say chocolate is essential to me in the first sense, and oxygen is essential in the second sense.)
3. Dating Service A gives you a short account of a person's past, and Dating Service B gives you a personal statement by the person of his or her values and goals. Which would be more helpful in getting to know the person? (Of course you would like to have both. But which would be *more* helpful?)
4. How does a psychoanalyst help a person get to know himself or herself? Do you think psychoanalysis undermines the Sartrean's theory, or supports it?

5. The Sartrean rejects the memory theory of identity because I don't remember much of my past, and I sometimes "remember" (falsely) things that didn't happen. A Lockean could say I am unaware of many of my values, and I sometimes believe I value something when actually I don't. Are those facts enough to reject the value theory of identity, in your opinion?

6. Was the Karla Faye Tucker who killed two people in Texas in 1983 identical with the Karla Faye Tucker who was executed in 1998?

7. Who decides who you really are—the people around you, or you yourself? Society, or the individual? Publicly known facts, or inner, personal feelings?

Methods and Techniques
FALSE DILEMMA

You face a dilemma when you have to make a difficult choice between two options. "Should I buy the computer now, or wait until the price comes down?" "Should I go out with Becky or Susan?" In these examples the choice is between two actions, but sometimes you must decide between two beliefs. "Will the Bears win or lose on Sunday?" "Was my allergic reaction caused by something I ate or by the new clothes I wore?" "Is there a God or isn't there?" Dictionaries usually define "dilemma" as a choice between two undesirable options, but I want to give the term a slightly broader meaning and use it to refer to a difficult choice between any two possibilities.

Dilemmas are very common, both in our day-to-day activities and in philosophy. Obviously I have arranged the essays in this book in a pattern of dilemmas. In the section on personal identity, you are presented with a choice between memories as the basis of identity or values as the basis of identity. To create your own worldview, you have to decide what to believe and which explanation is more convincing. In other sections you read about other dilemmas.

In both day-to-day activities and in philosophy it is very important to understand that you can face real dilemmas and false dilemmas. A false dilemma is an oversimplification of a situation. It is a description of a situation that makes it seem that you must choose between two options, when actually you have more than two choices. For example, a person might say "Should I give up all deserts and be miserable, or should I continue to gain weight and be miserable?" Actually there is a third choice: give up some deserts but not all of them, and lose weight that way. You can probably think of even more possibilities in this situation.

Here's another example of a false dilemma: "Will I get the best grade in the class on the exam, or will I be a complete failure?" This is a distortion of the situation because those are not the only two possibilities. Maybe I do not get the best grade in class, but I can still get a good grade—a grade to be proud of—and be successful that way.

But not all dilemmas are false dilemmas. Sometimes you must make a choice between two possibilities, and there really are no other options. Recently a man in New York City suffered an epileptic seizure and fell onto the subway tracks as a train was approaching. Another man saw what happened and had to make a snap decision: do I jump onto the tracks and try to help, or do I not? The bystander—Wesley Autrey—jumped down and held the sick man's body in the center of the tracks so his arms or legs wouldn't be severed by the train. Five cars passed over the two men before the train could stop, but both escaped unharmed (Cara Buckley, "A Man Down, a Train Arriving, and a Stranger Makes a Choice," *New York Times*, January 3, 2007, A1). In this situation you might say Autrey had other options: he could try to signal the driver of the train in time to stop, or he could call 911. But those are simply ways of "not jumping down to help." The real, gut-wrenching choice was to risk his life or not to risk it. Jumping down to help was risking it and anything else was not risking it.

So, we face real dilemmas and false dilemmas, and a very useful technique for improving your critical thinking is to learn to recognize false dilemmas when you see them. That is, ask yourself if the two possibilities presented to you are really the only two possibilities. If they aren't, and you have other options, then the dilemma is a false dilemma. This is a useful technique because we encounter false dilemmas far too often. Some people deliberately oversimplify a situation to create a false dilemma. For example, unscrupulous political leaders might say "Either you are with us or you are against us. Either you are a good friend or a deadly enemy." The demagogues want people to join their movement or party. By setting up the stark choice between friend or enemy, they are threatening to treat people as enemies if they don't go along with the movement. No one wants to be treated as an enemy, so many people will join the movement, if that is the only alternative. But of course that is not the only alternative. People can remain neutral, neither good friends nor deadly enemies. Or they can agree with part of the politician's position but reject other parts. The political leader is deliberately creating a false dilemma. (Two political activists wrote a book recently titled *We Are Right and They Are Wrong*.)

It isn't only unscrupulous politicians who oversimplify situations and create false dilemmas. As S.I. Hayakawa explains, whenever any of us is under the pressure of intense emotion, we tend to reduce our options to the minimum.

> If we are starving, there are only two kinds of things in the world so far as we are concerned at the moment: edible things and inedible things. If we are in danger, there are the things that we fear and the things that may help and protect us. At such basic levels of existence, in our absorption in self-defense or food-seeking, there are, in terms of those limited desires, only two categories possible. (S.I. Hayakawa, *Language in Thought and Action*, Fifth Edition, Harcourt, Inc., 1990, p. 113)

It is unfortunate that some people treat virtually every situation as a crisis, even if they aren't starving. They react in highly emotional ways when they don't need to, and that leads them to oversimplify matters and create false dilemmas.

The tendency to create dilemmas is even deeper than our emotions. It is probably an inborn, structural part of the human mind. Human beings naturally divide the world into "binary" (two-sided) opposites: male or female, light or dark, hot or cold, active or passive. (These were the opposites in the ancient Chinese concepts of *yin* and *yang*, whose opposition and interaction were the basis of all of reality.) We classify things as natural or artificial, human or animal, sacred or profane, good or evil, day or night, us or them. A person can be an introvert or an extrovert. Statements are true or false.

Dividing the world into binary opposites is part of the process of classifying things generally, and classifying things is necessary for survival. We treat the things we encounter as types—food, plate, friend, stranger, residence, office, doctor, automobile, etc.—rather than analyzing every object and situation as a new, unique, complex thing. If we didn't, we would be paralyzed. We would awaken in the morning, look in our closet, and spend hours examining every article of clothing we find, marveling at the details and differences and possibilities. Classifying is necessary. The question is whether binary classifications (e.g., male or female) really present us with two and only two choices, or whether they create false dilemmas.

As we have seen, some binary classifications are legitimate. If someone asks "Is Jane pregnant or not pregnant?," you can't say "She's a little of both," or "Neither," or "She's in between." She can't be in between or a little of both or neither. She must be pregnant or not pregnant. Johnny's answer on the multiplication test is either correct or incorrect. If he says "$11 \times 12 = 144$," then his answer is incorrect. Not "a little correct and a little incorrect" or "neither right nor wrong."

On the other hand, many binary classifications create false dilemmas. We often assume that everything must go in one category or the other category, when actually we have many more choices. The yin and yang classifications are like that. Is the soup hot or cold? Well, it's neither; it's in between. Is it light or dark outside? It's twilight, a little of both. Male and female is the most interesting and instructive example because it's controversial. Is every human being either male or female? Most people probably say yes. You have to be one, and you can't be both, they say. Others say this is a false dilemma. Some people are born with indeterminate organs, part male and part female. Some people have indeterminate chromosomes. Some people say they are physically male but psychologically female or vice versa. Are all these people definitely male or female? Or are they "in between," "a little of both," or "neither"? The answer isn't clear. So if someone asks "Is Jackie male or female?," is that a real dilemma or a false dilemma?

In each section of this book you are presented with a dilemma, and you must decide whether it is a real dilemma or an oversimplification. In other words, you must decide whether the two choices in each section are the only two choices you have, or whether there are other possibilities, compromises, "in-between" positions, and so on. Everyone wants to find alternatives to dilemmas because it's hard to make a decision when we are faced with a real dilemma. "Do I risk my life to save another person, or do I not (and watch him die)?" That decision would be very hard, and I hope you never have to make it. But I'm pointing out a different kind of decision you must make. You must decide if you have only two choices or not. When you are faced with a dilemma, first you must decide it if is a real dilemma or a false dilemma (only two choices or more than two). And then you must decide which choice is the best one, whether it is one of the two, or a combination, or in between, or something else.

In the two essays on personal identity, the authors argue for their explanation of identity, and they also try to show that alternatives won't work. For example, the Lockean considers the body criterion of identity as an alternative and tries to show that it can't explain our normal experience of identity. The Sartrean considers the Lockean's alternative and argues that it is not acceptable, not a real alternative. Many of the essays in the book do the same thing. The writers are aware of the dilemma, they are aware of alternatives, and they often try to show that the so-called alternatives really aren't believable or acceptable. It is up to you to decide how successful or unsuccessful they are, and whether there really are other choices besides the ones presented in the two essays.

Understanding the Dilemma
LOCKEAN OR SARTREAN?

One difference between the Lockean's point of view and the Sartrean's view is clear. The Lockean looks to the past and the Sartrean looks to the future. The Lockean believes people have histories, they have records, they have lives, and they remember those things. It's those memories that determine a person's identity. The Sartrean doesn't deny that people have pasts, but claims that the future is more important for a person's identity. When a person values something—a relationship, or playing sports, for example—that means he or she wants to continue enjoying that thing, wants to preserve it and maybe increase it in the future. And people care more about the future than the past, so the future is more essential to identity.

One obvious response to this disagreement is to propose a compromise. Maybe personal identity depends on *both* the past and the future. We can be open-minded and say that the Lockean and the Sartrean are both right. Then we don't have to disagree with either side and everyone is happy. Looking for a compromise is usually a good strategy. Often two people disagree about something because one sees only one part of a complex situation, and the other sees another part of the same situation, and neither can acknowledge the other's perception. For example, one group says men and women are alike and another group says they are different. Who is right? Well, they're both right. Men and women are alike in many ways but different in other ways. Is capitalism just? If we look at some cases we will say yes, but if we look at other cases we will say no. Maybe the best answer is that it can be both, depending on circumstances.

But this obvious strategy may not work with the disagreement in this section. The problem is that the Sartrean specifically considers the memory theory and criticizes it. The Sartrean says that we don't remember most of our past, and we have false memories. Memory isn't important anyway: insofar as memory is relevant at all, it's what we think we remember that gives us our sense of identity, not what we accurately remember. Furthermore, the Sartrean uses the example of Karla Tucker to claim that one individual can become a distinct, different person, even if the new person does remember the old person's actions. Tucker remembered killing people, but the Sartrean argues that the murderer was a different person, not identical with the present woman in prison. On the other side, the Lockean would say that a person's future goals may feel important to him or her, but they don't tell us if a present person is identical with a past person or not. So it may not be possible to say that both the Lockean and Sartrean are right.

The two positions in this section are different in another way, besides looking to the past and the future. The Lockean asks how we can know that another person is the same as someone in the past. For example, how can we know the woman at the high school reunion is the same as our former friend? Or how can we know the present Terri Schiavo is the same as the former Terri Schiavo? But the Sartrean takes a different approach. This writer asks how I can know myself. What makes me the person I am? What is essential to me? If I can answer that question for myself, then I can extend the answer to you and to others. But I begin with my own identity, not Terri Schiavo's or imaginary friends at reunions. Another way to put this difference is to say the Sartrean takes a first-person perspective on the question of identity, whereas the Lockean takes a third-person perspective.

Underlying the Sartrean's point of view is the assumption that people are different from other kinds of things. I can know what people are like "from the inside," so to speak. I'm a person, and so I can know at least one person directly, by being that person. I cannot know other people in the same manner. Nor can I know trees or animals or stars or molecules that way. I can only know about those things from the outside, objectively. I see their external properties, and others can see those properties as well as I can. But in my own case, I have a whole different window of access that other people do not have. It is only reasonable, then, that we should decide the identity of persons differently from the way we decide the identity of other things. When I ask myself what makes me the person I am, and I consider the inside (i.e., personal experience, priorities, self-awareness) as well as what others see, I conclude that my values define me much more definitely than my memories.

Does the Lockean really take a different approach? Memories are psychological states, after all. And the Lockean rejects the body—a physical object—as the standard of identity. Should we say both writers are taking a first-person approach? Probably not, because the Lockean applies an objective test to determine a person's identity. To decide if the present person ("Ms. Jones") is identical with some past person ("Kathy," from high school), the Lockean tests the present person's memories to see if she really does remember sneaking into the basketball game, or really does remember the things "Kathy" did years ago. The Lockean isn't thinking about himself or herself at all, but is applying an objective standard (accurate memory) to another person. The standard involves psychological states, but it's a standard that anyone could apply, and doesn't depend on the view "from the inside."

So far I've mentioned two basic differences between the memory theory and the value theory, and you can probably think of more. I'll conclude briefly with a third difference. The Sartrean says that people change. They actually change into different individuals. An example is Karla Tucker, and the Sartrean would say she is not alone. After twenty years of marriage one partner can be a different person, literally, from the one who originally married, according to the Sartrean. The Lockean says we can imagine a change in identity like that—if a person's memories changed completely—but it never actually happens. It only happens in movies and strange novels where people "switch bodies." (Perhaps it doesn't actually happen because memories are dependent on the brain. But that hypothesis isn't part of the memory theory itself.) The two writers agree that people's personalities change, and they agree that, in principle, the person inhabiting one body could disappear and be replaced by a different person. The difference is that the Sartrean says we can see this happening in the real world, but the Lockean says that while it's theoretically possible, it never actually happens.

So who are you? Are you the same person you were years ago? And how do you decide? Do you look within yourself at your core values? Or do you find a thread of memories connecting you to the past? Are you a Sartrean or a Lockean?

LOCKEAN

1. The question is what makes a present person identical with a person in the past, in spite of many deep changes and differences between the present person and the past person.
2. Having the same body is not proof, because a person's body can change completely.
3. We rely more on a person's memories than her body to decide is she is the same as a past person.
4. Remembering the past person is a criterion of identity, whereas bodily similarity is only evidence of identity.

SARTREAN

5. Memory can't be the standard of identity because memories are set and fixed, but my identity is open and within my control.
6. The things I value are more essential to me than my memories; I am what I care about.
7. The deepest and truest understanding of another person is an understanding of her values and visions of the future, not her memories of the past.

8. The number of individuals named Karla Tucker in Texas was two, not one; the individual who was executed was not the individual who killed people in 1983.

FOR FURTHER STUDY

Historical Examples

LOCKEAN: John Locke. *Essay Concerning Human Understanding*, Dover Publications, 1959 [originally 1690], Vol. 1, Book 2, chapter 27. Locke discusses the identity of substances, of "men" (i.e., human beings) as biological creatures, and of persons.

SARTREAN: Jean-Paul Sartre. "Existentialism Is a Humanism." In Walter Kaufmann, ed., *Existentialism from Dostoevsky to Sartre*. Plume, 1975. Sartre explains his idea that each individual must create himself or herself, and the consequences of our condition.

OTHER SOURCES

John Perry. *A Dialogue on Personal Identity and Immortality.* Hackett Publishing Company, 1978. A dialogue in the style of Plato between a dying philosophy professor who believes she is identical with her body and a minister who tries to convince her she is not.

John Perry, ed. *Personal Identity.* University of California Press, 1975. Excerpts from historical figures, including Locke, Hume, and Reid, as well as contemporary discussions.

Godfrey Vesey. *Personal Identity: A Philosophical Analysis.* Cornell University Press, 1974. Readable survey of several aspects of the problem of personal identity, organized around Hume's idea of the self as a bundle of experiences tied together by cause and effect.

Harry Frankfurt. *The Importance of What We Care About.* Cambridge University Press, 1987. A collection of essays defending the (Sartrean) view that our core values are the most important elements in our identity.

Sydney Shoemaker, Richard Swinburne. *Personal Identity.* Blackwell, 1984. Two opposing essays. Swinburne defends the possibility of disembodied survival.

Henry W. Johnstone, Jr. *The Problem of the Self.* Pennsylvania State University Press, 1970. A discussion of a variety of theories about the nature of the self, showing how different and irreconcilable they are.

Raymond Martin, John Barresi. *The Rise and Fall of Soul and Self.* Columbia University Press, 2006. Argues that in every epoch people have tried to empower the self and set it above and apart from the natural world, but have always encountered obstacles to that attempt.

Current Controversy

4.7   ARE THE DIFFERENCES BETWEEN MEN AND WOMEN PHILOSOPHICALLY SIGNIFICANT?

Unifier or Complementer?

A big part of philosophy is trying to organize all the questions we want to ask in some sort of order. On the topic of human nature, people ask many questions: What does it mean to be human? How are people different from animals? Can we make any broad generalizations about people? Are people basically good or basically bad? Do people have instincts, or are they entirely shaped by their environments?

Formulating the right questions is an important step in developing your worldview. In my classes students often resist the idea that we can find general laws of human nature. Many insist that every individual is unique, and any laws of human nature would overlook important features of some people's individuality. General laws restrict our freedom.

Of course they are right that everyone is unique and different from everyone else. On the other hand, all humans are human by definition, and therefore similar to other people. My students understand that people are different in some ways and similar in others. They do not want to say that we cannot find any general laws of human nature, but that differences are *more important* than similarities. Even if we find a common human nature, it doesn't matter. What matters is individuality, freedom, and self-realization.

They may be right, or they may not. But before entering that debate, it is important to recognize that we are asking a different question. We began by asking what it means to be human, or whether we can find general laws of human nature. But now we are asking whether the similarities among people are *important.* When we ask how all humans are alike, we are asking a factual, scientific question. Biologists, anthropologists, and psychologists try to answer it. But when we ask what similarities and differences are important, we are asking a more complicated, philosophical question.

Human nature is a very broad topic, and one way to narrow the focus is to think about men and women. Gender is one difference among people, but how important is it? The first essay in this section argues that it is not important. The writer wants to emphasize the unity among all people, so anyone who agrees can be called a "unifier." The second essay claims that differences between men and women are important, especially for philosophy. Men and women do not have the same talents, but complementary talents. Each can help the other. So one who accepts the second point of view can be called a "complementer."

NO: UNIFIER

"Men, Women, and People"

When I was in elementary school, my favorite part of the day was recess. All the students could go outside and play games. But one thing puzzled me. Boys and girls were always segregated. Boys played softball or soccer, and girls played volleyball or badminton, or skipped rope. I wanted to play softball. I was better at it than some of the boys, as I proved on weekends when the neighborhood kids played. I didn't look so different from boys. Boys came in all sizes and shapes, and in fact the differences between large and small boys were greater than the differences between medium boys and medium girls. When I asked why I wasn't allowed to play with the boys, I received all the usual question-begging answers: "Softball is a boys' game," "Boys and girls are different," "You wouldn't enjoy playing soccer with the boys," "Volleyball is better for girls."

Perhaps it was that experience with classifying people as boys and girls that led me to study law, because law depends so much on classifying people and actions. For example, if one person kills another, the person is guilty of homicide. But there are different types of homicide. If the person kills maliciously, the law says it is murder. But if the person kills accidentally, it is manslaughter. And there are further subdivisions within those categories.

I have always been intrigued by the ways we classify people, particularly men and women. The more I thought about it, the more it seemed to me that our classifications are socially constructed. That does not mean they are arbitrary, but it does mean they depend on choices we make as a society, and we could make other choices if we wanted to. People are similar and different in countless ways. Society decides which differences are important and which aren't, and society's decisions change over time.

To understand how gender is socially constructed, we need to think about the process of classifying in general. Classifying things is one of the most basic psychological operations. To classify means to divide a group of things into subgroups. For example, I classify the clothes in my closet into the subgroups of skirts, blouses, pants, and shoes. Colleges classify students by the number of courses they have taken: seniors have taken more than juniors, juniors more than sophomores, and sophomores more than freshmen. Librarians use the Dewey Decimal system, or the Library of Congress system, to classify books by their subject matter: philosophy, religion, social science, and so on. Each of these groups can be divided even further. The world is so complex that we must continually classify things to make sense of it all.

The same group of things can be classified in different ways. When I wash my clothes, I sort them into light and dark, not skirts and blouses. I could also classify them by color, as blue, green, brown, and yellow. Or by fabric: cotton, wool, silk, nylon, and rayon. Or size, or weight, or many other ways. Books can be classified not by subject but by difficulty or intended audience. Some are suitable for children, some for adolescents, some for adults. And students can be classified in hundreds of ways: by country or state of origin, by age, size, job experience, favorite music, hair style, and many others. Each classification is independent of the others. If I divide students into citizens and noncitizens, each of those two groups might include seniors, juniors, sophomores, and freshmen.

Everyone understands the basic process of classification, but some people have never thought about the most important point of all: none of the different ways of classifying a group of things is inherently better than another. The usefulness of a classification depends on one's purpose. If my purpose is to find clothes in the morning, then I classify them by function (skirt, blouse), but if my purpose is to wash them, a different classification is better. If my purpose is not to read books but to pack them in boxes for storage, then the best classification is by size: 5 inches long, 9 inches, 12 inches. Colleges sort students into majors to encourage them to acquire specialized knowledge in one area. If a college wants to recognize academic excellence, it can classify students by grades and place some on the dean's list.

Which classification of students is natural, the classification based on courses taken, area of specialization, age, or grades? None is "natural." They are all legitimate. Each classification serves a particular purpose. Some classifications may be more difficult to apply than others, or may allow separate classes to overlap. For example, sorting students into those with and without work experience is not easy. What counts as "work experience"? But employers are very interested in that quality and ask students about their work experience just so they can classify them. Their classification is just as "natural" or real as a classification based on age or courses taken.

Are *any* classifications more "natural" than others? The word "natural" makes us think of the natural world, so let's consider animals. Biologists classify animals as single-celled and multicellular, as vertebrates and invertebrates, as fish, reptiles, birds, and mammals. But a cook might classify animals as fatty or lean, a good or poor source of protein, expensive or cheap, or best broiled, baked, or fried. A farmer might classify them by their fur, their skin, or the type of leather they provide. A hiker might classify them as aggressive or shy, swift or slow, poisonous or harmless. Different people are *interested* in different aspects of animals. Biologists are interested in the evolution of animals, so their classification reflects the development of animals over the centuries from simple to complex. But the characteristics biologists emphasize are no more "natural" than any other characteristics. Being poisonous or harmless is just as natural as having a backbone or not. The hiker's purpose is different from the biologist's, but both classifications are equally "natural."

Since classification is such a basic psychological operation, and since humans are social beings, we take a strong interest in classifying ourselves. The group of human beings can be divided in an infinite number of ways, by age, appearance, native language, income, and others. Our basic purposes and goals will determine which classification we use and which we take as fundamental.

One of our basic purposes is reproduction, and therefore we classify people as male and female. In fact, our drive to reproduce is so strong that we elevate a simple biological feature above all others, and even suppress others to make the biological functions stand out. Men women in most societies are taught to accentuate the physical traits that distinguish them from the opposite sex. Women have often been taught to develop their caring, nurturing, childrearing side, and men have been taught to develop their competitive, moneymaking side. Women wear cosmetics and men grow facial hair. Many societies in different periods of history have encouraged this division of labor. Even in the United States, women were not allowed to vote until 1920; they were not allowed to work in many jobs until we needed their labor in the Second World War. Today women still face discrimination. Many people assume that all a women can do, or even wants to do, is bear children. All her other characteristics and talents are ignored. Men are victims of this simple-minded classification as well. They are sometimes taught that their identity is "being a real man," where that is defined as fathering a child, or engaging in sex. The ability and desire for sex becomes their obsession. They are psychologically reduced to sex machines, just as women are psychologically reduced to baby-making machines.

But it is crucial to understand that we do not have to think this way. Classification changes over time. Our basic purposes, such as survival and reproduction, do not change, but our *means* of achieving those ends do change. And since no system of classification is inherently natural or better than another, the ways we sort things change as well. In the future, we may not sort people into male and female. The biological traits related to reproduction may be as unimportant in classifications of people as the length of legs or the size of muscles are now. We won't even notice them.

In the past, people classified other people on the basis of what they could do with their hands. They were carpenters, weavers, cobblers, blacksmiths, and so on. The purpose was to organize labor in the most efficient way to increase everyone's prosperity. We still have the same goal, but our means of reaching it are different. Now we classify most people on the basis of what they can do with their minds, not their hands. We are engineers, accountants, lawyers, sales people, computer programmers. The old classification is changing and becoming obsolete, even though our basic purpose is the same.

Another example is transportation. Two hundred years ago if you wanted to travel you had three choices: you could walk, go by horse or carriage, or sail. Journeys were classified in those three ways: foot, horse, boat. But the steam engine created a new means of transport. Then came the internal combustion engine and the airplane. Now, if you want to travel you consider plane, train, or car (possibly ship, but probably not a sailing ship). Our means of traveling have changed, and that has inevitably changed our classifications. We think of walking more as a form of exercise and less as a practical means of travel. We can recognize a horse when we see one, but we never think of it or classify it as a way to get to work. The same radical changes in perception can occur with the categories "man" and "woman."

Our means of traveling changed gradually over many decades, but our means of having children are changing more rapidly. Humans will always want to reproduce, but like everything else, the ways in which we reproduce are changing. One of the biggest changes was the birth control pill. Before the 1960s, sexual intercourse was inextricably linked to having children. Thinking about having sex meant thinking about having children, and vice versa. But now these activities are separate. People can engage in sex without pregnancy, and can get pregnant without sexual intercourse. In vitro fertilization (i.e., in a laboratory) and artificial insemination are just two of the common techniques available. Our whole way of thinking about reproduction is changing.

Another step is surrogate mothers. Some women want to separate having children from getting pregnant, and we now have the means to do that. A woman can supply an egg and her partner can supply the sperm to fertilize it in vitro, and the fertilized egg can be implanted in another woman's uterus. The surrogate mother, or "birth mother," carries the growing embryo and fetus for nine months and gives birth to the couple's child. The genetic mother makes the same contribution to the new child as the father. She provides her sex cells containing half the genetic material. Once the child is born, she and her husband or partner could continue to share the child-rearing duties equally as well.

Soon we will have artificial wombs, just as we have artificial hearts, artificial kidneys, artificial lungs and limbs. We won't need to pay a woman to bear a child in her own womb. Then reproduction will be completely separated from sex and pregnancy, and men and women can play equal roles. Women can continue to work while the fetus grows, as men do now, and both mother and father can take maternity leave, or work part-time, during the child's early years.

Reproduction will still be important to us, but when the means of reproduction change, our ways of classifying people will change as well. Instead of focusing on the biological, reproductive features of individuals, we can attend to other characteristics, other talents, and other traits of personality. We will still recognize males and females, as we recognize physically strong and weak people now, or sharp-sighted and near-sighted people. In the distant past, when prehistoric humans were fighting for survival, those classifications were vitally important for hunting and protection. But now we have better means of protecting ourselves. Those classifications do not help us achieve our goals, and most people ignore them or are completely unaware of them. The same evolution could occur with the physical differences between men and women. In the future, being male or female may be as unimportant as being left-handed, or blonde, or over 6 feet tall.

Key Concepts

classification	means and ends	surrogate mother
categories	reproduction	artificial womb

Critical Questions

1. According to the unifier, is it better to classify students by number of courses taken, by income, or by grades?
2. Is there no difference between natural classifications and artificial or "human-made" classifications?
3. Do you think the changes in our common means of transportation have changed our ways of perceiving things such as horses, boats, or the act of walking? Could our perceptions of human males and females change fundamentally?
4. If one of your female classmates wore "men's clothes," or a male classmate wore "women's clothes," how would you feel about it? Are people who challenge traditional classifications dangerous to society?
5. If scientists developed a safe, reliable artificial womb, like the incubators hospitals use now, would the majority of women who wanted children use the machine, or would the majority get pregnant as women always have, in your opinion?
6. Do you think a unifier would approve of same-sex marriages?

YES: COMPLEMENTER

"Who's Afraid of Difference?"

Is philosophy sexist? The answer is obviously yes, in one sense of the question. All of the well-known philosophers in the Western tradition (and in other traditions as well) were men. Plato, Aristotle, Aquinas, Descartes, and so on to the twentieth century, were all men. Women were almost never permitted to study or teach philosophy, and if some natural philosophical genius appeared, her writing was not published. Female mystics and poets were permissible, but not philosophers. Thus philosophy is an exclusive male club.

But is philosophy itself sexist? Are the methods and concepts and theories in philosophy biased against women? I want to argue that the answer to this question is also yes, although it isn't as obvious. Concepts and methods cannot intentionally exclude women, or oppress them, as men can. But concepts and methods can be biased. To uncover the sexism in philosophy itself, we must first recognize some fundamental features of male and female psychology. And then we will see how those psychological tendencies biased philosophy against women.

In discussing men and women we must be very careful about making generalizations. Women have been victimized forever by unfounded generalizations, or stereotypes, that say that women in general are weak, excessively emotional, gossips, or addicted to childish fantasies of romance. History should make everyone, especially women, aware of how damaging and painful stereotypes can be. On the other hand, the fact that most generalizations are false does not imply that all are. If we are careful, we can make sound generalizations about the physical world, culture, and men and women. We simply have to base our generalizations on the broadest range of accurate data that we can, recognize exceptions, and always remember that additional observation might overturn any generalization.

With these caveats in mind, I will describe some general features of men's and women's experience that have far-reaching consequences. One feature is that women get pregnant, carry the fetus for nine months, go through labor and birth, and nurse babies. Men do none of these. In most societies—probably all societies—these biological connections lead women to interact with young children much more than men do. Until the children are weaned, women must nurse them several times a day. They continue feeding, cleaning, and comforting children more frequently then men do throughout childhood. They shape children through rewards and reprimands. Even when fathers help, most children's early, crucial experiences are primarily with their mothers. Cultures differ in small details, but everywhere women are the primary care-givers for infants and toddlers.

Everyone's early experiences influence his or her personality. One vital challenge infants face is to develop an identity, or a sense of themselves as distinct beings with their own feelings and choices. A major part of creating a self is imitation. Little boys try to imitate their fathers and little girls try to imitate their mothers. Also important is learning what not to do or feel. Boys and girls distinguish themselves from the opposite parent. But these processes are different for boys and girls. The emotional ties of security and dependence between young children and their mothers are very strong. Boys must struggle to separate themselves and think of themselves as different from the mother. They must learn to suppress their natural feelings, their tendency to cling to her and depend on her for absolutely everything, including their emotions and choices.

Instead, as males, they must identify with the father, who is comparatively absent and distant. The father has less physical contact, offers less comfort, less play, and less control than the mother.

Little girls, in contrast, learn to identify with the mother, who is constantly present. They do not need to separate themselves from their mothers to the degree that boys do. Consequently, their sense of self is more relational: their own thoughts, feelings, and desires are intertwined with their mother's, and later, with other people's. They do not feel the boy's need to draw sharp boundaries between self and other. On the contrary, the little girl must experience the merging with her mother as the most natural and satisfying way of finding herself. She wants to be just like her mother, and share in her mother's thoughts and feelings.

Furthermore, the emotional environment of 1- and 2-year-old children is the most intense imaginable. Living in the moment, and lacking interpretive concepts or knowledge, each experience creates the purest joy or the starkest terror, blissful contentment, or overwhelming desire, often in rapid succession. The center and source of these feelings is the mother. At this early stage of development, children do not distinguish between self, mother, and world; all are interdependent. Since the little girl identifies herself with her mother, and her mother continually elicits strong feelings in her, she accepts strong emotions and the emotional coloration of the world as normal and necessary. The little boy, on the other hand, must loosen the tie to the mother and dampen the strong emotional interactions. By shifting his focus to the father, he learns to suppress some of his feelings.

The results of these psychodynamics of family life are important. We are not discussing the fact that boys and girls internalize the values and behaviors that their culture expects of them. The process we are examining is deeper. Unlike culturally determined gender roles, it is virtually universal. In the earliest formation of a self, boys must identify with a comparatively distant parent, and girls must identify with a present parent. As a result, the structures of men's and women's personalities are different. The differences are a matter of degree, but they are important. Men see themselves as independent and self-directing; any dependency or merging with others is perceived by men as a threat. Women tend to value relationships with others, and define themselves in terms of their personal relationships. They seek interdependency. Men tend to suppress their emotional responses, whereas women regard them as a natural part of the world. To many women, men seem cold and lonely; to many men, women seem emotional and dependent. Of course there are exceptions to these generalizations. But since the mother-centered pattern of child rearing is so pervasive, and the process of forming an identity is so fundamental to personality, the generalizations probably apply in some degree to most people.

Recognizing the differences between men and women could help us improve and balance our understanding of ourselves. In particular, it could have a liberating effect in philosophy. Women's distinctive experience has been excluded from Western philosophy. In metaphysics, ethics, and the theory of knowledge, among other areas, the male perspective and masculinist assumptions have dominated. Indeed, many women have even been persuaded to accept masculinist assumptions and values as their own, and have denigrated or suppressed their distinct feminine nature. But uncovering male bias in traditional philosophy can only benefit it and remove a limitation. By adding their own contrasting voices and ideas to the dialogue, women can correct and improve our understanding of human nature, morality, and knowledge.

Modern philosophy, it is often said, began with Descartes, and Descartes held a very masculinist concept of the self. Descartes wanted to find something he could be absolutely certain of, and he began his search for certainty by discarding things he could *not* be certain of. He could not be certain that what he read in books was true, or even that what others told him directly was true. He could not be certain of what he saw with his own eyes, because sometimes his eyes tricked him. He said he couldn't even be certain that he was awake instead of dreaming, because when he was dreaming he thought that he was awake. He finally decided that the only thing he could be certain of was his own mind, or his own thinking. Even if he was dreaming, he was conscious and his mind was active. Even if he was mistaken about what he saw, at least he was thinking. "I think, therefore I am," he said. Descartes was sure of his own thinking, and decided he *was* his own thinking.

Descartes' reasoning reveals what an extremely masculinist sense of self he has. He sees himself as completely cut off from the world. Other people cannot be trusted. His senses fail to establish a firm connection. He even tries to repudiate his own body, and says he cannot be sure that he has arms and legs; maybe he is only dreaming them. The self he accepts is a sort of mathematical calculator, since he won't admit his emotions or desires as part of his self. He has taken the boy's task of separating himself from the enveloping mother to an extreme. And philosophers—almost all men—have elevated this biased sense of self to the norm. They have devalued women's ways of thinking of the self as dependent upon relations with other people, as embodied, and as emotional. No woman who has felt a child grow within her own body can take Descartes' point of view completely seriously. If women had been allowed to study philosophy, and if their ideas had been respected, Western philosophy would have a more realistic, balanced conception of the self.

Another part of philosophy skewed by a masculinist bias is ethics. A good illustration is a famous study of moral development by Harvard psychologist Lawrence Kohlberg. Kohlberg interviewed a large number of children of different ages. He described a moral problem and asked them how they would solve it. Some thought only in terms of avoiding punishment, some thought in terms of agreements and contracts among people, some thought about making the most people happy, and a few thought about universal principles of justice. According to Kohlberg, these approaches represent stages of moral growth, from the lowest egotism to the highest concern for what is right in itself. They also represent most of the major theories of morality in Western philosophy, such as egotism, social contract theories, utilitarianism, and Kantian formalism. We can disregard the details of these theories and recognize what they all have in common. All assume that being moral means finding a rule to apply in a situation. Kohlberg and others argue that as one's moral rules become more universal and more abstract, one ascends to "higher" levels of moral thinking. Moral development, therefore, means becoming more impersonal.

An interesting aspect of Kohlberg's study was that almost all his subjects were boys. Does that make any difference? Actually it was crucial. Another psychologist named Carol Gilligan noticed the imbalance in Kohlberg's study and decided to examine women's moral thinking. She presented a moral issue to a number of young women and found that they were reluctant to apply abstract rules. They assumed that every case was different, and wanted to know more specific details of each situation. They also seemed to believe that morality revolved around human relationships. They assumed that the best solution to the problem was one that preserved and strengthened caring, personal relationships among the people involved. The contrasts between Kohlberg's and Gilligan's results suggests that in moral thinking men emphasize fairness, justice, and respect for autonomous individuals, whereas women emphasize compassion, sympathy, and involvement with people. Men are more comfortable with general laws, whereas women consult their feelings about particular people and actions.

Gilligan's subjects do not fit Kohlberg's categories very well, nor do they rank very highly on his moral scale. But that only shows that Kohlberg relied on the standard moral theories of Western philosophy. The fact that boys neatly fall into the categories and girls do not suggests that the standard theories reflect masculinist values and biases. Their one-sidedness isn't surprising, since women were historically excluded from philosophy and never had the opportunity to express their distinctive approach to moral problems. If they had, we would now have a more balanced understanding of moral values and moral thinking.

Finally, in the theory of knowledge and the philosophy of science, Western philosophers have held up the ideal of objectivity. Objectivity is said to be an essential component of the proper scientific method. It is a necessary precondition of genuine knowledge of any kind. And what is objectivity? It is simply the core of the male personality structure. Being objective means separating oneself from the world, as the 1-year-old boy must separate himself from the mother. It is the attempt to eliminate or deny any connection between self and object. An objective description of something is a description of it "as it really is," without any input or influence from the person doing the describing. Philosophers have been particularly insistent that no desires or feelings can play any role in science or genuine knowledge. Being subjective, according to this tradition, means having a particular perspective, or allowing desires, goals, and emotional responses to be part of one's investigation of something.

It is difficult to describe the ideal of objectivity without realizing at once that it is unrealistic. Everyone has a personal perspective. We are all situated in a web of personal relations to the world around us. All scientists have emotions and values, which influence their choices of what phenomena to investigate and their interpretations of the results. Recognizing these facts would give us a more accurate understanding of science and the pursuit of knowledge. But as with Descartes' isolated self and Kohlberg's abstract principles, in science Western philosophers have taken the masculinist style and made it the norm, and even the ideal. Objectivity is clearly an inadequate guide in many areas, such as understanding people. To understand another person, I must be fully aware of my own thoughts and feelings. I understand another person by discovering what I would feel in similar circumstances. Understanding literature, social institutions, music, and the whole world of human culture depends upon empathy, recognizing different perspectives, and feelings. Good scientists—whether male or female—do use their feminine side in all sorts of ways: when they share ideas and hunches with colleagues, trust their intuition, use their fantasy to create novel hypotheses, indulge in the joy of discovery and understanding, and rely on friends for support and encouragement.

Men have a preferred style of thinking and women have a different style, although each gender can learn to appreciate the other's style. But in the past, men in positions of power have denigrated women's perceptions and asserted that only one way of thinking—the male way—was correct. But recognizing differences is not threatening; it is liberating. It promises a more balanced and realistic understanding of human experience.

Key Concepts

sexist	generalization	identity formation
the self	moral principles	objectivity

Critical Questions

1. Is the complementer's factual starting point correct? That is, in virtually all cultures and times, do women spend more time with small children than men do?

2. Why does a little boy try to imitate his father rather than his mother? Does the boy know he is a boy instead of a girl? If the complementer says yes, isn't she or he begging the question (i.e., assuming the boy's male identity to explain how male identity is created)?

3. Why do boys learn to suppress their emotions, according to the essay? Why don't girls learn the same thing?

4. According to the complementer, men and women have different types of personalities. Are those differences caused by genetic, biological factors or by social, historical factors, in the author's view? Could the causes be changed?

5. On the basis of Kohlberg's and Gilligan's studies, the complementer says that boys and girls think about moral issues in different ways. How does the

writer get from that fact to the conclusion that Western philosophy exhibits a male bias?

6. Is objectivity a male bias, in your opinion? Can the complementer say that his or her position is subjective, in the sense that it expresses personal wishes and a limited point of view? Is the complementer being objective?

Methods and Techniques
CLASSIFICATION

Classification is one of the most basic cognitive operations. It is valuable to look into a mental mirror, so to speak, and examine our own thinking so that we can try to improve it. Psychologists call the awareness of one's own thinking "metacognition."

First we should clarify the term. To classify means to arrange a group of items into smaller subgroups. It is to take a set of things, such as people, objects, words, or anything else, and divide it into two or more subsets. For example, human beings are normally divided into the subsets of men and women. Silverware is divided into forks, knives, and spoons. Furniture can be classified by style: colonial, Mediterranean, Victorian, contemporary, and so on. The term "classify" also has a related but slightly different meaning. I can look at a single object and decide what class it belongs in. For example, a bookseller may have to decide whether to classify a new book as biography or history or travel. This second kind of classification depends on the first kind. We begin with a group and divide it into classes, and only then can we put individuals into those classes.

How do we divide a group into subsets? For example, consider the following list of ten objects: (1) rose, (2) dollar bill, (3) basketball, (4) ivy, (5) stop sign, (6) Christmas tree, (7) Mars, (8) pumpkin, (9) tiger, (10) matador's cape. Do you see any way to arrange these objects into classes? One way is by color: red (1,5,7,10); green (2,4,6); and orange (3,8,9). Or by shape: spherical (3,7,8); flat (2,5,10); and other (1,4,6,9). Or as plant (1,4,6,8); plant product (2,10); animal (9); and other (3,5,7). And there are other ways. When we classify things in this manner we are simply recognizing similarities and differences. A dollar bill, ivy, and a Christmas tree are all similar in being green. A basketball, Mars, and a pumpkin are all similar in being spherical. When we put similar things together, we form a class, and with a large group of things, we can form several classes within the group.

Seeing similarities and differences means focusing on certain properties, such as color or shape. We analyze objects in the sense that we break them down into their properties and find the same property—red, green, spherical—in different objects. The property is the key. Classification depends upon extracting the defining property, and then grouping things on the basis of whether they have the property. The term for such a defining property is "criterion" (plural, "criteria"). In other words, the property of being red can be a criterion, establishing a class of things.

Any property can be used as a criterion, and criteria can be complex. We might try to classify the ten objects into those that smell good, those that smell bad, and those that have no smell. Or a criterion might be "objects I would like to have in my living room but not in other rooms, so long as they aren't too expensive." Boxers are classified by weight, and competitive runners by the distance they run.

Recognizing the criteria that define classes is an important skill. It requires us to look at the objects in a class and extract the property they all have in common. In fact, some standardized tests use problems of this sort. They present lists of objects and ask which object doesn't belong. For example,

1. moose,   2. mouse,   3. hammer,   4. cat,   5. eagle

Obviously "hammer" doesn't belong in this class because it is not an animal like the other objects. Another example:

1. Lincoln,   2. Reagan,   3. Monroe,   4. Franklin,   5. Adams

Franklin doesn't belong because all the other people were U.S. Presidents. Recognizing criteria means stepping up to a higher level of abstraction. One thinks of properties rather than particular objects.

Various problems can arise in classifying things. One problem is vagueness. The criterion that defines a class may be a matter of degree. For example, "red." Matadors' capes and American Beauty roses are definitely red, but is salmon red? Not exactly, although it is closer to red than to green or blue. Or "chubby." How much body fat must one have to be classified as chubby? There is no precise answer. The boundary between "average" and "chubby" is vague. Other vague terms are "cold," "the Midwest," "offensive," "child," "athlete," and "free." Examples of terms for classes with definite boundaries are "hydrogen," "robin," "pregnant," "state capitol," "licensed," and "metal."

Another practice that can lead to confusion is using subjective criteria. For example, I might say that most of the people in my history class in college are "likable," while most of those in my English class are "not very likable." By "likable" I simply mean that I enjoy being with them. A friend in the same classes who tries to distinguish the likable and not likable students probably wouldn't get very far, because the criterion—I enjoy being with them—is subjective and personal to me. My friend cannot apply it. He has no way of knowing whom I like and don't like. I could avoid confusion if I provide more objective criteria, such as "smiles often," "listens to people," and "has diverse interests." If those are the criteria for the class of likable people, then it will be easier to reach agreements on who is likable and who isn't.

These are only a few aspects of a fascinating topic. A final point to note is that one of the founders of Western philosophy, Socrates, believed that the essential task of philosophy was to find the underlying criteria that guide us when we classify some actions as "morally right" and others as "morally wrong." He asked what criteria define the class of just societies, the class of wise people, and the class of brave actions. In other words, he believed philosophy was the investigation of our concepts and the bases for our classifications of people and actions.

Understanding the Dilemma
UNIFIER OR COMPLEMENTER?

Are men and women fundamentally different? The unifier says no and the complementer says yes. The unifier says that even biological differences are not important, whereas the complementer says deep psychological differences divide men and women.

According to the unifier, we use biological differences as a basis for classifying people as male and female. But classifications are flexible, not written in stone. As technology provides us with more and better methods of reproduction, the biological differences will become less important, and less noticeable. In the future the categories "male" and "female" may not become obsolete, but certainly other categories, such as "creative," "ambitious," "sociable," and "generous," will become more important and receive more attention than "masculine" or "feminine."

A complementer, on the other hand, thinks it would be a tragedy if we lost sight of the differences between men and women. Women's distinctive perspective and insights have been suppressed and ignored in the past, and it's about time that we acknowledged them and recognized how valuable they are. Especially in philosophy, and in our most basic assumptions about human nature, morality, and knowledge, women's experience and the feminine point of view can correct the biases that limit our thinking.

Where do you stand? You have years of experience with many men and women. Are the differences diminishing and ultimately unimportant? Or do men and women think and feel and relate to others in fundamentally different ways?

When faced with philosophical dilemmas like this one, most people look for the middle ground. Most people would probably say some men and women are different and some aren't. We can imagine the possibilities as a horizontal line, and say there is a spectrum of types of people. On the far left, let's say, are "highly feminine women" and on the far right are "highly masculine men." In the middle are people who are both, or mixed, or feminine in some ways and masculine in others.

Is this an accurate picture of humanity? A unifier would probably say it is not. We do not need to label some behaviors as "feminine" or "masculine." In our society most women are pressured into moving toward the left side, the "feminine" side, and men are pressured into moving toward the right, the "masculine" side. But the ideal would be for most people to line up in the middle, which is neither male nor female, but "androgynous." At the present time, however, our rigid classifications of people drive them to one side or the other.

The ultimate pressure is being a mother or father. Men and women today may think and behave in similar ways—in school, in sports, in friendships, in jobs—until they start a family. Then the differences increase. The great majority of women get pregnant and give birth. Carrying the fetus, bonding with the newborn, and accepting responsibility for a helpless person pushes women to the feminine side, especially when society insists on it. Then the division of people into male and female becomes clearer and more pronounced. But it doesn't have to be that way, the unifier claims. Men and women can remain in the middle of the spectrum, with more options available to them. Alternative forms of reproduction will allow men and women to play equal roles in having children and rearing them.

A complementer disagrees, and claims that differences are valuable. Women should be proud of their differences from men. What the world needs is more caring, more communication and compromise, more empathy, and more creativity—the characteristics that are typically associated with women. The masculine traits of assertiveness, suppression of feelings, and extreme independence are nothing to envy.

At first glance, a complementer seems similar to a traditional conservative who believes men and women are very different. However, the conservative says that women are naturally suited to remain at home, support their husbands, and raise children. Men are natural leaders and women are natural followers. Nothing could be further from the complementer's point of view. The complementer says women's distinctive skills and talents belong in government, schools, the marketplace, and everywhere. Women's concern for relationships and understanding people make them better leaders and organizers than men. Their antipathy to conflict and violence makes them more trustworthy citizens than men. Their ability to work together and share things makes a more equitable, productive economy possible. Women are different from men, and their differences will lead to a better world.

In thinking about the differences between men and women, many people focus on the question of nature and nurture. Are the differences innate and unalterable, or are they culturally determined and changeable? No one who has studied the matter takes an "either/or" view. People are products of their genes *and* their environment, which constantly interact in countless ways we do not understand.

Neither the unifier nor the complementer has a simple answer to the question of nature and nurture. The unifier claims that the important factor is not nature or cultural roles, but human perception and classification. *Any* two things—a pencil and a blue whale—are similar in some ways and different in others. Human beings decide to emphasize and attend to a similarity or difference depending on their purposes and goals. There are innumerable innate similarities and differences between men and women, and innumerable cultural similarities and differences. We decide which ones to emphasize and which to ignore. People have always believed that the biological differences were the most important and the basis for classifying individuals as men or women. But it is possible to ignore biological differences and emphasize similarities, or ignore biology entirely as a basis for classifying and perceiving people. The future of the sexes doesn't depend on facts about biology or culture, but on what we choose to make of those facts. And technology is changing the way we think about the facts.

The complementers' view of nature and nurture is another example of looking for interactions. The complementer asserts that, because of biological facts about pregnancy and nursing, in almost all cultures children are reared by women. As a result, men and women form their sense of self in different ways and have different types of personalities. Facts about pregnancy and childbirth are biological and innate, but facts about family structure and ways of socializing children are cultural. The complementer claims these two sets of facts are interconnected. Is the need for a sense of identity innate or learned? Is the method of forming an identity through imitating authority figures innate or learned? These psychological processes are probably on the border between the inherited capacity and the acquired content. The complementer isn't so much concerned with disentangling the interconnections of genetics and culture—which is probably impossible—as with understanding the psychological processes and their consequences.

The dispute between a unifier and a complementer is not just a disagreement about nature and nurture. As with many philosophical dilemmas, both facts and values are at stake. What in fact are the differences between men and women? Are they artificial, based on outdated types of classification? Or are they deeply rooted in biology and child development? And *should* we encourage women to develop their differences from men, so they can apply their superior skills to all the problems we face? If you think differences are small and should be minimized, even in family structure, then you are a unifier. If you think women are psychologically different from men, and that after centuries of oppression, allowing feminine traits to flourish is the best hope for progress, then you are a complementer.

UNIFIER

1. The classification of things depends on our purposes; categories change with changing means of achieving our purposes.
2. The only real differences between men and women are the ability to impregnate and to give birth.
3. With developments in reproductive technology, such as an artificial womb, the biological difference between men and women will become negligible.
4. When the means of reproduction are available to anyone, classifications of people as "male" and "female" will decline, and classifications based on more important traits of personality will take their place.

COMPLEMENTER

5. Identifying with the relatively absent father shapes boys' personalities, and identifying with the nurturing mother shapes girls' personalities.

6. In general, men are more independent and less emotional than women, whereas women are more social and more sensitive than men.
7. Men's competitive and alienating nature has caused many problems in economics, society, and politics, and as women gain positions of power and apply their distinctive skills, we can look forward to progress.
8. The psychological differences between men and women have influenced basic philosophical conceptions of the self, morality, and knowledge, since philosophy has been dominated by men.

FOR FURTHER STUDY

Historical Examples

UNIFIER: Mary Wollstonecraft. *A Vindication of the Rights of Woman.* Edited by Carol H. Poston. Norton, 1988. Originally published in 1792. Criticism of degrading attitudes and behavior toward women, and a plea for human rights for all humans, including women.

COMPLEMENTER: Shulamith Firestone. *The Dialectic of Sex: The Case for Feminist Revolution.* Morrow, 1970. Critique of sexism in many areas, starting from the claim that biology leads to an unjust division of labor and psychological differences (but agreeing with the unifier that the means of reproduction should be changed).

OTHER SOURCES

Nancy Holmstrom, "Human Nature." In Alison M. Jaggar, Iris Marion Young, eds. *A Companion to Feminist Philosophy.* Blackwell, 1998. Brief survey of historical and contemporary positions on the question "Does human nature take sex-differentiated forms?," showing the multiplicity of feminist ideas.

Eve Browning Cole. *Philosophy and Feminist Criticism: An Introduction.* Paragon House, 1993. Clear, basic discussion of feminist ideas in epistemology, metaphysics, ethics, and political philosophy.

Rosemarie Putnam Tong. *Feminist Thought.* 2nd Edition. Westview Press, 1998. Lively, critical presentation of various schools of feminism, including liberal, radical, Marxist, socialist, psychoanalytic, existentialist, and postodernist feminism.

Leslie Stevenson, David L. Haberman. *Ten Theories of Human Nature.* 3rd Edition. Oxford University Press, 1998. Elementary discussion of religious, philosophical, and psychological views, including their diagnoses of the main problems we face, and their prescriptions.

Roger Trigg. *Ideas of Human Nature: An Historical Introduction.* 2nd Edition. Blackwell, 1999. Concise, informative essays on twelve great philosophers, each chapter concluding with a section on "contemporary relevance."

Peter Loptson. *Theories of Human Nature.* Broadview, 1995. Survey of eleven theories from Aristotle to Marvin Harris, considering questions of our place in nature, our malleability, our sociability, and the possibility of a science of human nature.

George Mandler. *Human Nature Explored.* Oxford University Press, 1997. Interesting chapters on evolution, consciousness, emotion, aggression, gender, and other topics, by a psychologist.

Germaine Greer. *The Whole Woman.* Knopf, 1999. Angry denunciation of all aspects of society as sexist and exploitative, by a complementer; rejects "equality" as a trap.

CONNECTIONS

REDUCTIONIST OR SPIRITUALIST?

The basic division in Chapter 4 is relatively clear. It is much simpler than the complex similarities and differences we discovered in Chapter 3 among beliefs about values. Having said that, I should also remind you that nothing in philosophy is simple. When someone claims to have a simple answer to a philosophical question, you should automatically be suspicious. However, some answers are simpl*er* than others. And the relationships among the positions in Chapter 4 are simpler than those among the positions in Chapter 3.

The basic issue regarding human nature is this: are human beings subject to natural or social laws, or are we not? Do the laws that govern the movements of physical objects also govern human beings? Or can people rise above those forces, perhaps by understanding them? Are human beings subject to social or psychological laws, applicable to us but not to physical objects? Or are the (rare) laws of the social sciences merely generalizations based on human actions, which are admittedly similar, but which are not rigidly determined beforehand? If we knew everything about an individual, could we predict what she or he would do in the future? Or is that impossible? (That is, granting that we *could* know everything, would it still be impossible to predict the person's actions?)

If you believe that human beings *are* subject to natural or social laws, then you are a "reductionist." And if you believe we are not controlled by natural or social laws, then you are a "spiritualist." I am proposing the name "reductionist" because it suggests that human actions can be "reduced" to lawful regularities. A reductionist believes that the bewildering, profuse variety of human behavior is ultimately explainable in terms of laws. The confusion and unpredictability can be reduced to order and predictability. On the other hand, a "spiritualist" believes that human beings are not just additional pieces of the world, but are different and special. People are "spiritual" beings, in the sense that some part of us is forever beyond the reach of science, measurement, prediction, complete understanding, and even lawful regularity. As the mentalist says in "People vs. Machines," we are ultimately a mystery to ourselves.

We could use different labels. If you do not like the terms "reductionist" and "spiritualist," you can find different ones. For example, you could call the first position "holism" and the second "exceptionalism" (or something like that), because the first sees human beings as integral parts of the larger whole of nature, while the second sees human beings as exceptional, fundamentally different from systems that are governed by laws. Or you could call the first group "explainers" and the second group "searchers," or something else.

But the important thing is the ideas, not the labels. I am suggesting that a certain idea runs through some of the positions in Chapter 4, and an opposite idea runs through some of the others. In other words, some of the positions are similar to each other and different from the others. Thinking about those contrasting ideas is a first step in seeing similarities and differences in the various positions. The similarities and differences are the connections among the parts of your worldview. They are the tendons, ligaments, and cartilage that hold your worldview together and allow it to function. Without them, your worldview is just a shapeless blob, like a dying jellyfish on the beach.

After reading this introduction, probably the first section of Chapter 4 that comes to mind is Section 4.1, "Are We Free?" Remember that a hard determinist says no, and a metaphysical libertarian and a soft determinist say yes. The hard determinist argues that human beings are part of the natural world, and that the whole world is governed by laws. We know it is lawful because of the many laws, in many different areas, that we have already discovered. So human behavior is subject to natural laws, too, even if we haven't yet discovered them. But a libertarian claims that we are free, and we know that we are free by simply introspecting our own thoughts and feelings as we make a decision. We can see that nothing coerces us. The libertarian is a good example of a spiritualist, while the hard determinist is a reductionist.

Does a soft determinist fit this classification? A soft determinist is a type of determinist. He or she agrees with the hard determinist about natural laws and the regularity of human behavior. Everything we do and think and feel is caused, according to the soft determinist. So he or she is a reductionist. She simply insists that we are still free, because the word "free" means caused by myself. It does not mean uncaused, or mysterious, or spiritual.

Another pair of opposites that fits the pattern is materialists and dualists. Reductionism is closely related to materialism, although they are not identical, and dualism is related to spiritualism. You read about materialists and dualists in Section 4.3, "Is the Mind Nothing but the Brain?" A materialist believes that human beings are complex organisms with remarkable brains. And that is all we are. Our minds, personalities, emotions, moods, creative insights, and consciences are just aspects of the physical brain. The remarkable correlations between brain events and mind events supports this materialistic view, as does the trend of reduction in all the sciences. Now if the human mind is just the brain—a physical organ—then the actions of the mind are all determined by physical events, because everything that happens in the brain is determined by prior physical events. Therefore materialists are reductionists.

But dualists have a different outlook. They believe that thoughts and feelings and all the experiences that make up your mind cannot be physical events because they are private. Only you can feel your toothache, but anyone (in principle) can observe events in your brain. Since mental processes are private and physical processes are public, they cannot be the same things. A human being is made of two distinct parts, mental and physical. This conclusion is relevant to the reductionist/spiritualist distinction. If the mind is not physical, then it may not be subject to laws as the physical world is. Dualists see the mind as a fundamentally different kind of entity from physical objects. So dualists are normally spiritualists.

But the connections here are not one-to-one, not perfect. A dualist *could* believe that the mind is nonphysical, but *is* subject to laws. Maybe the mind is governed by "mental laws," which are different from physical laws. In that case, the dualist would be a reductionist. It is also possible, though unlikely, that a materialist could be a spiritualist. That is, a person could believe that the mind is a physical organ, the brain, but could also believe that the physical world is *not* governed by laws. Maybe the laws that scientists have discovered are all illusions, or something like that. As I said, this is a possible belief, but not many people will hold it. It is contrary to too much evidence. Most materialists are reductionists, and most dualists are spiritualists.

While materialists try to show that the mind is the same thing as the brain, mechanists try to show that the mind works mechanically, like a computer. In Section 4.4, "Can Computers Think?," the mechanist pointed out many similarities between what people can do and what computers can do. For example, both can calculate, store information, and solve problems. Since they are similar in their output, they are probably similar in their operation as well. Computers are physical systems that operate according to instructions from a programmer. All the operations are strictly determined. If the mind works the same way as a computer, then all its operations are strictly determined, too. Therefore, mechanists are reductionists.

Mentalists, however, reject the mechanistic view of the mind. The mentalist in Section 4.4 argues that we cannot build machines that think like humans, because we do not know how humans think. We do not know any laws governing the operations of the mind, so we cannot embody them in a machine. And we never will be able to build a thinking machine, because if we do understand how we think, that knowledge will change the way we do it. So the machines can never catch up with the human way of thinking. Mentalists believe that human thought can never be captured in laws and rules. They are spiritualists.

In Section 4.5, "Are We Always Selfish?," the issue is whether or not people are subject to psychological laws. A psychological egoist believes that at least one law governs all human actions—the law of self-interest. That is, the egoist says that everything a person does is aimed at some benefit for himself or herself. No one does anything strictly for others or for any selfless principle. The evidence for this law is all the examples of actions that can be interpreted as selfish. Whenever an action appears to be altruistic, we can always find an unconscious motive, or a concern for the distant future, or a desire to avoid a greater pain, or some self-centered concern that makes the action selfish in reality.

In contrast, a psychological altruist believes that sometimes people act without any desire to benefit themselves, either in the long run or the short run or in any way. There are cases that cannot be reinterpreted as selfish, the altruist says, and therefore people are not bound by a universal law of selfishness. An altruist is a spiritualist because he or she rejects the idea of such a psychological law governing human behavior. On the other hand, an egoist accepts reductionism.

Another section in Chapter 4 is Section 4.2, "Are We Responsible for Our Actions?" The excuser says no and the judge says yes. At first glance, it might seem that an excuser is obviously a reductionist—people are not responsible because they are governed by inescapable laws—and a judge is obviously a spiritualist. But that would be too hasty. If we examine the actual details of the positions in Section 4.2, we see a more complicated picture. The excuser says people are not responsible whether their actions are caused or not. An excuser does not say people's actions are always caused, or subject to laws. Maybe actions are not caused. But the key point is that, either way, it makes no sense to say the person is responsible for the action. Thus an excuser does not necessarily hold the central belief of reductionism. But an excuser is similar to a reductionist, because most reductionists would agree that people cannot be responsible for their actions.

A judge is not simply a spiritualist either. A judge says that we have a clear and established set of rules for excusing people. We ask if the person caused an action, if the person was sane, if the person did it intentionally, and if the person did it freely. A person who does not have any of these recognized excuses is responsible, according to the judge. The judge in Section 4.2 does not say that people are outside the scope of natural or social laws. On the contrary, he says people's actions are probably caused. But we do not *know* the complex, remote causes. Since we do not know the ultimate causes, we make a decision on the basis of the causes we do know, and that is the person himself. The robber did cause the bank to be robbed, and therefore he is responsible. This position is similar to spiritualism in a practical sense because it says we do not know of any causes of human action. There may be causes, but our social and legal decisions must rest upon what we know, not upon what might be true. For all practical purposes, there are no laws governing normal human behavior.

The example of excusers and judges shows that the beliefs about human nature are complicated and hard to classify. The two positions represented in Section 4.6 by Lockeans and Sartreans, are a little more similar to the other contrasts in this chapter. Lockeans are reductionists and Sartreans are spiritualists. Lockeans believe that your identity depends on your memory of your past, and you can't change your past. It's fixed and immutable. In that sense, your identity is determined. You can try to learn more about yourself by reviewing the events of your life and reflecting on how you behaved. But the data are in. You are the person you were. The unbreakable link is your memory. You can also try to change the type of person you will be in the future. You can make New Year's resolution, and talk to a counselor to learn how to change. You can practice new behaviors. But you are still identical with the individual who did the things in your past because that's what you remember. You are like Aeneas escaping from Troy carrying his father on his back. You cannot throw off the burden of your past.

Sartreans, however, are similar to other spiritualists in this chapter. The Sartrean in Section 4.6 claims that it is absolutely essential to his identity that he have real choices and an open future. If he believed that every decision and thought and feeling he will ever have is already determined, he says, he would no longer be human. He can't believe in determinism even if he tries. Furthermore, what is essential to him as an individual—what makes him who he is—are the things he cares about most, whether it is people or projects or things. If those somehow changed, he would be literally a different person. His values make up his identity, and his values are up to him.

One contrast between Lockeans and Sartreans shows clearly that they are reductionists and spiritualists, respectively. The Lockean relies on a public, objective test of identity, applied by society, and the Sartrean relies on a private, subjective test, applied by each individual. In other words, if a person such as Karla Faye Tucker in 1997 remembers killing two people in 1983, and her memory can be verified by others, then the present Tucker is identical with the killer. The test is what she actually remembers. It may seem that memory is a subjective thing. But memories must be accurate if they are really memories, and objective observers decide whether or not a person's memories are accurate. If Tucker didn't remember the murders but said she remembered being somewhere else at the time (even though witnesses put her at the scene of the crime), we would decide she had "lost her mind" or "didn't know who she was."

Sartreans do not believe memory is the test of identity. The judicial system should not decide whether or not Tucker in 1997 is the same person as the person who committed the crime. Only Tucker can decide who she is. If what is essential to her has changed—if she is now loving and kind and humble—then her personality has changed. But has her identity changed? Sartreans say the real question is "Who decides?"And they say the individual should decide, not the state. Therefore, since individuals can choose their own identity, Sartreans are spiritualists, not reductionists.

The current controversy in Chapter 4 revolves around the question "Are the differences between men and women philosophically significant?" The unifier says no, and the complementer says yes. You will recall that a unifier claims that the process of classifying things is flexible. The categories we use, such as "mammal" and "reptile," or "dangerous" and "harmless," depend on our purposes and interests, and these change over time. The categories "male" and "female" are important because reproduction is important, but as our methods of creating new people change, these categories will matter less and less. Eventually, the biological difference between men and women will become insignificant, and other classifications of people will be more important.

The complementer in this section disagrees. Not only are men and women psychologically different, but the differences are important and we ought to take advantage of them in the future. The complementer begins with what he or she regards as basic facts about family structure and child development. In almost all families, women spend more time rearing children than men do. People can quibble over small exceptions, but the basic pattern is clear. Furthermore, children develop their personalities by imitating or identifying with the parent of the same sex. But since children interact with their mothers much more than with their fathers, the identification process is very different for boys and girls. However, the resulting strengths and assets of women have been ignored, especially in philosophy. In the future, we should celebrate these differences and benefit from them, according to the complementer.

Are these two positions similar to others in Chapter 4? The complementer's point of view is similar to other reductionist positions because the complementer believes people are subject to certain universal laws of behavior. Almost all families are organized in the same way—with female care-givers—and almost all children grow up in the same ways. We can understand ourselves and our potential for growth and happiness by understanding the forces that shape our lives. We can achieve a greater balance and harmony between men and women by recognizing the inevitable differences between them and by accepting their complementary roles.

Unifiers, in contrast, are similar to spiritualists, at least in their belief that human beings can design the kind of lives they want to have, and can even define themselves to a certain degree. Unifiers reject permanent categories, such as "male" and "female," and claim that all categories depend on our own purposes. Unifiers are not exactly like other spiritualists, such as libertarians, dualists, or mentalists, because those spiritualists believe that human nature is ultimately mysterious and irreducible to scientific law. Unifiers believe human nature is extremely complex and diverse, but that we can understand how we emphasize some qualities and not others in classifying people. The complexity, however, gives us the capacity to develop in virtually any direction we choose, including complete equality, and that faith in our open-ended future makes unifiers similar to spiritualists.

Classifying the positions in Chapter 4 as reductionist and spiritualist should help you think about the connections among your beliefs about human nature.

The classification certainly isn't the last word, but it is a start. Moreover, some positions do not fit into the scheme as well as others. Hard determinists are paradigmatic reductionists, and metaphysical libertarians are perfect spiritualists, but the classification of the other positions is only approximate. These discussions of connections at the end of each chapter are not supposed to provide you with simple answers. They are intended to suggest some possible relationships among your beliefs, but you must make up your own mind about how close (or distant, or irrelevant) those relationships are. The discussions are also intended to show you a whole part of philosophy that is not covered in the rest of the book. The other parts of the book discuss particular answers to traditional questions. But you should not forget that the connections among your answers are just as important as the individual answers themselves.

Reductionist	**Spiritualist**
determinist	metaphysical libertarian
materialist	dualist
mechanist	mentalist
psychological egoist	psychological altruist
excuser	judge
Lockean	Sartrean
complementer	unifier

REDUCTIONIST

1. Human beings are made of the same stuff as everything else and follow the same laws as everything else.
2. We can understand more and more of human behavior by learning about the physical and social causes that make each of us what we are.
3. The mind, or consciousness, is a natural phenomenon, and we will eventually discover its laws of operation (perhaps by modeling the mind on a computer).
4. Since humans are animals and obey similar laws, we probably have a drive to preserve ourselves and desire what benefits us.

SPIRITUALIST

5. Human beings are not just nerves and muscle, not just objects; our consciousness sets us apart from the natural, physical world.
6. People are so complex that we cannot generalize about them; every individual is unique.
7. We can never completely understand a person.
8. We choose our own behavior; it isn't determined by anything, and therefore we should accept responsibility for it.